# THE *MARZĒAḤ* IN THE PROPHETIC LITERATURE

# SUPPLEMENTS

TO

# VETUS TESTAMENTUM



VOLUME LXXXVI

# THE *MARZĒAḤ* IN THE PROPHETIC LITERATURE

*References and Allusions in Light of the Extra-Biblical Evidence*

BY

JOHN L. McLAUGHLIN



BRILL
LEIDEN · BOSTON · KÖLN
2001

This book is printed on acid-free paper.

**Library of Congress Cataloging-in-Publication Data**

McLaughlin, John L.
The *marzēaḥ* in the prophetic literature : references and allusions in light of the extra-biblical evidence / by John L. McLaughlin.
p. cm. — (Supplements to Vetus Testamentum, ISSN 0083-5889 ; v. 86)
Includes bibliographical references and index.
ISBN 9004120068
1. Bible. O.T. Prophets—Criticism, interpretation, etc. I. Title. II. Series.

BS1505.2 .M37 2001
224'.067—dc21

2001025261
CIP

**Die Deutsche Bibliothek – CIP-Einheitsaufnahme**

**McLaughlin, John L.:**
The *marzēaḥ* in the prophetic literature : references and allusions in light of extra-biblical evidence / by John L. McLaughlin. – Leiden ; Boston ; Köln : Brill, 2001
(Supplements to Vetus testamentum ; Vol. 86)
Zugl. : Toronto, Univ., Diss., 1998
ISBN 90-04-12006-8

ISSN 0083-5889
ISBN 90 04 12006 8



PRINTED IN THE NETHERLANDS

To my parents,

John and Rita McLaughlin:

With love,
For their love

CONTENTS

# ACKNOWLEDGEMENTS

This volume is a revision of my doctoral dissertation accepted by the Faculty of Theology at the University of St. Michael's College in October of 1998. The greatest changes are found in Chapter 1, where I have combined all the extra-biblical *marzēaḥ* texts in the original language with an English translation in order to facilitate easy reference. The subsequent chapters have been edited and revised in light of a few works that appeared after the dissertation was completed.

First and foremost, I wish to thank William H. Irwin for agreeing to direct this dissertation and for his assistance in all its stages. Throughout my doctoral program Bill was a model of caring scholarship, combining a concern for the person as well as the project. He allowed me the freedom to work out my ideas for the dissertation while gently pointing out the shortcomings and false directions. In the final year of writing in particular, he returned my submissions with great speed without sacrificing insight or depth in his responses. I am grateful for his mentoring and friendship over the years. I also deeply appreciate the contributions by the other members of my examination committee: Michael Kolarcik, Brian Peckham and J. Glen Taylor, who teach at member colleges of the Toronto School of Theology, and Dennis Pardee of the Oriental Institute in Chicago. I have benefited greatly from their insightful comments, suggestions and critiques.

A number of organizations provided financial assistance during my doctoral program and/or during the preparation of this volume. I received regular bursaries from both the Franciscans of Montreal and the Faculty of Theology at St. Michael's. The Catholic Biblical Association of America granted me a Memorial Stipend for five years. The Government of Ontario awarded me two Ontario Graduate Scholarships plus The Queen Elizabeth II Scholarship. A John B. Stephenson Fellowship from the Andrew W. Mellon Foundation, through the Appalachian College Association, provided the financial means to take a one-year leave of absence from my teaching responsibilities at Wheeling Jesuit University and finish writing the dissertation, while Wheeling Jesuit kindly gave me the time to do so. The revision and editing to produce this volume was supported by a Wheeling Jesuit University Summer Research Grant, a one-semester appointment as Scholar-in-Residence by WJU, and by a West Virginia Humanities Council Fellowship. For all this support I am deeply grateful.

Many people helped with various aspects of the dissertation and the subsequent revision. The library staff of both the Kelly Library at St. Michael's and the Bishop Hodges Library at Wheeling Jesuit located material in their own collections or through inter-library loan; Barb Julian of WJU was especially diligent in quickly locating obscure items from other institutions at short notice. Hami Verbin helped me with rabbinic Hebrew for that part of chapter 1. A number of individuals provided me with references, and/or double-checked ones I already had, on occasions when I could not easily do so; special thanks are due to Anne Anderson, Richard Ascough, Bob Derrenbacker, Brian Irwin, John Kloppenborg and Glen Taylor. Connie Crecion, the WJU secretary for McHugh Hall faculty handled details like photocopying and returning library books. Nancy Wagner, our departmental graduate assistant at Wheeling Jesuit, proof-read the final copy and double-checked the indexes. As much as all these contributions are appreciated, however, I alone am responsible for the end result; any shortcomings are my own.

This dissertation would never have been completed without those who supported and encouraged me through the good times and the bad. Michael Fahey, Dean of the Faculty of Theology at St. Michael's from 1986 to 1996, took an interest in my academic career, encouraging me to publish and to present papers at professional meetings, and giving me the opportunity to develop my teaching skills as a Sessional Lecturer. Sharon McGhie, the Administrative Assistant to the Dean and the Advanced Degree Director and Wilma Stoyanoff, the Registrar, helped make my years at St. Michael's easier and certainly more enjoyable and memorable. Richard Ascough, Jo-Ann Badley, Alicia Batten, Cathy Clifford, Bob Derrenbacker, Susan Lochrie-Graham, Dennis O'Hara, Connie Price, Caroline Whalen-Donaghey and Tyler Williams began as co-learners in the Ph.D. program and continue as friends and colleagues to this day. Last, but not least, Anne Anderson and John Kloppenborg were ongoing sources of support, encouragement and friendship during my years at St. Michael's and since. Dave Hammond, Norm Paulhus, Michael Steltenkamp and Kris Willumsen of the Department of Theology and Religious Studies at Wheeling Jesuit University have been a source of inspiration and encouragement over the last five years. That spirit extends to the entire faculty of WJU; the support I have received from virtually every academic department makes WJU a wonderful place to teach, work and live. Dennis O'Hara and Anne Marie Quinn graciously opened their home during numerous research trips Toronto over the last few years, giving me a place to work and relax. I also appreciate the deep and lasting friendship of Vera Bratuz, Paula and Terry Dobbelsteyn, and Cheryl and Paul Grady over the years.

Finally, I wish to thank my family. My eight brothers and sisters didn't always understand what I was doing in my academic career, but supported me through it all. I especially want to thank my parents, who raised us all to do our best at what we wanted. It is with great appreciation for their efforts that I dedicate this work to them.

John L. McLaughlin
Wheeling Jesuit University
Wheeling, West Virginia
September, 2000

# ABBREVIATIONS

| | |
|---|---|
| *AAAS* | *Annales archéologiques arabes syriennes* |
| AB | Anchor Bible |
| *ABD* | *The Anchor Bible Dictionary*. Ed. David Noel Freedman *et al.*; 6 vols.; New York/London/Toronto: Doubleday, 1992. |
| ABRL | Anchor Bible Reference Library |
| *AcOr* | *Acta Orientalia* |
| *AfO* | *Archiv für Orientforschung* |
| ALASPM | Abhandlungen zur Literatur Alt-Syrien-Pälastinas und Mesopotamiens |
| *ANET* | *Ancient Near Eastern Texts Relating to the Old Testament.* 3rd ed.; ed. J. B. Pritchard; Princeton: Princeton University Press, 1969. |
| AnOr | Analecta orientalia |
| *Anton* | *Antonianum* |
| AOAT | Alter Orient und Altes Testament |
| ARET | Archivi reali di Ebla: Testi |
| AS | Akkadica Supplementum |
| ATD | Das Alte Testament Deutsch |
| *BA* | *Biblical Archaeologist* |
| *BARev* | *Biblical Archaeology Review* |
| *BASOR* | *Bulletin of the American Schools of Oriental Research* |
| BBB | Bonner biblische Beiträge |
| BDB | Francis Brown, S. R. Driver and Charles Briggs. *The New Brown-Driver-Briggs-Gesenius Hebrew and English Lexicon with an Appendix Containing the Biblical Aramiac.* Peabody: Hendrickson Publishers, 1979. |
| BETL | Bibliotheca ephemeridum theologicarum lovaniensium |
| BFCT | Beiträge zur Förderung christlicher Theologie |
| BHR | Bibliotheca Helvetica Romana |
| *BHS* | *Biblia Hebraica Stuttgartensia.* 4th ed.; ed. K. Elliger, W. Rudolph *et al.*; Stuttgart: Deutsche Bibelgesellschaft, 1990. |
| *Bib* | *Biblica* |
| *BibLeb* | *Bibel und Leben* |
| BibOr | Biblica et orientalia |
| BIS | Biblical Interpretation Series |
| BKAT | Biblischer Kommentar, Altes Testament |
| *BN* | *Biblische Notizen* |
| *BRev* | *Bible Review* |
| BRS | Biblical Resource Series |
| *BSac* | *Bibliotheca Sacra* |
| BWANT | Beiträge zur Wissenschaft von Alten und Neuen Testament |
| BZAW | Beihefte zur *Zeitschrift für die alttestamentliche Wissenschaft* |
| *CAD* | *The Assyrian Dictionary of the Oriental Institute of the University of Chicago.* Ed. I. E. Gelb, T. Jacobsen, B. Landsberger and A. L. Oppenheim; Chicago, Oriental Institute, 1956–. |
| CahRB | Cahiers de la *Revue biblique* |

| | |
|---|---|
| CAT | Commentaire de l'Ancien Testament |
| *CAT* | *The Cuneiform Alphabetic Texts from Ugarit, Ras Ibn Hani and Other Places (KTU: Second, Enlarged Edition).* Ed. Manfried Dietrich, Oswald Loretz and Joaquín Sanmartín; ALASPM 8; Münster: Ugarit-Verlag, 1995. |
| CBC | Cambridge Bible Commentary |
| *CBQ* | *Catholic Biblical Quarterly* |
| CFTL | Clark's Foreign Theological Library |
| *CIS* | *Corpus inscriptionum semiticarum* |
| ConBOT | Coniectanea biblica, Old Testament |
| *CRAIBL* | *Comptes rendus de l'Académie des inscriptions et belles-lettres* |
| CT | Cahier théologique |
| *DDD* | *Dictionary of Deities and Demons in the Bible (DDD).* 2nd ed.; ed. Karel van der Toorn, Bob Becking, and Pieter W. van der Horst; Leiden/Boston/Köln: E. J. Brill, 1999. |
| *EA* | *Die El-Amarna Tafeln.* Ed. Jörgen Alexander Knudtzon; VB 2; Leipzig: J. C. Hinrichs, 1910-15. |
| EBib | Études bibliques |
| *EI* | *Eretz-Israel* |
| *ETL* | *Ephemerides theologicae lovanienses* |
| *EvT* | *Evangelische Theologie* |
| *ExpTim* | *Expository Times* |
| *FO* | *Folia Orientalia* |
| FOTL | Forms of the Old Testament Literature |
| FRLANT | Forschungen zur Religion und Literatur des Alten und Neuen Testaments |
| GKC | *Gesenius' Hebrew Grammar.* Ed. E. Kautzsch; 2nd Eng. ed. rev. A. E. Cowley; Oxford: Clarendon Press, 1910. |
| *HAR* | *Hebrew Annual Review* |
| HAT | Handbuch zum Alten Testament |
| HBS | Herders biblische Studien |
| Heb | Hebrew |
| *Hen* | *Henoch* |
| HSM | Harvard Semitic Monographs |
| HSS | Harvard Semitic Studies |
| *HTR* | *Harvard Theological Review* |
| *HUCA* | *Hebrew Union College Annual* |
| *IB* | *The Interpreter's Bible.* 12 vols.; ed. G. A. Buttrick *et al.*; New York: Abingdon Press, 1956. |
| ICC | The International Critical Commentary |
| *IEJ* | *Israel Exploration Journal* |
| *Int* | *Interpretation* |
| ITC | International Theological Commentary |
| *JA* | *Journal asiatique* |
| *JAOS* | *Journal of the American Oriental Society* |
| *JBL* | *Journal of Biblical Literature* |
| *JQR* | *Jewish Quarterly Review* |
| *JSOT* | *Journal for the Study of the Old Testament* |
| JSOTSup | *Journal for the Study of the Old Testament* Supplement Series |
| *JSS* | *Journal of Semitic Studies* |

| | |
|---|---|
| *JTS* | *Journal of Theological Studies* |
| *KAI* | *Kanaanäische und aramäische Inschriften.* 2nd ed.; 2 vols.; ed. Herbert Donner and W. Röllig. Wiesbaden: Otto Harrassowitz, 1966. |
| KAT | Kommentar zum Alten Testament |
| KHAT | Kürzer Hand-kommentar zum Alten Testament |
| *KTU* | *Die Keilalphabetischen Texte aus Ugarit.* Ed. Manfred Dietrich, Oswald Loretz, and Joaquín Sanmartín; AOAT 24; Kevelaer: Verlag Butzon und Bercker; Neukirchen-Vluyn: Neukirchener Verlag, 1976. |
| LAPO | Littératures anciennes du Proche-Orient |
| LBI | Library of Biblical Interpretation |
| LXX | Septuagint |
| MEE | Materiali epigrafica di Ebla |
| *MGWJ* | *Monatsschrift für Geschichte und Wissenschaft des Judentums* |
| MHeb | Mishnaic Hebrew |
| *MIO* | *Mitteilungen des Instituts für Orientforschung* |
| MRS | Mission de Ras Shamra |
| MT | Masoretic Text |
| *MVAG* | *Mitteilungen der vorderasiatischen Gesellschaft* |
| *NAB* | *New American Bible* |
| NCBC | New Century Bible Commentary |
| *NEB* | *New English Bible* |
| NICOT | New International Commentary on the Old Testament |
| *NJBC* | *The New Jerome Biblical Commentary.* Ed. Raymond E. Brown, Joseph A. Fitzmyer and Raymond E. Murphy; Englewood Cliffs: Prentice-Hall, 1990. |
| *NRSV* | *New Revised Standard Bible* |
| OBO | Orbis biblicus et orientalis |
| OBT | Overtures to Biblical Theology |
| OLA | Orientalia lovaniensia analecta |
| *OLZ* | *Orientalistische Literaturzeitung* |
| *OrAnt* | *Oriens antiquus* |
| OTL | Old Testament Library |
| OTMS | Old Testament Message Series |
| *OTS* | *Oudtestamentische Studiën* |
| PA | Palestina antiqua |
| *PAT* | *Palmyrene Aramaic Texts.* Ed. Delbert Roy Hillers and Eleonora Cussini; Baltimore/London: Johns Hopkins University Press, 1996. |
| PFAT | Palästinische Forschungen zur Archäologie und Topographie |
| *PIBA* | *Proceedings of the Irish Biblical Association* |
| PLO | Porta linguarum orientalium |
| *PRU* | *Le Palais royal d'Ugarit.* 6 vols.; ed. Claude F. A. Schaeffer *et al.*; Paris: Imprimerie Nationale, 1955-70. |
| *PSBA* | *Proceedings of the Society of Biblical Archaeology* |
| PTMS | Pittsburgh Theological Monograph Series |
| *RA* | *Revue d'assyriologie et d'archéologie orientale* |
| *RB* | *Revue biblique* |
| *RBR* | *Richerche Bibliche e Religiose* |
| *REJ* | *Revue des études juives* |

| | |
|---|---|
| *RES* | *Répertoire d'épigraphie sémitique* |
| *RESB* | *Revue des études sémitiques et babyloniaca* |
| *Revsém* | *Revue sémitique* |
| *RHPR* | *Revue d'histoire et de philosophie religieuses* |
| *RIDA* | *Revue internationale des droits de l'antiquité* |
| *RSF* | *Rivista di studi fenici* |
| RSO | Ras Shamra - Ougarit |
| *RSO* | *Rivista degli studi orientali* |
| *RSV* | *Revised Standard Version* |
| SBA | Studies in Biblical Archaeology |
| SBLDS | Society of Biblical Literature Dissertation Series |
| SBLMS | Society of Biblical Literature Monograph Series |
| SBLSBS | Society of Biblical Literature Sources for Biblical Studies |
| *SBLSP* | *Society of Biblical Literature Seminar Papers* |
| SBLSS | Society of Biblical Literature Semeia Series |
| SBLWAW | Society of Biblical Literature Writings from the Ancient World |
| SBOT | The Sacred Books of the Old Testament |
| *SEÅ* | *Svensk exegetisk årsbok* |
| *SEL* | *Studi epigrafici e linguistici* |
| *Sem* | *Semitica* |
| SHR | Studies in the History of Religions |
| SOTSMS | Society of Old Testament Studies Monograph Series |
| SS | Studi Semitici |
| *SSR* | *Studi storico-religiosi* |
| SWBA | Social World of Biblical Antiquity |
| *TADAE* | *Textbook of Aramaic Documents from Ancient Egypt: Newly Copied, Edited and Translated Into Hebrew and English.* 4 vols; ed. Bezalel Porten and Ada Yardeni; The Hebrew University Department of the History of the Jewish People, Texts and Studies for Students; Winona Lake: Eisenbrauns, 1986-99. |
| *TDNT* | Gerhard Kittel, *Theological Dictionary of the New Testament.* 10 vols.; Eng. trans. and ed. Geoffrey W. Bromiley; Grand Rapids: Wm. B. Eerdmans Publishing Co., 1964-76. |
| *TDOT* | *Theological Dictionary of the Old Testament.* 11 vols. to date; ed. G. Johannes Botterweck, Helmer Ringgren and Heinz-Josef Fabry; Grand Rapids: Wm. B. Eerdmans Publishing Co., 1974–. |
| *ThT* | *Theologisch Tijdschrift* |
| *TM* | *Tell Mardikh (Ebla)* |
| TSJTSA | Texts and Studies of the Jewish Theological Seminary of America |
| *TTZ* | *Trier theologische Zeitschrift* |
| *TWAT* | *Theologisches Wörterbuch zum Alten Testament.* Ed G. Johannes Botterweck and Helmer Ringgren. Stuttgart: W. Kohlhammer, 1973–. |
| UBL | Ugaritisch-biblische Literatur |
| *UF* | *Ugarit-Forschungen* |
| UUÅ | Uppsala universitets årsskrift |
| VB | Vorderasiatisches Bibliothek |
| *VT* | *Vetus Testamentum* |
| VTSup | *Vetus Testamentum*, Supplements |

| | |
|---|---|
| VWGT | Veröffentlichungen der Wissenschaftlichen Gesellschaft für Theologie |
| WBC | Word Biblical Commentary |
| WMANT | Wissenschaftliche Monographien zum Alten und Neuen Testament |
| *WO* | *Die Welt des Orients* |
| *ZAH* | *Zeitschrift für Althebraistik* |
| *ZAW* | *Zeitschrift für die alttestamentliche Wissenschaft* |
| *ZNW* | *Zeitschrift für die neutestamentliche Wissenschaft* |

# INTRODUCTION

The word *marzēaḥ*[1] occurs in literary and epigraphic references spanning three thousand years and a number of locations. The texts range from Ebla in the third millennium BCE to Madeba in the 6th century CE, with intervening attestations at Ugarit, Emar, Moab, Phoenicia, Elephantine, Nabatea, Palmyra and in rabbinic literature.[2] The word also occurs twice in the biblical literature, at Amos 6:7 and Jer 16:5. Much of this material was considered by David Bryan a quarter-century ago.[3] Nonetheless, a fresh examination of the material would be beneficial for a variety of reasons:

1) Scholarly interest in the *marzēaḥ* in general and individual texts in particular remains high,[4] and reconsideration of the ma-

---

[1] The word is vocalized differently from place to place, and at Ugarit even has a different final letter in some texts (see further in chapter 1). For the sake of uniformity and simplicity, I will use this transliteration of the Hebrew spelling (מַרְזֵחַ) to indicate the word and its referents in general, but will present the various spellings when discussing the individual texts.

[2] Against including *ma-ar-ṣa-ú* from El Amarna (*EA* 120:21) see W. L. Moran, *The Amarna Letters* (Baltimore: Johns Hopkins University Press, 1992) 199n11.

[3] D. B. Bryan, "Texts Relating to the *Marzēaḥ*: A Study of an Ancient Semitic Institution" (Ph.D. diss., Johns Hopkins University, 1973).

[4] Cf. the bibliography. Recent publications include a return to *CAT* 1.114 by three of its early commentators, a study of the *marzēaḥ* in relationship to other aspects of religious life at Ugarit and a discussion of Amos 6:7 and Jer 16:5, including a brief survey of the extra-biblical evidence: see K. J. Cathcart, "Ilu, Yariḫu and the One with the Two Horns and a Tail," *Ugarit, Religion and Culture: Proceedings of the International Colloquium on Ugarit, Religion and Culture: Edinburgh, July 1994. Essays Presented in Honour of Professor John C. L. Gibson* (UBL 12; eds. N. Wyatt, W. G. E. Watson and J. B. Lloyd; Münster: Ugarit-Verlag, 1996) 1-7 and compare K. J. Cathcart and W. G. E. Watson, "Weathering a Wake: A Cure for Carousal. A Revised Translation of *Ugaritica V* Text 1," *PIBA* 4 (1980) 35-58; M. Dietrich and O. Loretz, "'Siehe, da war er (wieder) munter!' Die mythologische Begründung für eine medikamentöse Behandlung in KTU 1.114 (RS 24.258)," *Boundaries of the Ancient Near Eastern World: A Tribute to Cyrus H. Gordon* (JSOTSup 273; eds. M. Lubetski, C. Gottlieb and S. Keller; Sheffield: Sheffield Academic Press, 1998) 174-98; D. Pardee, "*Marziḫu*, *Kispu*, and the Ugaritic Funerary Cult: A Minimalist View," *Ugarit, Religion and Culture: Proceedings of the International Colloquium on Ugarit, Religion and Culture: Edinburgh, July 1994. Essays Presented in Honour of Professor John C. L. Gibson* (UBL 12; eds. N. Wyatt, W. G. E. Watson and J. B. Lloyd; Münster:

terial as a whole in light of those more restricted studies published since Bryan's work will contribute to this ongoing research.

2) Additional extra-biblical instances of the word *marzēaḥ* have come to light since Bryan's study, namely two references from Ebla, one from Emar, *CAT* 4.399 from Ugarit, a Moabite text, a Phoenician *phialē* (drinking bowl) and a Palmyrene contract. While none of these alters the substance of his work, they do confirm some aspects and develop others and should be taken into account in order to develop the fullest possible picture of the *marzēaḥ*.

3) The frame of reference for considering the biblical *marzēaḥ* has changed. Since Bryan only dealt with occurrences of the word itself, the biblical *marzēaḥ* constituted a minor part of his study. However, in the last quarter-century, a number of scholars have suggested that various biblical texts, mostly in the prophetic literature, allude to a *marzēaḥ* without using the word itself. Thus, Amos 2:7b-8; 4:1; Hos 4:17-19; 9:1-6; Isa 5:11-13; 28:1-4; 28:7-8; 56:9-57:13; Ezek 8:7-13; 39:17-20 have all been interpreted in terms of biblical and extra-biblical *marzēaḥ* references.[5] This entails a significant expansion beyond the scope of Bryan's dissertation, so considering possible allusions[6] as well will result in a more extensive, and therefore more comprehensive, picture of the *marzēaḥ* in general, and within the prophetic literature in particular.

4) The various *marzēaḥ* texts have never been combined into a

---

Ugarit-Verlag, 1996) 273-87; C. Maier and E. M. Dörrfuß, "'Um mit ihnen zu sitzen, zu essen und zu trinken': Am 6,7; Jer 16,5 und die Bedeutung von *marzēaḥ*," *ZAW* 111 (1999) 45-57.

[5] The proponents of the various proposals are identified in Chapters 2-6 as each is considered in turn, along with the two biblical references in Amos 6:7 and Jer 16:5; see Chapters 3 and 4 respectively for reasons against considering Hos 7:3-7 and Isa 65:4. In addition to the prophetic texts, Cavalletti views Ps 78:15 as comparable to El's drinking at Ugarit (*CAT* 1.114), Pope interprets the entire Song of Songs as a *marzēaḥ*, and Jackson seems to suggest a *marzēaḥ* forms the background to Wisd 1:16; see S. Cavalletti, "Il dio ebbro di vino," *RBR* 15 (1981) 135-36; M. H. Pope, *Song of Songs: A New Translation with Introduction and Commentary* (AB 7C; Garden City: Doubleday, 1977), *passim*, but especially pp. 210-29; J. J. Jackson, "Style in Isaiah 28 and a Drinking Bout of the Gods (RS 24.258)," *Rhetorical Criticism: Essays in Honor of James Muilenburg* (PTMS 1; eds. J. J. Jackson and M. Kessler; Pittsburgh: Pickwick, 1974) 97.

[6] Henceforth, I use the word "reference" to indicate an instance where the word *marzēaḥ* actually appears and "allusion" for texts that involve a *marzēaḥ* but do not contain the word itself.

single, easily accessible volume. Bryan did present the texts known at that time in transliteration and English translation, but his work was not published. Moreover, as noted above, after his work was completed additional evidence concerning both the biblical and extra-biblical *marzēaḥ* has come to light. Since the following study presents all the extra-biblical *marzēaḥ* texts together with the biblical references and possible allusions in the original languages and English translation, it is hoped that the present volume can serve as a convenient single point of reference for the ongoing discussion concerning the *marzēaḥ* in the ancient Near East.

The purpose of the present study is to evaluate the validity of the various proposed *marzēaḥ* allusions mentioned above. In order to do this, however, it is necessary to establish some basic criteria by which such proposals can be evaluated. Those proposals have been advanced on a variety of grounds and usually in isolation from each other. Virtually all, however, entail a synchronic reading of the extra-biblical evidence, which does not allow for differences from place to place or development over the centuries, and often involves reading features of later *marzēaḥ*s into earlier ones. Yet, as Jonas C. Greenfield notes, "it would be methodologically wrong to assume a static institution, nonchanging and uninfluenced by the social, ethnic and political structure of the societies in which it flourished and not reflecting the influences of surrounding cultures and changing economic conditions."[7] This means that features present only in late attestations of the *marzēaḥ* could simply be more recent developments that were not characteristic of earlier *marzēaḥ*s. Nonethless, one can still assume some continuity over the millennia with respect to the *marzēaḥ*'s basic nature. In an effort to obtain a greater degree of certainty with respect to *marzēaḥ* allusions, I will focus on that continuity. By identifying elements of the *marzēaḥ* that are attested in both early and late instances, it will be possible to establish a minimal but fairly certain collection of *marzēaḥ* allusions.

[7] J. C. Greenfield, "The *Marzeaḥ* as a Social Institution," *Wirtschaft und Gesellschaft im Alten Vorderasien* (eds. J. Harmatta and G. Komoróczy; Budapest: Ákadémiai Kiadó, 1976) 455; cf. his admission that, "we have . . . read back into the *mrzḥ* at Ugarit some of the . . . features of the later *mrzḥ*" (ibid.).

The first step is an examination of the extra-biblical *marzēaḥ* references, including the new data that have appeared. That is the focus of the first chapter. My analysis of the material is guided by three principles. First, I only consider occurrences of the word *marzēaḥ* itself. While there may be *marzēaḥ* allusions in extra-biblical literature,[8] by establishing the constitutive features of the *marzēaḥ* from explicit references only, the criteria for evaluating biblical allusions will have a much higher degree of certainty. Similarly, although there are undoubtedly cross-cultural parallels, such as the Greek *thiasos* and *symposium*, these will not be considered either, so as to ensure that the criteria reflect only the *marzēaḥ* as it was known in the semitic world.

This relates to the second principle by which the extra-biblical references will be evaluated: my approach to those texts and inscriptions is "minimalistic." That is to say, I focus on the direct evidence from each successive attestation, accepting only what is explicit in the texts themselves. In doing so, I reject information

[8] E.g., a son's obligation to support his drunken father (*CAT* 1.17.I.30-31) was linked to the *marzēaḥ* by O. Eissfeldt, "Sohnespflichten im Alten Orient," *Syria* 43 (1966) 39-47; B. Margalit, *The Ugaritic Poem of AQHT: Text, Translation, Commentary* (BZAW 182; Berlin/New York: Walter de Gruyter, 1989) 276-77 (cf. *CAT* 1.114.18-19); *CAT* 1.15.IV.21-27 was viewed as a *marzēaḥ* by B. Margalit, "K-R-T Studies," *UF* 27 (1995) 249; and the funerary liturgy in *CAT* 1.161 is related to a *marzēaḥ* banquet by M. Dietrich and O. Loretz, "Neue Studien zu den Ritualtexten aus Ugarit (II)-Nr. 6-Epigraphische und inhaltliche Probleme in KTU 1.161," *UF* 15 (1983) 23; Margalit, *AQHT*, 273. References that require major restoration are also not considered (except where the term occurs undamaged in the immediate context). This excludes, for example, the restoration at *CAT* 1.1.IV.4 in J. C. L. Gibson, *Canaanite Myths and Legends* (2nd ed.; Edinburgh: T. &. T. Clark, 1978) 39; M. S. Smith, *The Ugaritic Baal Cycle. Vol. 1: Introduction with Text, Translation and Commentary of KTU 1:1-1.2* (VTSup 55; Leiden/New York/Cologne: E. J. Brill, 1994) 131; *idem*, "The Baal Cycle," *Ugaritic Narrative Poetry* (SBLWAW 9; ed. S. B. Parker; Atlanta: Scholars Press, 1997) 88, which is rejected by N. Wyatt, *Religious Texts from Ugarit: The Words of Ilimilku and His Colleagues* (The Biblical Seminar 53; Sheffield: Sheffield Academic Press, 1998) 47n41; at *CAT* 1.22.II.2 by K. Spronk, *Beatific Afterlife in Ancient Israel and in the Ancient Near East* (AOAT 219; Kevelaer; Neukirchen-Vluyn: Verlag Butzon and Bercker; Neukirchener Verlag, 1986) 176; T. J. Lewis, "The Rapiuma," *Ugaritic Narrative Poetry* (SBLWAW 9; ed. S. B. Parker; Atlanta: Scholars Press, 1997) 201; Wyatt, *Religious Texts*, 319; and in a Palmyrene inscription by C. Dunant, *Le sanctuaire de Baalshamin à Palmyre 3: Les inscriptions* (BHR 10; Rome: Institut suisse de Rome, 1971) 33, No. 21. Regardless of the relative merits of such proposals, without the term in the surrounding lines such texts will affect the certainty for which I am aiming.

from later *marzēaḥ*s or from non-*marzēaḥ* contexts that is not clearly reflected in each text itself. While this runs the risk of overlooking some subtle nuances, for the purpose of this study that risk is outweighed by the end result, namely identification of the essential elements of all *marzēaḥ*s. Put succinctly, minimalism will establish the minimal features of any and all *marzēaḥ*s, which should also be reflected in proposed allusions.

Third, the extra-biblical material will be grouped both geographically and chronologically. References with a common geographic provenance will be treated in relationship to one another; since such references can be dated within a relatively short time-frame relative to the *marzēaḥ*'s three-thousand year history,[9] it is less likely they will display radical change in the nature of a *marzēaḥ* in that place. At the same time, there is very little chronological overlap between references from different places, which means the evidence from the various locations can be treated successively in relation to other places in a roughly chronological order. Thus, distinctions can be made where necessary between *marzēaḥ*s in different places and at earlier and later stages of the *marzēaḥ*'s overall history.

Once the constitutive features of the *marzēaḥ* have been established, the subsequent chapters will consider the *marzēaḥ* in individual prophetic books. This will include both the references in Amos 6:7 and Jer 16:5 and an evaluation of all proposed allusions using the minimal criteria from Chapter 1. The prophetic literature provides an appropriate body of material for this study. To begin with, the only two instances of the word *marzēaḥ* in the Bible occur in prophetic books, and the majority of the proposed allusion are also found there,[10] so it makes sense to combine the latter with the former. While the prophetic literature is not monolithic, the various books do have some commonalities which enable one to speak in general terms of a shared "tradition," within which common themes and concerns appear; as such it would not be surprising to find the *marzēaḥ* reflected elsewhere in the prophetic literature beyond the two instances of the word itself.

[9] The biggest span is about two hundred years with respect to both Phoenician and Palmyrene references.

[10] Cf. n. 5 above.

Finally, the prophetic books in question are traditionally dated to a period of about two to three centuries, which happens to coincide with a major chronological gap in the extra-biblical attestations.[11]

Analysis of the prophetic references and allusions to the *marzēaḥ* will also be minimalistic and chronological (although for the sake of convenience, Isa 56:9-57:13 will be included with the other Isaiah texts). The first element is especially important in dealing with allusions, which must be established on the basis of an individual text's content. Therefore, care will be taken not to read *marzēaḥ* elements into possible allusions when such elements cannot be supported from the specific text or its context. On the other hand, the chronological aspect is more difficult to establish, due to the uncertain dating of the prophetic books themselves. It is widely recognized that the dates given in the opening verses of the various prophetic books and in the headings of many oracles are later editorial additions. Although they may be an accurate indication of the general period of composition, some scholars have emphasized the redactional nature of the prophetic books and argued that most of their content also stems from a much later date.[12] But since the *marzēaḥ* is clearly attested prior to the prophetic period (and in one instance at the same time in Moab) there is no reason to assume the *marzēaḥ* references and allusions are necessarily late. Yet at the same time, *marzēaḥ*s endured after this time elsewhere in the semitic world, so it may also have continued in post-exilic Judah, and later influence cannot be ruled out either.

Fortunately, this study does not require an exact date for any of the texts considered. The goal is to develop a *rough* chronology of the prophetic references and allusions, both in relationship to

---

[11] With the exception of the Moabite text, all of the extra-biblical *marzēaḥ* references can be dated either before Amos or after Ezekiel.

[12] For this approach to Isaiah see O. Kaiser, *Isaiah 1-12: A Commentary* (OTL; 2nd ed., revised and completely rewritten; trans. J. Bowden; Philadelphia: Westminster Press, 1983); for Jeremiah see R. P. Carroll, *Jeremiah: A Commentary* (OTL; Philadelphia: Westminster Press, 1986); W. McKane, *A Critical and Exegetical Commentary on Jeremiah. Vol. I: Introduction and Commentary on Jeremiah I-XXV* (ICC 20; Edinburgh: T. & T. Clark, 1986); *idem, A Critical and Exegetical Commentary on Jeremiah. Vol. II: Commentary on Jeremiah XXVI-LII* (ICC 20; Edinburgh: T. & T. Clark, 1996).

each other and to the extra-biblical references. To that end, some consideration will be given to the date of the relevant texts, but for the task at hand it is sufficient to establish a *relative* dating in relationship to the other prophetic texts. Therefore, I assume the traditional chronology of the biblical prophets as an initial, working hypothesis, and treat the various texts in the order of that chronology. In the course of that analysis, if it is determined that a text does contain a *marzēaḥ* allusion (or, obviously, a direct reference in Amos 6:7 and Jer 16:5) the date will then be addressed.[13] At that point I will look at whether the text's content reflects what is known about the context and setting of that particular prophet. In other words, is a particular *marzēaḥ* reference or allusion consistent with the traditional time of that prophet's ministry? If so, that establishes a plausible date by which to relate it to the other texts in other prophetic books.

The issue of consistency raises the matter of editorial additions. Since the focus of this study is not the editorial history of various texts but whether they allude to a *marzēaḥ*, I do not intend to present a full redaction-critical analysis of any of the texts which will be studied in the following chapters.[14] Nevertheless, redactional considerations cannot be dismissed if the aim is to determine whether the earlier text alluded to a *marzēaḥ*. Specifically, if constitutive elements of a *marzēaḥ* are only present as a later addition, then it is not a constitutive component of the original text, thereby invalidating the proposed allusion. In keeping with this, when discussing individual texts, only those deletions that directly affect the issue of a *marzēaḥ* allusion will be considered at any length.

Once the *marzēaḥ* references and allusions in the prophetic literature have been determined, it will be possible to draw some conclusions concerning the extent of the *marzēaḥ* during the prophetic period, its nature as it appears in the prophetic literature, the attitude of the individual prophets to it, and possible develop-

---

[13] Since texts that are determined not to allude to a *marzēaḥ* are irrelevant to the latter's chronology, their dating is also irrelevant to my purpose and will not be discussed.

[14] Such treatments can be found to varying extents in most commentaries, and in monographs dedicated to that purpose.

ments during that period of time and in relationship to the extra-biblical evidence. But first, the texts themselves must be considered, so I turn now to that task.

CHAPTER ONE

# THE EXTRA-BIBLICAL *MARZĒAḤ*

In this chapter all the extra-biblical references to the *marzēaḥ* will be examined according to the principles outlined in the Introduction. In an effort to establish the context for the *marzēaḥ* in the prophetic literature, I group the extra-biblical references into those which can be dated before and after the prophetic use of the term. The individual *marzēaḥ* references in each half are grouped according to their time and place of origin, and the results from each half will be summarized separately. This enables the features of the pre-biblical *marzēaḥ*, which forms the primary background for the prophetic references and allusions, to be established in isolation from the post-biblical *marzēaḥ*. In the final section of the chapter, I draw conclusions concerning the constitutive features of the *marzēaḥ* throughout its history, in order to establish criteria by which to evaluate the *marzēaḥ* in the prophets.

## I. The Pre-Biblical *marzēaḥ*

### A. *Ebla*

The word *marzēaḥ* has been identified in two texts from Ebla, dating to the second half of the third millennium.[1] Given the administrative nature of these texts it is difficult to determine much with any certainty, although they do provide a limited amount of general information.

#### 1. *TM* 75.G.1372[2]

| | | |
|---|---|---|
| 1 íbx4-túg 2-NI | 1 | 1 2-NI gown |
| *a-da-ti-gú*$^{ki}$*-sù* | 2 | to Adatigu |
| *wa* | 3 | and |

[1] For recent discussions of Ebla and the texts found there, including issues of dating, see G. Pettinato, *Ebla: A New Look at History* (trans. C. F. Richardson; Baltimore; London: Johns Hopkins University Press, 1991); R. D. Biggs, "Ebla Texts," *ABD* 2.263-70.

[2] Published as "Testo 46" in G. Pettinato, *Testi amministrativi della biblioteca L. 2769* (MEE 2; Napoli: Instituto Universitario Orientale di Napoli, 1980) 309.

| | | |
|---|---|---|
| 1 íbx3-túg-dar | 4 | 1 multi-coloured gown |
| dumu-nita | II 1 | to the child |
| *munu*$_x$*-ma-ni* | 2 | of Munu-Mani; |
| 4 íbx3-túg-dar | 3 | 4 multi-coloured gowns |
| NE.DI | 4 | as property |
| *a-mu-tù* | 5 | Amutu |
| šu ba$_4$-ti | 6 | has received |

| | | |
|---|---|---|
| Reverse | Reverse | |
| *in* ud | I 1 | on the occasion |
| *mar-za-u*$_9$ | 2 | of the *marzēaḥ*. |
| itu-*i*-SI | 3 | Month of *i*-SI. |

Here, gowns are given to three different individuals "on the occasion of the *marzēaḥ* in the month of *i*-SI." The word *marzēaḥ* seems to refer to an event of some sort, but it is not clear whether a *marzēaḥ* occurred every month, and this text refers to the one in the month of *i*-SI, or whether no intrinsic connection exists between the *marzēaḥ* and the month mentioned. In any case, the *marzēaḥ* seems to be an appropriate time for giving clothing. Nothing further can be established from this text alone, although some have made claims about this *marzēaḥ* on other grounds. For instance, noting similar wording in *TM* 75.G.1264:IV.15-17, where garments are given "on the day of the drinking feast of his son" (ud *maš-da-ù* dunu-nita-*šu*), Dahood equates the *marzēaḥ* and the *maš-da-ù*.[3] While he is probably correct as to the role of drinking in the *marzēaḥ*, the uncertain connection between these two Eblaite words is insufficient grounds for such a conclusion.[4] Similarly, Archi identifies this *marzēaḥ* as a funerary feast simply on the basis of his prior assumptions as to its nature.[5]

[3] M. J. Dahood, "The Minor Prophets and Ebla," *The Word of the Lord Shall Go Forth: Essays in Honor of David Noel Freedman in Celebration of His Sixtieth Birthday* (eds. C. L. Meyers and M. O'Connor; Winona Lake: Eisenbrauns, 1983) 54; *idem*, "Love and Death at Ebla and Their Biblical Reflections," *Love and Death in the Ancient Near East: Essays in Honor of Marvin H. Pope* (eds. J. H. Marks and R. M. Good; Winona Lake: Eisenbrauns, 1987) 99. For the text of *TM* 75.G.1264:IV.15-17 see Pettinato, *Testi amministrativi*, 22, 29.

[4] He appeals to a perceived parallel between בֵּת מַרְזֵחַ and בֵּת מִשְׁתֶּה in Jer 16:5, 9, but they are in fact distinct (see in Chapter 5 below). On the role of alcohol in the *marzēaḥ* see pp. 69-70.

[5] A. Archi, "Cult of the Ancestors and Tutelary God at Ebla," *Fucus: A Semitic/Afrasian Gathering in Remembrance of Albert Ehrman* (Current Issues in Linguistic Theory 58; ed. Y. L. Arbeitman; Amsterdam/Philadelphia: John Benjamins Publishing Company, 1988) 103n2. Against a funerary connection for the *marzēaḥ* throughout most of its history, see pp. 70-79 below.

2. *TM* 75.G.1443 XI.1-3[6]

| | |
|---|---|
| 1 gu-dùl-TÚG 1 aktum-TÚG 1 íb+ III-TÚG-sa$_6$-GÚN | 1 robe, 1 shirt, 1 coat are given to |
| *Du-da-sa* | 2 Dudasa |
| ugula *mar-za-u*$_9$ | 3 superintendent of the *marzēaḥ*. |

The "superintendent" in this text is almost certainly the predecessor of the *marzēaḥ* leader (*rb*/רב) mentioned at Ugarit, Nabatea and Palmyra, but there is not enough context to indicate whether here *marzēaḥ* refers to an event, as in the first text, or a group, as in the later references mentioning a leader. Nevertheless, as in the previous text, the *marzēaḥ* is again linked with giving clothing.

## B. *Ugarit*

The word *marzēaḥ* occurs in nine texts from Ugarit dating to ca. 1200 BCE.[7] Four are in Akkadian and five in alphabetic Ugaritic; seven are legal texts and two are mythological. For convenience, I group them by the language of composition.

### 1. *Akkadian Texts*

a. RS 14.16[8]

1 [iš-tu ûmi$^{\text{m}}$]$^{\text{i}}$ *an-ni-i-im*
2 [a-na pa-ni $^{\text{awi}}$]$^{\text{lê pl.}}$ *šibûti* $^{\text{pl. ti}}$
3 [ ] $^{\text{awilê pl.}}$ *ma-ar-zi-ḫi*
4 [ ] *mârê* $^{\text{pl.}}$ *Ti-su-pa-ri*
5 [ ]*-nu-me-na u* $^{\text{n}}$ *Abdi-an-ta*
6 [ ]*-nu-me-nu aḫu rabû u Abdi-an-tù aḫu ṣiḫru*
7 [ ]*-be-la* $^{\text{f}}$ *A-na-ti-um-me*
8 [ ... *i-na*] *be-ri-šú-nu*

---

9 [ ] $^{\text{n}}$ *Abdi-an-tù*

---

[6] Published in A. Archi, *Testi amministrativi: assegnazioni di tessuti (archivio L. 2769)* (ARET I; Roma: Missione archeologica italiana in Siria, 1985) 31.

[7] For an overview of the Ugarit texts see D. Pardee and P. Bordreuil, "Ugarit: Texts and Literature," *ABD* 6.706-21.

[8] The text is transliterated, with commentary, in C. Virolleaud, "Six textes de Ras Shamra provenant de la XIV$^{\text{e}}$ campagne (1950)," *Syria* 28 (1951) 173-79. Cf. the discussion in D. B. Bryan, "Texts Relating to the *Marzeaḥ*: A Study of an Ancient Semitic Institution" (Ph.D. Dissertation; Johns Hopkins University, 1973) 144-47.

10 [ ]*-na aḫê* $^{\text{pl}}$*-šu*
11 [ ... *m*]*a-al-li*
12 [ ]*i-ba-ṭar*[9] *i-na sûqi*
13 [ ]*i-zi-ir*
14 [ ...*š*]*u*(?) *išten* $^{\text{en}}$ *li-im kaspim* $^{\text{pl}}$
14b[10] ]*i-na eqlêti* $^{\text{ZUN}}$*-šu*[
15 [ ]*-ti*

Reverse

16 [ ] *sûqi*
17 [ ... *Ki-ir*(?)]*-ru-na*
18 [ ] *mâr Ti-ya-rum*
19 [ ] *bu-qa-na*
20 [pân – – – – – mâr] *Mu-na-ḫi-me*
21 [pân – – – – ] *mâr Ku-ut-ta-na*
22 [pân – – – – ] *mâr Šu-wa-an-da-na*
23 [pân – – – ]*-nu mâr Ḫu-ta-ši*
24 [pân – – – d]*a-nu mâr Ši-ku-ti*
25 [pân – – – ]*-du mâr Abdi-Ḫa-wa*
26 [pân – – – ]*-ia-nu mâr Ki-ir-ru-na*
27 [pân Mu – ]*na-ḫi-mu mâr Gur-pa-na*
28 [pân Ta – m]*ar*(?)*-te-nu mâr Ḫu-da-ši*
29 [pân – – –]*-bi-mu mâr Ta-me-ia*
30 [pân – – –]*bi-bi-lu mâr Ia-ku-un-ni*
31 *Warad* $^{\text{d.}}$ NIN-URTA $^{\text{awil}}$ *ṭup-sar-rum*

1 [From] this [day],
2 [before] witnesses,
3 . . .] the men of the *marzēaḥ*
4 . . .] the sons of Tisupari
5 . . .]-numena and Abdiantû
6 . . .]-numenu, the elder brother, and Abdiantû, the younger brother
7 . . .]-bela Anatiumme
8 . . . among] them

---

9 . . .] Abdiantû
10 . . . nume]na their brothers
11 . . . ful]fill
12 . . .] he will go out into the street

---

[9] Probably to be read as *i-pá-ṭar*; see Virolleaud, "Six Textes," 177.
[10] This line is reversed on the tablet.

13 . . .] he honoured
14 . . .] 1 silver *lîm*
14b . . .] in their fields
15 . . .]-ti

Reverse

16 . . . . . . . ] the street
17 . . . Kiir]runa
18 ] son of Tiyarum
19 ]-buqana
20 [before son of] Munaḫime
21 [before ] son of Kuuttana
22 [before ] son of Šuwaandana
23 [before ]nu son of Ḫutaši
24 [before d]anu son of Šikuti
25 [before ]du son of Abdiḫawa
26 [before ]ianu son of Kiirruna
27 [before Mu]naḫimu son of Gurpana
28 [before Tam]artenu son of Ḫudaši
29 [before ]bimu son of Tameia
30 [before ]bibilu son of Iakuunni
31 Warad $^{d.}$ NIN-URTA was the scribe

In RS 14.16 the phrase, "the men of the *marzēaḥ*" occurs after a lacuna at the beginning of line 3, and the next few lines contain portions of names (also after lacunae), which may be an actual list of those *marzēaḥ* members. The gaps are indicative of the tablet's fragmentary condition, which makes it difficult to determine exactly what is at issue in the text. The list of witnesses (perhaps as many as fourteen) at the end, however, indicates it is a juridical document of some sort while the monetary sum (a *lîm* of silver) in line 14 suggests a financial matter. Whether the text is a contract, a legal suit, or something else is not clear.

The lack of any substantial context prevents definitive statements concerning this *marzēaḥ*'s nature or function, but some observations are possible. First, a definable group of people, the "men of the *marzēaḥ*," is treated as a recognizable collective entity under the law. Second, the amount of money involved[11] indicates the group was

[11] Virolleaud, "Six Textes," 177, valued a *lîm* at 10,000 shekels and was followed by P. D. Miller, Jr., "The *MRZḤ* Text," *The Claremont Ras Shamra Tablets* (AnOr 48; ed. L. R. Fisher; Rome: Biblical Institute Press, 1971) 44; Bryan,

involved in significant financial matters. Third, these dealings, combined with the number of witnesses,[12] suggests this *marzēaḥ* was an important group in Ugarit.

b. RS 15.88[13]

| | | |
|---|---|---|
| *iš-tu* $_{2}$*ûmi an-ni-im* | 1 | From this day, |
| $^{l}$*níq-me-pa mâr níq-ma-*$^{il}$*adu* | 2 | Niqmepa, son of Niqmadu, |
| *šàr* $^{al}$*u-ga-ri-it* | 3 | King of Ugarit, |
| *it-ta-ši bît* $^{amilM}$ *mar-za-i* | 4 | has produced the house of the men of the *marzēaḥ* |
| *ù id-din-šu* | 5 | and he has granted it |
| *a-na* $^{amilM}$ *mar-za-i-ma* | 6 | to the men of the *marzēaḥ* |
| *a-na mârî*$^{M}$*-šu-nu* | 7 | (and) to their "descendants" |
| *a-na da-ri-ti* | 8 | forever. |
| *ma-am-ma iš-tu qâti*$^{ti}$*-šu-nu* | 9 | No one, from their hands |
| *ú-ul i-laq-qi* | 10 | shall take it. |
| $^{aban}$*kunuk šarri rabû* | 11 | Seal of the Great King. |
| $^{lil}$*šamaš-šarru ṭupšarrum*$^{um}$ | 12 | Šammaššarru, scribe. |

This text is a royal document issued over the seal of King Niqmepa, son of Niqmadu. It confirms the eternal ownership of a "house of the men of the *marzēaḥ*" (line 4) by them and their "descendants" (lines 6-7) as inviolable. Again, the text says nothing directly concerning this *marzēaḥ*, yet some information can still be gleaned from it. Since the term probably refers to a group rather than a place,[14] the text confirms that a *marzēaḥ* was a legally recognized collective that could own property. Its social importance, or at least that of its

"Texts," 147, 208; J. C. Greenfield, "The *Marzeaḥ* as a Social Institution," *Wirtschaft und Gesellschaft im Alten Vorderasien* (eds. J. Harmatta and G. Komoróczy; Budapest: Ákadémiai Kiadó, 1976) 452. Lewis reduces this amount to 1000 shekels on the basis of the *CAD*; see T. J. Lewis, *Cults of the Dead in Ancient Israel and Ugarit* (HSM 39; Atlanta: Scholars Press, 1989) 81n5.

[12] Compare the fourteen witnesses here with *CAT* 3.9 below, which lists only two witnesses.

[13] For transliteration and a French translation see *PRU* III, 88. Cf. Bryan, "Texts," 148-52.

[14] Lewis, *Cults of the Dead*, 83n16, states that, "the phrase . . . 'the house of the men of the *marzēaḥ*' . . . would be redundant if *marzēaḥ* were an architectural entity." This is not conclusive, since the men could have lived together separately from their meeting place, with the latter being the *marzēaḥ* proper. But without evidence of quasi-monastic lifestyles at Ugarit, the more plausible conclusion is that *bît* refers to a building owned and used as a gathering place by the members of a *marzēaḥ* association. Contrast Bryan, "Texts," 209-10, who argues that the word *marzēaḥ* indicates either the house itself or a specific part thereof.

members, is implied by the royal recognition of their property rights.[15]

A second point to consider is the extension of those property rights to the "descendants" forever. On the surface, this means "a member's ownership in the society's holdings was passed on to his sons,"[16] but some unarticulated presuppositions underlie this interpretation. Unless the prerequisites and personal qualifications for membership were hereditary, the *marzēaḥ* ran the risk of group property being owned in part by someone unsuited, or even unwilling, to be a member. Moreover, if an individual had no offspring, or at least no male offspring, how would his share of the assets be handled? The *marzēaḥ*'s political importance in this text indicates these and comparable scenarios could engender serious economic and legal difficulties. Thus, I suggest that *mârî*$^{M}$*-šu-nu* does not refer to biological progeny, but to subsequent members of the association.[17]

c. RS 15.70[18]

| | | |
|---|---|---|
| [i]*š-tu ûmi*$^{mi}$ *an-ni-i-im* | 1 | [F]rom this day, |
| [a-n]*a pa-ni* $^{l}$*a-miš-tam-ra mâr* $^{l}$*níq-me-pa* | 2 | [be]fore Ammištamru, son of Niqmepa, |
| [š]*àr* $^{al}$*ú-ga-ri-it* $^{amil}$*sākinu*[19] *il-te-qí* | 3 | [K]ing of Ugarit, the vizier has taken |
| bît $^{amilM}$*mar-ze-i ša ša-at-ra-na* | 4 | the house of the men of the *marzēaḥ* of Šatrana |
| *ù it-ta-din bît* $^{l}$*ib-ra-mu-zi* | 5 | and has granted the house of Ibramuzi |
| [ki-i-m]*a bîti-šu-nu* | 6 | [as] their house. |
| [bît $^{am}$]$^{ilM}$*mar-ze-i ša ša-at-ra-na* | 7 | [The house of the m]en of the *marzēaḥ* of Šatrana |
| *ṣa-mi-id a-na* $^{amil}$*sākini* | 8 | is given to the vizier, |
| *ù bît* $^{l}$*ib-ra-mu-zi* | 9 | and the house of Ibramuzi |
| *ṣa-mi-id a-na* $^{amilM}$*mar-ze-i* | 10 | is given to the men of the *marzēaḥ* |

---

[15] Greenfield, "Social Institution," 453; J.-M. de Tarragon, *Le culte à Ugarit d'après les textes de la pratique en cunéiformes alphabétiques* (CahRB 19; Paris: J. Gabalda, 1980) 147.

[16] Lewis, *Cults of the Dead*, 83.

[17] For this nuance see *CAD* 10.I.315; see further in n. 22.

[18] Transliteration and a French translation of the text are given in *PRU* III, 130. See also the discussion in Bryan, "Texts," 153-55.

[19] Written as *râbiṣu* in the original publication, but Buccellatti has established that MAŠKIM is to be read as *sākinu*; see G. Buccellati, "Due noti di testi accadici di Ugarit: MAŠKIM-*sākinu*," *OrAnt* 2 (1963) 223-228. For a discussion of the *sākinu*'s role at Ugarit see M. Heltzer, *The Internal Organization of the Kingdom of Ugarit (Royal Service-Systems, Taxes, Royal Economy, Army and Administration)* (Weisbaden: Reichert, 1982) 141-52.

| | | |
|---|---|---|
| *ša ša-at-ra-na ù a-na mârî*$^{M}$*-šu-nu* | 11 | of Šatrana and to their "descendants." |
| *ur*$_{5}$*-ra še-ra amîlu ma-am-ma-an* | 12 | In the future, no one |
| *la-a i-la-qí* | 13 | will take |
| *bît* $^{I}$*ib-ra-mu-zi* | 14 | the house of Ibramuzi |
| *iš-tu qâti* $^{amilM}$*mar-ze-i* | 15 | from the hands of the men of the *marzēaḥ* |
| *ša ša-at-ra-na* | 16 | of Šatrana |
| *ù iš-tu qâti mârî*$^{M}$*-šu-nu* | 17 | or from the hands of their sons |
| *a-di da-ri-ti* | 18 | forever. |
| $^{aban}$*kunuk* $^{I}$*a-miš-tam-ra mâr níq-me-pa* | 19 | Seal of Ammištamru, son of Niqmepa, |
| [š]*à*[r] $^{al}$*ú-ga-ri-it* | 20 | [K]in[g] of Ugarit. |

Although RS 15.70 is numerically prior to RS 15.88, the ascription to King Ammištamru, son of Niqmepa,[20] indicates it is a later text. It states that the vizier had taken over the "house of the men of the *marzēaḥ* of Šatrana" (lines 3-4) and given them Ibramuzi's house in its place. The text duplicates the phrase from the preceding text (but with the spelling *mar-ze-i* and the added association with the god Šatrana[21]), and repeats the reference to the men and their descendants from RS 15.88.6-7 in lines 10-11 and 15-17. Thus, this text supports the conclusions drawn above concerning property ownership and its preservation by the *marzēaḥ* members, while adding the information that a *marzēaḥ* could be connected with, or even dedicated to, a particular deity, perhaps recognizing him or her as its patron.[22]

The identical vocabulary in RS 15.70 and 15.88 raises the question whether the two texts deal with the same *marzēaḥ*. If so, both the king's involvement in an underling's dealings and the need to reimburse the loss in RS 15.70 would be explained by his predeces-

[20] This is probably Ammištamru IV and the king in RS 15.88 is probably his father, Niqmepa VI. For a discussion of dynastic succession at Ugarit on the basis of *CAT* 1.113 see K. A. Kitchen, "The King List of Ugarit," *UF* 9 (1977) 131-42.

[21] The determinative for a god is missing, but it is present in RS 16.157.5 (transliteration and French translation in *PRU* III, 83-84). On this deity see the works cited in O. Eissfeldt, "Kultvereine in Ugarit," *Ugaritica VI* (MRS 17; ed. C. F. A. Schaeffer; Paris: Geuthner, 1969) 191n23.

[22] This has interesting implications for the nuance of the term *mârî*$^{M}$*-šu-nu*. On one hand, lack of devotion to the god in question could render a member's son both unsuitable for and undesirous of membership. On the other hand, the religious context a divine patron provides might point to *marzēaḥ* initiates as the "spiritual" children of the "men of the *marzēaḥ*."

sor's decree. If they are distinct, the need to compensate this particular *marzēaḥ* for the alienation of its property increases its social and political importance. This reimbursement's full significance is highlighted by the lack of comparable recompense, either in kind or in money, to Ibramuzi for the house he has lost.[23]

d. RS 18.01[24]

| | | |
|---|---|---|
| *iš-tu* ${}_{2}$*ûmi an-ni-i* | 1 | From this day, |
| *aš-šum eqlât*$^{M}$ *iṣi iskarâni* | 2 | concerning the vineyards |
| *ša* $^{il}$*ištar ḫur-ri* | 3 | of the Hurrian Ishtar |
| *ša i-na* $^{al}$*šu-uk-sí* | 4 | situated in Šuksu: |
| *eqil* $^{is}$*karâni* | 5 | the vineyard |
| $^{il}$*ištar ḫur-ri* | 6 | of the Hurrian Ishtar |
| *be-ri* $^{amil\ M}$*mar-zi-i* | 7 | (is divided) between the men of the *marzēaḥ* |
| *ša* $^{al}$*a-ri* | 8 | of Aru |
| *ù be-ri* | 9 | and between |
| *amil* $^{M}$*mar-zi-i* | 10 | the men of the *marzēaḥ* |
| *ša* $^{al}$*si-i̯a-ni* | 11 | of Siyannu; |
| *amîlum a-na amîlum* | 12 | men against men |
| *la-a ub-bal-kat* | 13 | will not transgress. |
| $^{aban}$*kunuk* $^{I}$*pa-di-i̯a* | 14 | Seal of Padiya, |
| *šàr* $^{al}$*si-i̯a-ni* | 15 | King of Siyannu. |

The final Akkadian text to consider is an international document bearing the seal of Padiya, the King of Siyannu, in which a vineyard dedicated to the Hurrian Ishtar in the village of Šuksu is divided between the "men of the *marzēaḥ* of (the village of) Aru," and the "men of the *marzēaḥ* of (the village of) Siyannu" (lines 7-11). Royal involvement in this case cannot be attributed to their importance *per se*, since the text's focus is the resolution of a border dispute that only incidentally involves them.[25] Nonetheless, we do learn that

[23] This is even more significant if he is the same Ibramuzi who is called the king's "servant" and given another's property in RS 16.189 (*PRU* III, 90-91) and whose own property is declared inviolable in RS 16.285 (*PRU* III, 106-07), both times by Niqmepa. There is no indication in RS 15.70 that he is a *nayyālu* ("defaulter"); on this term see M. Heltzer, *The Rural Community in Ancient Ugarit* (Weisbaden: Reichert, 1976) 52-57.

[24] Transliteration and French translation can be found in *PRU* IV, 230. Cf. Bryan, "Texts," 155-57.

[25] Cf. the division of Šuksu between the kings of Ugarit and Siyannu in RS 17.123 (*PRU* IV, 230-31). Aru appears in a number of administrative texts listing Ugaritic villages; see the references in W. van Soldt, "Studies in the Topography of Ugarit (1): The Spelling of the Ugaritic Toponyms," *UF* 28 (1996) 660.

*marzēaḥ*s could be attached to particular geographical locations, and more than one could exist in relatively close proximity.[26] Furthermore, there is yet another reference to *marzēaḥ* members and property. Here that property has a triple significance: in addition to the possession of communal property encountered in previous texts, the vineyard suggests that wine consumption may have played a role in the *marzēaḥ*'s activities while the vineyard's dedication to a particular deity is (indirect) evidence that a *marzēaḥ* could have a divine patron.[27]

## 2. *Alphabetic Texts*[28]

The term *marzēaḥ* occurs in five alphabetic texts from Ugarit, namely two fragmentary economic texts, a legal document in much better condition and two mythological texts.

### a. *CAT* 4.399[29]

| | | |
|---|---|---|
| [ ]ġ*b* . xx *b* . *šrm* | 1 | [ ]? ?? among princes |
| [ ]*šd* . *irpn* . *ṯ*[ ] | 2 | [ ] fallow field ?[ |
| [ ]*š*[ ]*ṯtn* . *šd* . | 3 | [ ]? [ ] two fields |
| xx*š* . xx*ga* . *ḫmš* | 4 | ? five |
| *šd* . *ʿmn* . *irm* . | 5 | fields with him I erected. |
| [t]n . *ʿšrh* . *šd* . *ṯlṯ* | 6 | [You] give his banquet three |
| *zt* . ʿxx . *šbʿ* . *š*[d] | 7 | olive trees xxxx seven fie[lds] |
| *ʿmy* . *bn* . *mrzḥ* | 8 | with me. The men of the *marzēaḥ* |
| *ṯn* . *ʿšr* . *šd* . *b* . *i*xx[ ] | 9 | two, ten fields in ? |
| [a]r*bʿ* . *šd* . *b* . *šr* | 10 | four fields to the prince |
| [ ]x*i* . *šir* . *kbd* | 11 | [ ]? bountiful produce |
| [ ]*prt* . *ubyn* | 12 | [ ]? I will establish |
| *š*[i]*r* . *w* . *arbʿ* [30] | 13 | pr[o]duce and four |

[26] Lewis, *Cults of the Dead*, 84, suggests there might be only one *marzēaḥ* per city.

[27] Eissfeldt, "Kultvereine," 192, is uncertain whether Ishtar was the patron of both *marzēaḥ*s.

[28] The alphabetic (Ugaritic) texts will be cited according to their number and (except where noted) the transliteration in *The Cuneiform Alphabetic Texts from Ugarit, Ras Ibn Hani and Other Places (KTU: Second, Enlarged Edition)* (ALASP 8; eds. M. Dietrich, O. Loretz and J. Sanmartín; Münster: Ugarit-Verlag, 1995). In keeping with the practice there, damaged or poorly legible letters are printed in roman script while undamaged and legible signs are in italics.

[29] This text has not been published other than in *CAT* and thus was not discussed by Bryan.

[30] This line is written on the lower edge of the tablet.

| Reverse | Reverse |
|---|---|
| [ḥ]*m*[š . šd ]*n* | 14 [f]iv[e fields ] |
| š*d* . [ ] | 15 field [ ] |
| *g*x[ ]*šd* | 16 ?? [ ] field |
| [ ]*ṯ*xx | 17 ? |
| *k*x[ ] | 18 ? |
| *šd* . [ ] | 19 field [ ] |

Due to the fragmentary nature of *CAT* 4.399, the translation given above must be considered provisional, and any conclusions drawn from it taken as tentative until confirmed by other *marzēaḥ* texts. Nevertheless, it is fairly certain that it contains a register of fields and an enumeration of their produce.[31] The word *marzēaḥ* appears in line 8 within the phrase *bn* . *mrzḥ*. This is comparable to the Akkadian phrase [amilM]*mar-za-i* (and its variants), referring to one or more of the *marzēaḥ*'s members.[32] It probably indicates the owners of at least some of the fields. The nobility are mentioned in lines 1 and 10, but it is not clear what, if any, connection they have to this *marzēaḥ*, or whether there is any link between either them or the *marzēaḥ* and the banquet mentioned in line 6.

b. *CAT* 4.642[33]

| | |
|---|---|
| [ ]x[ ] | 1 [ ] ? [ ] |
| [ mr]*zḥ* . ʿ*n*[t ] | 2 [ the *mar*]*zēaḥ* of ʿAn[at ] |
| [ ]*šir* . *šd* . *kr*[m] | 3 [ ] fruit of the field, the vineya[rd] |
| [ ]*l* . *mrzḥ* . ʿ*n*[t] | 4 [ ] to the *marzēaḥ* of ʿAn[at] |
| [ ]l . *mrzḥ* . ʿ*n*[t] | 5 [ ] to the *marzēaḥ* of ʿAn[at] |

[31] There are references to fields (*šd*) in lines 2, 3, 5, 6, 7, 9, 10, 15, 16, 19 and to olive trees (*zt*) in 7; *šir* in lines 11 (and 13?) literally means "flesh" but is probably used metaphorically in the sense of "produce" of the fields, as in *CAT* 4.282.5, 6, 7, 8, 10, 12, 14 (note the numbers in that text as well); cf. [d]m . ʿ*ṣm* (literally "blood of trees" = sap) in *CAT* 1.4.III.44 and *dm zt* ("blood of olives" = olive oil) in *CAT* 1.114.31. In *CAT* 4.399 various numbers are present in lines 4 (*ḫmš*), 6 (*ṯlṯ*;), 7 (*šb*ʿ), 9 (*ṯn* . ʿ*šr*) and 10 (*[a]rb*ʿ).

[32] The *bn* could be either a singular or a construct plural, i.e., either "son" or "sons of the *marzēaḥ*." The classic case of "son" meaning "member of a group" is the biblical "sons of the prophets": e.g., 1 Kgs 20:35; 2 Kgs 2:3, 5, 7, 15, etc.

[33] Transliterated in *PRU* V, no. 32; it is discussed by Bryan, "Texts," 138-39.

| | | |
|---|---|---|
| [ l] . *mrzḥ* . ʿ[nt] | 6 | [ to] the *marzēaḥ* of ʿA⌊nat] |
| [ mr]*zḥ* . ʿ*n*[t] | 7 | [ *mar*]*zēaḥ* of ʿAn[at] |
| ... | 8 | ... |

The greatest concentration of the term *marzēaḥ* in a single Ugaritic text is in *CAT* 4.642. Unfortunately, the tablet is very badly damaged, but the word *marzēaḥ* is present or reconstructed a total of five times, on lines 2 and 4-7.[34] The tablet's advanced state of disrcpair provides minimal context from which to clarify the word's meaning, but two points can be determined. First, Otto Eissfeldt suggested restoring a *t* after each occurrence of ʿ*n*,[35] which yields the phrase, "the *marzēaḥ* of Anat," providing another instance of a *marzēaḥ* with a divine patron. Secondly, the only variation in what remains of the tablet is line 3, which refers to a vineyard's produce. The context suggests a relationship between the vineyard and the *marzēaḥ* of Anat, and the obvious one is that the latter owns the former.[36] This constitutes another example of a *marzēaḥ* owning property, which is indicative of a certain social status, and the fact that this property is a vineyard, the source of wine, should not be overlooked.

c. *CAT* 3.9[37]

| | | |
|---|---|---|
| *mrzḥ* | 1 | The *marzēaḥ*, |
| *d qny* | 2-3 | which Šamūmānu established |

[34] The word appears in full in each of lines 4-6, in the first two instances preceded by ]l or *l* and followed by a word divider plus ʿ*n*[. In line 6 there are no signs visible before the first word divider and only ʿ[ after the second one, but the *l* before *marzēaḥ* and the *n* at the end of the line can be supplied from the preceding two lines, and by comparison with [mr]*zḥ*.ʿ*n*[t] in lines 2 and 7. Moreover, the similarity among all of these lines supports restoration of the letters *mr* in the initial gap in lines 2 and 7.

[35] O. Eissfeldt, "Etymologische und archäologische Erklärung alttestamentlicher Wörter," *OrAnt* 5 (1966) 175; *idem*, "Kultvereine," 192. This proposal's widespread acceptance is exemplified by its restoration in *CAT* in all five instances.

[36] Eissfeldt, "Etymologische," 175; *idem*; "Kultvereine," 192. Pope supports this from the phrase "the field(s) of the gods, the field(s) of Aṯirat and *rḥmy*" in *CAT* 1.23.13,28, where *rḥmy* is taken as an epithet of Anat; see M. H. Pope, "A Divine Banquet at Ugarit," *The Use of the Old Testament in the New and Other Essays: Studies in Honor of W. F. Stinespring* (ed. J. M. Efird; Durham: Duke University Press, 1972) 192.

[37] Published in Miller, "The *MRZḤ* Text," 37-48; see also M. J. Dahood,

| | | |
|---|---|---|
| *šmmn* | | |
| *b . btw* | 4 | in his house. |
| *w št . ibsn* | 5 | "Now I have set up our dining area[40] |
| *lkm . km . ag* | 6 | for you; if I drive |
| *rškm .* | 7 | you out |
| *b . bty* | 8 | from my house |
| *ksp ḫmšm* | 9 | the fifty silver (shekels) |
| *is‘* [38] | 10 | I will pay." |
| Reverse | | Reverse |
| *w šm{.}mn* | 11 | Šamūmānū |
| *rb . al . ydd* | 12 | is the leader. Let not arise |
| *mt . mrzḥ* | 13 | a man of the *marzēaḥ* |
| *w yrgm . l* | 14 | and say to |
| *šmmn . tn .* | 15 | Šamūmānū: "give |
| *ksp . ṯql d ‘mnk* | 16 | silver, the shekels which you have." |
| *ṯqlm . ys‘* | 17 | They paid the shekels. |
| *ypḥ . iḫršp* | 18 | Witness: Iḫirašpu |
| *bn . uḏrnn* | 19 | son of Uḏrnn[41] |
| *w . ‘bdn* | 20 | and ‘Abdinu |
| *bn . sgld*[39] | 21 | son of Sigilda. |

This text is a legal document drawn up before two witnesses. The first line contains only the word *marzēaḥ*, even though there is ample room for the next word (the one-sign relative particle *d*) and part of the next word;[42] it is separated from what follows by a solid line. Lines 2-4 specify that this particular *marzēaḥ* is the one "which Šamūmānu established in his house," after which another solid line occurs. Thus, these four lines introduce, in general and then specific terms, what is at issue in the following lines.[43] Exactly what does follow is disputed, however, with scholars divided as to whether this

"Additional Notes on the *MRZḤ* Text," *The Claremont Ras Shamra Texts* (AnOr 48; ed. L. R. Fisher; Rome: Pontifical Biblical Institute, 1971) 51-54. Cf. the discussion in Bryan, "Texts," 136-39.

[38] This line is written on the lower edge of the tablet.

[39] This line is written on the upper edge of the tablet.

[40] On this translation of *ibsn* see p. 23.

[41] The commentators are unanimous in not vocalizing this name.

[42] The scribe does divide a single word over lines 6-7.

[43] Miller, "The *MRZḤ* Text," 43; R. E. Friedman, "The *MRZḤ* Tablet from Ugarit," *Maarav* 2 (1979-1980) 192.

is a contract establishing the *marzēaḥ* and spelling out the obligations and rights of those involved, or a legal suit between those same parties. Since some points of this debate are relevant to the nature of this *marzēaḥ*, they will be examined, but it is beyond the scope of this study to resolve every detail.

Proponents of the lawsuit interpretation point to the word *rb* in line 12, which they take as a verb cognate with the Hebrew verb ריב, meaning "to conduct a lawsuit." They argue that if this were a substantive designating Šamūmānu the leader the construct chain *rb mrzḥ* would be present.[44] Two points can be made in response. First, the text indicates at the outset that it is concerned specifically with a *marzēaḥ*, so a reference simply to "the leader" would naturally be taken as referring to the leader of that *marzēaḥ*,[45] especially since the designated individual established the *marzēaḥ* in the first place. Second, nothing in the text's format or structure requires interpreting it as a legal suit.[46] On the other hand, the opening lines indicate that the central issue is Šamūmānu's establishment of a *marzēaḥ* in his house. If this were a legal controversy we would expect some indication of that at the outset.[47] Since there is none, it is better to take *rb* as a noun rather than a verb, which means we have a nominal clause designating Šamūmānu as the one in charge of the *marzēaḥ*.

The question remains whether *marzēaḥ* here refers to a place or an association. The fact it is established inside Šamūmānu's residence does not rule out the former possibility, since the term could refer to a specific part of the house set aside for the *marzēaḥ*.[48] However, the introduction to a contract should give some indication of the parties involved, namely the collective known as a *marzēaḥ* (represented later in the text by the 2nd person plural address in line 6 and the phrase *mt . mrzḥ*) and Šamūmānu himself.[49] Also, the designation of Šamūmānu as *rb* makes more sense with respect to a group

---

[44] Dahood, "Additional Notes," 54. He builds on a suggestion by Miller, "The *MRZḤ* Text," 41, and is followed by B. Halpern, "A Landlord-Tenant Dispute at Ugarit?" *Maarav* 2 (1979-80) 131, 133.

[45] Friedman, "The *MRZḤ* Tablet," 197-98.

[46] Dahood and Halpern appeal to the witnesses at the end as indicative of court proceedings (Dahood, "Additional Notes," 54; Halpern, "Dispute?" 140), but we would expect to find them in a contractual document as well, especially in light of the money mentioned in the text (cf. n. 55 below).

[47] For example, "The lawsuit against Šamūmānu by the *marzēaḥ* set up in his house."

[48] Miller, "The *MRZḤ* Text," 43.

[49] Friedman, "The *MRZḤ* Tablet," 192.

than to a place. Therefore, this *marzēaḥ* is an association for which Šamūmānu provides a portion of his house.

But what function did that portion of his house serve? Most commentators translate *isbn* as "storehouse" on the basis of the Akkadian *abūsu*.[50] Fenton, however, correctly argues that a *marzēaḥ* association would require more than just a place to store provisions, and in particular would need a place to gather in order to consume those provisions. Thus he translates the word as "dining complex."[51] This rendering has three advantages. First, it is consistent with the *marzēaḥ*'s nature as reflected in other texts. Second, it helps to determine the function of the *n* in *ibsn*. Commentators generally view this as an(other) example where an Ugaritic substantive has an afformative *-n* but the Hebrew cognate does not.[52] However, this explanation is obviated if one takes the letter as the suffixed pronoun "our."[53] This leads to the third point, namely that such a rendering fits the overall context of the tablet. Šamūmānu has provided a room for a *marzēaḥ*. If this was merely a storage place, then Šamūmānu functions simply as a landlord, and there is no sufficient reason why he should be named as the *marzēaḥ* leader (lines 11-12). But since he is the leader, he is also a member of the *marzēaḥ* association, so it is natural for him to refer to "our" *isb*. Within this context, the word makes more sense if it refers to the location for the *marzēaḥ* gatherings rather than simply a storage room, since their gatherings would require a place separate from a storage room.

A final point to note is the amount of money involved. In lines 6-10 Šamūmānu promises to pay "the fifty silver (shekels)" if he evicts the *marzēaḥ* from his house. This amount probably refers to either a deposit or the full rent received for the use of his house, which he agrees to forfeit if he breaks the lease.[54] The Reverse of the tablet

---

[50] Thus, Miller, "The *MRZḤ* Text," 39-40; Dahood, "Additional Notes," 52-53, renders it as "stall" on the same basis. Halpern, "Dispute?" 137, is unique in deriving it from *ibissû*, a Sumerian loan-word into Akkadian meaning "damages (indemnified); financial loss." This is consistent with his idiosyncratic interpretation of the entire text.

[51] T. L. Fenton, "The Claremont 'MRZḤ' Tablet, Its Text and Meaning," *UF* 9 (1977) 72-73; cf. Miller, "The *MRZḤ* Text," 43 and n. 5. Fenton appeals to the *qal* passive participle אָבוּס ("fattened") at 1 Kgs 5:3; Prov 15:17, suggesting it is a small semantic step from animals to humans being fed.

[52] Thus Miller, "The *MRZḤ* Text," 40; Dahood, "Additional Notes," 52; for all intents, Halpern ignores the letter (see Halpern, "Dispute?" 122-23, 137 and 139n54).

[53] Thus Friedman, "The *MRZḤ* Tablet," 193; cf. Halpern, "Dispute?" 139.

contains the other side of the bargain, stipulating that Šamūmānu cannot be challenged for summary payment of this money, an action tantamount to the tenants breaking the lease. The text concludes with the statement that the deposit was made, as witnessed by two individuals.[55]

To summarize, in this text the term *marzēaḥ* refers to a voluntary association, initiated at a specific point in time,[56] and requiring money for its institution and/or maintenance. In addition to having specific members, as in other texts, a *marzēaḥ* could have a designated leader, although there is insufficient information here to determine the exact nature of that role.[57]

### d. *CAT* 1.114[58]

| | |
|---|---|
| (1) *il d*bḥ . *b bth* . *mṣd* . | El slaughtered game in his house, |
| *ṣd* . *b qrb* (2) *hkl*h . | Beasts in the midst of his palace; |
| ṣḥ . *l qṣ* . *ilm* . | He invited the gods to the carving: |
| *tlḥmn* (3) *ilm* . *w t*š*t*n . | "Eat, O gods, and drink, |
| *tštn y*<n> *'d šb'* | Drink wine to satiety, |
| (4) *trṯ* . 'd . škr . | New wine to drunkenness." |

[54] Fenton, "The Claremont 'Mrzḥ' Tablet," 75, views it as a fine levied against Šamūmānu, but that leaves the money he has (line 16) without an antecedent. It is probably synonymous with the funds mentioned in line 17. See further in n. 55 below.

[55] Translating *ṯqlm . ys'* as "they paid the shekels" with Friedman, "The *MRZḤ* Tablet," 203, who notes, "we would expect a statement in the witnessed tablet that such lease payment was paid." Miller, "The *MRZḤ* Text," 42, 44, following Albright, takes *ṯqlm* as a dual, interpreting this as a fine levied against anyone who might challenge Šamūmānu; see also M. Dietrich and O. Loretz, "Der Vertrag eines MRZḤ-Klubs in Ugarit. Zum Verständis von KTU 3.9," *UF* 14 (1982) 75. In response, note the call for consistency with respect to the text's monetary references in Halpern, "Dispute?" 133; Friedman, "The *MRZḤ* Tablet," 199.

[56] Obviously, both a group and its use of a particular meeting place must have had starting points, but these could have been in the distant past with no alteration in living memory.

[57] Possibilities include a business manager, chairperson at meetings, etc.

[58] In addition to the initial publication and discussion in C. Virolleaud, "Les nouveaux textes mythologiques et liturgiques de Ras Shamra (XXIV[e] campagne, 1961)," *Ugaritica V* (MRS 16; ed. C. F. A. Schaeffer *et al.*; Paris: Geuthner, 1968) 545-51 and the transliteration in *CAT*, see more recently D. Pardee, *Les textes paramythologiques de la 24[e] campagne (1961)* (RSO IV; Paris: Éditions Recherche sur les Civilisations, 1988) 13-74; T. J. Lewis, "El's Divine Feast," *Ugaritic Narrative Poetry* (SBLWAW 9; ed. S. B. Parker; Atlanta: Scholars Press, 1997) 193-96; N. Wyatt, *Religious Texts from Ugarit: The Words of Ilimilku and His Colleagues* (The Biblical Seminar 53; Sheffield: Sheffield Academic Press, 1998) 404-13. See also the discussion in Bryan, "Texts," 123-36.

| | |
|---|---|
| *yʿdb . yrḫ* (5) *gbh . km .* k[l]b[59] | Yariḫ arched[64] his back like a dog, |
| *yqṯqṯ . tḥt* (6) *ṯlḥnt .* | Scavenged[65] beneath the tables. |
| *il . d ydʿnn* | Any god who recognized him |
| (7) *yʿdb . lḥm*[60] *. lh .* | Prepared food for him, |
| *w d l ydʿnn* | But whoever did not recognize him |
| (8) *y*{.}*lmn*[61] *ḫtm . tḥt . ṯlḥn* | Struck him with sticks beneath the table. |
| (9) *ʿṯtrt . w ʿnt . ymġy* | He approached Athtart and Anat. |
| (10) *ʿṯtrt . tʿdb . nšb lh* | Athtart prepared a haunch for him, |
| (11) *w ʿnt . ktp* [[x]] | Anat a shoulder . . . |
| *bhm . ygʿr . ṯġr* (12) *bt . il .* | The porter of El's house chided them, |
| *pn . lm . klb*[62] *. tʿdbn* (13) *nšb .* | "Look, why have you prepared a haunch for a dog, |
| *l inr . tʿdbn . ktp* | For a cur have you prepared a shoulder?" |
| (14) *b i*l . ab*h . gʿr .* | He chided El, his father. |
| *yṯb* .il . kr (15) *a*šk[rh][63] | El sat, he assembled his drinking feast; |

[59] The original publication had a lacuna at this point; the restoration of *klb* was first suggested by S. E. Loewenstamm, "Eine lehrhafte ugaritische Trinkburleske," *UF* 1 (1969) 72, 74, and is followed by most scholars. *CAT* and Pardee, *Les textes para-mythologiques*, 17, both now indicate traces of the first and last letters of *klb*.

[60] Under the *m* can be read x[[x]]*dmṣd*. For this text as a palimpsest see *CAT*, p. 129; M. Dietrich and O. Loretz, "KTU 1.114, ein 'Palimpsest'," *UF* 25 (1993) 133-36.

[61] Under *lm* can be read ]*bqr*[.

[62] Rather than *rlb*. Hillers read *hn . lm . klb* in place of the original transcription of *pn . lmgr lb*; see D. R. Hillers, "Some Books Recently Received (Cont.)," *BASOR* 198 (April 1970) 46. The difference between *p* and *h* and between *r* and *k* is a matter of one and two horizontal wedges respectively; the *g* is probably an oversized word divider (thus, A. F. Rainey, "The Ugaritic Texts in Ugaritica 5," *JAOS* 94 [1974] 186). *CAT* and Pardee, *Les textes para-mythologiques*, 52-53, retain the initial *pn* but concur with the rest of Hiller's emendation. The resulting *klb* ("dog") provides a fitting parallel for *inr* ("cur") and coheres with the restoration of *klb* in line 5 (see n. 59).

[63] *CAT* restores three uncertain letters here; this restoration was first proposed by D. Pardee, "Ugaritic," *AfO* 28 (1981-82) 267n36; see further *idem*, *Les textes para-mythologiques*, 17-18, 54-55 and below. Pardee is followed by K. J. Cathcart, "Ilu, Yariḫu and the One with the Two Horns and a Tail," *Ugarit, Religion and Culture: Proceedings of the International Colloquium on Ugarit, Religion and Culture: Edinburgh, July 1994. Essays Presented in Honour of Professor John C. L. Gibson* (UBL 12; eds. N. Wyatt, W. G. E. Watson and J. B. Lloyd; Münster: Ugarit-Verlag, 1996) 5 [compare in n. 71 below]; Wyatt, *Religious Texts*, 409n31. In contrast, the second half of the poetic line is left blank in Lewis, "El's Divine Feast," 195.

[64] This extrapolation from the root meaning of *ʿdb* as "make, prepare, set, do" is called for by Yariḫ's canine activity.

[65] The root *qṯqṯ* probably means "glean"; cf. *yqṯ* at *CAT* 1.2.IV.27; Heb קָשַׁשׁ, "glean"; MHeb קִשְׁקֵשׁ, "move back and forth." Again, this particular rendering, proposed by Wyatt, *Religious Texts*, 407n13, is in keeping with Yariḫ's impersonation of a dog.

| | |
|---|---|
| *il* . *y*ṯb . *b mrzḥh* | El sat in his *marzēaḥ*. |
| (16) *y*št . [y]n . *ʿd šbʿ* . | El drank wine to satiety, |
| *trṯ* . *ʿd škr* | New wine to drunkenness. |
| (17) *il* . *h*l*k* . *l bth* . | El went to his house, |
| *yštql* . (18) *l ḥẓrh* . | He stumbled to his court. |
| *yʿmsn.nn* . *ṯkmn* (19) *w šnm* . | Thukamuna and Shunama supported him. |
| *w ngšnn* . *ḥby* . | The "creeper"[66] approached him, |
| (20) *bʿl* . *qrnm* . *w ḏnb* . | The one having two horns and a tail. |
| *ylšn* (21) *b ḫrih* . *w ṯnth* . | He floundered[67] in his (own) feces and urine, |
| *ql* . *il* . *k*m mt | El collapsed like the dead, |
| (22) *il* . *k yrdm* . *arṣ* . | El was like those who descend to the underworld. |
| ʿ*n*t (23) *w ʿṯtrt* . *tṣ*dn . | Anat and Athtart went hunting. |
| šxxd/lt (24) qdš . *bʿ*l[ ] | ? holy Baʿal(?) |
| . . . | . . . |
| Reverse | Reverse |
| . . . | . . . |
| (25) [xx x]xn . d[ ] | ? |
| (26) [ʿṯ]tr*t* . *w ʿn*t[ ]x[ ] | Athtart and Anat... |
| (27) w *bhm* . *tṯtb* . [x]xd*h* | And with them they brought back... |
| (28) km . *trpa* . *h*n *nʿr* | When they healed, look, he awoke. |
| (29) *d yšt* . *l lṣbh* . *šʿr klb* | What one should put on his brow: hairs of a dog |
| (30) *w riš* . *pqq* . *w šrh* | and the top of a *pqq*-plant and its stem.[68] |
| (31) yš*t aḥdh* . *dm zt* . *ḫrpnt* | Put it together with virgin olive oil. |

[66] *ḥby* may be either a noun or a personal name. For a survey of possible meanings of the word see K. J. Cathcart and W. G. E. Watson, "Weathering a Wake: A Cure for Carousal. A Revised Translation of *Ugaritica V* Text 1," *PIBA* 4 (1980) 39-40. This figure is identified as the Egyptian *ḥpy*, (the bull) Apis, by M. Liverani, "Review of *Ugaritica V*," *OrAnt* 8 (1969) 339; P. Xella, "Studi sulla religione della Siria antica I: El e il vino (RS 24.258)," *SSR* 1 (1977) 246n33; Pardee, *Les textes para-mythologiques*, 60-62.

[67] For this translation of *ylšn* see n. 88 below.

[68] Lines 29b-30 are translated "Soll gleichzeitig Leib und Kopf, Brustbein(?) und seinen Unterleib . . ." by M. Dietrich and O. Loretz, "'Siehe, da war er (wieder) munter!' Die mythologische Begründung für eine medikamentöse Behandlung in KTU 1.114 (RS 24.258)," *Boundaries of the Ancient Near Eastern World: A Tribute to Cyrus H. Gordon* (JSOTSup 273; eds. M. Lubetski, C. Gottlieb and S. Keller; Sheffield: Sheffield Academic Press, 1998) 179. This requires reading *(ḫš) ʿrk lb klb w riš . pqq . w šrh*, a radical departure from both Pardee and their own reading in *CAT*. Most agree that *pqq* is an unidentified plant.

With this tablet we move from legal affairs to mythology. The text deals with a banquet given by El, to which he invites an unspecified number of other gods. A *marzēaḥ* is mentioned in line 15 as the object of the phrase, "El sat in his *marzēaḥ*." Since the preceding poetic line also begins with "El sat," one expects some insight into the term's meaning from the corresponding parallel line, but the tablet is damaged at precisely that point. The word parallel with *marzēaḥ* begins with an *a*, but commentators have differed as to what can be read of the preceding and following signs, where and how extensive any lacunae are, and how to fill in those gaps. For instance, Virolleaud identified the second sign as a *ṯ*, restored *rt* immediately afterwards and read the line as *yṯb . il .* [b(?)] *aṯ*[rt] (". . . le Dieu s'assied à côté (?) de Aše[rat]").[69] Marvin Pope altered this slightly, restoring a final *h* rather than a *t* to produce *aṯ*[rh] ("his shrine") as the parallel term to *marzēaḥ*.[70] De Moor initially read *wb*[n] *aṯ*[rt.] at the damaged spot, which he rendered as "(but) Ilu and the sons of Aṯiratu remained seated."[71] Finally, Dietrich and Loretz read *yṯb* il wl *a*ṯr[bnh] and translated "El sitzt da und wacht nicht über seine Söhne."[72]

[69] Virolleaud, "Les Nouveaux Textes Mythologiques," 547; followed by H. P. Rüger, "Zu RS 24.258," *UF* 1 (1969) 205. Virolleaud's hesitant reading of a *b* before *aṯ*[rt] differs from the *k* in the transcription by Liliane Courtois published with his essay. In the first edition (*KTU*), the editors of *CAT* had read *wl* (both letters uncertain) before the *a*, found traces of both a *ṯ* and an *r* afterwards, and transcribed as *a*ṯr[t . . .]. In a separate article they filled the gap with a space plus *ym*, an epithet of Aṯirat, and translated, "Es sitzen El und auch Aṯira[t Jam]"; see M. Dietrich, O. Loretz and J. Sanmartín, "Der Stichometrische Aufbau von RS 24.258 (= Ug. 5, S. 545 NR. 1)," *UF* 7 (1976) 110, 112.

[70] Pope, "Divine Banquet," 190; he appealed to the word's presence in the Rephaim texts in close proximity to the word *mrzʿ*, which most commentators take as an alternative form of *mrzḥ* (see n. 94). Pope was followed by B. Margalit, "The Ugaritic Feast of the Drunken Gods: Another Look at RS 24.258 (KTU 1.114)," *Maarav* 2 (1979-80) 98-99; *idem, The Ugaritic Poem of AQHT: Text, Translation, Commentary* (BZAW 182; Berlin/New York: Walter de Gruyter, 1989) 276-77; E. T. Mullen, Jr., *The Assembly of the Gods: The Divine Council in Canaanite and Early Hebrew Literature* (HSM 24; Chico: Scholars Press, 1980) 266. Margalit read {*w*} *l* instead of [b?], and the whole line replaces his earlier reading of *yṯb . il . k*[s]*a . ṯ*[bth] in B. Margulis, "A New Ugaritic Farce (RS 24.252)," *UF* 2 (1970) 136; cf. Bryan, "Texts," 133.

[71] J. C. de Moor, "Studies in the New Alphabetic Texts from Ras Shamra," *UF* 1 (1969) 168, 172; followed by Cathcart and Watson, "Weathering a Wake," 37. De Moor and Cathcart both subsequently abandoned this reading (see notes 76 and 63 respectively).

[72] M. Dietrich and O. Loretz, "Neue Studien zu den Ritualtexten aus Ugarit (I). Ein Forschungsbericht," *UF* 13 (1981) 90. This replaced their reading in *KTU*

All these proposals can now be rejected in light of Dennis Pardee's reading of *kr ašk*[rh] at the relevant point, based on a direct examination of the tablet.[73] Although his translation as "il rassemble [sa] beuve[rie]" fits the context[74] and provides an acceptable parallel to the word *marzēaḥ*, he admits it is not absolutely certain. He appeals to 2 Kgs 6:23 and the south-Arabic root *krw* in support of the first word and its translation, but admits there is no Semitic parallel for the precise form of the second word, which he derives from the root *škr*. As a result, he acknowledges his interpretation of it as a noun meaning "drinking feast" must remain tentative.[75] Nevertheless, it is superior to de Moor's restoration of a final *r*, instead of Pardee's *h*; de Moor identified the resultant *aškrr* with the hallucinogenic plant henbane.[76] The word appears elsewhere at Ugarit,[77] but presents many problems in this text. For instance, de Moor also reads *kb* rather than Pardee's *kr* before this word,[78] and his rendering, "as with henbane," is grammatically problematic.[79] Also, hen-

---

and an earlier article (see n. 69). In a recent essay they propose *yṯb . il w l ašk*[r] and translate "El Sitzt da, und zwar wahrlich volltrunken"; see Dietrich and Loretz, "Die mythologische Begründung," 178, 184.

[73] See n. 63.

[74] It is more appropriate than "[El] calls to order his drinking feast" offered in his initial article. Although that is consistent with the preceding disruption by some of the guests, it does not make sense that El would make the effort to restore order only to leave almost immediately after.

[75] Pardee, *Les textes para-mythologiques*, 55. 2 Kgs 6:23 reads "He prepared a great feast for them" (וַיִּכְרֶה לָהֶם כֵּרָה גְדוֹלָה). Pardee notes the Arabic root's connections with hunting and the reference to game (*mṣd/ṣd*) in the first line of this text.

[76] J. C. de Moor, "Henbane and KTU 1.114," *UF* 16 (1984) 355.

[77] RS 17.120, line 244; this is acknowledged by Pardee, *Les textes para-mythologiques*, 55. Cathcart, "Ilu," 5, calls de Moor's proposal "interesting" but opts for Pardee's reading.

[78] In a note added just before the volume's final printing Pardee indicates *kbt* is also a possible reading based on what is left of the damaged signs (Pardee, *Les textes para-mythologiques*, 18n8), but that would make little sense ("like a house?" "like a daughter?") in either Pardee's or de Moor's interpretation.

[79] His subsequent translation as, "Ilu is sitting as if he is on the henbane drug" goes well beyond this. Pardee, *Les textes para-mythologiques*, 55n245, notes that in de Moor's reading (found on his p. 356) the preposition *b* indicates instrument or accompaniment, but the transitive verb *yṯb* does not normally take such complements. In fact, the construction *yṯb b* is idiomatic in Ugaritic, always referring to a place; see D. Pardee, "The Preposition in Ugaritic," *UF* 7 (1975) 352; 8 (1976) 245; M. H. Pope, "Notes on the Rephaim Texts from Ugarit," *Essays on the Ancient Near East in Memory of Jacob Joel Finkelstein* (Memoirs of the Connecticut Academy of Arts and Sciences 19; ed. M. de Jong Ellis; Hamden: Archon Books, 1977) 170.

bane provides a poor parallel to his subsequent, "Ilu is sitting with his society,"[80] and this sudden and solitary reference to drugs, even if only a simile, is inconsistent with the statement immediately following (line 16) that El's primary activity is drinking to the point of intoxication. On the other hand, intoxication is completely consistent with a "drinking party." Thus, despite his own reservations, Pardee's reading is superior on both epigraphic and contextual grounds.[81]

The parallel to "his *marzēaḥ*," therefore, is "his drinking feast," and it is clear from Pardee's translation of *kr* as "rassemble" that he understands this in terms of the participants.[82] This is consistent with the word *marzēaḥ* elsewhere at Ugarit, where it means a group, but the idiom *y<u>t</u>b b* requires that the indirect object ("his *marzēaḥ*") refer to a place rather than an association.[83] However, a drinking party is not a place, so it is best to read the two lines as concurrent rather than identical: El hosts a group of drinkers while sitting in his *marzēaḥ*.[84] Moreover, this *marzēaḥ* was a room within El's palace. Virolleaud took the statement that "El went to his house" (line 17) as evidence that the *marzēaḥ* was located apart from El's "house,"[85] but there is no indication that he left the latter after inviting the gods there in lines 1-4.[86] Moreover, the description of El's activity in the

[80] de Moor, "Henbane," 356. Pardee, *Les textes para-mythologiques*, 55n245, also notes that his own restored *-h* provides a better syntactic parallel with the same pronoun in *mrzḥh* (line 15)

[81] The most recent proposal by Dietrich and Loretz (see n. 72) does fit the context, but substitutes *w l* for Pardee's *kr*, which they accepted in their *CAT* collation.

[82] See also Cathcart, "Ilu," 5; Wyatt, *Religious Texts*, 309, who both translate as "his drinking companions." Elsewhere, however, Pardee implies that *ašk*[rh] refers to the feast itself, rather than to those in attendance. For instance, he says that the sense of *kr* is "'offrir . . .' ou 'inviter à un festin'" (Pardee, *Les textes para-mythologiques*, 54) and later comments that El "convie encore à une beuverie" (p. 73). His earlier translation as "[El] calls to order his drinking feast" (Pardee, "Ugaritic," 267n36), could be understood either way.

[83] See n. 79 above.

[84] Pardee, *Les textes para-mythologiques*, 54, translates the last term as "son festin-*mrzḥ*," preserving a more exact parallel with the preceding line.

[85] C. Virolleaud, "Les nouveaux textes mythologiques et liturgiques de Ras Shamra," *CRAIBL* (1962) 112; *idem*, "Les nouveaux textes mythologiques," 550; see also Pope, "Divine Banquet," 194; Cathcart, "Ilu," 2.

[86] Miller, "The *MRZḤ* Text," 43. Klaas Spronk distinguishes between the feast in line 1 and the *marzēaḥ* in line 15 but without supporting arguments; see K. Spronk, *Beatific Afterlife in Ancient Israel and in the Ancient Near East* (AOAT 219;

*marzēaḥ* (line 16) is identical to his earlier exhortation to drink at the feast he was having in his house. It seems more likely, therefore, that the *marzēaḥ* was located in a specific part of his palace set aside for the purpose, and line 17 simply indicates that he retired to his personal quarters.[87]

Two other points about this *marzēaḥ* can be made briefly. First, El's primary activity in his *marzēaḥ* is drinking until inebriated, which is also the main reason he invited the gods in the first place (lines 2-4, 16). El is so successful in this endeavour that he has to be helped from the room and flounders in his own waste.[88] In other words, in

---

Kevelaer: Verlag Butzon and Bercker; Neukirchen-Vluyn: Neukirchener Verlag, 1986) 200. Against Spronk, note the identical activity in lines 3-4 and 16; see also concerning Pardee in n. 87 below.

[87] Thus de Moor, "Studies," 172; Dietrich and Loretz, "Neue Studien I," 95; cf. the translation as "El (then) departs to his domicile // He retires to his quarter," in Margulis, "Farce," 133. The different terms paralleled with *bt* in lines 1-2 and 17-18 (*qrb hkl* and *ḥẓr* respectively) indicates just such a distinction within El's "house." This would be analogous to *CAT* 3.9, wherein Šamūmānu provides part of his house as a meeting place for the *marzēaḥ* association (see the discussion of this text on pp. 20-24 above).

Pardee, *Les textes para-mythologiques*, 57-59, also considers the *marzēaḥ* part of El's palace, but distinguishes it from the location of the feast in lines 1-13. He draws an analogy with the temple of Baalshamen at Palmyra, which contains an area for sacrifice, a banquet hall and an inner sanctuary, and suggests that in this text El moves from the first (lines 1-2) to the second (line 15) and then the third (lines 17-18). However, his own caution about using information from more than a millennium later is most appropriate. Moreover, El's activity in the (supposed) first and second locations is nearly identical, the only difference being the lack of references to "slaughter" and eating in the *marzēaḥ*. This is not surprising, however. Although El does invite the gods to "eat and drink" (lines 2-3), the emphasis even there is on drinking to the point of "satiety" and "drunkenness" (lines 3-4), so when the almost identical wording is predicated of El in line 16, only the focal point of this text is mentioned. Granted, one could drink excessively in two different locations in two different contexts (thus Pardee, *Les textes para-mythologiques*, p. 59), but the only reference to El moving comes in lines 17-18, between his *marzēaḥ* and his (inner) court. Also, if the intent was to itemize three different locations in El's house one would expect all to be so specified, yet "his house" only occurs in connection with "the midst of his palace" and "his court"; the failure to identify the *marzēaḥ* as a third subsection of "his house" is another reason for placing the activity in lines 1-16 within a single location. In short, El hosts a drinking feast that is located "in the midst of his palace," specifically "in his *marzēaḥ*," from whence he stumbles off to his private quarters.

[88] *ˌlšn* was derived from *l(w)š* ("knead") by Virolleaud, "Les nouveaux textes mythologiques," 550; he is followed, *inter alia*, by Rüger, "Zu RS 24.258," 206; Margulis, "Farce," 136; *idem* (Margalit), "Another Look," 110; Dietrich and Loretz, "Die mythologische Begründung," 188. In contrast, Pope, "Divine Banquet"

this text the *marzēaḥ* is a place dedicated to the consumption of large amounts of alcohol. Secondly, since the text projects human activity into the divine realm, by virtue of his presidency in the divine *marzēaḥ*, El probably functions as the patron of its human counterpart.[89]

e. *CAT* 1.21.II[90]

| | |
|---|---|
| (1) [ ]m*rzʿy*. | [ ] my *marzēaḥ* |
| *lk* b*ty* (2) [ ] | Come to my house [. . .] |
| [ b]t*y* . *aṣ*ḥk*m* [.] | [ ] my [hou]se I invite you |
| *iqra* (3) [ h]*kly*. | I call [ ] my [pa]lace. |
| *aṯrh* . *rpum* (4) [l tdd . | To its shrine, O shades, [hasten,] |
| aṯr]h . *l tdd* . *ilnym* | [To its shrine,] hasten, O deities |

196, derived it from Arabic *lšš*, which in the form *lašlaš* means "run to and fro in fear," "defecate with fear." He argued that this meaning fits the context in terms of both El's reaction to the sudden encounter and the incontinence that often accompanies excessive drinking. Xella's renderings from the root *l(w)š* as "impastare, rotolarsi, avvoltolarsi" ("mix, roll, wallow") and "impastare, imbratta" ("mix, dirty") are comparable, but since he thinks El is too far away syntactically to be the subject he considers *ḥby* the subject and El the object of the action; see Xella, "El e il vino," 240; *idem*, "Un antecedente eblaita del 'demone' ugaritico *ḥby*?" *SEL* 3 (1986) 18, 23n6; he is followed by Pardee, *Les textes para-mythologiques*, 64. It is not clear from Xella who is the source of the excrement, but Pardee attributes it to El while Cathcart, "Ilu," 5, links it to *ḥby* and takes him to be both the subject and the object of the verb.

As for the subject of the verb, El is mentioned in the next two lines, and placing him in his own excretions is consistent with the text's emphasis on drunkenness. This traditional interpretation of the lines is presented most recently in Lewis, "El's Divine Feast," 195; Wyatt, *Religious Texts*, 411 and his n. 42.

[89] Eissfeldt, "Kultvereine," 193; Miller, "The *MRZḤ* Text," 45; Pope, "Divine Banquet," 201-202; C. E. L'Heureux, *Rank Among the Canaanite Gods: El, Baʿal and the Repha'im* (HSM 21; Missoula: Scholars Press, 1979) 219; de Tarragon, *Le Culte*, 145; Pardee, *Les textes para-mythologiques*, 55-56. Margalit, "Another Look," 119-20, also correlates the earthly and divine realms but emphasizes El's role as the divine *marzēaḥ* leader rather than the earthly *marzēaḥ*'s patron.

[90] First published in C. Virolleaud, "Les Rephaïm: Fragments de poèmes de Ras Shamra," *Syria* 22 (1941) 8-11. For more recent presentations of the Rephaim texts (*CAT* 1.20-22) see W. T. Pitard, "A New Edition of the Rāpi'ūma Texts: *KTU* 1.20-22," *BASOR* 285 (February 1992) 33-77; T. J. Lewis, "Toward a Literary Translation of the Rapiuma Texts," *Ugarit, Religion and Culture: Proceedings of the International Colloquium on Ugarit, Religion and Culture: Edinburgh, July 1994. Essays Presented in Honour of Professor John C. L. Gibson* (UBL 12; eds. N. Wyatt, W. G. E. Watson and J. B. Lloyd; Münster: Ugarit-Verlag, 1996) 115-149; *idem*, "The Rapiuma," *Ugaritic Narrative Poetry* (SBLWAW 9; ed. S. B. Parker; Atlanta: Scholars Press, 1997) 196-205 (this text is found on pp. 199-200); Wyatt, *Religious Texts*, 314-23 (for this text see pp. 317-18). Cf. the discussion in Bryan, "Texts," 140-44.

| | |
|---|---|
| (5) [ ]m*rzʿy* . | [ ] my *marzēaḥ* |
| *apnnk* . *yrp* (6) [u | Then, O sha[des] |
| ]*km* . *rʿy* . | [ ] like a shepherd |
| *ht* . *alk* (7) [ym . wṯn . | Now I shall journey, [one day and two; |
| aḫr špšm . b[91]]*ṯlṯt* . | after sunrise on] the third |
| *amġy* . *l bt* (8) [y | I shall reach [my] house. |
| b qr]b . *hkly* . | [ in the mid]st of my palace. |
| *w yʿn* . *il* | Again El spoke: |
| (9) [ mrzʿ]y[92] . | [ ] my [*marzēaḥ*]. |
| *lk* . *bty* . *rpim* | Come to my house, O shades. |
| (10) [ aṣ]ḥ*km* . | [ I inv]ite you, |
| *iqrakm* (11) [ b hk]l*y* . | I call you [into] my [pal]ace. |
| *aṯrh* . *rpum* (12) [l tdd . | To its shrine, O shades, [hasten |
| aṯ]r*h* . *l tdd* . i[lnym] | To its sh[rine], hasten, O spi[rits.] |
| (13) [ ]xrn[ ] | [ ] ? [ ] |

In this text El invites the Rephaim to "my *mrzʿ*" (lines 1 and 5, and conjecturally in line 9[93]), which is probably a variant of the spelling *mrzḥ* found in the passages already examined.[94] Pardee rejects this on literary and philological grounds,[95] but the vocabulary shared with *CAT* 1.114[96] suggests a comparable content in the two texts. *CAT* 1.21.II must be used with caution, however, not only because of the variant spelling[97] but especially because the tablet is damaged and

[91] This restoration, absent from *CAT*, is made on the basis of *CAT* 1.14.IV.31-34; cf. Lewis, "The Rapiuma," 200; Wyatt, *Religious Texts*, 318.

[92] This restoration is not present in *CAT*, but is made on the basis of line 1: since *lk* . b*ty* follows m*rzʿy* there, restoration of *mrzʿ* before ]y *lk* . *bty* in line 9 is probable. The restoration is accepted by most scholars; see most recently, Pitard, "A New Edition" 285; Lewis, "The Rapiuma," 200; Wyatt, *Religious Texts*, 318.

[93] See n. 92 above. El is designated the speaker in line 8, but some emend this to Danel; see the discussion on pp. 71-73. On the Rephaim see n. 238.

[94] Following the suggestion of Eissfeldt, "Kultvereine," 194-95, who refers to the different spellings in the Akkadian texts discussed above; see further L'Heureux, *Rank*, 142n43.

[95] Pardee, *Les textes para-mythologiques*, 176n48; *idem*, "*Marziḫu*, *Kispu*, and the Ugaritic Funerary Cult: A Minimalist View," *Ugarit, Religion and Culture: Proceedings of the International Colloquium on Ugarit, Religion and Culture: Edinburgh, July 1994. Essays Presented in Honour of Professor John C. L. Gibson* (UBL 12; eds. N. Wyatt, W. G. E. Watson and J. B. Lloyd; Münster: Ugarit-Verlag, 1996) 278n6; see also B. B. Schmidt, *Israel's Beneficent Dead: Ancestor Cult and Necromancy in Ancient Israelite Religion and Tradition* (Winona Lake: Eisenbrauns, 1996) 65-66.

[96] Lewis, *Cults of the Dead*, 87, notes the repetition of *bt*, *bqrb hkl* and the verb *ṣḥ* in connection with a *marzēaḥ*. Comparable activity and terminology in the two texts is also noted by L'Heureux, *Rank*, 142; Margalit, "Another Look," 100; Mullen, *Assembly of the Gods*, 266-67.

[97] See Lewis, *Cults of the Dead*, 82n7 and the references in n. 95 above.

all instances of the term involve varying degrees of restoration.

Nevertheless, despite the text's fragmentary state, it is possible to get a general sense of the content. El issues an invitation to the Rephaim, mentioning three different destinations in sequence: a house (*bt*), a palace (*hkl*), and a shrine (*a̱tr*). The pronominal suffixes attached to these words indicate that the third is a specification of the first two: "house" and "palace" consistently have a first person singular suffix attached, while "shrine" has the third masculine singular suffix. This means an invitation is issued to "my house/palace" and specifically to "its (i.e., the house's or palace's) shrine."[98] The word *mrzʿ* appears at the beginning and end of this sequence. Since *bt* and *hkl* function as parallel terms in Ugaritic poetry,[99] they should be linked, which suggests that the words *mrzʿ* and *a̱tr* also correspond.[100] In other words, the house's "shrine" is El's *marzēaḥ*. The result is that, as in *CAT* 1.114, the *marzēaḥ* designates a specific portion of El's house/palace.

## C. *Emar*

1. *Emar* 466[101]

85 iti *Mar-za-ha-ni i-na* u$_4$ 14 *bu-qá-ra-tu*$_4$
86 *i-na* u$_4$ 16 *ina* sila.lím *ar-ba ú-ṣi*
87 udu *ša* uru.ki *ù ha-ṣí*$^{!}$*-nù ša* dingir "lì"
88 egir *i-*<*na*> sila.lím *ar-*<*ba*> *i-la-ak i-na*
89 <u$_4$> *šu-wa-tu-ma ṣa*$^{!}$*-du ša* $^{d}$*Iš*$_8$*-tár*$^{!}$ *i-na*
90 u$_4$ 17 *ṣa-du ša* $^{d}$*Iškur* 1 udu *ša nu-pu-ha-*<*an-ni*>
91 <*ina*> é *maš*$^{!}$*-ar*$^{!}$*-ti i-ša*$_{10}$*-ra-pu* lú.meš
92 *mar-za-ḫu ša mi-Ki*$^{!}$[102] ninda *na-ap-ta-na*
93 *i-na* dingir.meš *ú-ba-lu mi-iš-li* 1 udu
94 lú.máš.<šu>.gíd.gíd

---

[98] Lewis, "The Rapiuma," *passim*, attributes the third invitation to a narrator, and translates "his shrine" throughout; since "he" is El, the difference is slight.

[99] M. J. Dahood, "Ugaritic-Hebrew Parallel Pairs," *Ras Shamra Parallels I: The Texts from Ugarit and the Hebrew Bible* (AnOr 49; ed. L. Fisher; Rome: Biblical Institute Press, 1972) 153.

[100] Margalit, "Another Look," 102, considers the two terms a fixed pair, but this is dependent on reading *a̱trh* in *CAT* 1.114.15, which is no longer tenable in light of Pardee's collation.

[101] Published in D. Arnaud, *Recherches au pays d'Aštata. Emar VI.3: textes sumériens et accadiens* (Synthèse 18; Paris: Éditions Recherche sur les Civilisations, 1986) 422, 424.

[102] Reading with D. E. Fleming, *The Installation of Baal's High Priest at Emar:*

85 During the month of the *marzēaḥ*, the 14th day: cows.
86 On the 16th day, he goes out into the street.
87 The sheep of the city and the divine ox
88 go in the street behind. On the
89 same (day) is the hunt of Ishtar. On the
90 17th day is the hunt of Adad: one sheep . . . (?)
91 is burnt (in) the house of the *maš'artu* priestess. The men of the
92 *marzēaḥ* of mi-Ki(?) some naptanu bread
93 bring to the gods. Half of the sheep
94 (goes to) the diviner.

The word *marzēaḥ* is also found in a ritual calendar from the Syrian city of Emar, dating from the 13th century BCE,[103] although the reading is disputed at one point.[104] Daniel Fleming's more recent reading, according to which the "men of the *marzēaḥ*" bring offerings of bread to the gods (lines 91-93), fits the context, since this section of the text deals with "the month of the *marzēaḥ*";[105] Fleming's reading also approximates the designation for *marzēaḥ* members in the Akkadian texts from Ugarit. Thus, this text indicates a definable group of men associated with the *marzēaḥ*, as well as a link between the latter and an undefined number of deities. At the same time, the month name in line 85 suggests the *marzēaḥ* occurred yearly and was important enough to have a month named after it.

### D. *Summary*

We cannot assume complete uniformity in the pre-biblical *marzēaḥ*, especially since there is so little information available from Ebla and Emar. Nonetheless, it is possible to paint a composite picture as long as one remembers that not every feature was present in all instances. At Ebla the word refers to both a group and an event, but only the

*A Window on Ancient Syrian Religion* (HSS 42; Atlanta: Scholars Press, 1992) 269, 270; *idem*, "More Help From Syria: Introducing Emar to Biblical Study," *BA* 58 (1995) 146; see also Schmidt, *Israel's Beneficent Dead*, 126. The original publication of the text read ninda[!] *za-ri* $sa_x$*-mi-di*[!] ("Les hommes du pain-*zariu* de farine fine"); see Arnaud, *Emar VI.3*, 422, 424.

[103] On the city, the texts and the dating, see J.-C. Margueron, "Emar," *ABD* 2.488-90.

[104] See n. 102.

[105] Both authors agree on this reading at line 85; see Arnaud, *Emar VI.3*, 422; Fleming, *Installation*, 269, 270. Arnaud simply transliterates the word in his translation (p. 424).

former is in evidence at Emar. At Ugarit, with the exception of the mythological texts, where the word refers to a place, *marzēaḥ* refers to an association, with a single individual as its chief; terminology comparable to that used of the general membership and the leader at Ugarit occurs at Emar and Ebla respectively. At Ugarit this group often had a specific deity as its patron, engaged in financial transactions and usually owned property; houses[106] and vineyards are mentioned most frequently. The repeated reference to vineyards, as well as the content of *CAT* 1.114, suggests that consumption of alcohol in copious quantities, perhaps as part of a larger feast, was a major feature of the group's gatherings.

## II. The Post-biblical *marzēaḥ*

### A. *Moab*[107]

כה אמרו אלהן לסרא לך המרזח והרחין וה
בית וישעא רחק מהם ומלכא השלש

Thus the gods said to Sara': To you (belongs) the *marzēaḥ* and the millstones and the // house; Yiš'a' has renounced them. Milka' is the "third."[108]

[106] For the possible identification of an actual *marzēaḥ* house at Ugarit see M. Yon, "The Temple of the Rhytons at Ugarit," *Ugarit, Religion and Culture: Proceedings of the International Colloquium on Ugarit, Religion and Culture: Edinburgh, July 1994. Essays Presented in Honour of Professor John C. L. Gibson* (UBL 12; eds. N. Wyatt, W. G. E. Watson and J. B. Lloyd; Münster: Ugarit-Verlag, 1996) 405-16, especially p. 416, followed by Pardee, "*Marziḫu*," 280. The building is neither a temple nor a house; both Yon and Pardee suggest the stepped platform could have held an image of a *marzēaḥ*'s divine patron.

[107] The text is published in P. Bordreuil and D. Pardee, "Le papyrus du *marzeaḥ*," *Sem* 38 (1990) 49-68, pl. VII-X, which appeared well after Bryan's dissertation. Bordreuil and Pardee date it to the late seventh to early sixth century BCE (p. 61).

Since they worked only from photographs and did not directly examine the papyrus, have it tested or even know its whereabouts at the time of publication (see their pp. 49-50), some have questioned its authenticity. André Lemaire, for example, suggests it is a forgery "inspired" by the Balaam inscription from Deir 'Alla; see A. Lemaire, "Oracles, politique et littérature dans les royaumes araméens et transjordaniens," *Oracles et prophéties dans l'antiquité: Actes du Colloque de Strasbourg 15-17 juin 1995* (Publications du Centre de Recherce sur le Proche-Orient et la Grèce Antiques 15; ed. J.-G. Heintz; Paris: Diffusion de Boccard, 1997) 181n22. Contrast this with the arguments for authenticity on internal grounds by Bordreuil and Pardee, pp. 65-68. In balance, I think it acceptable to consider the text, with caution, to the extent that it reflects *marzēaḥ* elements known from assured references, but not to introduce features unknown elsewhere.

[108] I.e., the witness.

The first reference to consider in this section is, properly speaking, not post-biblical but contemporary with the prophetic literature. In a trans-Jordanian (probably Moabite[109]) papyrus, the gods confirm Sara''s possession of "the *marzēaḥ*, the millstones and the house." The reference to the *marzēaḥ* in sequence with types of property suggests it is "an architectural entity,"[110] possibly a *marzēaḥ* house,[111] and Sara' may be a leader in whose name group possessions were held. Since the text appears to be an oracular decision in response to an inquiry, the unnamed deities cannot be definitively associated with the *marzēaḥ* itself, but neither can a possibile link be ruled out. Finally, the papyrus is accompanied by a damaged bulla that reads, "belonging to the king (of?) *'kt*[ ] ([ ]אכת // למלך),[112] which suggests that this *marzēaḥ* was of sufficient importance to attract royal attention.

## B. *Elephantine*[113]

| | | |
|---|---|---|
| על חגי אמרת | 1 | To Haggai: I spoke |
| לאשן על כסף | 2 | to 'Ashina about the money |
| מרזחא[114] כן אמר | 3 | of the *marzēaḥ*. This he said |
| לי לם לאיתו[115] | 4 | to me (namely, to 'Ito): |

[109] For the language involved and probable geographic origin see Bordreuil and Pardee, "Le papyrus du *marzeaḥ*," 62-65.

[110] Lewis, *Cults of the Dead*, 89.

[111] Bordreuil and Pardee, "Le papyrus du *marzeaḥ*," 56, suggest a portion of a building on analogy with *CAT* 3.9. This is possible but not certain.

[112] For discussion of the bulla see Bordreuil and Pardee, "Le papyrus du *marzeaḥ*," 50-52; they are uncertain whether the second word is a royal name or a city.

[113] Ostracon Cairo Museum 35468a, first published in A. H. Sayce, "An Aramaic Ostracon from Elephantine," *PSBA* 31 (1909) 154-55. For recent editions of the text with English translation see J. M. Lindenberger, *Ancient Aramaic and Hebrew Letters* (SBLWAW 4; ed. K. H. Richards; Atlanta: Scholars Press, 1994) 39; *TADAE* 4.177 (D7.29). See also the discussion in Bryan, "Texts," 168-69.

[114] Sayce read the beginning of this line as אlll מר and translated lines 2-3 as "about the price of the myrrh, 3 a(rdebs)." For this corrected reading see M. Lidzbarski, *Ephemeris für semitische Epigraphik* (New York: Stechert, 1902-1915) 3.119-21; B. Porten, *Archives from Elephantine: The Life of an Ancient Jewish Military Colony* (Berkeley: University of California Press, 1968) 179, 184; P. Grelot, *Documents araméens d'Égypte: introduction, traduction, présentation* (LAPO 5; Paris: Les Éditions du Cerf, 1972) 371-73; Lindenberger, *Letters*, 39.; *TADAE* 4.177.3.

[115] *TADAE* 4.177.4 reads לאיתי but the translation as "There isn't (any)" makes no sense in light of the next line, where "he" promises to return it to Haggai or Yigdal. Thus I follow the original publication and Lindenberger, *Letters*, 39, in reading a (damaged) ו as the final letter.

| | | |
|---|---|---|
| כען אנתננה[116] | 5 | "Now I will give it |
| לחגי או | 6 | to Ḥaggai or |
| יגדל דבר | 7 | to Yigdal." Speak |
| עלוהי | 8 | to him |
| וינתנהי | 9 | and make him give it |
| לכם | 10 | to you. |

In this ostracon from a 5th century BCE Jewish military colony in Egypt, a certain Ito informs Haggai that he has spoken with ʾAshina concerning money in relationship to a *marzēaḥ*, and that ʾAshina has agreed to pay it to either Haggai or Yigdal. Porten initially considered Ito the *marzēaḥ* leader who has requested that ʾAshina pay his share of the cost for "a banquet in memory of a late member" to Haggai, the treasurer, or another official, namely Yigdal.[117] Nothing in the text indicates such leadership roles, but they do fit the context. The role of treasurer would be more secure if כסף מרזח is translated as "the *marzēaḥ*'s money" rather than "money for the *marzēaḥ*."[118] In that case, it does not refer to individual dues but to the association's common fund, and ʾAshina is being relieved of, or has resigned, his position as financial overseer and the position is being transferred to Haggai. In either case, money played a role in the administration of the Elephantine *marzēaḥ*, which had some form of official leadership, and by extension a general membership.

## C. *Phoenicia*

### 1. *A phialē*[119]

A *marzēaḥ* is mentioned in three Phoenician contexts. The first is a bronze drinking bowl from Lebanon, measuring 18.4 cm across and

---

[116] The addition of a final י in *TADAE* 4.177.5 is unnecessary; I retain the original reading, with Lindenberger, *Letters*, 39.

[117] Porten, *Archives from Elephantine*, 184; contrast his later reading in n. 115 above. His assumption that the *marzēaḥ* is a funerary association will be addressed in this chapter's conclusion.

[118] Thus, Eissfeldt, "Etymologische," 168, *contra* Porten, *Archives from Elephantine*, 184 (but contrast his later translation as "the silver of the *marzeaḥ* [*sic*]" in *TADAE* 4.177); Lindenberger, *Letters*, 39. This possibility is also raised by both Lidzbarski, *Ephemeris*, 3.120-21 and Miller, "The *MRZḤ* Text," 48, but neither reaches a definite conclusion. The absence of a preposition to indicate instrumentality favours this translation.

[119] Published in N. Avigad and J. C. Greenfield, "A Bronze *phialē* with a Phoenician Dedicatory Inscription," *IEJ* 32 (1982) 118-28. This article appeared after Bryan's work.

3.6 cm. deep, dated to the early fourth century BCE with a dedicatory inscription that reads קבעם אנחן II ערבת למרזח שמש.[120] Avigad and Greenfield transposed the two vertical lines, representing the number two, to a position after the first word (the objects being enumerated) and linked the personal pronoun אנחן with ערבת, which they took to be a verb; this yielded the translation "2 cups we offer to the *marzēaḥ* of Šamaš."[121] However, Guzzo Amadasi has shown on the basis of ancient Greek, Etruscan and Italic parallels that the pronoun probably refers to the cups, which means the numeral is in the correct place, and that ערבת is a plural substantive that also refers to the cups. As such the inscription should be translated as, "we 2 cups are offerings for the *marzēaḥ* of Šamaš."[122]

The inscription reflects a couple of elements encountered at Ugarit, namely consumption of liquids and the *marzēaḥ*'s dedication to a deity, in this case to Šamaš. The *marzēaḥ* here might be a group, in which case the bowl is simply given to them, but most take the inscription to mean the drinking bowl is dedicated for use during some activity, such as a drinking party.

2. *The Marseille Tariff*[123]

1 בת בעל[...] ב[עת המש]אתת אש טנ[א האשם ש על המשא]תת
עת [ר חלץ]בעל השפט בן בדתנת בן בד[אשמן וחלצבעל]
2 השפט בן בדאשמן בן חלצבעל וח[ברנם]
3 באלף כלל אם צועת אם שלם כלל לכהנם כסף עשרת 10 באחד
ובכלל יכן לם עלת פן המשאת ז ש[אר משקל שלשת מאת 300]
4 ובצועת קצרת ויצלת יכן הערת והשלבם והפעמם יאחרי השאר
לבעל הזבח
5 בעגל אש קרני למבמחסר באטומטא אם באיל כלל אם צו[עת]
אם שלם כלל לכהנם כסף המשת [5 באחד יבכלל יכן לם על]

[120] For the dating on epigraphic grounds see Avigad and Greenfield, "A Bronze *phialē*," 121; M. G. Guzzo Amadasi, "Under Western Eyes," *SEL* 4 (1987) 124-25. Catastini read אנסך for the original אנחן, but the latter is confirmed by Guzzo Amadasi; see A. Catastini, "Una nuova iscrizione fenicia e la 'Coppa di Yahweh'," *Studi in onore di Edda Bresciani* (ed. S. F. Bondi *et. al.*; Pisa: Giardini, 1985) 111-18; Guzzo Amadasi, "Under Western Eyes," 121-22.

[121] Avigad and Greenfield, "A Bronze *phialē*," 121.

[122] Guzzo Amadasi, "Under Western Eyes," 122-24.

[123] *KAI* 69; the text can be found in vol. I, p. 15 and a German translation and commentary in vol II, p. 83-87; for an English translation see *ANET*, 656-57. See also Bryan, "Texts," 158-63.

6 ת פן המשאת ז שאר משקל מאת וחמשם 150 ובצועת קצרת
ויצלת וכן הערת והשלבם והפע[מם ואחרי השאר לבעל הזבח]
7 ביבל אם בעז כלל אם צועת אם שלם כלל לכהנם כסף שקל 1 זר
2 באחד ובצועת יכ[ן לם עלת פן המשאת ז קזרת]
8 ויצלת יכן הערת והשלבם והפעמם ואחרי השאר לבעל הזבח
9 באמר אם בגדא אם בצרב איל כלל אם צולת אם שלם כ[ל]ל
לכהנם כסף רבע שלשת זר [2 באחד ובצועת יכן לם על
10 ת] פן המשאת ז קצרת ויצלת וכן הערת והשלבם והפעמם ואחרי השאר
לבעל [הזבח
11 בצ]פר אגנן אם צץ שלם כל[ל] אם שצף אם חזת לכהנם כסף רבע שלשת
זר 2 באחד וכן הש[אר לבעל הזבח
12 ע]ל צפר אם קדמת קדשת אם זבח צד אם זבח שמן לכהנם כסף א[גרת
10 לבאחד . . . . .
13 [ב]כל צועת אש יעמס פנת אלם יכן לכהנם קצרת ויצלת ו[ב]
צועת . . . . .
14 [ע]ל בלל ועל חלב ועל כל זבח אש אדם לזבח
במנח[ת]י . . . .
15 בכל זבח אש יזבח דל מקנא אם דל צפר בל יכן לכהנ[ם מנם]
16 כל מזרח וכל שפח וכל מרזח אלם וכל אדמם אש יזבח . .
17 האדמם המת משאת על זבח אחד כמדת שת בכתב[ת . . .
18 [כ]ל משאת אש איבל שת בפס ז ונתן לפי הכתבת אש [כתב . . . .
האשם אש על המשאתת עת ר חלצבעל בן בדתנ]
19 ת וחלצבעל בן בדאשמן וחברנם
20 כל כהן אש יקח משאת בדץ לאש שת בפס ז ונענ[ש . . . .
21 כל בעל זבח אש איבל יתן את כ . .[ע]ל המשאת א[ש . . . .

(1) Temple of Baʿal-[Zaphon]. Ta[riff of pay]ments e[rected by the overseers of pay]ments in the time of [the lord Ḥilleṣ-]baʿal the judge, son of Bod-tanith, son of Bod-[eshmun, and of Ḥilleṣ-baʿal] (2) the judge, son of Bod-eshmun, son of Ḥilleṣ-baʿal and their col[leagues].

(3) For an ox: a whole-offering[124] or a *ṣwʿt*[125] or a complete whole-

[124] A. van den Branden argues that the first instance of כלל in this line (as well as in lines 5, 7 and 9) is to be distinguished from the second instance, where it clearly refers to a type of sacrifice. He links the first occurrence to the Aramaic word כְּלָל ("general rule"): see A. van den Branden, "Lévitique 1-7 et le tarif de Marseille, *CIS* I 165," *RSO* 40 (1965) 115-16; he is followed by D. W. Baker, "Leviticus 1-7 and the Punic Tariffs: A Form Critical Comparison," *ZAW* 99 (1987) 191. However, Creason has shown on syntactical grounds that it is the first of a series of sacrifices; see S. Creason, "The Syntax of אם and the Structure of the Marseille Tariff," *RSF* 20 (1992) 143-59.

[125] Although there is widespread agreement that this word denotes a type of sacrifice, the precise meaning is disputed. For a convenient summary of scholarly

offering, to the priests ten—10—silver (shekels) for each; and for a whole-offering they shall have, besides this payment, m[eat weighing three hundred—300—(shekels)]; (4) and for a *ṣwʿt*, the neck and the joints, but the skin and the ribs and the feet and the rest of the meat shall belong to the sacrificer.

(5) For a calf whose horns are missing, or for a ram: a whole-offering or a *ṣw*[ʿt] or a complete whole-offering, to the priests five—5—silver (shekels) [for each; and for a whole-offering they shall have, besides (6) this payment, meat weighing one hundred and fifty—150—(shekels); and for a *ṣwʿt* the neck and the joints, but the skin and the ribs and the fe[et and the rest of the meat shall belong to the sacrificer].

(7) For a he-goat or a goat: a whole-offering or a *ṣwʿt* or a complete whole-offering, to the priests one—1—silver shekel and 2 *zars* for each; and for a *ṣwʿt* they shall h[ave, besides this payment, the neck] (8) and the joints, but the skin and the ribs and the feet and the rest of the meat shall belong to the sacrificer.

(9) For a lamb or for a kid or for the young of a hart: a whole-offering or a *ṣwʿt* or a com[pl]ete whole-offering, to the priests three-quarters of a silver (shekel) [2] *zars* [for each, and for a prayer-offering (?) they shall have, besides] (10) this payment, the neck and the joints, but the skin and the ribs and the feet and the rest of the meat shall belong to the sacri[ficer.

(11) For a b]ird, an *ʾgnn* or a *ṣṣ*:[126] a complete whole-offering or a *šṣp*-sacrifice or a divinatory (sacrifice), to the priests three quarters of a silver (shekel) and 2 *zars* for each; but the me[at shall belong to the sacrificer.

(12) Fo]r a bird or sacred first-fruits or sacrifice of game or sacrifice of oil: to the priests 10 silver *a*[*gorahs* (?)] for each . . . .

(13) [For] every *ṣwʿt* that is offered before the gods, the priests shall have the neck and the joints, and for a *ṣwʿt* . . . .

(14) [Fo]r a cake, for milk and for fat and for every sacrifice which a man sacrifices as a meal-offering, . . . shall . . . .

(15) For every sacrifice which a man may sacrifice who is poor in cattle or poor in birds, the priests shall receive nothing [from them].

(16) Every clan and every family and every *marzēaḥ* of the nobles,[127] and all men who shall sacrifice . . ., (17) such men (shall give) a payment for each sacrifice, according to what is established in the document . . . .

(18) [Ev]ery payment which is not established on this table shall be

opinions see M. G. Guzzo Amadasi, *Le iscrizioni fenicie e puniche delle colonie in Occidente* (Studi Semitici 28; Roma: Università di Roma, Instituto di studi del vicino Oriente, 1967) 175-76.

[126] The meaning of this and the previous term is disputed. For a convenient survey of opinions see M. Delcor, "Le tarif de Marseille (CIS I, 165). Aspects du système sacrifiel punique," *Semitica* 38 (1990) 89-92.

[127] For this translation see p. 42 below.

given according to the document which [...the overseers of payments drew up in the time of the lord Ḥilleṣ-baʿal, son of Bodtan](19)ith, and of Ḥilleṣ-baʿal, son of Bod-eshmun, and their colleagues.

(20) Every priest who takes a payment other than that which is established on this tablet, shall be fin[ed . . . .]

(21) Every sacrificer, who shall not give . . . [for] the payment wh[ich . . . .

The second Phoenician text is the Marseille Tariff, two stone blocks discovered near the French city in 1845. However, the type of stone is similar to that found at Carthage, and epigraphic considerations confirm that provenance for the inscription;[128] it is usually dated to the fourth or the third century BCE.[129] The tariff lists payments due to the priests of the temple of Baʿal-Zaphon in connection with sacrifices. Line 15 exempts the poor from such requirements, while line 16 mentions four other groups: clans (כל מזרח), families (כל שפח), *marzēaḥ*s (כל מרזח אלם) and every (group of) men who sacrifice (כל אדמם אש יזבח).[130] A. van den Branden takes the first three terms as participles enumerating cultic functionaries who are also exempt because of their profession,[131] but the plural אדמם in the final phrase indicates they are collectives. Moreover, the text's structure and the summary statement in line 17 that such people shall pay the prescribed fee calls for a contrastive rather than successive reading of lines 15-16.[132] As such, the Tariff spells out the financial obligations of individuals, while those of the groups mentioned in line 16 are contained elsewhere.

---

[128] B. Peckham, "Phoenicia and the Religion of Israel: The Epigraphic Evidence," *Ancient Israelite Religion: Essays in Honor of Frank Moore Cross* (eds. P. D. Miller, P. D. Hanson and D. S. McBride; Philadelphia: Fortress Press, 1987) 83.

[129] E.g., *KAI* vol. II, p. 83 and *ANET*, p. 502 ascribe it to the end of the third century BCE; Peckham dates it ca. 325 BCE; see B. Peckham, "Phoenicia," 94n50; J. B. Peckham, *The Development of the Late Phoenician Scripts* (Cambridge: Harvard University Press, 1968) 100, 211, 217.

[130] For this translation of the first two terms see G. A. Cooke, *Textbook of North-Semitic Inscriptions: Moabite, Hebrew, Phoenician, Aramaic, Nabataean, Palmyrene, Jewish* (Oxford: Clarendon Press, 1903) 121.

[131] A. van den Branden, "Notes phéniciennes," *Bulletin du Musée de Beyrouth* 13 (1956) 94-95; he translates מרזח as, "one who serves at the feast."

[132] Up to this point the text has specified the fees for specific types of sacrifice, with each type introduced by either ב or ל, and line 15, mentioning the poor, also follows this pattern. Beginning with line 16, however, the prepositions are missing and the precise fees are not specified; instead the reader is referred in lines 17 and 18 to another written document, line 20 indicates the penalty if a priest accepts a different fee than what is set out, and line 21 deals with people who refuse to pay. See also the comments of Bryan, "Texts," 160.

Thus, the third phrase refers to a *marzēaḥ* association. A clue concerning the group's membership is found in the phrase's final word, אלם (literally, "gods"). Both *KAI* and *ANET* take it as a general reference to Ba'al-Zaphon, who is mentioned at the beginning of the text, but Février claims that in Phoenician the plural refers to the nobility (thus, "the *marzēaḥ* of the nobles").[133] While the plural does not always have this sense,[134] Février's appeal to *KAI* 19.2 for the meaning "nobles" is correct. Three contextual considerations favour that meaning as well. First of all, it is unlikely that a *marzēaḥ* dedicated specifically to Ba'al-Zaphon would be mentioned in a list of general sacrificial responsibilities, or that they would need such responsibilities spelled out for them. Secondly, a non-religious meaning provides a better parallel with the preceding secular social groups. Finally, the contrast with the poor, who are mentioned in the preceding line, supports a reference to the upper class. Therefore, in this text the word *marzēaḥ* refers to an upper-class group which was expected to meet certain financial obligations in the religious sphere.

3. *The Piraeus Inscription*[135]

1 בים 4 למרזח בשת 14 לעם צדן תם בד צדנים בנאספת לעטר
2 אית שמעבעל בן מגן אש נשא הגו על בת אלם ועל מבנת חצר בת אלם
3 עטרת חרץ בדרכנם 20 למחת כ בן אית חצר בת אלם ופעל אית כל
4 אש עלתי משרת אית רעת ז לכתב האדמם אש נשאם לן על בת
5 אלם עלת מצבת חרץ ויטנאי בערפת בת אלם ען אש לכנת גו
6 ערב עלת מצבת ז ישאן בכסף אלם בעלצדן דרכמנם 20 למחת
7 לכן ידע הצדנים כ ידע הגו לשלם חלפת אית אדמם א{.}ש פעל
8 משרת את פן גו

[133] J. G. Février, *La religion des Palmyréniens* (Paris: J. Vrin, 1931) 208. Miller, "The *MRZḤ* Text," 45n7, proposes that אלם may "be read as *'ēlīm* 'rams,' i.e. leaders, chieftains" rather than "gods," which yields the same nuance as Février's proposal. Lewis, *Cults of the Dead*, 89n40, discounts this because of the *marzēaḥ*'s frequent link with deities elsewhere (Porten, *Archives from Elephantine*, 181, also relates אלם to a deity), but it is just as often linked to the upper class. Bryan, "Texts," 213, thinks the plural points to more than one *marzēaḥ* in the city, but in that case the first term should be plural, not the second.

[134] Note the phrase בת אלם ("house of the gods" = "temple") in the Piraeus inscription, discussed below.

[135] *KAI* 60; see vol. I, p. 13 for the text and vol. II, pp. 73-74 for the German translation and commentary. An English translation and commentary is given in Cooke, *Textbook*, 94-99. It is discussed in Bryan, "Texts," 163-67.

*Τὸ κοινὸν τῶν Σιδωνίων*
*Διοπείθ(η)ν Σιδώνιον*

(1) On the 4th day of the *marzēaḥ*, in the 14th year of the people of Sidon, the Sidonians in assembly decided to crown (2) Shemaba'al, son of Magon, who (has been) leader of the community in charge of the temple and the building of the temple court, (3) with a gold crown of 20 full-weight darics, because he built the court of the temple and did all (4) the service he was charged with; this decision is to be written (by) the men who are our leaders in charge of the temple (5) upon a carved stele, and they shall set it up in the portico of the temple in the eyes of anyone; and to designate the community as (6) surety for this stele. Let them take from the money of the god Ba'al of Sidon 20 full-weight drachmae. (7) Thus the Sidonians shall know that the community knows how to reward the men who have done (8) service before the community.

The community of the Sidonians
Diopeithan the Sidonian.

The final Phoenician text is the Piraeus inscription, an eight-line Phoenician text followed by two lines in Greek, dating from the mid-third century BCE.[136] This text records a decision made on "the fourth day of the *marzēaḥ*" (line 1) by the *marzēaḥ* members[137] to present

[136] The opening lines date the inscription to "the 14th year of the people of Sidon"; since the Sidonian era was thought to have begun in 111 BCE, the inscription was traditionally dated to 97 or 96 BCE (e.g., by Cooke, *Textbook*, 95; cf. also J. B. Peckham, *Late Phoenician Scripts*, 78). In contrast, after comparing the monetary terms in this text with Greek inscriptions, Baslez and Briquel-Chatonet opt for a "Sidonian era" beginning with Alexander the Great, and date this text to 320/319 BCE; see M. F. Baslez and F. Briquel-Chatonnet, "Un exemple d'integration phénicienne au monde Grec: les Sidoniens au Pirée à la fin du IVe siècle," *Atti del II congresso internazionale di studi fenici e punici: Roma, 9-14 Novembre 1987* (Instituto per la civiltà fenicia e punica. Collezione di studi fenici 30; eds. E. Acquaro, P. Bartoloni, *et al.*; Roma: Consiglio nazionale delle richerche, 1991) I.229-40. However, Donner and Röllig argued that the formation of the Greek letters points to a date in the second half of the 3rd Century BCE, as does the reference to Persian currency (darics; line 3): see *KAI* II, 73. Teixidor draws the same conclusion from the epigraphic evidence, and on analogy with the cities of Tyre and Arados suggests Sidon had begun an earlier system of dating during the second quarter of the third century BCE; see J. Teixidor, "L'assemblée législative en Phénicie d'après les inscriptions," *Syria* 57 (1980) 457-60, who is followed by W. Ameling, "ΚΟΙΝΟΝ ΤΩΝ ΣΙΔΩΝΙΩΝ," *ZPE* 81 (1990) 190-92.

[137] J. Teixidor, "L'assemblée," 455, 460, considers "the Sidonians in assembly" (צדנים בנאספת) a legislative body distinct from the general population (גו), while B. Peckham, "Phoenicia," 94n51, feels that the text "distinguishes between citizens and members of the association (*ḥṣdnym/gw*)." However, Ameling, "ΚΟΙΝΟΝ ΤΩΝ ΣΙΔΩΝΙΩΝ, 194-98, has shown on the basis of contempo-

Shemaba'al with a gold crown and to erect a stele commemorating the fact. Since the inscription mentions "the fourth day of the *marzēaḥ*," the word as used here cannot refer to a group as it does elsewhere. Rather, it denotes some kind of celebration, and in light of the role feasting played in earlier *marzēaḥ*s, I suggest such a meaning here. This feast spanned at least four days, and the unqualified reference to "the *marzēaḥ* in the 14th year . . .," with no further specification necessary for the reader to establish the precise date, implies there was only one such celebration in a given year.[138] At the same time, the *marzēaḥ* was considered a suitably prestigious occasion for conferring public honours, such as this presentation of a gold crown to Shemaba'al.[139] Shemaba'al is designated a leader (line 2), as are other unnamed individuals (line 4), albeit with the word נשא rather than the usual רב, and the general membership is mentioned frequently in the text with the term גו ("community"). Although only the leaders were involved in the actual governance of the temple,[140] which makes them part of the city's upper-class, the *marzēaḥ* "community" itself is able to dictate the use of funds dedicated to the god Ba'al (line 6). If this is the temple treasury, then the *marzēaḥ* "community" itself has a connection with the temple and therefore comprised important members of society. In any case, it appears that Ba'al was their patron, and the amount of funds involved points to a certain economic status.

---

rary Greek parallels that κοινὸν, which corresponds to the phrase צדנים בנאספת, refers to a religious group such as a *marzēaḥ* and that צדנים בנאספת and גו refer to the same group.

[138] *KAI* II, 73; Porten, *Archives from Elephantine*, 181; B. Peckham, "Phoenicia," 94n54.

[139] Greenfield, "Social Institution," 454; see also Février, *La religion des Palmyréniens*, 202; Porten, *Archives from Elephantine*, 181.

[140] Based on the parallel with line 4, where the other leaders are said simply to be "in charge of the temple," line 2 should be read as indicating Shemaba'al was a leader of the community *and* in charge of the temple, not that the community itself was. B. Peckham, "Phoenicia," 94n51, considers Shemaba'al the *marzēaḥ*'s representative to the temple, but the preposition על is more naturally translated as "over" (with the sense "in charge of") rather than "to" or "at" as required by Peckham's proposal; for the latter we would expect ל (on the two prepositions see the discussions in S. Segert, *A Grammar of Phoenician and Punic* [Munich: Verlag C. H. Beck, 1976] §56.22; R. S. Tomback, *A Comparative Semitic Lexicon of the Phoenician and Punic Languages* [SBLDS 32; Missoula: Scholars Press, 1978] 153-54, 242-43. Moreover, in line 3 he is honoured for constructing the temple courtyard, not representing the *marzēaḥ* group.

## D. *Nabatea*

### 1. *Petra*[141]

דכיר עבידו בר וקיהאל[142] וחברוהי מרזח עבדת אלהא

> May ʿObaidu son of Waqih'el be remembered and his companions, the *marzēaḥ* of ʿObodat the god.

The first piece of Nabatean evidence is this brief memorial inscription from Petra. It is quite straightforward, confirming *marzēaḥ* elements encountered previously. The term itself is in apposition to "ʿObaidu and his companions,"[143] yet another instance of an identifiable membership with one individual, probably the leader, singled out. This *marzēaḥ* also has a specific deity as its patron, the divinized dead king ʿObadas.[144]

### 2. *ʿAvdat*[145]

1 דנה מדדא[146] [די קרב][147] ...טו בני . ה .

---

[141] First published, with discussion, in G. Dalman, *Neue Petra-Forschungen und der heilige Felsen von Jerusalem* (PFAT 2; Leipzig: J. C. Heinrich, 1912) 92-94; see also Lidzbarski, *Ephemeris*, 3.278. Cf. the discussion in Bryan, "Texts," 198-99.

[142] Dalman, *Neue Petra-Forschungen*, 92, read זיקא and Lidzbarski, *Ephemeris*, 3.278, left it blank; it was corrected to וקיהאל on the basis of a closer inspection of the inscription by R. Savignac, "Chronique: notes de voyage de Suez au Sinaï et à Pétra," *RB* 10 (1913) 440.

[143] The word "companions" (חברו) in this and subsequent *marzēaḥ* texts may be a technical term for *marzēaḥ* members; see the discussion in M. O'Connor, "Northwest Semitic Designations for Elective Social Affinities," *JANES* 18 (1986) 72-80.

[144] He is generally identified as ʿObadas I, e.g., by J. Starcky, "Pétra et la Nabatène," *Supplément au Dictionaire de la Bible 7* (eds. L. Pirot, A. Robert, H. Cazelles and A. Feuillet; Paris: Librairie Letouzey et Ané, 1966) vol. 7, cols. 906, 1015; Porten, *Archives from Elephantine*, 181; J. Teixidor, "Bulletin d'épigraphie sémitique," *Syria* 48 (1971) 458. However, Eissfeldt, "Etymologische," 169, suggests ʿObadas II and ʿObadas III is proposed by J. Cantineau, *Le Nabatéen* (Paris: Ernest Leroux, 1930-1932) 1.6, 2.125; C. R. du Mesnil du Buisson, *Les tessères et les monnaies de Palmyre: un art, une culture et une philosophie grecs dans les moules d'une cité et d'une religion sémitiques* (Inventaire des Collections du Cabinet des Médailes de la Bibliothèque Nationale; Paris: Éditions E. du Boccard, 1962) 467. Any of these would place the inscription in the First Century BCE. For a possible funerary aspect to this *marzēaḥ* see pp. 78-79 below.

[145] Published as Inscription #10 in A. Negev, "Nabatean Inscriptions from ʿAvdat (Oboda) II," *IEJ* 13 (1963) 113-17. Cf. the discussion in Bryan, "Texts," 199-207.

[146] A. Negev, "Nabatean Inscriptions from ʿAvdat (Oboda) I," *IEJ* 13 (1961)

2 דה [וחברוהי][148] בני מרזחא[149] דנא מרזח
3 דושרא אלה גאיא בשנת יח(?)
4 ...אל לרבאל מלכא מלך נבטו די אחיי ושיזב עמה

> (1) This trough [which was dedicated] . . . . . X, sons of Y (2) [and his companions], the members of the *marzēaḥ*, which is the *marzēaḥ* of (3) Dushara, the god of Gaia, in the 18th year . . . (4) . . . of King Rab'el, king of the Nabateans, who brought life and deliverance to his people.

References to the *marzēaḥ* also occur at ʿAvdat, in fragmentary inscriptions on the side of four large stone trough-shaped objects.[150] The four-line partial inscription above is representative of the others. It mentions "X, son of Y" (the names are damaged), followed by a reference to "his companions, the members of the *marzēaḥ*." The singular masculine suffix on וחברוהי points to an individual and his companions, echoing the references to a *marzēaḥ*'s leader and members seen before, including at Petra. There is also the further speci-

---

137; *idem*, "Nabatean Inscriptions II," 114, read סכרא here and in the other inscriptions from ʿAvdat, linked the word with irrigation systems unearthed in the area, and translated the word as "dam" (Negev, "Nabatean Inscriptions I," 131-33); his assertion that, "The absence of the noun סכרא in the Nabatean Inscriptions hitherto discovered may indicate that farming in arid lands had not been practiced by the Nabateans until then" (Negev, "Nabatean Inscriptions II," 117), is special pleading. J. Naveh, "Some Notes on Nabatean Inscriptions from ʿAvdat," *IEJ* 17 (1967) 187-88, corrected this to מדרא (he showed that the first letter is a מ and the next two could each be either a ר or a ד) and suggested that the objects were some type of receptacle for liquid. O. Eissfeldt, "Neue Belege für nabatäische Kultgenossenschaften," *MIO* 15 (1969) 233-35, further clarified their purpose when he proposed reading מדדא, from the root מדד ("to measure") and interpreted the objects as stone troughs used to serve wine; he also noted the remains of vineyards and wine presses in the vicinity of ʿAvdat on p. 224. Bryan, "Texts," 174, 204, compares Hebrew דוד ("cauldrons") and the phrase בת דודא at Palymra; see also p. 56 below.

[147] Negev, "Nabatean Inscriptions II," 113, restored די בנא here, but Naveh, "Some Notes," 188, proposed די קרב here and in inscription 8 on the basis of #7a (cf. Negev, "Nabatean Inscriptions I," 133, 134).

[148] This restoration is supported by inscriptions 8 and 9b (see Negev, "Nabatean Inscriptions I," 135, 137); in the latter the word is followed by the same phrase as here (on which see n. 149).

[149] Negev, "Nabatean Inscriptions II," 113, 114, read סרותא, which he took as a name. This correction is made by Starcky, "Pétra et la Nabatène," 919, 1014; Naveh, "Some Notes," 188. It is supported by Negev's admission that the name Saruta' is unknown in the extant Nabatean sources (Negev, "Nabatean Inscriptions I," 137) and by his misreading of a מ as a ס in line 1 (see Naveh, "Some Notes," 187).

[150] See Negev, "Nabatean Inscriptions I," 131-33, for a description of these objects and their physical context.

fication that they are "the *marzēaḥ* of Dushara, the god of Gaia."[151] Thus, here the word *marzēaḥ* denotes a group with a leader and members who together are linked with a patron deity.

This *marzēaḥ*'s divine patron gives some insight into the group's activities. In Nabatean religion Dushara is equated with, among others, the Greek god Dionysus,[152] whose associations with intoxication suggest that heavy drinking played a role in the association. This view is reinforced by the purpose of the stone objects themselves. Their designation in the inscriptions,[153] combined with the large cup mark in the bottom of each,[154] indicates they were used for serving liquid, and in light of wine's role in *marzēaḥ*s in general and in this one in particular through its dedication to Dushara/ Dionysus, it is reasonable to surmise that was the kind of liquid served. Furthermore, the size of the objects indicates significant amounts of wine were used.[155]

A few other points may be made briefly by comparing this inscription (No. 10) with Nos. 7-9. First, inscriptions 8 and 10 are both dated to "the 18th year of Rab'el, who brought life and deliverance to his people," but the former also mentions an individual, different from the one in #10, and his companions.[156] Therefore, specification of the *marzēaḥ*'s patron in #10 may reflect a desire to distinguish it from at least one other *marzēaḥ* in the vicinity. Second, the fragmentary #7b may contain the title for a *marzēaḥ* leader, רב מרזחא,[157] paral-

---

[151] Dushara was the national deity of the Nabateans as well as the patron of various localities. On this deity see H. Niehr, *Religionen in Israels Umwelt: Einführung in die nordwestsemitischen Religionen Syrien-Palästinas* (Die Neue Echter Bibel, Ergänzungbund zum Alten Testament 5; Würzburg: Echter Verlag, 1998) 220-22.

[152] G. Dalman, *Petra und seine Felsheiligtümer* (PFAT 1; Leipzig: J. C. Hinrichs, 1908) 50; Starcky, "Pétra et la Nabatène," 990; Eissfeldt, "Neue Belege," 225.

[153] See n. 146 above.

[154] See the description in Negev, "Nabatean Inscriptions I," 132.

[155] Negev gives the dimensions of the sides of various troughs as follows: 7a - 90 cm. X 75 cm.; 7b - 190 cm. X 95 cm.; 8 (inscribed area only) - 63 cm. X 46 cm.; 9b - 56 cm. X 45 cm.; 10 - 132 cm. X 80 cm.; see Negev, "Nabatean Inscriptions I," 133, 134, 135, 137; *idem*, "Nabatean Inscriptions II," 113.

[156] Whether one reads "Garmo built" (בנא גרמו; Negev, "Nabatean Inscriptions I," 135), or "son of Adarmo" (בר אדרמו; Naveh, "Some Notes," 188), in #8, either must be distinguished from the fragmentary name in #10, which has the letters -דה immediately before "his companions." The expected identification of "his companions" as "members of the *marzēaḥ*" is obliterated in #8, but its presence in inscriptions 9 and 10 (according to Naveh's corrected reading; see n. 149) supports its restoration in #8.

[157] Following Naveh, "Some Notes," 188, against Negev's "this house"

leling the reference to an individual and his companions in our inscription. Finally, the stone objects were "dedicated" (קרב), reinforcing that *marzēaḥ*'s religious connection.

To summarize, there may have been more than one *marzēaḥ* at ʿAvdat at the same time. At least one had a recognizable leader and membership, a patron deity and its members drank wine in abundance from "dedicated" drinking troughs.

## E. *Palmyra*

### 1. *Tesserae*[158]

References to the *marzēaḥ* at Palmyra fall into two categories: tesserae and inscriptions. To begin with the former, the term occurs on nine of over twelve hundred tesserae (terra-cotta coins) dating from the first to third centuries CE, and probably employed as tokens of admission to banquets.[159] Six contain a name followed by the usual title for a *marzēaḥ*'s leader (רב מרזחא),[160] one refers to an individual's leadership of a *marzēaḥ* (ברבנות מרזחא),[161] another mentions the members (בני מרזחא)[162] and the final one uses the term absolutely in reference to "the *marzēaḥ* of Beʿeltak and Taymaʾ, day 5" (מרזח בעלתך ותימא יום 5).[163] As with the Piraeus inscription, the men-

---

(דנה דרחא; Negev, "Nabatean Inscriptions I," 134). Negev admits his second term is unattested in Nabatean inscriptions.

158 Most of the tesserae were initially published in H. Ingholt, H. Seyrig and J. Starcky, *Recueil des tessères de Palmyre* (Institut Français d'Archéologie de Beyrouth, Bibliothèque Archéologique et Historique 58; Paris: Imprimerie Nationale, 1955); an additional one mentioning a *marzēaḥ* is C. Dunant, "Nouvelles tessères de Palmyre," *Syria* 36 (1959) No. 12. The tesserae have recently been collated in *Palmyrene Aramaic Texts* (eds. D. R. Hillers and E. Cussini; Baltimore/London: Johns Hopkins University Press, 1996), and references to them will be to that volume by number alone. For a comprehensive discussion of the tesserae in general see du Mesnil du Buisson, *Les tessères*; for their relationship to the *marzēaḥ* see Bryan, "Texts," 220-25.

159 H. Seyrig, "Les tessères palmyréniennes et le banquet rituel," *Memorial Lagrange* (Cinquantenaire de L'École Biblique et Archéologique Française de Jerusalem (15 Novembre 1890 – 15 Novembre 1940); ed. L. Vincent; Paris: J. Gabalda, 1940) 55; du Mesnil du Buisson, *Les tessères*, 21.

160 Nos. 2033, 2036-2039, 2041; only No. 2038 is dated, to 132/133 CE.

161 No. 2040; the leader, Shalman Yarhibolaʾ Maliku ʾAʿabai, is also named on No. 2037.

162 No. 2279.

163 No. 2807. In the original publication of this tessera (Dunant, "Nouvelles

tion of "day 5" means that this particular *marzēaḥ* was a feast lasting a number of days and dedicated to the deities named, rather than a group devoted to them.[164] This raises the possibility of the same nuance for the other tesserae, but while such a meaning is plausible for the first two phrases,[165] it is more likely that בני in the third phrase designates members of a group rather than participants in a feast. Thus, I retain the denotations for רב/בני מרזח(א) found in earlier attestations[166] and interpret *marzēaḥ* in the three composite phrases as referring to one or more *marzēaḥ* associations.

The first seven tesserae depict a priest on the other side and Nos. 2033, 2039-2041 also have some form of the individual's name there.[167] This suggests that the image depicts the leader and, by extension, that such leadership was an honour worthy of publication; in fact, a major purpose of the Palmyrene *marzēaḥ* may have been bestowal of this honour.[168] With the exception of No. 2040,[169] in these seven tesserae the priest is reclining beneath a vine and in No. 2039 he is also holding a cup, pointing once again to the significance of wine for the *marzēaḥ*. Since No. 2033 also has the phrase "the priests of Bel" on the front, it is likely the other six should be similarly linked and that Bel is the patron of a *marzēaḥ* made up of his priests. At the same time, other gods are also mentioned on *marzēaḥ* tesserae. No. 2039 depicts Pan, the second line of No. 2279 is probably to be restored as "Ne]bo" while its opposite side de-

---

tessères," No. 12) it was translated as "thiase, à ton autel, et Taima, jour 5$^{e}$." This is quite awkward; cf. n. 164 below.

[164] The second name is identified with a member or even the leader of the *marzēaḥ* by du Mesnil du Buisson, *Les tessères*, 364-67, while Milik takes it as a diminutive derived from בני תימרזו, a group associated elsewhere with the goddess Be'eltak and in one instance identified as priests; see J. T. Milik, *Recherches d'épigraphie proche-orientale I: Dédicaces faites par des dieux (Palmyre, Hatra, Tyr) et des thiases sémitiques a l'époque romaine* (Institut Français d'Archéologie de Beyrouth, Bibliothèque Archéologique et Historique 92; Paris: Librairie Orientaliste Paul Geuthner, 1972) 111, 219; cf. J. Cantineau, "Textes palmyréniens provenant de la fouille du temple de Bêl," *Syria* 12 (1931) No. 12 (pp. 132-33); Ingholt, Seyrig and Starcky, *Recueil des tessères*, No. 66. However, a reference to two deities is more likely than a combination of divine and human individuals.

[165] I.e., "leader/during the leadership of the *marzēaḥ*-feast."

[166] See especially n. 32 and p. 22 above.

[167] No. 2033 contains the name in full, with only "the priests of Bel" on the front, while Nos. 2039-2041 present a shortened form of the full name already given on the front.

[168] Bryan, "Texts," 221-22.

[169] On which see p. 60 below.

picts a nude Apollo, and No. 2807 mentions the *marzēaḥ* of Beʿeltak and Tayma'. Thus, *marzēah*s dedicated to other deities co-existed with Bel's.[170]

However, unless a *marzēaḥ* was the only type of banquet celebrated at Palmyra, in the absence of a more explicit designation it would be wrong to identify every tesserae mentioning "Bel's priests" with the *marzēaḥ*.[171] In fact, consideration of all twenty tesserae referring to them provides strong reasons not to do so.[172] Half of them (which I will call Group A), also show a reclining priest plus a name on the other side,[173] and the parallels with the tesserae discussed in the preceding paragraph suggest the individual depicted is being honoured. The other ten (Group B) contain a variety of iconographic motifs, but only two are accompanied by names.[174] This second group lacks the banqueting motif, proving in and of itself that not all tesserae with the inscription "the priests of Bel" need necessarily be linked with banquets in general, never mind the *marzēaḥ* in particular. At the same time, whether the honour bestowed in Group A is because of a role in a *marzēaḥ* or even during the course of one is an open question. Henri Seyrig has published a Greek inscription dealing with a boy's consecration to the Palmyrene priesthood, and suggested just such an event would be an appropriate occasion on which to acknowledge an individual by issuing a tesserae depicting him as the honoured member of a banquet.[175] Although that could occur as part of a *marzēaḥ*, there is no indication this was the case. In sum, although a *marzēaḥ* comprising the priests of Bel was an important one at Palmyra, this is not the only type of banquet with which they were associated, and for my purposes the discussion above of only those tesserae specifying a *marzēaḥ* is sufficient.

---

[170] See further on p. 58.

[171] *Contra* du Mesnil du Buisson, *Les tessères*, 468-70 and *passim*.

[172] Of those twenty, only one (No. 2033) has the word *marzēaḥ* on it. The following discussion is dependent on Bryan, "Texts," 222-24.

[173] Nos. 2016, 2018-2020, 2023, 2025, 2028, 2029, 2033, 2035.

[174] Nos. 2017, 2021, 2022, 2024, 2026, 2027, 2030-2032, 2034; the first two contain the names.

[175] H. Seyrig, "Antiquités syriennes: 37—Postes romains sur la route de Médine; 38—Inscriptions grecques de l'agora de Palmyre," *Syria* 22 (1941) 267-70. Cf. tessera No. 887, which has 2 columns (a temple?) a priest's cap (imposed during the consecration?) and a name (noted by Bryan, "Texts," 223).

## 2. *PAT* 0991[176]

1 בירח אדר שנת 300[ . . .
2 כמריא די בלעסתר ובעל[שמן . . .
3 אנש מנהון יומא די יהון סמ[כי. . . גברא די]
4 מרזח די יהא ברשהון למקל[תא . . .
5 אלא גבר די יהוא אחיד ברש[הון . . .
6 ס<לען> 3 צרי לדהבי ומן מנהון[. . .
7 באדרונא או יושט ידה על[ . . .
8 ומן די יעד שביניהון יחו ל[ . . .
9 די יהוא אחיד על דהבא ויהימ[ן . . .
10 די הימן בשתה ואף אשרו [די ל]א ישלט אנש [ . . .
11 מומא באדרונא ומן די ימא [ל]חמן יחוב חטיא דד[ינרן
. . . ואף]
12 אשרו די כל גבר מן בני עתעקב די יגנב מן בת
ב[לעסתר . . .
13 עלוהי די יחוב חטיא דדינרן לדהבא ואחר שבע [ . . .
14 יהא שליט גברא די יג[ור] למשתא בעדרונא עד די [ . . .
15 די הן יחשח אפר על ב[י]ת בל ובני עתעקב כמרי[א . . .
16 או למנתן לבלעסתר מדען די ימד לגברא די [מרזח . . .
17 ימד מצעת גוא על [חש]בנא ומדען אחרן לאים[. . . .
18 למבקרו ולמו[דא מן די] חטיו ולמעבד פת[ . . .
19 אנשא די שנ[. . .]ר/ד ומן מן די אזל[ . . .
20 מן מן די י[. . .]א קדמיא די ב[. . .
21 ודי יהו[. . .]אכי ינ[. . .
22 אעל[. . .
23 הי[. . .
24 ל[. . .

(1) In the month of Adar, in the year 300[. . .] (2) the priests of Belastor and Baʿal[shamen . . .] (3) those among them the days when there will be a ban[quet . . . the member of] (4) the *marzēaḥ* who will be at their head for the sacri[fice . . .] (5) but the member who will be elected at their [head . . .] (6) 3 Tyrian s(hekels) to the treasurer and the one from among them [. . .] (7) in the banquet hall the agreement will be inscribed on [. . .] (8) and the one who will collect their votes will notify [. . .] (9) who will be elected over the treasury and will be in charg[e . . .] (10) of the one who will be in charge during his year

[176] The text plus preliminary discussion was presented in J. Teixidor, "Le thiase de Bêlastor et de Beelshamên d'après une inscription récemment découverte à Palmyre," *CRAIBL* (1981) 306-14. This appeared after Bryan's dissertation.

and also they have decided [that] a person will [no]t have the power . . .] (11) an oath in the banquet hall and anyone who swore (an oath but) did not keep it will pay a fine in de[narii . . . and also] (12) they decided that anyone from the sons of ʿAteʿaqab who steals from the temple [of Belastor . . .] (13) concerning he who pays a fine in denarii to the treasurer after seven [. . .] (14) will have the rights of a member who will remain at the banquet in the banquet hall until [. . .] (15) that if food is needed for the te[mp]le of Bel, then the sons of ʿAteʿaqab, the pries[ts . . .] (16) or for an offering to Belastor portions which will be determined for the members of the [*marzēaḥ* . . .] (17) will be determined among the community according to the [acc]ount and the other portions for a sign [. . .] (18) to examine and to determine those who have sinned and to make an open[ing(?) . . .] (19) those who chan[ge(?) . . .] ? and from whomever has gone [. . .] (20) from whomever [. . .] first of those in [. . .] (21) and who will be [. . .] because ? [. . .]
lines 22-24 are too fragmentary to yield any meaning

The *marzēaḥ* also figures in a number of inscriptions from Palmyra. The earliest is also the most recently discovered: this contract regulating various aspects of a *marzēaḥ* association. Teixidor dates it to the beginning of the Common Era, but greater precision is impossible due to the text's fragmentary nature.[177] After a reference to the priests of Belastor and Baʿalshamen (line 2), the text mentions "[the member of] the *marzēaḥ* who will be at their head for the sacri[fice . . .]" (lines 3-4) being elected (line 5) and paying three Tyrian shekels to the treasurer (line 6). The third person plural pronominal suffix ("*their* head") confirms that here the term *marzēaḥ* refers to a group, and that the surrounding words refer to the selection of their leader. Teixidor thinks the money is in return for the honour of the leadership role[178] but it may be meant to fund the banquet mentioned in line 14. Lines 8-11 outline responsibilities incumbent upon other members[179] and specifies that a fine be paid if they do not live up to their duties. In short, this *marzēaḥ* is a highly structured collective. The masculine גברא, used for the individuals in the contract, *may* indicate a gender-exclusive membership,[180] but the election of

[177] Line 1 breaks off after the number 300, which corresponds to 11 BCE, but Teixidor, "Le thiase," 306, dates it later, although not precisely, on paleographic grounds.

[178] Teixidor, "Le thiase," 310.

[179] Since the text is broken it is not possible to identify any specific role beyond that of treasurer in line 9: "the one who is elected over the treasury"; for this rendering of דהבא see Teixidor, "Le thiase," 311.

[180] Thus Teixidor, "Le thiase," 312. Although the term has to be supplied

the leader and lesser functionaries in that *marzēaḥ* points to an otherwise democratic and voluntary institution. A "banquet hall" (אדרונא) plays a major role as the place where the contract is to be deposited (line 7), the oaths of office are taken (line 11) and, of course, the banquet itself is held (line 14).

Seven other inscriptions from Palmyra also deal with the *marzēaḥ*, but since they have been known and discussed for decades, the details can be presented in summary form.

3. *PAT* 0326[181]

בירח] שבט שנת 345 עלתא דה [עבדו 1
בני מ]רזחא אלן לעגלבול ולמלכבל אלה[יא] 2
[וה]בי בר עתנורי עודו וחגגו בר זבדלה כמרא 3
[ונ]בוזבד בר מלכו מתנא ותימו בר עגילו רבבת 4
[ו]מלכו בר ירחבולא חתי וירחבולא בר תימרצו 5
אברוק וזבדבול בר ידיעבל אלהו ועגילו בר 6
נורי זבדבול ומלכו בר מקימו תימעמד 7

> (1) [In the month of] Shebaṭ, the year 345. This altar [has been made (2) by] these [members of the *ma*]*rzēaḥ* for ʿAglibol and for Malakbel [their] gods: (3) [Waha]bai, son of ʿAthenurai (son of) ʿAudu, and Ḥagagu, son of Zabdilah (son of) Komoraʾ, (4) [and N]ebuzebad, son of Maliku (son of) Mathnaʾ, and Taimu, son of ʿAgailu (son of) Rababat, (5) [and] Maliku, son of Yarḥiboleʾ (son of) Ḥattai, and Yarḥiboleʾ, son of Taimarṣu (6) (son of) ʾAbroqa, and Zabdibol, son of Yedaiʿabel (son of) ʾElihu and ʿAgailu son of (7) Nurai (son of) Zabdibol and Maliku, son of Maqaimu, (son of) Taimoʿamad.

This altar inscription, dated to 34 CE, states it has been "made by] these [members of the *ma*]*rzēaḥ* (בני מרזחא) for ʿAglibol and Malakbel, [their] gods," after which nine names, presumably of those members,[182] occur. Once again we find here a definable *marzēaḥ* membership connected with patron deities.

---

at the end of line 3, it is present in lines 5, 12, 14, 16.

[181] Published in E. Littmann, "Deux inscriptions religieuses de Palmyre, le dieu שיע אלקום," *JA* 9e Sér 18 (1901) 374-81, with corrections in C. Clermont-Ganneau, "Note sur les deux inscriptions religieuses de Palmyre publiées par M. E. Littmann," *JA* 9e Sér 18 (1901) 521-25. The text is also presented in Lidzbarski, *Ephemeris*, 1.343-45; Cooke, *Textbook*, 302-03; *CIS* 2, §3980. Cf. Bryan, "Texts," 195-97.

[182] According to O'Connor, "Elective Social Affinities," 72, the membership of a *marzēaḥ* numbered either nine or twelve individuals. Pardee, *Les textes para-*

4. *PAT* 0265[183]

1 צלמא דנה די זבידא בר שעדו
2 תימשמש די עבדת לה בולא
3 [לי]קרה וסהד לה ירחבול אלהא
4 ברבנות מרזחותה די כמרי בל
5 בירח ניסן שנת 428

(1) This statue is that of Zebaida', son of Šaʿadu (2) (son of) Taimošamaš, which the Senate made for him (3) to honour him and witness to him, the god Yarḥibol, (4) during his leadership of the *marzēaḥ* of the priests of Bel. (5) The month of Nisan, year 428.

In 117 CE a statue of Zebaida' was erected by the senate "during his leadership of the *marzēaḥ* of the priests of Bel" (line 4). In addition to an individual leader, this inscription also provides evidence of a *marzēaḥ* comprising a specific group ("the priests of Bel") and a link with a deity, in this case the god Yarḥibol.

5. *PAT* 1357[184]

1 [או]טקרטור קס]ר . . . . . . . . . . .
2 [. . . . . . .]. די אקים לה מלכ]ו . . .
3 מתקרא מזבנא בר ב]. . . . . . . . . . .[
4 במרזחותה די כמ]רא די בל[185] . . .[ בירח אב שנת 504

(1) [Em]peror Caes[ar . . . (2) . . . ] who has raised for him, Malik[u . . .] (3) surnamed Mezabanna, son of B[. . .] (4) during his *marzēaḥ* leadership of the pr[iests of Bel.] In the month of Ab, year 504.

*mythologiques*, 58, argues for a minimum of eleven, at least at Palmyra; Niehr, *Religionen*, 184, suggests "ca." twelve.

[183] Published in M. Sobernheim, *"Palmyrenische Inschriften," MVAG* 10/2 (1905) 30, plate 4. He read line 2 to say that the statue was erected by Zebaida''s daughter, but this was corrected and the reference to his presidency of the *marzēaḥ* established by C. Clermont-Ganneau, "Épigraphie palmyrénienne," *JA* 10e Sér 5 (1905) 394-95; see also J.-B. Chabot, "Séance du 10 novembre," *CRAIBL* (1911) 670. The text is also in Lidzbarski, *Ephemeris*, 2.281-82; *RES* §2129; *CIS* 2, §3919. See also Bryan, "Texts," 192-93.

[184] Published in Cantineau, "Textes," 119-20, fig. 3; see also J. Cantineau, *Inventaire des inscriptions de Palmyre 9: Le sanctuaire de Bêl* (Publications du Musée National Syrien de Damas 1; Beyrouth: Imprimerie Catholique, 1933) §26 (pp. 38-39); Bryan, "Texts," 190-92.

[185] This restoration is assured from the Greek portion.

The form במרזחותה appears in a bilingual (Greek and Aramaic) inscription from 193 CE; the Aramaic text is fragmentary, but appears to refer to the Emperor's erection of some object, such as a stele or statue, in honour of Maliku during his leadership of the *marzēaḥ* of the priests of Bel. Here too the *marzēaḥ* comprises a specific membership with a named leader. The Emperor's role in creating something to honour Maliku may indicate some degree of importance for this particular *marzēaḥ*.

6. *PAT* 0316[186]

1 ברבנות מרזחות שלמא בר מלכו בר בלידע [עבד צלמי]א אלן שתא
2 מן כיסה בירח ניסן שנת 514

(1) During the leadership of the *marzēaḥ*, Shalma', son of Maliku, son of Belaida' [has made] these six [statue]s (2) from his own funds. In the month of Nisan, year 514.

A designated leader for a *marzēaḥ* is also evident in this text from 203 CE, where the phrase ברבנות מרזחות ("during the leadership of the *marzēaḥ*") is predicated of Shalma', son of Maliku. His ability to fund construction of six statues suggests he was a man of some wealth. The somewhat lengthier Greek portion also mentions three different emperors, which implies official recognition for this *marzēaḥ*.

7. *PAT* 2743[187]

1 [בי]רח תשרי שנת 555
2 ברבנות מרזחות ירחי אגרפא ירחי
3 ידיעבל עגא יעת די שמש אלהיא ויתב על
4 קסמא שתא כלה ואסק דמרא עתיקא
5 לכמריא שתא כלה מן ביתה וחמר בזקין
6 לא איתי מן מערבא דכירין ובריכין
7 פרטנכס ומלכוסא בנוהי ועגילו כתובא

[186] Published in Sobernheim, "Inschriften," 66-68; Clermont-Ganneau, "Épigraphie," 405-407; for the text see also Lidzbarski, *Ephemeris*, 2.303-305; *CIS* 2, #3970 and Tab 16. See too, the discussion in Bryan, "Texts," 193-95.

[187] See H. Ingholt, "Les thiases à Palmyre d'après une inscription inédite," *CRAIBL* (1925) 355-62; *idem*, "Un nouveau thiase à Palmyre," *Syria* 7 (1926) 128-41, pl. 34; *An Aramaic Handbook* (PLO 10; ed. F. Rosenthal; Weisbaden: Otto Harrassowitz, 1967) I/1.42-43; Bryan, "Texts," 170-76.

8 וזבי בר שעדא די הוא על בת דודא
9 וירחבולא ממזגנא ומסיענא כלהון

> (1) [In the mo]nth of Tishri, year 555 (2) during the leadership of the *marzēaḥ* by Yarḥai Agrippa', (son of) Yarḥai (3) Jedai'bel (son of) 'Aga' (son of) Ya'oth, who served the gods and presided over (4) the distribution[188] for the whole year and gave aged wine (5) for the priests the whole year from his house and old wine (6) that was not from the West. May they be remembered and blessed: (7) Pertinkas and Malkosa', his sons, and 'Agailu the secretary (8) and Zabai son of Šo'ada', who was over the cauldron house (9) and Yarḥibola', the wine steward, and all the helpers.

The phrase "during the leadership of the *marzēaḥ*" (ברבנות מרזחות) is also found in reference to a certain Yarḥai Agrippa' on a stone erected in 243 CE. The inscription goes on to describe Yarḥai's piety, specifies his role in terms of wine distribution, and mentions those who served under him: a secretary, a chef ("who is over the cauldron house") and a wine steward are each identified by name, plus some anonymous "helpers." Thus, as in *PAT* 0991, this particular *marzēaḥ* had a president as well as other officers, which indicates a well-organized group. The leadership role lasted for at least a year, so this *marzēaḥ* probably met more than once during that time, and one of the leader's roles was overseeing the use of wine during that time. Yarḥai's ability to provide quality wine from his own stores indicates he was a wealthy individual.

8. *PAT* 1358[189]

1 ברבנות מרזחות חדודן סנקלטיקא
2 בר עגילו מקי דכירין ובריכין אנשא די
3 הוו מהדמרין[190] ב[בת בל מ]לא בר ירחי מלא

---

[188] The words יתב על קסמא in lines 3-4 were translated as "présidé la divination" in Ingholt, "Un Nouveau Thiase," 132, 141, but Milik, *Recherches I*, 279-81 notes that קסמא means "distribution" in Arabic, which fits the context (see immediately below) better.

[189] Published in J. Cantineau, "Inscriptions palmyréniennes," *RA* 27 (1930) 45-48; see also *idem*, "Textes," 117-19; *idem*, *Le Sanctuaire*, 40-41; *An Aramaic Handbook*, I/1.43 and the discussion in Bryan, "Texts," 176-85.

[190] Cantineau, "Inscriptions," 46 and *PAT* read מהרקרין. Cantineau derived it from from a putative Old Persian loan-word that is only indirectly attested elsewhere, and translated "mages." However, he also indicated that מהדמרין was a possible reading, and that was adopted by M. Gawlikowski, "Inscriptions de Palmyre," *Syria* 48 (1971) 415, who parsed the word as a *haphel* participle of the

4 די הוא [. . . .]שעא בר אתעקב שעא
5 די חוא ע[ל . . . אד]ר?ונא ואתעקב בר ירחי על
6 תונא [. . . .] עגילו די הוא על אמודא
7 ונרקיס ועגילו בר מהרדד דהוא קים על
8 טליא ועגילו בר ורוד דהוא קים על אמודא
9 ובת נטרא ושמע טבית בירח אדר שנת 583

(1) During the leadership of the *marzēaḥ* by Ḥadudan, the Senator, (2) son of ʿAgailu Maggai. May they be remembered and blessed, the men who (3) are custodians in [the house of Bel: Ma]le', son of Yarḥai Male' (4) who was [. . .] Šaʿa', son of 'Atheʿaqab (son of) Šaʿa' (5) who was ov[er . . . the ban]quet hall and 'Atheʿaqab son of Yarḥai, who was over (6) the room [. . . ] ʿAgailu, who was over the porticos (7) and Narqis and ʿAgailu, son of Mihrdad, who has been established over (8) the young men[191] and ʿAgailu, son of Worod, who has been established over the porticos (9) and the house of the guards. (They are) well known.[192] In the month of Adar, year 583

## 9. *PAT* 2812[193]

1 ברבנות מרזחות ס[פ]טמ[יוס] חדודן [סנקלטיקא]
2 נהירא בר ספטמ[יו]ס עגילו מקי די עדר [חילא די
3 א]ורלינוס קסר [מ]ר[נ]א ואדמ[ר] עם ולדא [. . .[194]
4 והו]א עמהון בדי[רא בירח] אב שנת 500 [+ 83 . . .
5 ביר]ח אדר ד[י] ש[נת 584 . . .
6 ובריכ]ין ו[הבי] בר [שעא] בר אתעקב
7 [. . .] ע[ל] ב[ו]מא[ו. . .
8 . . .בר אתע]קב יר[חי די] על [. . .
9 ו. . . .בר] אתעק[ב ירחי] על תונא ועג[ילו בר . . .
10 די על ע[מ]ודא ו . . . על טליא
11 . . .
12 ו]ירחב[ולא בר ע]גי[לו די] על ב]ת [נטר]י [ו]שמ[ע
13 טבית . . .

root דמר, with the meaning "custodes." This has the double advantage of deriving from a root known from surrounding Semitic languages and fitting the subsequent enumeration of individuals who were in charge of ("over") various parts of the temple.

191 I.e., those being trained for temple service; see Cantineau, "Inscriptions," 47.

192 For this rendering of שמע טבית see Gawlikowski, "Inscriptions," 415.

193 Published in Gawlikowski, "Inscriptions," 416-21, pl. 23.

194 Gawlikowski, "Inscriptions," 420, restored די בני מרזח here. Although plausible in connection with the opening words of the inscription, his proposal is not followed in *PAT* and will not be used to establish the text's content.

> (1) During the leadership of the *marzēaḥ* of Se[p]tim[ius] Ḥadudan, [Senator], (2) illustrious one, son of Septim[iu]s ʿAgailu Maqai, who aided [the troops of (3) A]urelius Caesar, [ou]r L[or]d and guardi[an] of the people and the children [. . . (4) and wh]o was with those in the tem[ple in the month] of Ab, year 5[83. (5) In the mo]nth of Adar, that [is] ye[ar 584 . . . (6) [and be bless]ed: Wa[habai] son of [Šaʿaʾ] son of ʾAteʿaqab (7) [. . .] ov[er] the altar [. . . (8) . . . son of] ʾAteʿa]qab (son of) Yar[ḥai who was] over [. . . (9) and . . . son of] ʾAteʿaq[ab (son of) Yarḥai] who was over the room, and ʿAg[ailu son of . . . (10) [who was over the por]ti[cos and . . . over the young men] (11) [. . . . . . . . .] (12) [and] Yarḥib[oleʾ, son of ʿA]gai[lu who was] ov[er the hou]se [of the the guard]s. (They are) [well] (13) know[n . . .

Finally, ברבנות מרזחות occurs in these two inscriptions from 272/273 CE[195] dealing with Senator Ḥadudan's leadership of a *marzēaḥ*. Once again, this leader is a person of importance, namely a Senator. The majority of both texts honours various temple functionaries by name, and in light of other inscriptions they are probably members of the *marzēaḥ*[196] and Bel may have been their patron.

At this point, a few general observations concerning the Palmyrene evidence, in addition to the specifics of each text discussed above, are in order. The first thing to note is the various patron deities: the altar inscription in *PAT* 0326 was done by devotees of ʿAglibol and Malakbel, Yarḥibol is mentioned on the Zebaidaʾ statue (*PAT* 0265), while Bel is named in the Greek portion of the Shalmaʾ inscription (cf. *PAT* 0316), and the *marzēaḥ* members are officials in Bel's temple in the Ḥadudan texts (*PAT* 1358, 2812). Together with the diversity reflected in the tesserae,[197] this implies that more than one *marzēaḥ* existed in the city, although a comparison between the numerous references to Bel and the solitary references to other divine patrons shows that the *marzēaḥ* of Bel was the most significant one.[198]

---

[195] The first is clearly dated to 272 CE; the second is dated to the following year by Gawlikowski, "Inscriptions," 420. Although the years are damaged (or restored) in lines 4 and 5, he appeals to the (restored) praise of Ḥadudan because "he aided [the troops of] Caesar Aurelius." *PAT* also dates it to 273 CE.

[196] So too Gawlikowski, "Inscriptions," 415; *marzēaḥ* members are also "remembered" and/or "blessed" in the Petra inscription and *PAT* 2743, roles are itemized in *PAT* 0991, and members are simply listed in *PAT* 0326.

[197] See pp. 49-50.

[198] The assertions that all *marzēaḥs* in the city had Bel as the principle patron and that any others were the additional patrons of individual meetings (see du Mesnil du Buisson, *Les tessères*, 470, 472 and *passim*; Milik, *Recherches I*, 110 and

Secondly, the frequent references to priests in both the tesserae and the inscriptions raises the question whether the Palmyrene *marzēaḥ* was an association of priests and/or dedicated primarily to ritual worship. Teixidor argues for a lay membership in the *marzēaḥ* contract, distinct from the clergy mentioned in line 2, with the latter serving only as spiritual guides and ritual functionaries when needed.[199] However, although the inscription's broken state prevents certainty, the phrase "those from among them" at the beginning of line 3 seems to relate the priests to the following material dealing with the *marzēaḥ*. Similarly, since Yarḥai "presided over the distribution for a whole year" and served quality wine to the priests for the same time period, his *marzēaḥ* also seems to comprise primarily priests. On the other hand, there is no reason the functionaries associated with Yarḥai or in the Ḥadudan texts must be priests. More importantly, it is not certain that all *marzēaḥ* leaders at Palmyra, who would be expected to play a leading role during *marzēaḥ* activity, were priests.[200] Two inscriptions seem to imply that the leader fulfilled priestly duties, but other explanations are possible for both. The *marzēaḥ* contract, for instance, mentions an individual "who will be at their head for the sacri[fice . . .]" (line 4), but this could simply mean that he will preside at the banquet rather than play a liturgical role.[201] In the same way, since the Yarḥai inscription focuses on his distribution of wine rather than any cultic actions,[202] the statement that he "served the gods" may simply refer to his piety. It is also worth comparing the two Ḥadudan inscriptions (*PAT* 1358 and 2812) with those mentioning Maliku (*PAT* 1357) and Shalmaʾ (*PAT* 0316). The latter two have Greek parallels in which the *marzēaḥ* leader is designated "high priest and symposiarch (ἀρχιερεὺς καὶ συμποσιάρχος). Unfortunately, the Ḥadudan inscription is mono-

*passim*), goes far beyond the evidence of both types of references. If the references to the "symposion of ʿAglibol and Malakbel" published by J. Starcky, "Autour d'une dédicace palmyrénienne à Šadrafa et à Duʿanat" *Syria* 26 (1949) 60-61, are to be equated with a *marzēaḥ* (the inscriptions are in Greek only, so it is impossible to be certain on the matter) they may indicate a greater significance for the *marzēaḥ* of those deities as well.

199 Teixidor, "Le thiase," 312. Contrast Niehr, *Religionen*, 183, who thinks the leader here was a priest.

200 Milik's view that the leader of the priests' *marzēaḥ* was also the leader of all of them (Milik, *Recherches I*, 110 and *passim*) goes beyond the available evidence, as does Niehr's assertion that this leader was the chief priest (Niehr, *Religionen*, 181).

201 *Pace* Teixidor, "Le thiase," 310.

202 See n. 188 on the translation of קסמא.

lingual, but it is significant that he is identified as a Senator rather than by any priestly title. This parallels a Greek inscription honouring the Procurator Septimus Vorod, as the "συμποσιάρχος of the priests of Bel," with the word ἀρχιερεὺς notably absent.[203] Thus, the unnamed leader in the contract as well as Yarḥai and Ḥadudan may all have been laity rather than priests. Finally, there is no conclusive evidence that those *marzēaḥ* leaders who were priests performed priestly functions as part of their position. The six tesserae mentioning a *marzēaḥ* leader (רב מרזחא) also depict a priest,[204] but neither they, nor the bilingual Maliku and Shalma' inscriptions (which identify them as high priests), give any indication of ritual activity. This only leaves a single tessera (No. 2040), in which a priest is shown offering incense. However, this particular tessera lacks the banquet motif and emphasizes his term of office rather than his position.[205] As such, the depiction of an explicitly sacerdotal function might be attributed more to his priesthood than to his role within the *marzēaḥ*.[206]

To summarize, while the *marzēaḥ* comprising Bel's priests was the most important one at Palmyra, it is possible there were others in the city whose membership and/or leader were not cultic functionaries. Moreover, even when the leader was a priest, this leadership was distinct from his clerical state. Thus, the only real indication of a ritual component for the Palmyrene *marzēaḥ* comes from the altar inscription. The nine members of a *marzēaḥ* made the altar for their gods, 'Aglibol and Malakbel, but the former are not designated priests, nor does the inscription state that the altar was for use during their gatherings, although that is possible. In any case, this single, inconclusive inscription does not outweigh the silence in the other Palmyrene *marzēaḥ* references. I am not denying that rituals might have been performed in connection with the *marzēaḥ* here or elsewhere, only highlighting that such activity was not emphasized and that the *marzēaḥ*'s primary purpose was not worship.

What little evidence exists of other activities points to the role of alcohol. The centrality of the banquet hall in the *marzēaḥ* contract[207]

---

[203] See *CIS*, §4485; the few extant Aramaic letters shed no light on the text.

[204] Nos. 2033, 2036-2039, 2041.

[205] Its phrase, "during the presidency of the *marzēaḥ*" (ברבנות מרזחא) is unique among the *marzēaḥ* tesserae; in contrast, the individual who is named in No. 2040 is simply called a *marzēaḥ* leader (רב מרזחא) on No. 2037, which displays banqueting rather than cultic imagery on the reverse.

[206] Bryan, "Texts," 221.

[207] See p. 53 above.

illustrates the importance of feasting while Yarḥai's provisioning indicates that wine was consumed. The latter is reinforced by the banqueting iconography on the *marzēaḥ* tesserae as well as the depiction of a goddess with grapes on one of them (*PAT* 2807). Thus, lacking any indication of other activities, I tentatively conclude that banqueting in general, and drinking in particular, played a significant role in the Palymra *marzēaḥ*.

## F. *Rabbinic Literature*

The obvious place to begin an examination of the *marzēaḥ* in the rabbinic[208] tradition is with texts that utilize either of the two biblical references. The Targums to Amos 6:7 and Jer 16:5, where the Hebrew term מַרְזֵחַ occurs, simply use the Aramaic equivalent (מרזחא), but there are allusions to those texts elsewhere in the rabbinic literature. Two texts connect the *marzēaḥ* with mourning. In *Bab. Moʿed Qaṭan* 28b, Mar Zuṭra quotes Amos 6:7b to explain the custom of a mourner occupying the head place at a funerary meal: "The bitter and distraught will be made chief of the sprawlers" (מר רזח נעשה שר לסרוחים). However, this is a classic example of midrashic word-play adapted to the point under discussion[209] and of limited value for determining the *marzēaḥ*'s nature at that time. Similarly, in *Bab. Ketubah* 69ab Mar Uqba quotes Jer 16:5 to support his answer to the question "What is a *marzēaḥ*?" with the word "mourning" (מאי מרזיחא אבל), followed by a repetition of Mar Zuṭra's word-play on Amos 6:7. In contrast, three texts link the *marzēaḥ* to a far less somber setting. Commenting on Amos 6:7, *Midrash Leviticus Rabbah* 5:3 equates the *marzēaḥ* with the Maioumas feast by stating that there were many מיומסאות, such that each tribe had its own; *Midrash Numbers Rabbah* 10:3 and *Midrash Tanhuma* 8 make the same comment, but with respect to Amos 6:4.[210]

---

[208] For ease of reference, I use "rabbinic" to refer to all Jewish material from the early centuries of the Common Era, without prejudice as to the actual authorship.

[209] Reading שׂר for MT סר and dividing מרזח into two words, מר וזח ("bitter and distraught").

[210] A full analysis of the Maioumas is beyond the scope of this study, but note the rabbinic description of it as "confused feasts beside the sea" (משתאות הוללות לחוף הים). The Roman authorities considered it so excessive they tried to ban it. See further in the standard dictionary articles, such as W. Drexler, "Maioumas," *Ausfürliches Lexicon der griechischen und römischen Mythologie 2:2* (ed. W. H. Roscher;

Moving beyond citations of Amos 6:7 and Jer 16:5, another rabbinic tradition concerning the *marzēaḥ* is connected with the incident of Baʿal-Peor at Shittim.[211] In Num 25:2 the Moabites "invited the people to the sacrifices of their gods, and the people ate and bowed down to their gods." Targum Pseudo-Jonathan inserts "in their *marzēaḥ*s" (במרזיחיהון) after the reference to eating, while Sifre Numbers 131 notes that they "made *marzēaḥ*s for them" (עשות להן מרזיחים). It is not explicit whether these additions refer to a feast held by a *marzēaḥ* association or the buildings in which they were held, but in the preceding chapter of both texts other words are used for the edifices they construct (see below), which suggests a *marzēaḥ* banquet is intended here. Marvin Pope seeks to clarify the banquet's nature on the basis of Ps 106:28, which says that the Israelites "attached themselves to Baal-Peor // they ate the sacrifices of the dead" (וַיֹּאכְלוּ זִבְחֵי מֵתִים). For Pope, this is evidence that the feasts of Num 25:2 "are explicitly identified as funeral feasts."[212] While Pope is correct in his assessment of the Psalm,[213] neither the Targum nor Sifre share the Psalmist's perspective on Num 25:2. Although the meal is a sacral one linked with the Moabite gods, there is no indication in the MT, the Targum or Sifre that these were deified ancestors, for instance. In fact, in the rabbinic texts the deities are secondary to other aspects of the *marzēaḥ*, as Balaam's advice to Balak in Pseudo-

---

Leipzig: B. G. Teubner, 1894-1897; rpt. Hildesheim: Georg Olms, 1965) 2:2, cols. 2286-2288; K. Preisendenz, "Maioumas," *Paulys Real-Encyclopädie der classischen Altertumwissenschaft: Neue Bearbeitung begonnen von George Wissowa unter Mitwirkung zahlreicher Fachgenossen 14:1* (ed. W. Kroll; Stuttgart: Metzler, 1928) 14:1, cols. 610-12 and more recently, R. M. Good, "The Carthaginian MAYUMAS," *SEL* 3 (1986) 99-114. On the feast in rabbinic literature as a whole see J. Perles, *Etymologische Studien zur Kund der rabbinischen Sprache und Altertümer* (Breslau: Schletter, 1871) 96-100; *idem*, "Miscellen zur rabbinischen Sprach- und Altertumskunde," *MGWJ* 21 (1872) 251-54. A convenient summary of the Maioumas and its relationship to the *marzēaḥ* can be found in Bryan, "Texts," 34-67; he thinks the reference to it here is a scribal error derived from דימוסיא ("common") but acknowledges there must have been a plausible connection between the two for the mistake to have occurred (see his pp. 28-32, 67).

[211] See also the discussion in Bryan, "Texts," 74-112.

[212] M. H. Pope, *Song of Songs: A New Translation with Introduction and Commentary* (AB 7C; Garden City: Doubleday, 1977) 217.

[213] Older scholarship interpreted the Psalm to mean "lifeless idols," but this requires an unattested connotation for מֵתִים, which is, on the other hand, paralleled with "gods" in *CAT* 1.6.VI.47-48; Isa 8:19-20; cf. 2 Sam 28:13; thus Lewis, *Cults of the Dead*, 167; see also M. J. Dahood, *Psalms III: 101-150. A New Translation with Introduction and Commentary* (AB 17A; New York: Doubleday, 1970) 73-74 and the references in Schmidt, *Israel's Beneficent Dead*, 265n567.

Jonathan Num 24:14 shows. He suggests the Israelites can be overcome if the Moabites set up taverns (פונדקין, cf. Greek πανδοκεῖν) in which abundant food and drink will lead to drunkenness, making the Israelites susceptible to seductive women who can lead them into apostasy. In other words, in these rabbinic texts the most important feature of this *marzēaḥ* is drinking that leads to lasciviousness and culminates in idolatrous worship.[214]

In the remaining rabbinic uses of *marzēaḥ*, it is clear from the context that it designates a meal contrasted with mourning rather than a *marzēaḥ* building. In *Jer. Berakot* 6a, Rabbi Zeira orders his disciples not to mourn him one day and eat a *marzēaḥ* the next (לא תקבלון יומא דין אכילה למחר מרזחייא), and a joyous banquet[215] provides an appropriate contrast to mourning. Similarly, *Qohelet Rabbah* 7:4 denounces Nabal for "making" a *marzēaḥ* while the nation mourns Samuel (וזה הרשע עושה לו מרזיחין: "but this wicked one makes for himself a *marzēaḥ*") and nearly identical wording is used in *Esther Rabbah* 3:3 when Ahasuerus and Vashti host feasts despite the destruction of Jerusalem and the temple (ורשע זה עושה מרזיחין גם ושתי הרשעה עושה מרזיחין: "but this wicked one makes a *marzēaḥ*. Vashti, the wicked one, also makes a *marzēaḥ*"). In both cases, the contrast with mournful events requires that *marzēaḥ* refer to a joyful banquet rather than a *marzēaḥ* house. In the latter instance, this is confirmed by *Esther Rabbah* 1:10, which states that Ahasuerus "made" the *marzēaḥ* while seated (ורשע זה יושב ועושה מרזיחין: "but this wicked one sits and makes a *marzēaḥ*"). It is also in keeping with the biblical text (Esth 1:2-9), where these two hold feasts. At the same time, in light of elements seen elsewhere, it is worth noting the luxurious surroundings and copious amount of wine at Ahasuerus' feast (Esth 1:6-8).[216]

To summarize, then, with the exception of instances dependent on Jer 16:5 the rabbinic tradition understands the *marzēaḥ* to be a

---

[214] A causal connection between the incident and wine can also be found in *Midrash Tanhuma*, extrapolating from Gen 9:27.

[215] *Marzēaḥ* here is translated as a "Trauermahle" by O. Eissfeldt, "מַרְזֵחַ und מַרְזְחָא 'Kultmahlgenossenschaft' im spätjüdischen Schrifttum," *Kleine Schriften zum Alten Testament 5* (eds. R. Sellheim and F. Maass; Tübingen: J. C. B. Mohr, 1973) 5.139; see also, Porten, *Archives from Elephantine*, 184. However, the emphasis in the succeeding lines is clearly on celebratory drinking.

[216] The nearly identical wording in the other texts may suggest that the rabbis viewed the feast in those instances in a comparable light.

celebratory drinking feast which, at least in some cases, is characterized by its excesses.

## G. *The Madeba Map*

The latest epigraphic attestation of the *marzēaḥ* is in a 6th century CE mosaic map of the Middle East found on the floor of a Byzantine Church in Madeba, Jordan.[217] A building to the east of the Dead Sea is labelled, "*marzēaḥ* house, also (known as) the Maioumas" (ΒΗΤΟΜΑΡΣΕΑ Η Κ(ΑΙ) // ΜΑΙΟΥΜΑΣ). This is usually connected with the incident of Baʿal-Peor at Shittim.[218] Bryan discounts the connection, noting that the location is not quite correct and arguing that since the building resembles a theatre and pool it is meant to represent the site of a contemporary Maioumas near Madeba itself.[219] However, the map consistently depicts sites connected with biblical events, and the one in Num 25:2 is a far better candidate for this location than either the Samarian *marzēaḥ* denounced by Amos or the Jerusalem *marzēaḥ* house mentioned in Jer 16:5.[220] In any case, the connection of the *marzēaḥ* with a specific building remains, as does its association with the Maioumas feast, most likely under the influence of *Midrash Leviticus Rabbah* 5:3, *Midrash Numbers Rabbah* 10:3 and *Midrash Tanhuma* 8.

## H. *Summary*

There is a high degree of continuity in the post-biblical *marzēaḥ* references. In most locations the term refers to an association orga-

---

[217] On the map in general see M. Avi-Yonah, *The Madaba Mosaic Map with Introduction and Commentary* (Jerusalem: Israel Exploration Society, 1954); H. Donner and H. Cüppers, *Die Mosaikkarte von Madeba* (Abhandlungen des deutschen Palästinavereins; Tafelband; Weisbaden: Otto Harrassowitz, 1977); H. Donner, *The Mosaic Map of Madaba: An Introductory Guide* (PA 7; Kampen: Kok Pharos Publishing House, 1992).

[218] The connection was first made by A. Büchler, "Une localité énigmatique mentionnée sur la mosaïque de Madaba," *REJ* 42 (1901) 125-28 and is accepted by most scholars.

[219] Bryan, "Texts," 113-19.

[220] The dislocation of the site of Shittim may be the result of the artist's desire to shift such a negative episode away from the vicinity of Madeba itself; see R. T. O'Callaghan, "Madaba (Carte de)," *Supplément au Dictionaire de la Bible* (eds. L. Pirot, A. Robert and H. Cazelles; Paris: Librairie Letouzey et Ané, 1957) vol. 5, col. 677.

nized under an identifiable leader, with other officials also designated in the Piraeus inscription, at Palmyra and perhaps at Elephantine. The *marzēaḥ* is connected with property in the Moabite inscription, the Palmyrene contract and the Madeba Map, and in every location except Elephantine and Madeba it is explicitly linked with one or more deities. References and allusions to drinking are another common feature. Finally, there is evidence of development in the word's meaning, from a group of individuals who hold a banquet to the banquet itself. In two of the three Phoenician references, *marzēaḥ* designates a feast rather than a group, both meanings can be found on the Palmyrene tesserae, and in the rabbinic material it refers exclusively to a feast. At the beginning of this semantic shift, this was almost certainly a case of an activity deriving its name from those who performed it, i.e., the *marzēaḥ* feast was celebrated by *marzēaḥ* members. The rabbinic texts do not indicate whether the *marzēaḥ* groups themselves had ceased and only the memory of their parties remained.

## III. Conclusions: The Constitutive Features of the *marzēaḥ*

The task at this point is to draw some conclusions as to the *marzēaḥ*'s essential nature in the ancient world on the basis of the evidence presented in this chapter. This will provide the context for evaluating the *marzēaḥ* in the prophetic literature, particularly allusions that do not use the word itself. In doing so, I will emphasize points of continuity between the pre- and post-biblical *marzēaḥ* references in an effort to identify features that are consistently present in most instances, and especially in both early and late attestations. If a feature is only mentioned in later attestations, I will assume it is an innovation introduced around the time it is first mentioned in connection with a *marzēaḥ*. While such characteristics may have been present earlier, I resist retrojecting them onto prior *marzēaḥ*s without direct textual evidence. On the other hand, if an element is not mentioned in a particular instance yet is consistently present in earlier attestations, that does not necessarily mean it is not characteristic of that particular *marzēaḥ*; it may simply be that a text focuses on other matters. That probability is even greater when a missing element is regularly present both before and after a single attestation. An example of the former is the rabbinic material, which makes no reference to a *marzēaḥ* leader (רב מרזח) since it is concerned with negative aspects of the *marzēaḥ* feast, while Elephantine presents the latter case: Ito is not so designated, but in light of the term's use both earlier (at Ebla and Ugarit) and later (Nabatea and Palmyra), that is a legitimate interpretation of his role as presented in the inscription, which is more concerned with the proper transfer of funds than individual titles.

From this perspective three elements are consistently present in *marzēaḥ* references over three millennia, and can be taken as constitutive features of the *marzēaḥ* association and its gatherings: a definable upper-class membership, a religious connection, and alcohol. A fourth element, namely a funerary connection, is often claimed as an essential aspect of the *marzēaḥ*, but the evidence does not support that view. In what follows I justify inclusion of the first three and rejection of the last.

### A. *Definable Upper-Class Membership*

There is no doubt the *marzēaḥ* was a significant institution in the ancient semitic world. Its existence over three millennia in a variety of locations is, in itself, testimony to its importance, as is the determination of public dates simply by reference to a *marzēaḥ* as early as Emar and as late as the Piraeus inscription. Similarly, the *marzēaḥ* was considered a suitable context for bestowing honours at Ebla, Sidon, and Palmyra. Finally, a *marzēaḥ*'s financial dealings are confirmed by a large number of witnesses in one Ugaritic text and attract the attention of the king in another, the Moabite papyrus records royal approval for the disposition of *marzēaḥ* property, and the Senate and even Emperors are linked to the *marzēaḥ* at Palmyra.

The high degree of prestige accorded the *marzēaḥ* throughout its history is due primarily to the social standing of its membership. The earliest indication of the *marzēaḥ* members' elite status comes from Ugarit. A full analysis of Ugarit's social organization is beyond the scope of this study,[221] but a general sense of the *marzēaḥ*'s place in

---

[221] Preliminary general discussions can be found in P. C. Craigie, *Ugarit and the Old Testament* (Grand Rapids: Wm. B. Eerdmans Publishing Co., 1983) 26-43; A. H. Curtis, *Ugarit (Ras Shamra)* (Cities of the Biblical World; Grand Rapids: Wm. B. Eerdmans Publishing Co., 1985) 49-65; see further A. F. Rainey, "The Social Stratification of Ugarit" (Ph.D. Dissertation, Brandeis University; 1962). For treatments of more specific aspects see Heltzer, *The Rural Community*; *idem*, *Goods, Prices and the Organization of Trade in Ugarit (Marketing and Transportation in the Eastern Medi-*

its social structure can be derived from the locations where the tablets referring to it were found.[222] Not only is Ugarit the capital of a kingdom, but the tablets were discovered in either royal and temple archives or the private collections of obviously wealthy individuals. It is reasonable to assume legal documents reflect the concerns and ideology of those who kept them, while reinforcement and outright legitimation of one's lifestyle provides an even stronger motivation for preserving the mythological texts. Simply put, the sites where the various *marzēaḥ* tablets were excavated favour situating the *marzēaḥ* itself among the upper levels of society.

This is confirmed by details in the tablets themselves. The buildings and vineyards owned by Ugaritic *marzēaḥ* associations point to financial means beyond those of the average peasant or day-labourer. So too with the amounts of money connected with the *marzēaḥ*. RS 14.16 mentions one *lîm* (1000 shekels), although its precise relationship to the *marzēaḥ* is unclear, but the sum of 50 silver shekels in *CAT* 3.9 is more certain. Miller dismisses this as, "not a very large sum when compared with other transactions involving a *marziḥ* at Ugarit,"[223] but that amount of money would purchase between five and ten bulls, or as many as seventy-five sheep.[224] This also places the *marzēaḥ*'s social setting among Ugarit's elite.

Similar features can be found in subsequent *marzēaḥ* references. Buildings are linked to the *marzēaḥ* in the Moabite papyrus, the contract from Palmyra and the Madeba Map.[225] Money plays a role

---

*terranean in the Socond* [sic] *Half of the II Millenium* [sic] *BCE)* (Weisbaden: Reichert, 1978); *idem*, *Internal Organization*; for cautionary comments on the use of the second volume by Heltzer see Pardee, "Ugaritic," 270-72.

[222] For a convenient discussion of the texts' provenance see M. Yon, "Ugarit: History and Archaeology," *ABD* 6.695-706, especially p. 695.

[223] Miller, "The *MRZḤ* Text," 40, following Hillers and referring to RS 14.16.

[224] Cf. Heltzer, *Goods*, 21; R. R. Stieglitz, "Commodity Prices at Ugarit," *JAOS* 99 (1979) 16, 23. Two points help put this into perspective. Administrative texts from Ugarit list individual households owning anywhere between none and three bulls, and as many as sixty sheep (see Heltzer, *The Rural Community*, 84-88 for texts and discussion). The mention of only a few heads of households per village, and at times only one, suggests these are not comprehensive enumerations of entire villages but rather census lists of the leading (by virtue of their wealth) citizens of each. Secondly, although the amounts may not represent an entire year's levy, whole villages sometimes paid as little as twenty shekels in taxes (Heltzer, *The Rural Community*, 34). Thus, the amounts of money required of a *marzēaḥ*'s members would exceed the capacity of the average peasant.

[225] On the archaeological remains of what may have been a *marzēaḥ* house at Ugarit see n. 106. The building at Kuntillet ʿAjrud is identified as a *marzēaḥ* house

at Elephantine and in the Palmyrene contract, and the four and five day *marzēaḥ* feasts mentioned in the Piraeus inscription and the Beʿeltak tessera[226] would have required great financial resources, as would the wine consumption which seems to be characteristic of the *marzēaḥ*.[227] Furthermore, in the Marseille Tariff a *marzēaḥ* is identified with the nobility, in the Piraeus inscription the *marzēaḥ* leaders are involved with the temple's governance and at Palmyra, the only time social roles are specified they are priests, temple functionaries and a senator, all of which are members of the elite. Similarly, the rabbinic equation of Ahasuerus' feast with a *marzēaḥ* combines the nobility with the financial resources necessary for the luxurious setting and the free-flowing wine of that banquet.

Finally, the consistent terminology for the members and their leader points to an organized and easily identifiable group from among the elite of a region. The Palmyrene *marzēaḥ* dedicated to ʿAglibol and Malakbel had nine members, and the co-existence of more than one *marzēaḥ* at both Ugarit and Palmyra shows the group was not all-inclusive. When this is combined with the preceding discussion of social standing, it is clear the *marzēaḥ* association comprised a subsection of the upper-class in the majority of known cases.[228]

## B. *A Religious Connection*

The *marzēaḥ*'s religious aspect can be easily established on the basis of the consistent association with one or more deities. The *marzēaḥ*

---

by M. H. Pope, "Le *MRẒH* à l'Ugarit et ailleurs," *AAAS* 29-30 (1979-1980) 142 and one is claimed for Dura-Europos in the 2nd Century CE by du Mesnil du Buisson, *Les tessères*, 467-68. Similar proposals are made for Palmyra by Pardee, *Les textes para-mythologiques*, 58-59; C. Maier and E. M. Dörrfuß, "'Um mit ihnen zu sitzen, zu essen und zu trinken': Am 6,7; Jer 16,5 und die Bedeutung von *marzeªḥ*," *ZAW* 111 (1999) 53.

226 No. 2807; if "day five" is meant for admission on that specific day then those in attendance would have varied during the course of the feast, which may imply a large banquet as well.

227 See further on pp. 69-70.

228 Granted, the preserved evidence comes from the upper-class itself, and a parallel *marzēaḥ* comprising poorer members of society may have existed without leaving any record. However, the limited resources of such a group would not have permitted the same degree of consumption, especially of alcohol (see below). As such, it would have differed significantly from the *marzēaḥ* reflected in the extant texts, perhaps so much as to be unrecognizable. Thus, barring explicit reference to a lower-class *marzēaḥ*, the conclusions drawn here concerning the group's social status stands.

members bring offerings to the gods at Emar, while at Ugarit El himself hosts a *marzēaḥ*, and in other Ugaritic texts *marzēaḥ*s are associated with Šatrana, the "Hurrian" Ishtar and probably ʿAnat. It is not clear whether the gods mentioned in the Moabite papyrus are to be linked with that *marzēaḥ*, but the Phoenician drinking bowl refers to "the *marzēaḥ* of Shamash," the Sidonian *marzēaḥ* (the Piraeus inscription) is linked to Baʿal, the gods ʿObadas and Dushara are mentioned in Nabatean contexts and eleven different deities are linked to various *marzēaḥ*s at Palmyra.[229] Moreover, the drinking bowl is an "offering" and the ʿAvdat drinking troughs were "dedicated"; both terms suggest that they were used in a religious context. But at the same time there is no direct reference to rituals being performed during a *marzēaḥ*.[230] So while the various deities are best interpreted as divine patrons, worship of these patrons does not seem to be the primary purpose of the *marzēaḥ*s dedicated to them. The *marzēaḥ* and its gathering was religious, in the sense that it was connected with a patron deity or deities, but it was not cultic.

## C. *Alcohol*

Alcohol consumption, usually in the form of wine, is the only activity regularly connected to the *marzēaḥ*. The clearest example is at Ugarit, where El hosts a *marzēaḥ* for the other gods during which they and he "drink wine to satiety, new wine to drunkenness"; El imbibes so much he has to be helped from the room and ultimately collapses in his own bodily excretions. Most subsequent *marzēaḥ*s are also linked with alcohol in some way. The Phoenician drinking bowl and the serving troughs at ʿAvdat both reflect the role wine played in

[229] Bel is the most frequently mentioned, but various *marzēaḥ*s are also linked to Belastor and Baʿalshamem, ʿAglibol and Malakbel, Yarḥibol, Pan, Nebo, Appolo, Beʿeltak and Tayma.

[230] The funerary liturgy in *CAT* 1.161 was related to a *marzēaḥ* banquet by M. Dietrich and O. Loretz, "Neue Studien zu den Ritualtexten aus Ugarit (II)—Nr. 6—Epigraphische und inhaltliche Probleme in KTU 1.161," *UF* 15 (1983) 23. In the absence of the term itself, however, nothing connects that text to a *marzēaḥ*; cf. L'Heureux, *Rank*, 192; B. Margalit, *A Matter of "Life" and "Death": A Study of the Baal-Mot Epic (CTA 4–5–6)* (AOAT 206; Kevelaer: Verlag Butzon and Bercker; Neukirchen-Vluyn: Neukirchener Verlag, 1980) 199; Schmidt, *Israel's Beneficent Dead*, 102n278. *CAT* 1.161 is often associated with the Mesopotamian *kispum* ritual (see the discussion and references in Schmidt, *Israel's Beneficent Dead*, 102-105), but the latter is to be distinguished from the *marzēaḥ* (see p. 71 below). See also pp. 59-60 concerning the Palmyrene *marzēaḥ*.

the *marzēaḥ*. Furthermore, the ʿAvdat troughs were found near vineyards, and vineyards are also included in two different listings of property owned by Ugaritic *marzēaḥ* members. The identification of the Nabatean god Dushara, a *marzēaḥ* patron, with Dionysus is also consistent with an emphasis on heavy drinking. At Palmyra one text refers to quality wine being dispensed regularly under the supervision of a wine steward, and the tesserae include depictions of grape vines and wine cups. The *marzēaḥ* leader's designation as a συμποσιάρχος in two bilingual inscriptions from Palmyra is also significant in light of the *symposium*'s connections with drinking. Finally, in the rabbinic literature the *marzēaḥ* is explicitly linked to drunkenness at Baal-Peor, to the copious drinking of Ahasuerus' banquet and, along with the Madeba Map, is equated with the Maioumas, which included excessive drinking. Thus, the common identification of heavy drinking as a constitutive feature of the *marzēaḥ* is correct.[231] Moreover, in as much as drunkenness features in both early (El's *marzēaḥ*) and late (rabbinic material and the Madeba Map) *marzēaḥ* references, and is at least implied at ʿAvdat through the size of the drinking troughs and Dushara's identification with Dionysus, it is likely that a major purpose of the *marzēaḥ* itself was to get drunk.

## D. *Non-Funerary*

The *marzēaḥ* is often considered to be, in essence, a funerary banquet connected to the cult of the dead. The strongest statement is by Marvin Pope: "Despite unfounded scepticism in some quarters, there is scant reason to doubt that the West Semitic *marzēaḥ* was a feast for and with the departed ancestors . . . ."[232] Although recent scholarship has tended to reject this view,[233] it still has its proponents and so must be considered, if only to exclude it as an essential aspect of the *marzēaḥ*.

---

[231] See, e.g., Pardee, "*Marziḥu*," 278: "The only constant in the documentation regarding the *marziḥu* . . . is the consumption of wine." Contrast Schmidt, *Israel's Beneficent Dead*, 63-64.

[232] M. H. Pope, "The Cult of the Dead at Ugarit," *Ugarit in Retrospect* (ed. G. D. Young; Winona Lake: Eisenbrauns, 1981) 176.

[233] See. e.g., Bryan, "Texts", *passim*; L'Heureux, *Rank*, 206-12, 218-21; H.-J. Fabry, "מַרְזֵחַ *marzēaḥ*," *TWAT* 5.11-16; Lewis, *Cults of the Dead*, 80-94; Pardee, *Les textes para-mythologiques*, 54-57, 176-77; *idem*, *Marziḥu*," 277-79; J. L. McLaughlin, "The *marzeaḥ* at Ugarit: A Textual and Contextual Study," *UF* 23 (1991) 274-80; Schmidt, *Israel's Beneficent Dead*, *passim*.

On a general level, the *marzēaḥ* is frequently identified as the West Semitic equivalent of the Mesopotamian *kispum* banquet, at which food and drink were ritualistically shared with deceased ancestors.[234] However, there is no indication that ritual activity was an essential element of the extra-biblical *marzēaḥ*,[235] and this includes feeding the dead. Thus, there is no basis for equating the two terms.[236]

At the same time, there is little evidence of any other funerary concerns in the *marzēaḥ* references. Among the pre-biblical references, the Ebla and Emar texts clearly deal with other matters and the legal documents from Ugarit neither affirm nor deny the *marzēaḥ*'s association with the cult of the dead, but are simply silent as to its precise purpose.[237] This leaves the two Ugaritic mythological texts to consider.

Some scholars find a funerary connection for the *marzēaḥ* in the Rephaim texts (*CAT* 1.20-22) on the basis of a posited link between them and the Aqhat story (*CAT* 1.17-19), specifically as the lost ending of the latter. Under this interpretation, in *CAT* 1.21.II, Danel invites the Rephaim to a *marzēaḥ*, and since the latter are elsewhere connected with mourning rituals,[238] that *marzēaḥ* is considered a mourning banquet in honour of Danel's dead son Aqhat.[239] The designation of El as the speaker in *CAT* 1.21.II.8 is a problem for this proposal, but its proponents emend the line to conform with *CAT* 1.20.II.7,

---

[234] See, e.g., J. C. Greenfield, "Une rite religieux araméen et ses parallèles," *RB* 80 (1973) 46-52, especially pp. 48-49; Pope, "Le *MRZḤ*," 143; *idem*, "The Cult of the Dead," 176; Archi, "Cult of the Ancestors," 104. On the *kispum* itself see A. Tsukimoto, *Untersuchungen zur Totenpflege (kispum) im alten Mesopotamien* (AOAT 216; Kevelaer: Verlag Butzon and Bercker; Neukirchen-Vluyn: Neukirchener Verlag, 1985).

[235] See n. 230.

[236] See also Pardee, "*Marziḥu*," 277; Schmidt, *Israel's Beneficent Dead, passim.*

[237] Halpern, "Dispute?" 135-36, raises the possibility that in *CAT* 3.9.13, the word *mt* might be a reference to the dead (thus, "let not the *mrzḥ* bemoan its dead") but he rejects the idea.

[238] Note especially their invocation in *CAT* 1.161. On the Rephaim at Ugarit, including their relationship to the biblical רְפָאִים, compare the discussions in J. C. de Moor, "Rāpi'ūma—Rephaim," *ZAW* 88 (1976) 323-45; L'Heureux, *Rank*, 111-223; A. Cooper, "Divine Names and Epithets in the Ugaritic Texts," *Ras Shamra Parallels III: The Texts from Ugarit and the Hebrew Bible* (AnOr 51; ed. S. Rummel; Rome: Pontifical Biblical Institute, 1981) 460-67; S. Talmon, "Biblical *rĕpā'îm* and Ugaritic *rpu/i(m)*," *Biblical and Other Studies in Honor of Robert Gordis* (HAR 7; ed. R. Aharoni; Columbus: Ohio State University, 1983) 235-49; Schmidt, *Israel's Beneficent Dead*, 71-93, 267-73.

[239] Pope, "Divine Banquet," 192; *idem*, "Notes," 166; Margalit, "Another Look," 100; Lewis, *Cults of the Dead*, 87.

where Danel is the subject of the same verb.[240] The only author to provide arguments in support of the change is Klaas Spronk. He notes the almost identical wording in both *CAT* 1.20.II.5 and 1.21.II.6-7 (the *mrzʿ* text),[241] which leads him to expect *yʿn . dnil* to follow in both texts as well. Therefore, he argues that the letters *dn* were omitted before *il* in 1.21.II.8 by *homoioteleuton*.[242] Once *yʿn . dnil* is restored in the second text, making Danel the speaker, the first person pronominal suffixes attached to *mrzʿ* in lines 1, 5 and 9[243] refer to him, with the result that Danel invites the Rephaim to his *marzēaḥ*.

There are problems with Spronk's argument, however. To begin with, the *homoioteleuton* at *CAT* 1.19.II.12 to which he appeals is not a good parallel to this text. The former involves two identical letters rather than just one (it reads *ydn il* whereas our text has *yʿn . il*). It is easy to understand how a scribe could omit *dn* immediately after the exact same two letters, but that is not the same as omitting *dn* after *ʿn*. Also, our text contains a word divider, which separated *yʿn* from the supposedly lost *dn* and would have further decreased the chance of a mistake.[244] Moreover, the context for the former *requires* that the subject be Danel, whereas in the latter that is precisely the question at issue. Secondly, *CAT* 1.20.II.5 and 1.21.II.6-7 are not identical. Although the references to a three day journey are similar in both texts, the subjects of the verbs *hlk* and *mġy* are different, as are the destinations. In *CAT* 1.21.II an individual (note the first person verb forms) informs the Rephaim he will travel to and arrive at "my house" and "my palace," and the only plausible subject for these verbs is the speaker in line 8. On the other hand, in *CAT* 1.20.II the Rephaim (mentioned in line 6; note also the third person plural verbs) travel to "threshing floors" (*grnt*) and "plantations" (*mṭʿt*). At the same time, although Danel is the subject of *yʿn* in the next line, what follows differs from *CAT* 1.21.II. There the speaker repeats the invitation to "my *marzēaḥ*," but in *CAT* 1.20.II the verb

240 Pope, "Divine Banquet," 192; *idem*, *Song of Songs*, 219; *idem*, "The Cult of the Dead," 174; Margalit, "Another Look," 100.

241 The restoration of a three day journey in the differently damaged texts is assured from *CAT* 1.14.IV.31-34: *tlkn ym . w ṯn . aḫr špšm . b ṯlṯ* ym[ġy .] *l*.

242 Spronk, *Beatific Afterlife*, 169n6. He appeals to *CAT* 1.19.II.12 in support of the *homoioteleuton*.

243 Cf. n. 92.

244 The same argument was made separately by Pitard, "A New Edition," 71, but see already McLaughlin, "The *marzeaḥ* at Ugarit," 275.

is succeeded by a (restored) epithet of Danel[245] plus another parallel line before Danel actually speaks, at which point his words also differ. Rather than speak of "my *marzēaḥ*" in "my house/palace" and "its place" as the speaker in *CAT* 1.21.II does, in *CAT* 1.20.II Danel states that the Rephaim have arrived at the "plantations" and the "threshing floors." In short, in the latter text Danel does not travel and neither repeats nor confirms an invitation to a *marzēaḥ*.[246]

In sum, Spronk's argument for emending *CAT* 1.21.II.8 is weak on both text-critical and literary grounds. His explanation for a putative scribal error is not convincing, and despite points of contact, significant divergences between the two texts point to different speakers in *CAT* 1.20.II.7 and 1.21.II.8. Therefore, El should be retained in the latter.[247] This eliminates any explicit relationship between Danel in 1.20.II and the *marzēaḥ* mentioned in 1.21.II, which in turn removes the primary reason for associating the two tablets with the story of Aqhat. In other words, Danel's presence in *CAT* 1.20.II may be completely unrelated to the Aqhat legend, and without that connection it is debatable whether the Rephaim's involvement, by itself, is adequate grounds for a funerary aspect to the *marzēaḥ* in *CAT* 1.21.II. Despite their chthonic connections,[248] that is only part of their role in Ugaritic mythology. Their appellation as *ilnym* shows that they exist within the divine realm,[249] so it is not unreasonable for them to be invited to a feast by the head of the Ugaritic pantheon.[250]

---

[245] The restoration of *mt . rpi* is assured by the presence of its "standard parallel," *mt hrnmy*, in the next line (the quoted phrase is from Spronk, *Beatific Afterlife*, 168; he gives no indication in his transliteration of a lacuna at that point in the text, however [see his p. 165]).

[246] Danel's words are damaged, but what is present consists of a straight-forward acknowledgement of the Rephaim's arrival. There is an oblique reference to eating in the subsequent fragmentary lines, but no reference to a *marzēaḥ*. L'Heureux, *Rank*, 136-37, sees Danel's role as that of an attendant at the ancient equivalent of a parking lot, since the "plantations/threshing floors" are the only area large enough to receive the Rephaim's chariots.

[247] Thus Eissfeldt, "Kultvereine," 193; L'Heureux, *Rank*, 142; Mullen, *Assembly of the Gods*, 266-67; Pitard, "A New Edition," 71; Lewis, "The Rapiuma," 200; Wyatt, *Religious Texts*, 318.

[248] See n. 238.

[249] Thus Mullen, who considers *rpum* and *ilnym* to be fixed pairs, as does Dahood; see Mullen, *Assembly of the Gods*, 262; Dahood, "Parallel Pairs," 342.

[250] Mullen equates both the Rephaim Texts and *CAT* 1.114 with the annual meeting of the divine council, which was preceded by great feasting and drinking; see Mullen, *Assembly of the Gods*, 265-67 and especially the references to banquets in the Ugaritic texts he provides in n. 251. Note also the comparable language in this text and *CAT* 1.114 (see n. 96 above).

This brings us to *CAT* 1.114. Marvin Pope points to a number of places where he thinks the text reflects funerary matters, but only one has any support from other Ugaritic texts, and that support is weak. Lines 4-5 read *yʿdb . yrḫ gbh*; Pope took the word *yrḫ* as a verb cognate with Arabic *wariḫ* and *raḫḫ* and Akkadian *reḫū*, which relate to moisture, connected *gbh* with moist parts of the body, and referred the whole line to the "ancient and widespread custom" of consuming fluid from the deceased, here presumably on the part of El.[251] *CAT* 1.96 *might* support this view, but the meaning of that text is disputed.[252] In any case, Pope's reading of two juxtaposed but uncoordinated verbs (*yʿdb . yrḫ*) is without parallel in the text and requires an unanticipated and therefore confusing nuance for the fare being consumed. As a result, his proposal has not been followed and virtually all commentators see the moon god Yariḫ at this point.[253]

The rest of Pope's specific suggestions involve reading evidence from later material and geographically disparate practices into this text. For example, he compares the "wild game" (*ṣd*, line 1) served at El's meal with the Aramaic cognate *ṣûdnîtā*, which "is applied in rabbinic usage to the tasty dish served to mourners as the funeral meal."[254] Similarly, he links *qṣ* in line 2 with the Syriac *qĕṣā* and rabbinic *qĕṣāṣā*; the former is used in connection with the Christian Eucharist (thereby evoking the death and resurrection of Jesus) and the latter is "a designation of a ceremonial meal for occasions both

[251] Pope, "Divine Banquet," 179-80.

[252] According to Pope (and others), in *CAT* 1.96.1-5 ʿAnat eats the flesh and drinks the blood of "her brother" Baʿal. However, Lewis has shown that the first word in the text is *ʿnn* not *ʿnt*, and has suggested that the tablet is an incantation against the "(Evil) Eye"; see T. J. Lewis, "The Disappearance of the Goddess Anat: The 1995 West Semitic Research Project on Ugaritic Epigraphy," *BA* 59 (1996) 115-21. For an English translation of the text and discussion of the interpretational difficulties, including a possible emendation from *ʿnn* to *ʿnt*, see M. S. Smith, "*CAT* 1.96," *Ugaritic Narrative Poetry* (SBLWAW 9; ed. S. B. Parker; Atlanta: Scholars Press, 1997) 224-28. N. Wyatt, *Religious Texts*, 375n1, argues against emending the text.

[253] The sole exception appears to be Virolleaud, "Les nouveaux textes mythologiques," 547, 549, who left *yrḫ gbh* untranslated but suggested it was the name of the feast: "mois complet." Pope, "Divine Banquet," 179, explicitly rejects seeing the lunar deity here.

[254] Pope, "Divine Banquet," 175. In fairness to Pope, he does not explicitly connect the two terms, but the implication is obvious from his discussion of them in sequence. He also associates both with "venison" (his translation of the Ugaritic term) and notes Isaac's desire for the same on his death bed (Gen 27:1-4), as well as the midrashic identification of that event as a mourning meal for Abraham's death.

sad and joyful."[255] But the Ugaritic terms themselves never have funerary associations,[256] and since straightforward references to a specific type of meat and the meal at which it is served are consistent with the context, there is no need to give the words connotations from more than a millennium later.

There are comparable problems with two of Pope's other suggestions concerning this text. In line 8 someone strikes someone else under the table, which Pope interprets in light of rituals used by Russian Lapps and New Guinea tribes to drive away ghosts.[257] But apart from the problematic chronological and geographic distance between Ugarit and these modern practices, not to mention why the gods would want to scare away other spirits, line 8 is not a matter of indiscriminate striking. Most commentators derive *ylmn* from the root *hlm*, in which case it must be parsed as a 3rd masculine singular plus the 3rd singular pronominal suffix *n*. As such, the text describes a specific individual, namely Yariḫ,[258] being struck, not an anti-ghost technique. Similarly, Pope presents a fascinating survey of canines in various cultic settings, especially funerary ones, in

---

[255] Pope, "Divine Banquet," 177; note the two possible settings.

[256] For example, compare *ṣd* at CAT 1.17.V.39; 1.22.I.11; 4.408.5 and *qṣ* at *CAT* 1.4.III.42; 1.6.II.11; 1.147.12. See also the philological analysis of the two terms in Pardee, *Les textes para-mythologiques*, 27-35.

[257] Pope, "Divine Banquet," 181. He also took *yqṯqṯ* in line 5 as a 3rd masculine plural verb, associated it with Mishnaic and Talmudic *qišqēš* ("knock, strike, clap"), and drew another parallel with such incantational beating (Pope, "Divine Banquet," 172, 180). Cf. the criticism of this correlation by Lewis, *Cults of the Dead*, 85 and the translation of the term in n. 65 above.

[258] Pope's translation, "he / they knocked with staff under the table" (Pope, "Divine Banquet," 180), does not account for the suffix. In Lewis, "The Rapiuma," 194, Yariḫ is the subject of the verbs in lines 6-8; he prepares food "for the god he knows" and strikes "the god he does not know." However, if "the god" is the object of the verb "to know" (*ydʿ*) in both instances, the additional indication of an object through the pronominal suffix *n* attached to both is extremely awkward (for the introduction of an extra *n* before a suffixed pronoun attached to a verb see S. Segert, *A Basic Grammar of the Ugaritic Language with Selected Texts and Glossary* [Berkeley: University of California Press, 1984] §51.13; for a similar duplication of the *n* in this text see *yʿmsn . nn* in line 18 and *ngšnn* in line 19). Moreover, in Lewis' translation, Yariḫ is functioning as the chef for the feast, but in the very next lines, Athtart and Anat prepare food for him (the verb is the same, *ʿdb*) with no apparent explanation for the role reversal. It is more likely, therefore, that "the god" is the subject of lines 6-8 and Yariḫ is indicated by the pronominal suffixes. The result is that Yariḫ is struck by "the god who does not recognize him" (so also Pardee, *Les textes para-mythologiques*, 44-45; Wyatt, *Religious Texts*, 408 and his n. 18).

connection with the reference to a dog in l. 12.[259] On a methodological level, L'Heureux correctly objects that "all the comparative material in the world cannot of itself prove that this specific dog is associated with funerary rites."[260] An even more telling point, however, is that there is no actual dog in this text. Rather, in line 5 Yariḫ is compared to a dog (*km* . [klb]) and line 12 is a metaphorical insult.[261] As a result, canine connections with mourning are irrelevant to this text.

Thus, none of Pope's specific funerary connections in *CAT* 1.114 withstand scrutiny, and without them his general assertions in that regard lose their force. For instance, he argues that the tablet reflects "a human affair in which it was deemed proper or obligatory to drink to excess," noting that "mourning was such an occasion,"[262] but weddings, births, military victories and the passing of the New Year are other situations when alcohol can be, and is, consumed to excess.[263] Similarly, he suggests this may be a wake for Baʿal, since "he is not among the few named,"[264] yet this very paucity of divine names actually argues against Pope's position. A stronger case could be made if there were a fuller listing of the Ugaritic pantheon, but as it stands Baʿal's omission here could be a coincidence.[265]

To summarize, the cumulative effect of Pope's evidence for a con-

---

[259] Pope, "Divine Banquet," 183-89; *idem*, *Song of Songs*, 210-14.

[260] L'Heureux, *Rank*, 211, seconded by Lewis, *Cults of the Dead*, 85.

[261] See n. 59 for the restoration of *klb*. Loewenstamm's article appeared after Pope's had been completed (see Pope, "Divine Banquet," 170n2). Because the comparative *km* is absent from line 12, Pardee thinks Yariḫ actually becomes a dog in this text (see the discussion in Pardee, *Les textes para-mythologiques*, 39-42; on p. 73 he comments, "*Yariḫu* . . . ayant pris la forme du chien . . ."). However, the fact that Yariḫ is called a dog, or even treated like one by other gods (see lines 6-8), does not mean he has the physical characteristics of one. Yariḫ is acting like a dog under the table and the gods play along, so the porter refers to him accordingly. His remark is all the more disparaging precisely because the comparative particle is dropped. (Decorum prevents me from listing in print some of the modern insults in which individuals are identified with, rather than compared to, various animals or parts of their anatomy.)

[262] Pope, "Divine Banquet," 178.

[263] Cf. n. 250 above.

[264] Pope, "The Cult of the Dead," 178; cf. *idem*, "Divine Banquet," 179-80. Miller, "The *MRZḤ* Text," 47n1, cites a similar opinion held by Albright. Note the possible reference to Baʿal in line 24 of *CAT*; however, Pardee, *Les textes para-mythologiques*, 19, was not able to identify the third letter.

[265] Similarly, Baal's absence from "The Birth of the Beautiful Gods" (*CAT* 1.23) does not make El's sexual activity a mourning rite nor the references to wine at the beginning and end a wake.

nection between this *marzēaḥ* and mourning rites collapses under closer scrutiny. None of the specific elements he proposes can be supported from the text, and his more general arguments are not conclusive. In keeping with Pope's own admission that "there are no explicit references to the funeral character of the . . . banquet,"[266] the text is unable to bear the interpretive weight he places upon it.

The non-funerary nature of this *marzēaḥ* is reinforced by the character and larger context of the text. The final three lines, a prescription for a hangover,[267] should be taken into account when interpreting the mythological section. The two parts are separated by a single line, but their purposeful juxtaposition[268] constitutes an incantation and accompanying medicinal remedy.[269] This means the central concern of the tablet as a whole is the consumption of alcohol, its effects when taken in excess, and a remedy for the attendant discomfort. It has nothing to do with death and/or mourning rituals.[270] This does not mean that mourners could not attend a *marzēaḥ* and become similarly afflicted, but the Ugaritic *marzēaḥ* was not itself a mourning meal.

Funerary elements are lacking in the majority of the post-biblical *marzēaḥ* references as well. Only a few indicate any concern for the dead or mourning, which is unusual if that were a major purpose of the *marzēaḥ*. Porten identified the Elephantine *marzēaḥ* as a "funer-

---

[266] Pope, *Song of Songs*, 219.

[267] Loewenstamm, "Trinkburleske," 77; Pope, "Divine Banquet," 170, 198-201; Margalit, "Another Look," 112-18; Lewis, "The Rapiuma," 194; Wyatt, *Religious Texts*, 404.

[268] As indicated by the empty space afterwards on the Reverse (de Moor, "Studies," 168).

[269] de Moor, "Studies," 168; Bryan, "Texts," 136; Dietrich, Loretz and Sanmartín, "Stichometrische Aufbau," 114; Spronk, *Beatific Afterlife*, 200; Pardee, *Les textes para-mythologiques*, 73-74. Barstad argues that the entire tablet is a "medical text": H. M. Barstad, "Festmahl und Übersättigung. Der 'Sitz im Leben' von RS 24.258," *AcOr* 39 (1978) 23-30.

[270] The statement that "El collapsed like the dead // El was like those who descend to the underworld" (lines 21-22) notwithstanding. Although he disagrees with him, in discussing Pope's funerary associations for the text L'Heureux states, "the completely drunken stupor evidenced in the behaviour of El *can be* understood as an *Ersatz*-experience of death designed to establish community with the deceased and create the experience that the ordeal of death has been faced and overcome" (L'Heureux, *Rank*, 211; my italics for "can be"); cf. Spronk, *Beatific Afterlife*, 200, who accepts this view. On the other hand, this comparative phrase may have no greater connection with the cult of the dead than the contemporary English colloquialisms, "fall down dead-drunk" or "dead to the world."

ary association," but only on the basis of later *marzēaḥ*s.[271] Du Mesnil du Buisson defined the *marzēah* at Palmyra as an "association religieuse dont le but était d'assurer le salut à des membres et d'accomplir les rites appropriés, après leur décès."[272] In support of this claim he interprets the celestial imagery on some tesserae as the realm of the blessed, and vegetative iconography on others as symbolic of regeneration in the after-life. However, the rites to which he alludes are not mentioned in any Palmyrene *marzēaḥ* references, and most of the tesserae he describes are not explicitly connected to a *marzēaḥ*.[273] Moreover, the astral imagery also evokes the divine realm, a fitting association for tesserae connected with priests, and the botanical depictions could just as easily symbolize health and well-being in the here-and-now.[274]

Nonetheless, there are a few possible funerary connections in later *marzēaḥ*s. Lewis suggests that the Phoenician drinking bowl may be relevant in light of Šamaš's connections with the underworld.[275] The patron of the Nabatean *marzēaḥ* at Petra is a divinized king, and some think the main purpose of that *marzēaḥ* is to honour him in a form of ancestor worship.[276] Bryan dismisses this completely by stressing 'Obadas' current divine status as the reason for his patronage,[277] but his prior human existence sets him apart from other deities linked with earlier *marzēaḥ*s, and cannot be ignored or glossed over.[278] Nonetheless, other *marzēaḥ*s show little interest in ritual or worship,[279]

---

[271] Porten, *Archives from Elephantine*, 179-86.

[272] See du Mesnil du Buisson, *Les tessères*, 467 and *passim*, especially pp. 473-74.

[273] Cf. p. 50 above.

[274] See further the critique of du Mesnil du Buisson in Bryan, "Texts," 220-25.

[275] Lewis, *Cults of the Dead*, 90, see also his pp. 35-46. In contrast, Schmidt points to "the sun deity's function as judge in commercial legal matters" (Schmidt, *Israel's Beneficent Dead*, 136), but there is no evidence of the latter here. Catastini, "Una Nuova Iscrizione," 111-18, thinks the inscription refers to libations for the dead by the *marzēaḥ* of Šamaš; this requires reading אנסך for the original אנחך, but the latter is to be preferred (see n. 120 above).

Lewis' discussion of the sun god is restricted to mythological texts from Ugarit and Mesopotamia. For the Phoenician material, including a funerary role, see C. Bonnet, "Le dieu solaire Shamash dans le monde phénico-punique," *SEL* 6 (1989) 97-115; E. Lipiński, *Studia Phoenicia XII: Dieux et déesses de l'univers phénicien et punique* (OLA 64; Leuven: Peeters, 1995) 264-68.

[276] See the references to Porten, Eissfeldt and du Mesnil du Buisson in n. 144.

[277] Bryan, "Texts," 226, followed by L'Heureux, *Rank*, 209.

[278] See the criticism of Bryan and L'Heureux in Lewis, *Cults of the Dead*, 90-91.

[279] See n. 230.

and this inscription deals with the memory of the *marzēaḥ*'s leader and members, not its patron. As such, the specific deity being invoked may be co-incidental after all. Finally, a few rabbinic texts link the *marzēaḥ* with mourning, but most are dependent on the prior connection in Jer 16:5 and must also be balanced by other rabbinic texts where the *marzēaḥ* and mourning are explicitly contrasted.

In summary, although many have claimed the *marzēaḥ* is a mourning banquet, only the Phoenician drinking bowl dedicated to Šamaš, the *marzēaḥ* of the deified King ʿObadas at Petra and some rabbinic texts support any connection with the cult of the dead. None is conclusive, however, and the earliest is from the 4th century BCE, with the other two occurring centuries later. The most one can conclude, therefore, is that some late, individual *marzēaḥ*s may have developed funerary aspects, but the extra-biblical *marzēaḥ* as a whole was not, by nature, a funerary association or mourning banquet. Contrary to Pope's assertion, scepticism over the *marzēaḥ*'s link to the cult of the dead is not "unfounded."

In conclusion, extensive upper-class drinking within a religious connection are the only features that are consistently present throughout the history of the *marzēaḥ*. Those three features, therefore, constitute the basic criteria by which the *marzēaḥ* in the prophetic literature, especially allusions that do not use the word, should be evaluated. That is the task of the following chapters, each of which will consider references and possible allusions to the *marzēaḥ*[280] in different prophetic books. During the course of that examination, I will be specially attentive for antecedents to elements so far only attested in later references to the *marzēaḥ*.

---

[280] In light of the eventual overlap in meaning, henceforth I use the word *marzēaḥ* as a general term of reference, encompassing both the association and its feasts. When the evidence permits I will be more specific.

CHAPTER TWO

# THE *MARZĒAḤ* IN AMOS

One of two biblical references to the *marzēaḥ* occurs in Amos 6:7.[1] In addition, Hans Barstad has argued that two other passages in the book of Amos reflect the *marzēaḥ* without using the term. First, he considers the content of Amos 2:8 and 6:4-6 comparable, and identifies the "girl" in 2:7b as a *marzēaḥ* hostess.[2] Second, he considers Amos 4:1 a *marzēaḥ* allusion because of the similar form and content there and in Amos 6:4-6.[3]

It is logical to begin discussion of the *marzēaḥ* in the book of Amos with Amos 6:1, 3-7. Not only does the word itself occur in v. 7, but Barstad's proposals concerning Amos 2:7b-8 and 4:1 are based in part upon their similarity to the first passage. Once the features of the *marzēaḥ* in Amos 6 are established, those proposals can be evaluated on the basis of that text and the criteria developed in chapter 1. Unlike Barstad, however, I will consider Amos 4:1 before 2:7b-8 because it is more closely linked to Amos 6 in terms of form and the overall structure of the book.

## I. Amos 6:1, 3-7

The word *marzēaḥ* in Amos 6:7 occurs in the judgment section of a woe oracle.[4] Since that judgment is predicated upon the accusation in the preceding verses, in order to understand what the author meant by a *marzēaḥ* it is necessary to establish the extent and content of those verses.

---

[1] Amos 6:1-7, with the relevant versional and rabbinic evidence, is discussed in D. B. Bryan, "Texts Relating to the *Marzeaḥ*: A Study of an Ancient Semitic Institution" (Ph.D. diss., Johns Hopkins University, 1973) 13-34.

[2] H. M. Barstad, *The Religious Polemics of Amos: Studies in the Preaching of Am 2,7B-8; 4,1-13; 5,1-27; 6,4-7; 8,14* (VTSup 34; Leiden: E. J. Brill, 1984) 11-36, especially pp. 34-36.

[3] Ibid., 42.

[4] On the woe form see pp. 89-94.

## A. *The Text*

| | |
|---|---|
| הוֹי הַשַּׁאֲנַנִּים בְּצִיּוֹן | 1 a Alas, you[6] who are secure on Zion, |
| וְהַבֹּטְחִים בְּהַר שֹׁמְרוֹן | b you confident[7] ones on Mount Samaria; |
| נְקֻבֵי[5] רֵאשִׁית הַגּוֹיִם | c notables[8] of the first of the nations, |

[5] C. C. Torrey, "On the Text of Am 5:25; 6:1,2; 7:2," *JBL* 13 (1894) 62-63, emended this to the imperative נִקְפוּ, which he derived from נקף II, "go around, make a circuit." However, the root נקב is supported by Symmachus (οἱ ὠνομασμένοι ), Theodotion (οἳ ἐπεκλήθησαν) and the Vulgate (*optimates*), and should be retained; Harper's suggestion that the LXX's ἀπετρύγησας should be changed to ἀπετρύπησαν would provide even more support for the MT; see W. R. Harper, *A Critical and Exegetical Commentary on the Books of Amos and Hosea* (ICC 18; Edinburgh: T. & T. Clark, 1912) 141. The MT root is read as an imperative by A. B. Ehrlich, *Randglossen zur Hebräischen Bibel* (Leipzig: J. C. Hinrichs, 1912) 5.243-44; J. J. M. Roberts, "Amos 6:1-7," *Understanding the Word: Essays in Honor of Bernhard W. Anderson* (JSOTSup 37; eds. J. T. Butler, E. W. Conrad and B. C. Ollenburger; Sheffield: JSOT Press, 1985) 157. Their connection of v. 1 with the secondary v. 2 argues against this (on v. 2 see pp. 84-85 below).

[6] Form-critically, the woe oracle requires a direct address (see p. 94 below), which is expressed in most of this text through the article plus a participle (for this construction as a vocative see GKC §126e-f; R. J. Williams, *Hebrew Syntax: An Outline* [2nd ed.; Toronto: University of Toronto Press, 1976] §89; B. K. Waltke and M. O'Connor, *An Introduction to Biblical Hebrew Syntax* [Winona Lake: Eisenbrauns, 1990] §13.5.2a,c), and this article plus adjective construction should be understood as a vocative as well. The adjective and participles in this passage are interpreted as vocatives by W. Janzen, *Mourning Cry and Woe Oracle* (BZAW 125; Berlin/New York: Walter de Gruyter, 1972) 22-23; D. R. Hillers, "*Hôy* and *Hôy*-Oracles: A Neglected Syntactical Aspect," *The Word of the Lord Shall Go Forth: Essays in Honor of David Noel Freedman in Celebration of His Sixtieth Birthday* (eds. C. L. Meyers and M. O'Connor; Winona Lake: Eisenbrauns, 1983) 185-88; Roberts, "Amos 6:1-7," 156, 163n8; F. I. Andersen and D. N. Freedman, *Amos: A New Translation with Introduction and Commentary* (AB 24A; New York/London/Toronto: Doubleday, 1989) 556. Taking this verse as vocative eliminates the otherwise abrupt shift to a second person finite verb in 3b.

[7] For הַבֹּטְחִים as "confident" see Job 6:20; 11:18; 40:23; Prov 28:1; etc.

[8] The basic meaning of the root נָקַב is "to pierce," which can serve as the means of designating something or someone (see BDB 666; cf. Arabic *naqīb* ["chief, leader"]). Objects of the Hebrew verb in the latter sense include wages (Gen 30:28) and a name (נִקְּבוּ בְּשֵׁמוֹת): Num 1:17; 1 Chr 12:32; 16:41; 2 Chr 28:15; 31:19; cf. Isa 62:2; Ezra 8:20. Morgenstern, "Amos Studies IV: The Addresses of Amos—Text and Commentary," *HUCA* 32 (1961) 325, inserts שֵׁם between the participle and this phrase; cf. Symmachus and Theodotion. By extension, someone who has been so designated has been set apart or noted, hence the translation of the plural passive participle here as "notables." Cf. the discussion in H. W. Wolff, *Joel and Amos: A Commentary on the Books of the Prophets Joel and Amos* (Hermeneia; ed. S. D. McBride; trans. W. Janzen; Philadelphia: Fortress Press, 1977) 274.

| | | |
|---|---|---|
| וּבָאוּ לָהֶם[9] בֵּית יִשְׂרָאֵל[10] | d | the house of Israel comes to you.[12] |
| הַמְנַדִּים לְיוֹם[11] רָע | 3 a | You, excluding[13] an evil day, |
| וַתַּגִּישׁוּן שֶׁבֶת חָמָס | b | you bring near a rule of violence. |
| הַשֹּׁכְבִים עַל־מִטּוֹת שֵׁן | 4 a | You, lying on beds of ivory, |
| וּסְרֻחִים עַל־עַרְשׂוֹתָם | b | sprawling on your[14] couches, |
| וְאֹכְלִים כָּרִים מִצֹּאן | c | eating lambs from the flock, |
| וַעֲגָלִים מִתּוֹךְ מַרְבֵּק | d | and calves from the fattening stall; |

---

[9] Holladay sees a break-up of the "stereotyped phrase," "the first fruits of the harvest" (רֵאשִׁית תְּבוּאָה) between 1c and d, and emends these two words to תְּבֻאָה לָחֶם ("harvest of bread/food); see W. L. Holladay, "Amos VI 1bβ: A Suggested Solution," *VT* 22 (1972) 108; on p. 110 he offers his "idiomatic" translation: "the cream of the crop." On the break-up of composite phrases see M. J. Dahood and T. Penar, "The Grammar of the Psalter," *Psalms III: 101-150. A New Translation with Introduction and Commentary* (AB 17A; New York: Doubleday, 1970) 413-14; W. G. E. Watson, *Classical Hebrew Poetry: A Guide to Its Techniques* (JSOTSup 26; Sheffield: JSOT Press, 1984) 328-32. Holladay acknowledges minor problems with his proposal (e.g., the otherwise unattested misreading of ת for ו and the *scriptio defectiva* of תְּבֻאָה; see his pp. 108-09), but more serious is whether this is even a "stereotyped phrase." It only occurs at Prov 3:9 and Jer 2:3, and the two words are divided by כָּל־ in the former (they are separated by references to grain, wine, oil and honey at 2 Chr 31:5). Moreover, those examples split between a literal (Prov 3:9) and metaphorical (Jer 2:3) use of the phrase. Such limited and equivocal use is insufficient evidence of a "stereotyped phrase."

[10] This line is emended to וְכֵאלֹהִים (הֵמָּה) בְּבֵית יִשְׂרָאֵל ("[they are] like gods in the house of Israel") by S. Oettli, *Amos und Hosea. Zwei Zeugen gegen die Anwendung der Evolutionstheorie die Religion Israels* (BFCT 5; Gütersloh: Bertelsmann, 1901) 72, who also suggests וּבַעֲלֵי בֵית יִשְׂרָאֵל ("Lords of the House of Israel"). The former proposal is followed by E. Würthwein, "Amos-Studien," *ZAW* 62 (1950) 43; V. Maag, *Text, Wortschaft und Begriffswelt des Buches Amos* (Leiden: E. J. Brill, 1951) 37; R. Fey, *Amos und Jesaja: Abhängigkeit und Eigenständigkeit des Jesaja* (WMANT 12; Neukirchen-Vluyn: Neukirchener Verlag, 1963) 11; W. Rudolph, *Joel–Amos–Obadja–Jona* (KAT; Gütersloh: Gütersloher Verlagshaus/Gerd Mohn, 1971) 216; *BHS*. This radical alteration of the MT is without textual support, and reads an elevated self-importance on the part of the elite into 1d. So too Morgenstern's emendation (following Procksch) to ואלהים הם לבית ישראל; "they are gods *to* the house of Israel"; see J. Morgenstern, "Amos Studies IV," 325. K. Marti, *Das Dodekapropheton erklärt* (KHAT 13; Tübingen: J. C. B. Mohr [Paul Siebeck], 1904) 199, suggests וּבֵאלֹהֵי בֵית יִשְׂרָאֵל ("and in the gods of the house of Israel") as a continuation of 1b, but since the rest of the passage deals with self-assurance, I understand the ב in both 1a and b to be locative, with most commentators (cf. pp. 94-95).

[11] For a ל with the accusative see GKC 117n; Williams, *Hebrew Syntax*, §273.

[12] D. R. Hillers, "*Hôy* and *Hôy*-Oracles," 186-87, has shown that, just as in Classical Arabic, a third person pronoun is commonly used in biblical Hebrew to refer to an earlier vocative, and therefore requires translation as "your"; see also Waltke and O'Connor, *Biblical Hebrew Syntax*, §4.7d.

[13] הַמְנַדִּים is a *piʿel* participle from the root נָדָה; its only other occurrence (in Isa 66:5) confirms the translation as "excluding"; cf. BDB 622.

[14] See n. 12.

| | | |
|---|---|---|
| הַפֹּרְטִים עַל־פִּי הַנָּבֶל | 5 a | singing[17] to the sound of the lute, |
| חָשְׁבוּ[15] לָהֶם כְּלֵי־שִׁיר | b | they[18] compose on instruments of music; |
| הַשֹּׁתִים בְּמִזְרְקֵי יַיִן | 6 a | drinking from bowls of wine, |
| וְרֵאשִׁית שְׁמָנִים יִמְשָׁחוּ | b | they anoint with finest oils, |
| וְלֹא נֶחְלוּ עַל־שֵׁבֶר יוֹסֵף | c | but are not grieved over the ruin of Joseph! |
| לָכֵן עַתָּה יִגְלוּ בְּרֹאשׁ גֹּלִים | 7 a | Therefore, now they will be exiled, the first of the exiles, |
| וְסָר מִרְזַח סְרוּחִים[16] | b | and the sprawler's *marzēaḥ* shall cease.[19] |

[15] In the MT this line begins with "like David," but his association with music is often challenged as a post-exilic idea, originating with the Chronicler; the *plene* spelling of the name supports that conclusion. Thus the phrase is deleted by J. L. Mays, *Amos: A Commentary* (OTL; Philadelphia: Westminster Press, 1969) 113 note a; Wolff, *Joel and Amos*, 272-73, 276; G. Fleischer, *Von Menschen verkaüfern, Baschankühen und Rechtsverkehrern: die Sozialkritik des Amosbuches in historisch-kritischer, sozialgeschichtlicher und archäologischer Perspektive* (BBB 74; Frankfurt am Main: Athenäum Verlag, 1989) 232-233; Andersen and Freedman, *Amos*, 552, 563, 564. Morgenstern, "Amos Studies IV," 324, claims the name is "superfluous" and "seriously disturbs the meter." Elhorst divides כְּדָוִיד as כַּד וְיָד but his translation as "Pitcher and hand they clap . . ." requires an unacceptable meaning for חָשְׁבוּ; see H. J. Elhorst, "Amos 6 5," *ZAW* 35 (1915) 63. Weiser's reading of הֵידָד for כְּדָוִיד and לָשִׁיר for כְּלֵי־שִׁיר requires too much of a textual change; see A. Weiser, *Die Prophetie des Amos* (BZAW 53; Giessen: A. Topelmann, 1929) 240-41. The deletion does not substantially affect the passage.

[16] The LXX's καὶ ἐξαρθήσεται χρεμετισμὸς ἵππων ἐξ Εφραιμ ("and the horses' neighing is taken from Ephraim") has read סוּסִים for MT סְרוּחִים and derived מִרְזַח from the root רזח, "cry out"; see BDB 931; O. Eissfeldt, "Etymologische und archäologische Erklärung alttestamentlicher Wörter," *OrAnt* 5 (1966) 166-71. Eissfeldt's attempt to distinguish the biblical and extra-biblical *marzēaḥs* on the basis of homonymous but separate roots has not been accepted; cf., e.g., O. Loretz, "Ugaritisch-biblisch *mrzḥ* 'Kultmahl, Kultverein' in Jer 16,5 und Am 6,7. Bemerkungen zur Geschichte des Totenkultes in Israel," *Künder des Wortes. Beiträge zur Theologie der Propheten: Joseph Schreiner zum 60. Geburtstag* (eds. L. Ruppert, P. Weimar and E. Zenger; Würzburg: Echter-Verlag, 1982) 87-93]). In any case, the mention of Ephraim is clearly a gloss, making Bryan's emendation of the MT to וְסָר מִרְזַח שָׂרִים מֵאֶפְרָיִם ("the leaders' *marzēaḥ* has departed from Ephraim") unnecessary and unsupportable, *contra* Bryan, "Texts," 18-20; see also H.-J. Fabry, "מַרְזֵחַ *marzēaḥ*," *TWAT* 5.14.

[17] The Vulgate translates the *hapax legomenon* הַפֹּרְטִים as "those who sing" (*qui canitis*); for a plausible etymology of the Hebrew see J. Montgomery, "Notes from the Samaritan: The Root פרט—Amos 6:5," *JBL* 25 (1906) 51-52; he refers to M. Heidenheim, *Bibliotheca Samaritana* (Leipzig: Schulze, 1885) 2.110 and is followed by S. Daiches, "Amos VI.5," *ExpTim* 26 (1914-15) 521-22; Barstad, *Religious Polemics*, 127. The word is translated as "chant" without comment by R. Vuilleumier-Bessard, *La tradition cultuelle d'Israël dans la prophétie d'Amos et d'Osée* (CT 45; Neuchatel: Éditions Delachaux & Niestlé, 1960) 13; M. H. Pope, *Song of Songs: A New Translation with Introduction and Commentary* (AB 7C; Garden City: Doubleday, 1977) 214.

[18] The transition to third person verbs at this point is probably influenced by the constellation of third person pronouns referring to vocatives in the preceding lines (thus Roberts, "Amos 6:1-7," 156).

[19] The repetition of מ, ר, ה, and the sibilants ס and ז has given rise to a number

This text reproduces the MT, with the exception of two deletions. Neither verse 2 nor the reference to David in 5b directly affect the understanding of the *marzēaḥ* in this passage, but since the former involves a substantial deletion, some comment is in order.[20] The extensive debate over the verse's authenticity revolves around the intended perspective, which is then used to establish the date. If the verse is meant as a warning, the cities would have been conquered, but if it quotes the Samarian elite encouraging the populace to compare Samaria's superiority, then the cities would still be independent. Since Calneh (Akkadian Kullani) and Hamath, both located in Syria, were conquered by Tiglathpilesar III in 738 BCE, who also subdued Philistia, and thus Gath, in 734 BCE,[21] the first scenario points to a time after the traditional date for Amos[22] while the second permits a date during his ministry.[23]

---

of creative, alliterative translations, including, "Da verlernen das Lärmen die Lümmel" in B. Duhm, "Anmerkungen zu den Zwölf Propheten I: Buch Amos," *ZAW* 31 (1911) 1-18; "Da schwindet des Schwadronieren der Schwelger" in Rudolph, *Joel–Amos*, 215, (cf. "Dann ist es aus mit Saus und Braus" [p. 221]); "Suppressed is the sprawlers' spree" in Wolff, *Joel and Amos*, 273; "[Then will the] sound of their singing cease" in S. N. Rosenbaum, עָמוֹס הַיִּשְׂרְאֵלִי *Amos of Israel: A New Interpretation* (Macon: Mercer University Press, 1990) 66; "Spent will be the sprawlers' spree" in S. M. Paul, *Amos: A Commentary on the Book of Amos* (Hermeneia; ed. F. M. Cross; Minneapolis: Fortress Press, 1991) 199 (he comments, "Their wining shall give way to whining" [p. 210]); and "Aus ist das Gelage der Ausgelassenen" in E. Blum, "'Amos' in Jerusalem: Beobachtungen zu Am 6,1-7," *Hen* 16 (1994) 27. My more literal rendition highlights the word *marzēaḥ* itself.

[20] On the deletion of "like David" see n. 15.

[21] On the individual cities see S. A. Meier, "Calneh," *ABD* 1.823-34; M.-L. Buhl, "Hamath," *ABD* 3.33-36; J. D. Seger, "Gath," *ABD* 2.908-09.

[22] Thus, Harper, *Amos and Hosea*, 144-46; A. S. Kapelrud, *Central Ideas in Amos* (Oslo: W. Nygaard, 1956) 59; Fey, *Amos und Jesaja*, 11n2; Wolff, *Joel and Amos*, 275; G. H. Wittenberg, "Amos 6:1-7: 'They Dismiss the Day of Disaster but You Bring Near the Rule of Violence'," *JTSA* 58 (March 1987) 58; Fleischer, *Von Menschen verkaüfern*, 226-29, 243; Blum, "Am 6,1-7," 31-34; D. U. Rottzoll, *Studien zur Redaktion und Komposition des Amosbuchs* (BZAW 243; Berlin/New York: Walter de Gruyter, 1996) 155-56. Paul objects that by then Israel would have been an Assyrian vassal as well, and such a warning would have been irrelevant. He dates the verse to a period of Israelite peace and prosperity, and relates the conquests of Calneh and Hamath to Shalmaneser III's claims of victory in 858 BCE and 853 BCE respectively, and for Gath suggests either its defeat by Hazael ca. 815 BCE (2 Kgs 12:18) or its destruction by Uzziah of Judah ca. 760 BCE (2 Chr 26:6); see Paul, *Amos*, 202-04; see also M. Bič, *Das Buch Amos* (Berlin: Evangelische-Verlagsanstalt, 1969) 130; E. Hammershaimb, *The Book of Amos: A Commentary* (trans. J. Sturdy; New York: Schocken Books, 1970) 97-98; Andersen and Freedman, *Amos*, 558; G. V. Smith, *Amos: A Commentary* (LBI; Grand Rapids: Zondervan Publishing House, 1989) 201-02; on Gath see also M. Haran, "The Rise and Decline of the Empire of Jeroboam Ben Joash," *VT* 17 (1967) 269n1.

[23] E. Sellin, *Das Zwölfprophetenbuch übersetzt und erklärt* (KAT 12; 2nd ed.; Leipzig: Deichert, 1929) 242; Maag, *Text*, 39; Mays, *Amos*, 115. However, unlike elsewhere

This scholarly divergence illustrates the impossibility of certitude concerning the verse's precise historical reference or the intention behind it,[24] and it is not possible to determine the verse's status on that basis. Instead, literary considerations, namely how well the verse is integrated into the larger unit, are more useful. Various arguments for unity have been made,[25] but none demonstrate v. 2's originality, only its dependence on v. 1: v. 2 requires v. 1 to make sense, but the reverse is not true. The larger unit's meaning would not be impaired if v. 2 were absent, and, in fact, v. 3 flows quite naturally from v. 1. Also, the unit itself is a "woe oracle," characterized primarily by participles describing the addressees' actions,[26] whereas v. 2 uses imperatives and questions, which are otherwise absent from the passage.[27] Thus, v. 2 is most likely a later insertion.

## B. *Establishing the Unit*

Since some scholars use other parts of the chapter to interpret elements of the *marzēaḥ* in this passage, it is necessary to establish its limits as the primary interpretive context. The starting point is easily determined: the concluding formula אָמַר יהוה ("says Yahweh"), reinforced by the cultic phrase, אֱלֹהֵי־צְבָאוֹת שְׁמוֹ ("God of Hosts is his name") marks Amos 5:27 as the end of the preceding unit, and the initial הוֹי of 6:1 introduces a new section. A few scholars extend

in Amos, the verse is not marked as a quotation (see Blum, "Am 6,1-7," 31; in his n. 31 he contrasts Amos 6:2 with Amos 5:14; 6:13; 8:5; 9:10; see also 2:12; 3:9; 4:1; 8:14. More difficult is that by Amos' time Gath had been subdued by the Judean King Uzziah (Mays, *Amos*, 115). The reference to Gath is deleted by A. Weiser, *Das Buch der zwölf Kleinen Propheten* (ATD 24; Göttingen: Vandenhoeck & Ruprecht, 1949) 176; Morgenstern, "Amos Studies IV," 326; Rudolph, *Joel–Amos*, 216, but such minor surgery is no more acceptable in principle than deleting the entire verse.

[24] Rudolph, *Joel–Amos*, 219.

[25] E.g., Davies, Smith, Wood and Snyman each think "these nations" refers to Zion and Samaria in 1a-b (this requires switching the pronouns on the last two words of v. 2), Snyman and Wood note the proper names in both verses, and Wood feels "they go" in 1d leads naturally into the verbs of motion in v. 2; see G. H. Davies, "Amos—The Prophet of Re-Union: An Essay in Honour of the Eightieth Birthday of Professor Aubrey R. Johnson, F.B.A," *ExpTim* 92 (1981) 200; G. V. Smith, *Amos*, 202n60; J. R. Wood, "Amos: Prophecy as a Performing Art and Its Transformation in Book Culture" (Ph.D. diss., University of St. Michael's College, 1993) 77, 78, 79 and her p. 78n65; S. D. Snyman, "'Violence' in Amos 3,10 and 6,3," *ETL* 71 (1995) 40.

[26] See pp. 89 and 94.

[27] The argument here is not based upon the impossibility of direct address in a "woe oracle" (see n. 6 for taking the participles as vocatives) but the content of the address and the grammatical means of expressing it.

the unit to the end of the chapter,[28] but the majority end it at v. 7. A number of factors support this view. The phrase לָכֵן עַתָּה ("Therefore, now") in 6:7 introduces an announcement of judgment, and it is unlikely that it would extend for eight verses. Moreover, the divine oath in v. 8 (נִשְׁבַּע אֲדֹנָי יהוה בְּנַפְשׁוֹ; "The Lord Yahweh swears by himself") introduces a new line of thought.[29] Similarly, the rest of the chapter bears little connection with vv. 1-7,[30] and most commentators divide vv. 8-14 into smaller units separate from the earlier verses.[31] Rhetorical features in Amos 6:1, 3-7 that are absent from the succeeding verses also support taking it as a unit. The frequent use of participles, often with the definite article, unifies the passage, as do various lexical links. These include סְרֻחִים, repeated in vv. 4b and 7b, the paranomasia between שֶׁבֶת and שֶׁבֶר in 3b and 6c,[32] and the repetition of the root ראשׁ in 1c, 6b and 7a. Moreover, in vv. 1 and 7 ראשׁ forms an inclusion marking the beginning and end of the unit.

Within those boundaries, however, some part of almost every verse has been challenged as secondary to the original unit. If all such proposals were accepted, all that would be left as the "original" oracle would be "Alas" from 1a, plus vv. 1b, 4 and 6a. As indicated in the introductory chapter, it is not my intention to present a de-

[28] Barstad, *Religious Polemics*, 127, calls the chapter "a coherent unity"; J. H. Hayes, *Amos the Eighth-Century Prophet: His Times and His Preaching* (Nashville: Abingdon Press, 1988) 182, describes it as "a well structured and integrated whole"; G. V. Smith, *Amos*, 198, considers it "a fairly unified whole." Rosenbaum, *Amos of Israel*, 76, suggests 6:1-10 is a unit, but admits, "The first seven verses of chapter 6 are a complex literary unit nicely knit together . . . ."

[29] Hayes, *Amos*, 182, 187, explains the oath as a confirmation of the preceding verses, but acknowledges that the rest of the verse is concerned with Samaria's entire population, not just the elite as in the preceding verses. Some reinforce the separation between vv. 7 and 8 by transferring נְאֻם־יהוה אֱלֹהֵי צְבָאוֹת ("utterance of Yahweh, God of Hosts") from 8b to the end of v. 7 (see Harper, *Amos and Hosea*, 150; Morgenstern, "Amos Studies IV," 324; Wolff, *Joel and Amos*, 273, 279; Roberts, "Amos 6:1-7," 161-62), but that destroys the inclusion of v. 8 with the same words in v. 14.

[30] Rosenbaum, *Amos of Israel*, 65, 66, identifies the house in v. 9 as the *marzēaḥ* house known from Ugarit and Jer 16:5, but in vv. 9-10 the emphasis is on death as a result of war, not exile as in v. 7.

[31] In recent major commentaries, Wolff divides them as vv. 8-11,12,13-14 (*Joel and Amos*, 179-90), Andersen and Freedman as vv. 8-10,11-13,14 (*Amos*, 569-90) and Paul as vv. 8-11,12-14 (*Amos*, 213-21). G. V. Smith, *Amos*, 198, attempts to unify the chapter under the rubric of "a common concern for the nation's false security," but that characterization is appropriate to practically the whole book of Amos, to say nothing of other prophets.

[32] See M. D. Carroll, *Contexts for Amos: Prophetic Poetics in Latin American Perspective* (JSOTSup 132; Sheffield: JSOT Press, 1992) 262; Snyman, "'Violence,'" 40.

tailed redaction-critical analysis of this or any of the passages that will be considered.[33] Although notice will be taken of some proposals when discussing the passage as a whole, for my purposes it is sufficient to note that the text given above is consistent with what is known of the *marzēaḥ* and of the accepted time of Amos' ministry.[34]

Still, one proposed deletion must be considered because of its implication for the following discussion. Jacques Vermeylen and Gunter Fleischer both consider all of v. 7 secondary for slightly different reasons.[35] Vermeylen considers vv. 8-11 the original conclusion to Amos 6:1, 3-6 and notes both that the word *marzēaḥ* only occurs one other time, in a later text (Jer 16:5), and that the verb סָרַח is only applied to humans in Amos 6:4, 7; for him, the different orthography in the two verses "montre bien le procédé d'emprunt."[36] Fleischer, on the other hand, deletes v. 7 because he finds nothing in the preceding verses to justify the punishment announced in v. 7, thereby rejecting two of the main proposals in this regard: social injustice or pagan worship. He finds no evidence of non-Yahwistic cultic activity, and claims the passage describes luxury, not injustice. Since prosperity was considered a sign of divine blessing, that alone would not elicit the punishment of exile.[37] Thus, both Vermeylen and Fleischer suggest v. 7 was added at the same time as 6c,[38] and corresponds with it alone. This would mean the attitudes and actions described in vv.

---

[33] Although I do not agree with all of his conclusions, a thorough recent effort in this regard concerning Amos 6:1-7 can be found in Rottzoll, *Studien*, 153-68.

[34] On the content see pp. 94-103; for the dating see pp. 108-109.

[35] J. Vermeylen, *Du prophète Isaïe à l'apocalyptique: Isaïe I-XXXV, miroir d'un demi-millénaire d'expérience religieuse en Israël* (EBib; Paris: J. Gabalda, 1978) 563-64; Fleischer, *Von Menschen verkaüfern*, 237-40; the latter is followed by Rottzoll, *Studien*, 162-63. Oswald Loretz initially took the entire verse as redactional, but later accepted 7b as original; cf. Loretz, "'Kultmahl,'" 90; *idem*, "*Marziḥu* im ugaritischen und biblischen Ahnenkult: zu Ps 23; 133; Am 6,1-7 und Jer 16,5.8," *Mesopotamica, Ugaritica, Biblica: Festschrift für Kurt Bergerhof zur Vollendung seines 70. Lebensjahres am 7. Mai 1992* (AOAT 232; eds. M. Dietrich and O. Loretz; Kevelaer: Verlag Butzon and Bercker; Neukirchen-Vluyn: Neukirchener Verlag, 1993) 136-37.

[36] Vermeylen, *Du prophète Isaïe*, 564.

[37] He also wonders whether "exile" indicates knowledge of Israel's fate after the fact, but does not give an answer (see Fleischer, *Von Menschen verkaüfern*, 240); Vermeylen, *Du prophète Isaïe*, 564, considers it clear evidence of deuteronomistic editing. But since any astute observer of Assyrian foreign policy would realize exile was a very real possibility, a general reference to exile is not out of place. It should also be noted that this is far less specific than, for instance, "exile beyond Damascus" in Amos 5:27. Wolff, *Joel and Amos*, 151, suggests the latter destination actually points to deportations by the kingdom of Urartu prior to and contemporary with Amos.

[38] Cf. in n. 89 below.

1, 3-6 were not identified with a *marzēaḥ* by the original author, but at the same time, their content is such that a later editor did. If that is the case, Amos 6:1, 3-6 might fall into the category of a *marzēaḥ* allusion rather than a direct reference, in which case the criteria developed in Chapter 1 could be applied.

This view of v. 7 as secondary should be rejected however. With respect to Vermeylen's argument, on a form-critical level, the woe oracle is a subset of the Judgment Against the Nation, and as such an announcement of judgment is to be expected.[39] However, Vermeylen's proposed judgment section (vv. 8-11) does not cohere as well with vv. 1, 3-6 as does v. 7: vv. 8-11 focus on a house, which does not appear in vv. 1, 3-6 at all. At the same time, Vermeylen's supposedly later vocabulary is not convincing. In light of the extensive early use of the word *marzēaḥ* outside of the Bible, there is no reason Amos 6:7 must be dependent on Jer 16:5 for the term, or the reverse for that matter; both could simply reflect their contemporary situations. Similarly, although there is no easy explanation for the different orthography of סְרֻחִים/סְרוּחִים, if it results from redactional activity, why did the editor not either copy exactly or conform the original to his spelling?[40] Since there are numerous indications that v. 7 is integral to the passage, this one disputable point is insufficient reason to delete it.

As for Fleischer, the reason for judgment in this passage will be discussed in greater detail below,[41] but for now, while I agree Amos does not oppose the *marzēaḥ* for cultic reasons, Fleischer's position requires deleting virtually all references to both injustice and the cult. Moreover, he fails to consider the injustice underlying the text. Even though there is little *explicit* mention of injustice in 6:1, 3-7 (once Fleischer deletes 3b and 6c[42]), one of Amos' central concerns is the social inequities that had developed because of the elite's economic and judicial exploitation of the poor (see, e.g., Amos 2:6-8; 5:7, 10-12, 24; 8:4-6). The luxurious lifestyle enjoyed by the upper-class was only possible because of their injustice against the lower class. Thus,

---

[39] C. Westermann, *Basic Forms of Prophetic Speech* (trans. H. C. White, foreword by G. M. Tucker; 1967; rpt. Cambridge: The Lutterworth Press; Louisville: Westminster/John Knox Press, 1991) 190, 192. The "woes" of Isaiah 5 and 28 regularly include an announcement of punishment introduced by לָכֵן.

[40] The very fact that he would have felt able to add to the text shows he did not consider it "sacrosanct," and therefore could have altered the word in v. 4.

[41] See pp. 104-07.

[42] On the interpretation of these verses see pp. 95-97 below.

there is a connection between the prophet's description of the elite and the announced judgment, even if it is not as explicit as Fleischer would like. Furthermore, this conceptual coherence is reinforced by the lexical links between vv. 1, 3-6 and 7,[43] and so the link between the attitudes and actions in vv. 1, 3-6 and the *marzēaḥ* in v. 7 is original to the passage.

## C. *The Form*

The opening word (הוֹי) marks this passage as a woe oracle.[44] Because internal features of this form as well as its *Sitz im Leben* have a bearing on the discussion of this and other texts,[45] some consideration will be given to it.

The word הוֹי occurs 51 times in the First Testament,[46] all but once (1 Kgs 13:30) in the prophetic literature. Of the remaining occurrences, thirty-one times the word is followed immediately by a negative characterization of a group or individual, usually by means of a participle, although occasionally a noun or even an adjective appears.[47] The latter is the case with Amos 6:1a, although the sub-

[43] See p. 86.

[44] The form's traditional terminology is retained in the following discussion, even though I translate the word as "alas" (cf. p. 94 below).

[45] See the discussion of Amos 4:1 below, and of Isa 5:11-13; 28:1-4 in Chapter 4.

[46] Traditional terminology for the two main divisions of the Bible is problematic and has hermeneutic implications. "Old Testament" connotes "antiquated," "outdated" and even "replaced" for some. "Hebrew Bible" is popular in many circles, but designating the material by its (primary) language of composition does not take into account the Aramaic portions of Daniel or the extensive scholarly use of ancient versions in other languages, to say nothing of the second part of the Bible, which still tends to be called the "New Testament." "Hebrew Bible" also does not incorporate the deutero-canonical books, some written exclusively in Greek, which Roman Catholics and Eastern Orthodox Christians consider scriptural. Similarly, "Jewish Bible/Scripture" is inadequate for Christians, for whom the first part is also canonical. As an uneasy compromise I use First and Second Testament for the two main divisions of the biblical literature (this coincides with the editorial policy of the *Biblical Theology Bulletin*).

[47] In addition, the "woe" is applied directly to someone through a preposition 4 times: Jer 50:27; Ezek 13:3 [עַל]; Jer 48:1 [אֶל]; Ezek 13:18 [לְ]. Twice הוֹי is followed by a name: Isa 10:5; 29:1. In 8 instances it seems to function as an interjection, 4x with a negative connotation (Isa 1:24; 17:12; Jer 30:7; 47:6) and 4x (all in later texts) as a call for attention (Isa 55:1; Zech 2:10 [2x], 11). Finally, it occurs in a funerary lament 6 times: 1 Kgs 13:30; Jer 22:18 (4x); 34:5. This breakdown is dependent on the statistics of Christof Hardmeier presented in Wolff,

sequent participles carry on the characterization begun in v. 1, and are governed by the opening הוֹי.[48] But even though the word is almost exclusive to the prophets, there has been debate whether the form was developed by them or taken over from another setting. If it is original to the prophets, since Amos is the first to use it he might have invented it. Thus it is necessary to consider the form's original *Sitz im Leben*.

The earliest proposal was by Mowinckel, who saw the pronouncement of "woe" as "a formal variety of the curse."[49] However, since his main concern was the blessing and cursing Psalms it was left to Westermann to develop the proposal in greater detail.[50] In particular, Westermann notes the comparable structure (an introductory word [הוֹי or אָרוּר] plus a participle) in both the prophetic woes and the curses, and also draws a parallel between the curses clustered in Deut 27:15-26 and the prophetic woe sequences.[51] He concludes, therefore, that, "not only the form but also the content of the prophetic woe originated with the curse . . . ."[52] If so, by pronouncing a woe/curse the prophet would bring about what he proclaims.[53]

A closer examination of the woes and curses argues against dependence, however. In the curses, the participle is singular, whereas the prophetic woes developed from predominately plural participles in earlier texts to singular participles in later texts.[54] Secondly,

---

*Joel and Amos*, 242-43n108; cf. Wolff's own breakdown on p. 242 and the discussion by G. Wanke, "אוֹי und הוֹי" *ZAW* 78 (1966) 216.

[48] Andersen and Freedman, *Amos*, 559; Paul, *Amos*, 204.

[49] S. Mowinckel, *The Psalms in Israel's Worship* (1962; rpt. The Biblical Seminar 14; trans. D. R. Ap-Thomas; Sheffield: JSOT Press, 1992) 2.50; he discusses the curse in general on pp. 48-50. He first proposed this correlation in S. Mowinckel, *Psalmenstudien* (Kristiania: Jacob Dybwad, 1922) 119.

[50] Westermann, *Basic Forms*, 190-98.

[51] Ibid., 193. Woe sequences are found in Isa 5:8, 11, 18, 20, 21, 22; 28:1; 29:1, 15; 30:1, 31:1 and Hab 2:6, 9, 12, 15, 19. In Amos, woe oracles begin in 5:18 and 6:1; another was reconstructed in 5:7 by G. A. Smith, *The Book of the Twelve Prophets. Vol. I: Amos, Hosea, Micah* (The Expositors Bible, 8th Series; London: Hodder & Stoughton, 1896); he is followed by most commentators. Andersen and Freedman, *Amos*, 461-62, identify 19 participial statements in the book (6 within 6:1-6 and including 5:7) as "woes," thereby rendering the actual word הוֹי irrelevant.

[52] Westermann, *Basic Forms*, 198.

[53] On the inherent efficacy of the prophetic pronouncements see A. F. Key, "The Magical Background of Is 6:9-13," *JBL* 86 (1967) 198-204. A discussion of "performative language" in general can be found in J. L. Austin, *How to Do Things with Words* (Oxford: Oxford University Press, 1962).

[54] Wolff, *Joel and Amos*, 243 and n. 108. Cf. R. E. Clements, "The Form and Character of Prophetic Woe Oracles," *Semitics* 8 (1982) 22.

little significance should be attached to sequences of either the woes or the curses. The latter are clearly linked because of their initial word[55] and that is the most likely explanation for the woe sequences as well.[56] Furthermore, the woes and curses do not share any common content.[57] Finally, the early pre-exilic prophets never utter curses,[58] so it is less likely they would employ a derivative form.

A second view situates the prophetic woe oracles within clan wisdom. This was first suggested by Gerstenberger, and has since been vigorously advanced by H. W. Wolff.[59] Gerstenberger's starting point is the impersonal tenor of the woes, which he describes as "general and timeless indictments of historically unspecified evildoers."[60] Secondly, the woes share a concern for social justice and drunkenness with the wisdom tradition.[61] This leads Gerstenberger to see הוֹי as the opposite of אַשְׁרֵי ("happy"), a common wisdom term.[62] Just as אַשְׁרֵי introduced actions and attitudes acceptable in the established village wisdom, so too, he argues, descriptions of what was unacceptable would have begun with הוֹי. Since such wisdom statements were rooted in the positive and negative consequences of various actions, the prophetic use would be understood primarily in terms of cause and effect, namely, that "woe" will eventually come to those who perform the described negative actions.

However, no direct correlation between הוֹי and אַשְׁרֵי, or between הוֹי and wisdom in general, exists in the First Testament; with one exception, הוֹי is found only in the prophetic books. Gerstenberger

---

[55] Although there is some general similarity of content (e.g., vv. 20-23 deal with forbidden sexual relations, namely, "anyone who lies" with his father's wife, an animal, his sister or his mother-in-law), most of the curses in Deut 27:15-26 have little relationship among them, and even vv. 20-23 are probably juxtaposed simply because of the repeated "anyone who lies with . . . ."

[56] R. J. Clifford, "The Use of *HÔY* in the Prophets," *CBQ* 28 (1966) 459.

[57] E. S. Gerstenberger, "The Woe-Oracles of the Prophets," *JBL* 81 (1962) 258-60.

[58] J. G. Williams, "The Alas-Oracles of the Eighth Century Prophets," *HUCA* 38 (1967) 84.

[59] Gerstenberger, "Woe-Oracles," 249-63; H. W. Wolff, *Amos the Prophet: The Man and His Background* (ed. J. Reumann; trans. F. R. McCurley; Philadelphia: Fortress Press, 1973) 17-34; *idem*, *Joel and Amos*, 94, 243-45. They are followed by Clements, "Prophetic Woe Oracles," 24-25.

[60] Gerstenberger, "Woe-Oracles," 252; see also Wolff, *Joel and Amos*, 94; J. G. Williams, "Alas-Oracles," 82n19.

[61] Gerstenberger, "Woe-Oracles," 254-58; see also Wolff, *Joel and Amos*, 244, 245.

[62] Gerstenberger, "Woe-Oracles," 260-61; see also Wolff, *Amos the Prophet*, 25-29.

can only point to two places where the concepts "happy" and "woe" occur together, and both require emendation.[63] Moreover, even though these textual changes are commonly accepted, the counterpoint to אַשְׁרֵי in both instances is not הוֹי, but אוֹי, and Wanke has shown on syntactical grounds that the two words are to be distinguished.[64] As for Gerstenberger's other points, although the prophetic woes might appear "timeless" and "historically unspecified" to us, that does not mean they were to those who first heard them.[65] An audience did not need to hear a regnal year announced every time a prophet spoke to know he was talking about specific groups and times. It would have been clear to Amos' contemporaries who "the confident on Mount Samaria" were, especially since the participles in this passage constitute direct address.[66] As for the concern about social justice and drunkenness, these are not unique to a wisdom setting, but are part of a shared social system, and should not be equated exclusively with any one group or tradition.[67]

Because neither curses nor clan wisdom provide convincing pre-prophetic backgrounds for the woe saying, scholars eventually focused attention on the lone instance of הוֹי outside the prophetic literature. In 1 Kgs 13:30 the word is used during a funerary lament over the "man of God" from Judah. The same setting is found in Jer 22:18, where Jeremiah announces that the traditional lament (הוֹי is mentioned four times in the verse) will not be spoken when King Jehoiakim is buried, and in Jer 34:5, where such mourning is denied to King Zedekiah. All three passages contain the verb סָפַד ("la-

---

[63] From אִמְרוּ to אַשְׁרֵי in Isa 3:10-11 and from אִי to אוֹי in Qoh 10:16-17; see Gerstenberger, "Woe-Oracles," 261.

[64] Wanke, "אוֹי und הוֹי," 215-16. אוֹי occurs 25 times, 22x with the preposition ל, 19x with a personal pronoun or suffix, and often with a reason for the exclamation. Contrast the distribution of הוֹי presented in n. 47. The former is best translated as "woe to me/you/him (because) . . ." while the latter should be rendered as "Alas!" (see p. 94 below).

[65] See also the criticism in Janzen, *Woe Oracle*, 21, 41n3, that Gerstenberger's understanding of the woe oracle is valid only if over half of the word's occurrences are excluded from consideration.

[66] See n. 6 above.

[67] Matters of justice fall within the realm of the judiciary, for instance. For a common background for law and wisdom see J.-P. Audet, "Origines comparées de la double tradition de la loi et de la sagesse dans le Proche-Orient ancien," *Acten Internationalen Orientalistenkongresses (Moscow)* 1 (1960) 352-57. See also the warnings (*mutatis mutandis*) about casting too wide a net in the search for wisdom influence in J. L. Crenshaw, "Method in Determining Wisdom Influence Upon 'Historical' Literature," *JBL* 88 (1969) 129-42; cf. Janzen, *Woe Oracle*, 24.

ment"), which indicates that funerary lamentation was the original *Sitz im Leben* for a proclamation of הוֹי.[68]

This is significant for how the speaker and the audience would have understood the prophetic woe cry, and for the translation of הוֹי. A woe oracle mourns those whose actions are described after the opening הוֹי.[69] This is especially the case with Amos, who, as the first prophet to use the woe form is the closest to its funerary origins[70] and the expectations that background would create in his audience. In other words, by using the woe form Amos laments the impending fate of those he is describing in vv. 1, 3-6, in anticipation of their punishment announced in v. 7. Koch's formulation is especially apt: "Amos . . . publishes the people's obituary in advance."[71] Secondly, in the three verses with an explicit funerary con-

---

[68] This was first proposed, apparently independently, by Clifford, "*HÔY*," 458-64 and Wanke, "אוֹי und הוֹי," 215-18. See also H.-J. Kraus, "הוֹי als prophetische Leichenklage über das eigene Volk im 8. Jahrhundert," *ZAW* 85 (1973) 15-46; H.-J. Zobel, "הוֹי *hôy*," *TDOT* 3.361-62; and especially Janzen, *Woe Oracle*, 3-19 and Vermeylen, *Du prophète Isaïe*, 2.503-52, both of whom develop it in great detail, with comparative material from surrounding semitic cultures. Compare the double cry of הוֹ in the context of funeral lament in Amos 5:16-17, immediately before the הוֹי of 5:18.

Wolff, *Joel and Amos*, 243, links funerary lamentation with clan wisdom through the extended family, noting along the way Jer 9:16, where professional mourners are called "the wise [women]" (הַחֲכָמוֹת). But in a village, mourning was done by virtually everyone, and especially by relatives, "wise" or not (Kraus, "הוֹי," 19); in contrast, Jeremiah operated in the southern capital, Jerusalem. Moreover, in Jer 9:16 the root חכם denotes professional skill or expertise. If the words "wisdom" or "wise" are alone sufficient to indicate the wisdom tradition, then the latter includes artisans (Exod 35:31-36:1), tailors (Exod 28:3), scribes (Jer 8:8), sailors (Ps 107:27), shipbuilders (Ezek 27:8-9), warfare (Prov. 21:22, Isa 10:13), commerce (Ezek 28:4-5) and sorcery (Isa 47:9-13; cf. the Babylonian magicians in Daniel); in other words, everybody and everything. Wolff's proposal defines "wisdom" so broadly as to be useless. In any case, even Wolff is forced to admit, ". . . the הוֹי of Amos resonates much more strongly with the unnerving tone of the cry of funerary lamentation than is the case in our *postulated* pedagogical wisdom sayings." (Wolff, *Joel and Amos*, 245; emphasis added).

[69] Clifford, "*HÔY*," 460-61; J. G. Williams, "Alas-Oracles," 87; *idem*, "Irony and Lament: Clues to Prophetic Consciousness," *Semeia* 8 (1977) 55; Janzen, *Woe Oracle*, *passim*; K. Koch, *The Prophets, Vol. I: The Assyrian Period* (trans. M. Kohl; Philadelphia: Fortress Press, 1983) 44; Wittenberg, "Amos 6:1-7," 59; H. Wildberger, *Isaiah 1-12: A Commentary* (Continental Commentaries; trans. T. H. Trapp; Minneapolis: Fortress Press, 1991) 196; Zobel, "הוֹי *hôy*," 3.363-64. Note especially Kraus' statement: "Das vom Profeten angeprangerte Verhalten trägt den Tod in sich . . ." (Kraus, "הוֹי," 44).

[70] See Janzen, *Woe Oracle*, 84.

[71] Koch, *The Prophets I*, 47. See also Clifford, "*HÔY*," 464; Janzen, *Woe Oracle*, 48-49. Kraus, "הוֹי," 27, considers the unexpected עַתָּה in v. 7 as further evi-

text (1 Kings 13:30; Jer 22:18; 34:5), the syntax in all six instances of the word consists of הוֹי plus direct address to the dead individual.[72] As such, Williams' suggested translation of הוֹי as "Alas!" rather than the traditional "Woe"[73] seems more appropriate, in that it retains the element of direct address while counteracting a tendency to expand the simple cry of "Woe" into "Woe to," for which there are no textual grounds and which sounds too much like a curse.[74]

## D. *Discussion*

Amos 6:1, 3-7 easily divides into three parts on the basis of content. Verses 1 and 3a describe the elite's attitude with respect to themselves, while 3b and 6c indicate the implications of that attitude for others. Verses 4-6b describe the actions stemming from that attitude, and together vv. 1, 3-6 constitute a divine accusation against the Samarian upper class. Finally, v. 7 announces the punishment for the sins described in the preceding verses: they will be exiled and their *marzēaḥ* will end. It is not clear whether this means the end of a group or of its banquet; perhaps it reflects the beginning of a semantic overlap in which the word can designate both at the same time.

The addressees are characterized in v. 1a-b as "secure" and "confident." While some scholars think the ב preposition in both lines indicates the indirect object of, and reason for, the audience's confidence and security,[75] the rest of the passage focuses on them, not Zion or Samaria, as the basis for this attitude, which means the

---

dence that, as far as Amos is concerned, their death sentence is a present reality. Wolff and Paul consider it imminent; see Wolff, *Joel and Amos*, 277; Paul, *Amos*, 210. Weisman considers this use of the woe form satirical as well; see Z. Weisman, *Political Satire in the Bible* (SBLSS 32; Atlanta: Scholars Press, 1998) 83-84, 88-89.

[72] Note also the Greek addition at 1 Kgs 12:24 (LXX 3 Kings 12:24m): Οὐαι κύριε = הוֹי אָדוֹן (cf. Jer 22:18; 34:5).

[73] J. G. Williams, "Alas-Oracles," 75.

[74] At Amos 6:1, the *RSV* and the *NAB* translate as "Woe to . . .," the *NEB* renders "Woe betide . . ." and the *NJB* reads "Disaster for those . . . ." The *NRSV*'s "Alas for those . . ." is an improvement over the *RSV*. On the woe's possible development into a curse in the later prophetic literature see Clifford, "*HÔY*," 461-64; Janzen, *Woe Oracle*, 27-34.

[75] Andersen and Freedman, *Amos*, 553; P. Bovati and R. Meynet, *Le livre du prophète Amos* (Rhétorique Biblique 2; Paris: Les Éditions du Cerf, 1994) 205; Snyman, "'Violence,'" 43.

preposition should be taken as a locative. Lines 1c-d describe their status as the "notables" to whom the general populace comes, probably because they are the usual administers of justice.[76] Verse 3a goes on to state that they are able to "exclude the evil day." This may be the result of some activity,[77] but their description in v. 1 as "secure" and especially "confident" points instead to a description of their mental state.[78] The phrase יוֹם רָע is unique in the First Testament, but it fits the description of the "day of Yahweh" in Amos 5:18-20.[79] However, Amos 6:3a is the flip-side of 5:18-20, describing *their* view of the Day of Yahweh: they (incorrectly) think Yahweh will intervene on their behalf, delivering them from evil.

In 3b the focus shifts to the effect their attitude has on others. In contrast to their efforts to exclude the evil day, they bring near שֶׁבֶת חָמָס. The correct understanding of this phrase revolves around the first word. If it is a substantive derived from the verb שָׁבַת, it means "cessation,"[80] but this does not fit the context very well. Rudolph's rendition as "ein gewaltsames Ende"[81] is more appropriate, but does not fit the word's nuance elsewhere as "inactivity" rather than "termination." Reider's derivation from the Arabic *waṯbat* ("assault")[82] also fits, but is unparalleled in the First Testament.[83] A number of emendations have also been proposed,[84] but none have any textual

[76] Harper, *Amos and Hosea*, 143; S. R. Driver, *The Books of Joel and Amos* (The Cambridge Bible for Schools and Colleges; 2nd ed.; adapted and supplemented by H. C. O. Lanchester; Cambridge: Cambridge University Press, 1915) 195; Bič, *Amos*, 130; Hammershaimb, *Amos*, 96; Bovati and Meynet, *Amos*, 204n4. The latter consider בוא ל a technical term in the judicial process. The irony is that, as 3b and 6c in particular show, they do not care and are unwilling to help them.

[77] Some sort of ritual, perhaps magic, is adduced here by Maag, *Text*, 209; Bič, *Amos*, 131; C. Hauret, *Amos et Osée* (Verbum Salutis, Ancien Testament 5; Paris: Beauchesne, 1970) 82. οἱ εὐχόμενοι ("those praying") might lend some support to this proposal, but it is only found in later manuscripts (e.g., A, Q and the margin of the Hexaplar); the main LXX reading is οἱ ἐρχόμενοι. Wood, "Amos," 383, suggests "acts of worship and sacrifice"; cf. Amos 5:21-24.

[78] Thus BDB; Harper, *Amos and Hosea*, 146; Mays, *Amos*, 117; Hayes, *Amos*, 185.

[79] Thus Kraus, "הוי," 26; Wolff, *Joel and Amos*, 275; Andersen and Freedman, *Amos*, 561; G. V. Smith, *Amos*, 203; Paul, *Amos*, 199, 204.

[80] BDB 992. See Exod 21:19; Prov 20:2; cf. Isa 30:7.

[81] Rudolph, *Joel–Amos*, 216.

[82] J. Reider, "Etymological Studies in Biblical Hebrew," *VT* 2 (1952) 122.

[83] Wolff, *Joel and Amos*, 272; Paul, *Amos*, 205.

[84] שֶׁבֶר וְחָהָס ("destruction and violence") was proposed by W. Nowack, *Die Kleinen Propheten übersetzt und erklärt* (HAT 3; 3rd ed.; Göttingen: Vandenhoeck & Ruprecht, 1922); Weiser, *Propheten*, 175. Marti, *Dodekapropheton*, 200, changed it to שֹׁד וְחָמָס ("devastation and violence"; cf. Amos 3:10). שְׁנַת חָמָס ("A year of violence")

or versional support. However, the Vulgate does read *solio iniquitatis* ("throne of iniquity"). This suggests that שֶׁבֶת is, in fact, the infinitive construct of יָשַׁב, which means "sit, dwell," and by extension, "rule, reign."[85]

The second word (חָמָס) refers primarily to physical violence, but can also denote general wrongdoing, almost always by the powerful against the poor and weak.[86] Linked with שֶׁבֶת (as derived from יָשַׁב) it either refers to injustice at the place where they sat in judgment (cf. v. 1d) or to the effect of that injustice.[87] Whatever the precise nuance, the lexical link with חָמָס in Amos 3:10, combined with the antithetical parallelism in Amos 6:3, indicates that their actions affect the nation's internal situation.[88] This is further explicated by their lack of concern "over the ruin of Joseph" in 6c. This line is often interpreted in political terms,[89] but nothing in the phrase itself or

---

is suggested by Maag, *Text*, 37-38; S. Amsler, "Amos," *Osée Joël Amos Abdias Jonas* (CAT 11a; 2nd ed.; Genève: Labor et Fides, 1982) 218n3; Kraus, "הוי," 26. *BHS* suggests all three possibilities.

[85] BDB 442. Cf. J. Wellhausen, *Die Kleinen Propheten übersetzt und erklärt* (4th ed.; Berlin: Walter de Gruyter, 1963) 85, first proposed in the 3rd edition from 1898. He is followed by, *inter alia*, Harper, *Amos and Hosea*, 146; Wolff, *Joel and Amos*, 272; Hayes, *Amos*, 185; Andersen and Freedman, *Amos*, 562; Bovati and Meynet, *Amos*, 206; Snyman, "'Violence,'" 46.

[86] BDB 329; it occurs as part of the common phrase חָמָס וָשֹׁד in Amos 3:10. Cf. the discussions of Wolff, *Joel and Amos*, 194; Paul, *Amos*, 117.

[87] I have translated it as "rule of violence" in an attempt to capture both possibilities.

[88] *Contra* Hayes, *Amos*, 185-86, who understands Amos 6:3 as an invasion by an anti-Assyrian coalition. G. V. Smith, *Amos*, 203, also relates it to foreign attack. It is linked to internal oppression by Harper, *Amos and Hosea*, 146; Mays, *Amos*, 116; Wolff, *Joel and Amos*, 275; Wittenberg, "Amos 6:1-7," 62-63; G. V. Smith, *Amos*, 203; Bovati and Meynet, *Amos*, 208, 212. The disintegration of internal social bonds during this period because of the shift to latifundialization is discussed by R. B. Coote, *Amos Among the Prophets: Composition and Theology* (Philadelphia: Fortress Press, 1981) 24-39; W. Schottroff, "The Prophet Amos: A Socio-Historical Assessment of His Ministry," *The God of the Lowly: Socio-Historical Interpretations of the Bible* (eds. W. Schottroff and W. Stegemann; trans. M. J. O'Connell; Maryknoll: Orbis Books, 1984) 33-40; I. Jaruzelska, "Social Structure in the Kingdom of Israel in the Eighth Century B.C. as Reflected in the Book of Amos," *FO* 29 (1992-93) 91-117.

[89] Two proposals date the line after the traditional period of Amos' ministry. Wolff, *Joel and Amos*, 273-74, 277; Wittenberg, "Amos 6:1-7," 67; Fleischer, *Von Menschen verkaüfern*, 233-34, all relate it to the northern leaders' lack of concern for the nation's internal political strife in the years immediately prior to the Assyrian conquest. In contrast, J. M. Ward, *Amos and Isaiah: Prophets of the Word of God* (New York: Abingdon Press, 1969) 82-83; Roberts, "Amos 6:1-7," 160-61; Fleischer, *Von Menschen verkaüfern*, 234, 243; Wood, "Amos," 79, 81, 83, 85; Blum, "Am

the larger passage requires a political interpretation; it can just as easily point to the dissolution of covenantal bonds between the rich and the poor, against which the entire book of Amos protests.[90] This is consistent with their complacent self-indulgence in the preceding verses, and the paranomasia between שֶׁבֶת and שֶׁבֶר linking vv. 3b and 6c[91] also supports an internal, social interpretation of the latter line.

Following this, v. 7 announces an ironic reversal of the situation denounced in vv. 1, 3-6: those who considered themselves the elite of "the first of the nations" will be "the first of the exiles,"[92] bringing to an end their sprawling *marzēaḥ*. This reversal indicates that the preceding lines deal with the attitudes and actions of *marzēaḥ* members during their feast. As such, vv. 4-6b in particular describe an actual *marzēaḥ* feast that is consistent with what is known about the *marzēaḥ* from extra-biblical materials, including all three of the constitutive elements identified in Chapter 1. First of all, this *marzēaḥ* involves a specific upper-class group. Their identification as "the notables of the first of the nations" in 1c is confirmed by various indications of wealth in vv. 4-6b. For instance, they recline on ivory-inlaid beds[93] eating the choicest meats. Meat was not part of the

---

6,1-7," 34-35; Rottzoll, *Studien*, 160-61, 164, all interpret it as the south's rejection of the north afterwards. Explanations attributing the line to Amos include earlier internal political strife (Hayes, *Amos*, 187), imminent external attack (G. V. Smith, *Amos*, 205) and an allusion to the division of the kingdom after Solomon (Hammershaimb, *Amos*, 101-02).

[90] Thus Mays, *Amos*, 117; B. Vawter, *Amos, Hosea, Micah, with an Introduction to Classical Prophecy* (OTMS 7; Wilmington: Michael Glazier, 1981) 61; Koch, *The Prophets I*, 50; R. Martin-Achard and S. P. Re'emi, *God's People in Crisis: A Commentary on the Books of Amos and Lamentation* (ITC; Grand Rapids: Wm. B. Eerdmans Publishing Co., 1984) 48; Paul, *Amos*, 209.

[91] See n. 32.

[92] Note the punning reversal of fortune and the paranomasia of the second word in רֵאשִׁית הַגּוֹיִם and רֹאשׁ גֹּלִים.

[93] The "ivory beds" (מִטּוֹת שֵׁן) of v. 4a are not made completely of ivory, but contain ivory inlays and ornamentation. See P. J. King, *Amos, Hosea, Micah—An Archaeological Commentary* (Philadelphia: Westminster Press, 1988) 139; this is specified in the Targum. On ivory in the ancient world see R. D. Barnett, *Ancient Ivories in the Middle East* (Jerusalem: Institute of Archaeology, 1982); H. Shanks, "Ancient Ivory: The Story of Wealth, Decadence, and Beauty," *BARev* 11/5 (1985) 40-53; King, *Amos, Hosea, Micah*, 139-49; for Samaria in particular see J. W. Crowfoot and G. M. Crowfoot, *Early Ivories from Samaria* (Samaria-Sebaste 2; London: Palestine Exploration Fund, 1938); K. Kenyon, *Royal Cities of the Old Testament* (London: Barrie & Jenkins, 1971) 71-89. For the possible identification of Phoenician ivory-inlaid *marzēaḥ* beds see R. D. Barnett, *A Catalogue of the Nimrud Ivories, with*

average diet, and thus a luxury,[94] and the types of meat mentioned in 4c-d are of the highest quality; the phrase "calves from the middle of the fattening stall" (מַרְבֵּק)[95] is especially indicative of their affluence. They wash this down with "bowls"[96] (rather than the usual

*Other Examples of Ancient Near Eastern Ivories in the British Museum* (London: Trustees of the British Museum, 1957) 131n4; *idem*, "Assurbanipal's Feast," *EI* 18 (1985) 3*.

[94] T. H. Sutcliffe, *The Book of Amos* (London: SPCK, 1939) 50; R. S. Cripps, *A Critical and Exegetical Commentary on the Book of Amos: The Text of the Revised Version Edited with Introduction, Notes and Excursuses* (2nd ed.; foreword by R. H. Kennett; London: SPCK, 1955) 206; Mays, *Amos*, 116; H. McKeating, *The Books of Amos, Hosea and Micah* (CBC; Cambridge: Cambridge University Press, 1971) 49-50; M. Fendler, "Zur Sozialkritik des Amos: Versuch einer wirtschafts- und sozialgeschichtlichen Interpretation alttestamentlicher Texte," *EvT* 33 (1973) 45; Schottroff, "The Prophet Amos," 35; Andersen and Freedman, *Amos*, 563.

[95] This Hebrew word means "tying place" (cf. Arabic *rabaqa*, "tie up") and refers to stalls in which livestock were confined to be fattened without developing tough muscle by moving around. See BDB 918; Maag, *Text*, 167-68; Wolff, *Joel and Amos*, 276; King, *Amos, Hosea, Micah*, 149-51; Paul, *Amos*, 206. The phrase עֵגֶל־מַרְבֵּק also occurs literally in 1 Sam 28:24, and is used figuratively of the restored people of Israel (Mal 3:30) and of Egyptian mercenaries (Jer 46:21). On the basis of an Egyptian sarcophagus relief showing a cow being milked with a calf tied to her front leg, Weippert suggests the word refers to a practice in which a calf, unable to reach its mother's udders, is weaned by a farmer and taken while still very young, and therefore the meat tender; see H. Weippert, "Amos: Seine Bilder und ihr Milieu," *Beiträge zur prophetischen Bildsprache in Israel und Assyrien* (OBO 64; eds. H. Weippert, K. Seybold and M. Weippert; Freiburg: Universitätsverlag; Göttingen: Vandenhoeck & Ruprecht, 1985) 8-9; followed by C. Maier and E. M. Dörrfuß, "'Um mit ihnen zu sitzen, zu essen und zu trinken': Am 6,7; Jer 16,5 und die Bedeutung von *marzeaḥ*," *ZAW* 111 (1999) 46n5. This requires an unusual temporal, rather than locative, meaning for תָּוֶךְ, however. In any case, the essential point remains the same.

[96] The מִזְרָקִים in v. 6 are sacred vessels used in sprinkling rites (see King, *Amos, Hosea, Micah*, 157-58); the 31 other occurrences of the term in the First Testament are in a cultic context (see especially Exod 24:6.) They would have been wide and probably shallow (King, p. 158, suggests a diameter of up to eighteen inches). The Targum calls it a silver *pylwwn*, a loan word from the Greek *phialē*; see K. J. Cathcart and R. P. Gordon, *The Targum of the Minor Prophets: Translated, with a Critical Apparatus, and Notes* (The Aramaic Bible 14; Wilmington: Michael Glazier, 1989) 88n8. Barnett, "Assurbanipal's Feast," 6*n30, also connects the two terms. This calls to mind the Phoenician *phialē* dedicated to the *marzēaḥ* of Šamaš, measuring 18.4 cm across and 3.6 cm deep (see the discussion in Chapter 1). Thus the translation as "bowls."

The LXX reads τὸν διυλισμένον οἶνον ("strained wine"), reflecting a possible Hebrew *Vorlage* מְזֻקָּקֵי יַיִן (cf. Isa 25:6). Dahmen feels this provides a better parallel with the choice meats in v. 4 and the "finest oil" in the next line; see U. Dahmen, "Zur Text- und Literarkritik von Amos 6:6a," *BN* 31 (1986) 7-10; he is followed (with emendation to מְזֻקַּק יַיִן) by Fleischer, *Von Menschen verkaüfern*, 234-36; see already Morgenstern, "Amos Studies IV," 323, who refers to Procksch.

cups) of wine, which suggests large amounts were consumed.[97] This and the "finest oils"[98] for anointing also indicate that the participants enjoyed significant financial standing. Second, heavy drinking during the feast is also reflected in this passage. The amount of wine consumed has just been noted, and the resultant drunkenness is conveyed by the word סְרוּחִים in 4b and 7b. The verb סָרַח means "go free, be unrestrained, overrun, exceed."[99] Elsewhere it is always used of objects which can hang loose, such as curtains (Exod 26:12, 13), vines (Ezek 17:6) and turbans (Ezek 23:15). Used only here of humans, their physical position reflects both their mental attitude (vv. 1, 3) and their wine consumption (v. 6). Third, there are numerous indications this is a religious banquet, beginning with the opening specification of the feast's location as "on Zion."

This interpretation entails a radical departure from the usual understandings of this line, so some justification is required, beginning with the inadequacy of the traditional interpretations. Many reject the reference to Zion in Amos 6:1 on the assumption that Amos' words were directed to the north only,[100] and deal with the word by

However, since the *marzēaḥ* is a religious feast and there are numerous other religious allusions in the passage, the MT should be retained (see further on pp. 99-103).

[97] Thus Harper, *Amos and Hosea*, 149; Driver, *Joel and Amos*, 198; B. Thorogood, *A Guide to the Book of Amos with Theme Discussions on Judgment, Social Justice, Priest and Prophet* (Theological Education Fund Study Guides 4; London: SPCK, 1971) 69; Fendler, "Sozialkritik," 45; Wolff, *Joel and Amos*, 276; B. Lang, *Monotheism and the Prophetic Minority* (SWBA 1; Sheffield: The Almond Press, 1983) 122; J. A. Soggin, *The Prophet Amos: A Translation and Commentary* (trans. J. Bowden; London: SCM Press, 1987) 103, 105; G. V. Smith, *Amos*, 205; Paul, *Amos*, 122. In contrast, Hammershaimb, *Amos*, 101; Andersen and Freedman, *Amos*, 564; J. Jeremias, *Der Prophet Amos* (ATD 24; Göttingen: Vandenhoeck & Ruprecht, 1995) 88 and possibly Kraus, "הוי," 27, think the issue is the misuse of cultic items. Barstad, *Religious Polemics*, 127n5, simply says the bowl's size isn't the point while King, *Amos, Hosea, Micah*, 158, says it could be either. Cf. below concerning their "sprawling."

[98] As in v. 1, רֵאשִׁית refers to importance or quality, not time, yielding the translation "the finest oils." On the production of "the finest oil" see L. E. Stager, "The Finest Olive Oil in Samaria," *JSS* 28 (1983) 241-45; King, *Amos, Hosea, Micah*, 159-61.

[99] BDB 710.

[100] In itself, Oettli's question is still valid almost a century later: "Why should not Amos, a Judean, be allowed to touch on his own homeland?"; see Oettli, *Amos und Hosea*, 72; contrast the sustained and intriguing defense of a northern origin for Amos in Rosenbaum, *Amos of Israel*, *passim*; cf. also Kraus, "הוי," 28. However, the lack of consensus as to the answer is illustrated by comparing Paul, *Amos*, 200, who agrees with Oettli, and Wolff, *Joel and Amos*, 269, who does not. Most think Amos didn't address the south, but the opposite view is held by Martin-Achard

removing it, either by deletion,[101] emendation,[102] or the "restoration" of a word more closely corresponding to Samaria.[103] These are all hypothetical and require significant deviation from the MT, despite the lack of text-critical support for any reading other than Zion. Yet even when Zion is retained, there is little agreement as to the line's interpretation. Some consider the whole passage a post-Amos composition indicating that Samaria's fate awaits Judah as well.[104] The supposedly later historical references in v. 2 and in the phrase "the ruin of Joseph" (v. 6) are claimed as supporting evidence, but if v.

---

and Re'emi, *God's People in Crisis*, 48; G. V. Smith, *Amos*, 199-200; Andersen and Freedman, *Amos*, *passim*. Hayes, *Amos*, 182-83, thinks the reference to Zion reflects its status as a vassal to Israel.

[101] Simply deleting "Zion" would disturb the parallelism with the following line, but that difficulty is avoided by deleting the entire line yet retaining the initial הוֹי; thus Marti, *Dodekapropheton*, 198; he is followed by Wolff, *Joel and Amos*, 269; Wittenberg, "Amos 6:1-7," 67; Fleischer, *Von Menschen verkaüfern*, 226, 243; Loretz, "*Marziḥu*," 132, 134-35; Blum, "Am 6,1-7," 29, 34; Rottzoll, *Studien*, 154-55, 158.

[102] Ehrlich, *Randglossen*, 5.243 and the *BHS* suggest בְּגָאוֹן ("in pride"); cf. Maag, *Text*, 37, who specifies it as "*their* pride" (בִּגְאוֹנָם). Rudolph, *Joel–Amos*, 215, proposed בְּצָרוֹן ("in the fortress"); cf. Zech 9:12. בְּעִיּוֹן ("in Ijon") is offered by W. von Soden, "Zu Einigen Ortsbenennungen bei Amos und Micha," *ZAH* 3 (1990) 214-16; cf. 1 Kgs 15:20 and 2 Kgs 15:29, but note the critique in Loretz, "*Marziḥu*," 137-38. The word is revocalized as בְּצִיּוֹן ("in the rock; from the Arabic *ṣuwwa*) by P. Riessler, *Der Kleinen Propheten oder das Zwölfprophetenbuch nach dem Urtext übersetzt und erklärt* (Rottenburg: Bader, 1911) 85, 87.

[103] "In Tirzah" (בְּתִרְצָה) was proposed by T. K. Cheyne, "Gleanings in Biblical Criticism and Geography," *JQR* 10 (1898) 573, who is followed by Harper, *Amos and Hosea*, 141; K. Budde, "Zu Text und Auslegung des Buches Amos," *JBL* 43 (1924) 121-23. Vawter, *Amos, Hosea, Micah*, 60, suggests "in Bethel" (בְּבֵית אֵל). It was changed to "in the [capital] city" (בָּעִיר) by E. Sellin, *Das Zwölfprophetenbuch übersetzt und erklärt* (KAT 12; 1st ed.; Leipzig: Deichert, 1922) 198; in the 2nd (1929) and 3rd (1930) editions he retained "Zion." "In Joseph" (בְּיוֹסֵף) is read by H. L. Ginsberg, *The Israelian Heritage of Judaism* (TSJTSA 24; New York: The Jewish Theological Seminary of America, 1982) 31. Morgenstern, "Amos Studies IV," 325; Coote, *Amos Among the Prophets*, 13, simply state that an unknown reference originally stood here.

[104] Thus, e.g., Ward, *Amos and Isaiah*, 82-83; Wood, "Amos," 80-81. Cf. Roberts, "Amos 6:1-7," 159-61, who attributes it to Amos but extends his ministry well past Jeroboam's death. Jeremias takes all of Amos 5-6 as post-Amos; see J. Jeremias, "Amos 3–6: From the Oral Word to the Text" (trans. S. A. Irvine), *Canon, Theology, and Old Testament Interpretation: Essays in Honor of Brevard S. Childs* (eds. G. M. Tucker, D. L. Petersen and R. R. Wilson; Philadelphia: Fortress Press, 1988) 217-29; he is followed by Snyman, "'Violence,'" 44. In contrast, Wolff, *Joel and Amos*, 107, considers chaps. 3-6 to be the nucleus of Amos' preaching. Although various deletions are proposed, some portion of Amos 6:1-7 is attributed to Amos by virtually all commentators, as well as in Rottzoll's recent redactional study (see Rottzoll, *Studien*, 153-68).

2 is secondary[105] and "the ruin of Joseph" refers to societal breakdown rather than military conquest[106] then those arguments are moot. More importantly, one would expect a clearer indication of a southern audience, but nothing else in the passage points in that direction. Finally, the address in v. 1b to those who are "*confident* . . . on Mount Samaria" points to a date before any calamity.

Weiser and Bič also relate Zion to Jerusalem, but as the object of the northerners' attitude. Weiser renders הַשַּׁאֲנַנִּים בְּצִיּוֹן as "those who are proud of Zion," which he relates to the north's conquest of Jerusalem in the early 8th century.[107] However, as Wolff points out, "שׁאנן never means 'proud of,' but rather 'carefree, secure.'"[108] On the other hand, Bič thinks the words mean the elite of Samaria do not care about Zion ("sie seien *in bezug* auf Zion sorglos gewesen," italics in the original), reflecting their belief that the northern manifestation of Yahweh is satisfied with them, and they have nothing to fear from the Yahweh of Zion who sent Amos.[109] This seems dependent on the LXX, which reads οὐαὶ τοῖς ἐξουθενοῦσι Σιων ("those who detest Zion"), perhaps reading the root שׂנא from Amos 5:21 by metathesis. But the LXX drops the prepositional *beth* from "Zion," and the entire construction suggests the Greek translator also had difficulty with a reference to Zion (Jerusalem) here.[110] Moreover, the repetition of שַׁאֲנַנּוֹת and בֹּטְחוֹת in Isa 32:9 and 11 in the same order with roughly the same nuances support retaining the former here.

In contrast, Andersen and Freedman think representatives of the southern elite were present in Samaria for an important feast, perhaps a wake for a member of the royal or priestly classes.[111] However, not only is there no other indication Amos is addressing southerners, but those Judahites would also be subject to the threatened exile, a punishment the south did not experience until one hundred and eighty years after Amos. Most importantly, the "secure" are "in/

[105] See pp. 84-85 above.
[106] See pp. 96-97 above.
[107] Weiser, *Amos*, 229-31; cf. 2 Kgs 14:11-14
[108] Wolff, *Joel and Amos*, 269; it is derived from the verb שָׁאַן, which means "be at ease or at peace, rest securely" (BDB 983).
[109] Bič, *Amos*, 129; see Amos 1:2.
[110] Wolff, *Joel and Amos*, 270.
[111] Andersen and Freedman, *Amos*, 552. Whether or not this *marzēaḥ* has funerary connections is discussed on p. 104 below.

on Zion," which means they could not even be in the northern kingdom if Zion refers to Jerusalem.[112]

Since there are problems with the traditional understandings of the term, I follow Fohrer's proposal that Zion here is "a technical expression for the situation of the capital; Samaria is the 'Zion' of the Northern Kingdom."[113] Since he did not present arguments in support of this proposal, it has been criticized and rejected by most scholars.[114] However, there is evidence he may be correct. In Ps 133:3, the priestly anointing is compared to "dew of Hermon which descends on the mountains of Zion," and the geographical distance involved together with the plural "mountains" suggests the single sacred hill of Jerusalem is not intended. Moreover, if Sion (שִׂיאֹן) is a variant spelling of Zion, then Deut 4:48 directly identifies Zion as Mount Hermon.[115] Similarly, in Ps 48:3 Zion is described as "the extremities of the north" (יַרְכְּתֵי צָפוֹן). This is unusual in light of its association with Judah in v. 12, and together with the previous references is best explained as echoes of Zion's mythological origins as the holy mountain of the gods.[116] In most texts Zion's mythological setting has been transposed to the site of the Jerusalem temple as the place where God has "made his name to dwell," but such a restrictive view of the divine locus is a later deuteronomistic invention which an earlier northern audience would not share. For them, Yahweh dwelt in the northern temples, including in Samaria. Thus, these examples, although admittedly few, counter Wolff's objection that for Zion to refer to anywhere other than Jerusalem "would constitute a singular exception."[117] Moreover, the reference to Mount Samaria in the singular in Amos 6:1b distinguishes it from the plu-

[112] Although they do not comment on the first line, Andersen and Freedman think Samaria is the focus of trust in the second line (Andersen and Freedman, *Amos*, 553), but nothing in the subsequent lines supports that view. I consider the ב in both lines as locative; see pp. 94-95 above.

[113] G. Fohrer, "Zion-Jerusalem in the Old Testament," *TDNT* 7.295.

[114] Exceptions are Lang, *Monotheism*, 121 and Rosenbaum, *Amos of Israel*, 33-34, 91. The latter traces the proposal to J. P. Peters, *The Psalms as Liturgies* (New York: Macmillan, 1922) 210.

[115] Cf. Ps 133:3; in Deut 3:9 Siryon (שִׂרְיֹן) is given as the Sidonian name for Mt. Hermon (cf. Ps 29:6), but there is no textual-critical basis for emending Deut 4:48.

[116] Note especially Baʿal's home on Mt. Zaphon in the Ugaritic literature. See further R. J. Clifford, *The Cosmic Mountain in Canaan and the Old Testament* (HSM 4; Cambridge: Harvard University Press, 1972).

[117] Wolff, *Joel and Amos*, 269.

ral "mountains of Samaria" in 3:9.[118] This suggests a special significance in 6:1b, to which Zion provides an appropriate parallel: since the other terms in lines 1a-b are roughly synonymous, Zion and Mount Samaria should be as well, with the latter specifying which "Zion" is intended.

To summarize, the self-confident and secure nobility convene their *marzēaḥ* in a place with religious connections, namely "Mount Samaria," the "Zion" of the north. Furthermore, various aspects of Amos 6:4-6b are consistent with and reinforce the probability of a religious context for this *marzēaḥ*. First, as noted earlier, their drinking "bowls" are elsewhere mentioned exclusively in cultic contexts.[119] Second, the verb מָשַׁח is normally used of religious anointing.[120] Third, according to King, the נֵבֶל ("lute") mentioned in 5a was "ordinarily reserved for a religious function."[121] Finally, in light of the constellation of other religious elements in the passage, the meat in 4c-d may have been offered in sacrifice[122] and the songs may even have been religious ones.[123]

Thus, the constitutive features of a *marzēaḥ* are present in Amos 6:1, 3-7. In contrast, two elements commonly seen in connection with the extra-biblical *marzēaḥ* are not mentioned in this text: the *marzēaḥ* leader and the *marzēaḥ* house. Some consider the house mentioned in Amos 6:9-10 to be the latter,[124] but those verses are from a separate unit describing the effects of divine judgment; as such they are subsequent to, and therefore distinct from, the situation of Amos 6:1, 3-7.[125]

---

[118] The LXX's singular (τὸ ὄρος) incorrectly conforms that verse to the singular in Amos 4:1 and 6:1. The Targum and the Vulgate both reflect the plural in Amos 3:9.

[119] See n. 96.

[120] Harper, *Amos and Hosea*, 150; Mays, *Amos*, 116; Kraus, "הוי," 27n50; Paul, *Amos*, 208. In contrast, סוך is usually used for secular anointing.

[121] King, *Amos, Hosea, Micah*, 154. See also Vuilleumier-Bessard, *La Tradition Cultuelle*, 87.

[122] Kraus, "הוי," 26-27; B. Peckham, "Phoenicia and the Religion of Israel: The Epigraphic Evidence," *Ancient Israelite Religion: Essays in Honor of Frank Moore Cross* (eds. P. D. Miller, P. D. Hanson and D. S. McBride; Philadelphia: Fortress Press, 1987) 95n58; Andersen and Freedman, *Amos*, 563, 567; Wood, "Amos," 82; Jeremias, *Amos*, 88. Cf. "your fattened animals" (מְרִיאֵיכֶם; Amos 5:22).

[123] Vuilleumier-Bessard, *La Tradition Cultuelle*, 87; Kraus, "הוי," 27; Koch, *The Prophets I*, 53. Andersen and Freedman, *Amos*, 567, suggest the temple and court musicians may have been present.

[124] See, e.g., n. 30.

[125] See the discussion of the passage's limits on pp. 85-86 above.

Many consider this particular *marzēaḥ* a funerary banquet, but that is simply asserted on the basis of their presupposition concerning the nature of all *marzēaḥ*s, rather than argued on the basis of evidence.[126] However, since there is no indication of funerary elements in the earlier *marzēaḥ*s at Ebla, Emar and Ugarit, evidence of it here is required. Some point to the funerary language of vv. 9-10,[127] but it was noted above that those verses describe events subsequent to this passage, and in any case the funerary language derives from the general destruction, not the specific purpose of the house.[128] Others appeal to the funerary associations of the "woman at the window" motif from the Samarian ivories (and elsewhere).[129] Unfortunately, we have no information as to what, if anything, may have been on the specific ivory inlays mentioned in 4a, so any suggestions in that regard can only be speculation. Finally, some claim that 6c indicates this *marzēaḥ* should have been a mourning banquet in which they would "grieve over the ruin of Joseph,"[130] but this too is rooted in a prior understanding of the *marzēaḥ*'s nature and purpose. By itself, the line simply establishes a contrast between their attitude, described in vv. 1 and 3 and embodied in vv. 4-6b, and what that attitude should be. Any funerary associations in 6c are supplied by the interpreter, not the text. On the other hand, we do know that abstention from using oil was a mourning custom in ancient Israel, so its use in v. 6b argues against this *marzēaḥ* being a funerary banquet.[131]

The final point to consider is the reason for Amos' denunciation and rejection of this *marzēaḥ*. Since this would most likely be reflect-

---

[126] Thus, e.g., A. Neher, *Amos: contribution à l'étude du prophétisme* (Paris: Librairie Philosophique J. Vrin, 1950) 107-08; Bič, *Amos*, 134; Wittenberg, "Amos 6:1-7," 59.

[127] See J. C. Greenfield, "The *Marzeaḥ* as a Social Institution," *Wirtschaft und Gesellschaft im Alten Vorderasien* (eds. J. Harmatta and G. Komoróczy; Budapest: Åkadémiai Kiadó, 1976) 453; King, *Amos, Hosea, Micah*, 139; but contrast his "Using Archaeology to Interpret a Biblical Text—The *marzēaḥ* Amos Denounces," *BARev* 14/4 (July/August 1988) 37.

[128] My thanks to Dennis Pardee for pointing this out.

[129] Barnett, "Assurbanipal's Feast," 1*-6*, especially p. 3; E. Gubel, "À propos du *marzeaḥ* d'Assurbanipal," *Reflets des deux fleuves: volume de mélanges offerts à André Finet* (AS 6; eds. M. Lebeau and P. Talon; Leuven: Peeters, 1989) 47-53; King, *Amos, Hosea, Micah*, 146-48; E. F. Beach, "The Samaria Ivories, *Marzeaḥ* and Biblical Texts," *BA* 55 (1992) 136.

[130] Peckham, "Phoenicia," 95n58; see also Andersen and Freedman, *Amos*, 567, 568; G. V. Smith, *Amos*, 203, 206; Beach, "The Samaria Ivories," 130-39.

[131] H. E. W. Fosbroke, "The Book of Amos: Introduction and Exegesis," *IB* 6.824; Paul, *Amos*, 209. Even Andersen and Freedman, *Amos*, 567, admit this would be unusual in a mourning feast.

ed in allusions elsewhere in the book, it is worth considering the matter. However, scholars are divided as to the reason for Amos' opposition, with suggestions including cultic matters, immorality and injustice.

There are two opinions as to the precise cultic aspect the prophet opposes. The first sees the *marzēaḥ* as a non-Israelite institution associated with pagan deities.[132] Some claim the ivory inlays contained idolatrous images,[133] but that cannot be verified. Barstad points to Amos 5:26 and 8:14 as evidence that "polemics against foreign deities play a major role in the preaching of Amos."[134] However, those verses provide shaky ground for Barstad's position: the former is often deleted as a later addition and the latter, if not secondary, at least requires revocalization of the MT אַשְׁמַת ("the guilt/sin [of Samaria]") to אֲשִׁמַת in order to produce a reference to the goddess Ashima.[135] More importantly, *contra* Barstad, those verses do *not* reflect a major concern in the book. Even Barstad acknowledges that the issue is not Yahweh being replaced by other gods but their worship alongside him, which he understands as the syncretistic introduction of foreign gods.[136] This is not the place for a full-scale discussion of monotheism, but there is evidence it is a late development and that prior to the exile mainstream Yahwism was polytheistic.[137] With respect to the book of Amos in particular, apart from 5:26 and 8:14, there is no indication of any opposition to syncretism. Two exam-

---

[132] The strongest arguments are found in Barstad, *Religious Polemics*, 127-42, especially p. 141. He was anticipated by H. Gressmann, "Ἡ ΚΟΙΝΩΝΙΑ ΤΩΝ ΔΑΙΜΟΝΙΩΝ," *ZNW* 20 (1921) 229-30; Bič, *Amos*, 132 and is followed by Rosenbaum, *Amos of Israel*, 67; Blum, "Am 6,1-7," 27n12; Bovati and Meynet, *Amos*, 210.

[133] E.g., Vuilleumier-Bessard, *La Tradition Cultuelle*, 40. See also Bič, *Amos*, 132; King, "Using Archaeology," 40.

[134] Barstad, *Religious Polemics*, 141n96. He does not specify the deity involved here, but Bič, *Amos*, 132, as well as Bovati and Meynet, *Amos*, 210, suggest Ba'al is the *marzēaḥ*'s patron.

[135] 2 Kgs 17:30 narrates the introduction of Ashima's (note the spelling there: אֲשִׁימָא) cult by Hamathites resettled in Samaria by the Assyrians. Barstad's discussion of Amos 5:26 and 8:14 and the literature he cites (Barstad, *Religious Polemics*, 118-26, 143-201), should now be supplemented by Paul, *Amos*, 194-98 and 268-70; Rottzoll, *Studien*, 189-92 and 266-69. Reading Asherah (אֲשֵׁרַת) in 8:14 (thus Maag, *Text*, 55-56), requires both revocalization and alteration of the consonantal text.

[136] Barstad, *Religious Polemics*, *passim*.

[137] See M. S. Smith, *The Early History of God: Yahweh and the Other Deities of Canaan* (San Francisco: Harper & Row, 1990) especially pp. 145-60. For the wide-spread pre-exilic worship of Asherah in particular see S. M. Olyan, *Asherah and the Cult of Yahweh in Israel* (SBLMS 34; Atlanta: Scholars Press, 1988).

ples immediately prior to 6:1, 3-7 support this conclusion. Amos 5:18-20, although critical of a cultic concept, focuses on the Yahweh cult. Those verses seek to correct the people's improper understanding of the Day of Yahweh, but it is still *Yahweh's* Day that they await. Moreover, divine statements in Amos 5:21-23 such as "*I* reject", "*I* do not accept", "*I* do not look at" and "remove from *me*" indicate the rejected cultic actions were directed to Yahweh. The same conclusion would be reached from a close examination of other cultic passages in the book, such as 4:4-5, but that is beyond the scope of this study. Suffice it to say, if the northern cult was syncretistic there should be some reflection of that in such passages, but there is none. Although other deities probably were worshipped alongside Yahweh during Amos' time, the *only* places in the book of Amos this elicits an objection are Amos 5:26 and the revocalized 8:14. At the very least, this means polemics against foreign gods are not a *major* concern of the prophet; at the most, it suggests the former verse is, indeed, secondary and the latter should not be emended to introduce what is foreign to Amos' own concerns.

This does not mean the *marzēaḥ* in Amos 6 could not have a patron other than Yahweh, but that is not the reason for the prophet's opposition. In fact, since there is no clear reference to other deities in the preceding verses,[138] some suggest Yahweh himself was the patron. If so, the objection to the *marzēaḥ* might lie in the association of Israel's god with a Canaanite institution.[139] But since this runs counter to Israel's own Canaanite origins, others look to some other cultic aspect of this *marzēaḥ* to justify Amos' condemnation.[140] The use of the cultic מִזְרָקִים as over-sized wine glasses is considered blasphemous by some,[141] while Bič suggests the animals were the first of the flock and belonged completely to Yahweh.[142] Either view requires a degree of eisegesis, however, since there is no other indi-

---

[138] Fleischer, *Von Menschen verkaüfern*, 238; M. E. Polley, *Amos and the Davidic Empire: A Socio-Historical Approach* (New York: Oxford University Press, 1989) 89; B. B. Schmidt, *Israel's Beneficent Dead: Ancestor Cult and Necromancy in Ancient Israelite Religion and Tradition* (Winona Lake: Eisenbrauns, 1996) 146.

[139] Thus Polley, *Amos and the Davidic Empire*, 89. Fleischer, *Von Menschen verkaüfern*, 239, argues the *marzēaḥ* was permissible within Yahwism; see also Jeremias, *Amos*, 88.

[140] Soggin, *The Prophet Amos*, 105, is uncertain whether the issue is syncretism or profanation of Yahwistic practices.

[141] See the references in n. 97.

[142] Bič, *Amos*, 132. See also Jeremias, *Amos*, 88.

cation Amos is objecting to the perversion of pure Yahweh worship.

A second proposal is that Amos objects to the *marzēaḥ* because of immorality. Vuilleumeier-Bessard finds a reference to orgies in v. 4,[143] Freedman suggests they were singing "naughty" songs[144] and Loretz castigates them for their generally "lascivious conduct" (*laszive Verhaltern*).[145] The Targum and Talmud support this view, but that says more about what the rabbis thought concerning their own contemporary *marzēaḥ*s than its nature centuries earlier.[146] Taken in its own context, the passage describes inebriated sprawling rather than sexual misconduct.

Ultimately, both the cultic and moral interpretations ignore the clear indication of the prophet's concern in 6c: the leaders are unconcerned about the situation confronting the nation (which he calls Joseph). It is their attitude he finds objectionable, an attitude embodied in their drunken feast. He does not oppose the feast itself, but the disposition it expresses. I argued above that "the ruin of Joseph" refers to the break-down of the covenantal bonds that should have united the various social levels of the nation.[147] Instead, the Samarian elite exploited their fellow Israelites. The prophet condemns their lack of concern in 6b, which elicits punishment in v. 7. In short, he does not just oppose their luxurious lifestyle, but that lifestyle at the expense of, and with indifference to, the poor.[148]

---

[143] Vuilleumier-Bessard, *La Tradition Cultuelle*, 44. See also F. Briquel-Chatonnet, *Studia Phoenicia XII: Les relations entre les cités de la côte phénicienne et les royaumes d'Israël et de Juda* (OLA 46; Leuven: Departement Oriëntalistiek/Uitgeverij Peeters, 1992) 332.

[144] D. N. Freedman, "But Did King David Invent Musical Instruments?" *BRev* 1/2 (1985) 51. He suggests they were "scurrilous, obscene or blasphemous, and possibly all three."

[145] Loretz, "'Kultmahl,'" 91.

[146] See in chapter 1 under "Rabbinic Literature." Pope's effort to establish the *marzēaḥ* as essentially licentious, here and elsewhere, is also dependent on later rabbinic, christian and pagan literature; see M. H. Pope, "A Divine Banquet at Ugarit," *The Use of the Old Testament in the New and Other Essays: Studies in Honor of W. F. Stinespring* (ed. J. M. Efird; Durham: Duke University Press, 1972) 184-89; *idem*, *Song of Songs*, 211-14.

[147] See pp. 96-97.

[148] See further the discussions of Fendler, "Sozialkritik," 45-46; H. B. Huffmon, "The Social Role of Amos' Message," *The Quest for the Kingdom of God: Studies in Honor of George E. Mendenhall* (eds. H. B. Huffmon, F. A. Spina and A. R. W. Green; Winona Lake: Eisenbrauns, 1983) 114; Schottroff, "The Prophet Amos," 34-35; R. Bohlen, "Zur Sozialkritik des Propheten Amos," *TTZ* 95 (1986) 282-301; Wittenberg, "Amos 6:1-7," 62-65.

## E. *Dating the Text*

The prophet Amos is the first biblical prophet whose words were written down and collected into a book.[149] However, the book as we now have it does not derive from Amos himself. His words were probably collected by others, and that process involved editorial choices; moreover, the book as a whole, including Amos 6:1, 3-7, has undergone subsequent redactional development as well.[150] Nonetheless, only a few scholars deny all of this passage to Amos; rather, almost all trace at least some of it to the prophet himself.[151] The archaeological evidence supports the latter view. The emergence of an upper-class around the time of Amos' ministry is indicated by excavations in the northern kingdom, which reveal that fairly uniform buildings prior to that time were replaced by a cluster of large, luxurious homes in one part of a city and smaller, poorer dwellings elsewhere.[152] Similarly, details in this passage such as the elite's ivory-inlaid beds and the production of luxury items like oil and wine are also consistent with the archaeological record for the capital, Samaria.[153]

In short, the situation described in Amos 6:1, 3-7 is consistent with the known state of affairs in the northern kingdom, ca. 760 BCE, and the passage probably dates from around that time. As such, the reference to the *marzēaḥ* in Amos 6:7 is the earliest explicit mention

---

[149] Most date Amos' ministry to around 760 BCE. Those who diverge from the consensus generally do so by only a couple of decades. For example, Rottzoll, *Studien*, 16-18, dates the prophet's words to ca. 780 BCE; Andersen and Freedman, *Amos*, *passim*, suggest ca. 780-770 BCE; Coote, *Amos Among the Prophets*, 19-24, places Amos' ministry after the death of Jeroboam; Roberts, "Amos 6:1-7," 158-59, argues that Amos began during Jeroboam's reign but continued well past his death.

[150] A detailed redactional analysis of the entire book can be found in Rottzoll, *Studien*; he treats Amos 6:1-7 on pp. 153-68.

[151] See n. 104.

[152] See the discussions in J. W. Crowfoot, K. Kenyon and E. L. Sukenik, *The Buildings at Samaria* (Samaria-Sebaste 1; London: Palestine Exploration Fund, 1942); R. de Vaux, *Ancient Israel: Its Life and Institutions* (New York/Toronto: McGraw-Hill, 1961) 1.72-74; A. Mazar, *Archaeology of the Land of the Bible: 10,000–586 B.C.E.* (ABRL; New York: Doubleday, 1992) 411-15.

[153] On ivory see n. 93 above. A. Parrot notes the reference in the Samarian ostraca to oil and wine as taxes to support the royal court; see A. Parrot, *Samaria, the Capital of the Kingdom of Israel* (SBA 7; trans. S. R. Hooke; London: SCM Press, 1958) 75; see also Rosenbaum, *Amos of Israel*, 56n23, 65. The ostraca themselves are published in G. A. Reisner, *Israelite Ostraca from Samaria* (Cambridge: Harvard University, 1924). For a discussion of the oil's quality see Stager, "The Finest Olive Oil," 241-45.

in the prophets (Jer 16:5 is at least 150 years later). At the same time, it predates possible allusions in Hosea and Isaiah by a few decades.[154]

## II. Amos 4:1

Having established the nature of the *marzēaḥ* at the time of Amos, and his attitude toward it, the next step is to evaluate possible *marzēaḥ* allusions elsewhere in the book. The preceding discussion of 6:1, 3-7 provides a basis for analyzing Amos 2:7b-8 and 4:1, supplemented by the criteria derived from the extra-biblical evidence.

I begin with Amos 4:1 because it is more closely related to Amos 6:1, 3-7 in terms of structure and content than Amos 2:7b-8. First of all, Amos 4:1-3 and 6:1-7 are clearly associated in the structural arrangement of the whole book. Rottzoll identifies a concentric "ring structure" by which an editor has organized the book's contents, within which 4:1-3 and 6:1(2)3-7 balance each other.[155] Secondly, their relative position in this editorial structure is probably based on their initial composition in light of each other. This can be seen from individual points of contact between the two passages. Both describe the elite oppressing the poor, mention drinking and refer to a divine mountain (Bashan[156] and Zion) followed by a parallel specification of the audience's location as "on Mount Samaria" (בְּהַר שֹׁמְרוֹן).[157] Also, both passages use participles to express the two groups' actions. The woe form requires them in 6:1, 3-6, but there is no such formal requirement in 4:1,[158] which suggests they are used in 4:1 purposely in order to emphasize the connection with 6:1, 3-

[154] See in Chapters 3 and 4.

[155] Rottzoll, *Studien*, 152; he presents a chart showing the concentric structure of the entire book on p. 3. Rottzoll builds upon the work of de Waard with respect to chapter 5 and Lust concerning 4:1-6:7; see J. de Waard, "The Chiastic Structure of Amos V:1-17," *VT* 27 (1977) 170-77; J. Lust, "Remarks on the Redaction of Amos V 4-6, 14-15," *OTS* 21 (1981) 129-54.

[156] See further on p. 116 below.

[157] The singular "mountain" sets these two instances apart from Amos 3:9, where the plural refers to the surrounding area (cf. n. 118), and the references to "Samaria" alone in 3:12 and 8:14.

[158] Nine examples of the Judgment Against the Nation form are presented in Westermann, *Basic Forms*, 174-75. One is Amos 4:1-2, and Mic 2:1-4 begins with הוֹי and is therefore more properly classified as a woe oracle. In five of the remaining seven, finite verbs dominate for the people's actions, with participles occurring only after other verb forms (see Hos 2:5-7; Isa 8:6-8; 30:12-14; Mic 3:1-2:4; Jer 5:10-14). The two exceptions are Mic 3:9-12 and Jer 7:16-18, 20; the latter is governed by a command for the prophet to observe their actions at that moment.

6. Finally, in both units the punishment is exile (Amos 4:2-3 and 6:7).[159]

Hans Barstad was the first person to suggest the *marzēaḥ* as the background for this verse. Beginning from the expectation that a prophet who addressed the same audience repeatedly would treat the same topic more than once, he notes "great similarities both with regard to form and content" between Amos 4:1 and 6:4-6.[160] These include wine, which he finds suggestive of a meal, oppression, which points to the upper class, and the religious connotations of the phrase, "cows of Bashan." The first step in evaluating his proposal is to establish the text of Amos 4:1; the verse is part of a slightly larger unit, but since only 4:1 figures in Barstad's proposed *marzēaḥ* allusion, the following discussion will focus on that verse.

## A. *The Text*

| | | |
|---|---|---|
| שִׁמְעוּ הַדָּבָר הַזֶּה | 1 | a Hear this word |
| פָּרוֹת הַבָּשָׁן | | b you cows of Bashan |
| אֲשֶׁר בְּהַר שֹׁמְרוֹן | | c who are on Mount Samaria, |
| הָעֹשְׁקוֹת דַּלִּים | | d oppressing the poor, |
| הָרֹצְצוֹת אֶבְיוֹנִים | | e crushing the needy, |
| הָאֹמְרֹת לַאֲדֹנֵיהֶם | | f saying to your[161] lords, |
| הָבִיאָה וְנִשְׁתֶּה | | g "Bring, so that we can drink!" |

The Hebrew text above duplicates the MT exactly. There are some translational difficulties, however, which must be addressed. To begin with, there is a significant lack of gender agreement in the verse. The opening verb is a masculine plural imperative, but is followed by a feminine plural substantive (1b) and three feminine plural participles (1d-f). Introduced by the article, these participles are vocatives,[162]

---

[159] With the exception of Hayes, *Amos*, 141, virtually all commentators take Amos 4:2-3 as describing exile, although they differ on the exact translation and interpretation of the admittedly difficult lines. For a recent review of the issues see Paul, *Amos*, 130-36; on the terminology in v. 2 see also Rottzoll, *Studien*, 146-50.

[160] Barstad, *Religious Polemics*, 42; Amos 4:1 is also associated with the *marzēaḥ* by Peckham, "Phoenicia," 83, 94n57. The two passages are linked, with varying degrees of detail but without specifying Amos 4:1 as a *marzēaḥ*, by, *inter alia*, Mays, *Amos*, 71; Wolff, *Joel and Amos*, 207; J.-L. Vesco, "Amos de Téqoa, défenseur de l'homme," *RB* 87 (1980) 496; Koch, *The Prophets I*, 47; Andersen and Freedman, *Amos*, 421; Bovati and Meynet, *Amos*, 127, 128. Amos 4:1-3 is placed immediately after 6:4-7 by Morgenstern, "Amos Studies IV," 311-12, 324.

[161] See n. 12.

[162] See n. 6.

continuing the direct address initiated in 1a. But the third participle is followed by an indirect object consisting of a plural noun with a masculine plural suffix (אֲדֹנֵיהֶם, literally "their lords"). All of this raises questions concerning the gender, and by extension the identity, of those addressed, as does the succession of two masculine and one feminine suffixes in the next verse. Many eliminate the problem by changing the masculine suffixes to the feminine,[163] but without any text-critical or versional support. A second approach relates the masculine suffix in line f to the plural masculine nouns in lines d and e, yielding a reference to the "lords" of the "poor" and the "needy."[164] But while possible, this does not account for the masculine imperative at the beginning of the verse. A fairly straightforward solution is at hand, however, with the recognition of some peculiarities of grammar and syntax in biblical Hebrew. The masculine imperative addressing females can be explained on three principles: the tendency to avoid 2nd person plural feminine verbs,[165] the preference for a masculine verb in the initial position of a sentence,[166] and the use of masculine imperatives elsewhere to address females.[167] This leaves the masculine pronominal suffix in 1f, which can also be explained by the substitution of a masculine pronoun where a feminine one is expected.[168] Moreover, since it refers to the vocative participles, the pronoun continues the direct address and should be translated as "your."[169] Thus, the grammatical irregularities can be explained in such a way that females in a relationship with the "lords" of 1f are addressed throughout.

---

[163] E.g., M. Löhr, *Untersuchungen zum Buch Amos* (BZAW 4; Giessen: J. Ricker, 1901) 9, 13; Marti, *Dodekapropheton*, 179; Nowack, *Propheten*, 133; Weiser, *Propheten*, 156; Morgenstern, "Amos Studies IV," 324; Wellhausen, *Propheten*, 78; T. H. Robinson and F. Horst, *Die zwölf Kleinen Propheten* (HAT 1; Tübingen: J. C. B. Mohr, 1964) 14, 84.

[164] Bič, *Amos*, 85; Fleischer, *Von Menschen verkaüfern*, 82; Rottzoll, *Studien*, 144. Fleischer points out that the "lords" could still be in a relationship with the women, but that the emphasis is on the former's connection with the "poor" and "needy."

[165] R. J. Williams, *Hebrew Syntax*, §234. Cf. Ruth 1:8; Joel 2:22.

[166] GKC §145o-p; Waltke and O'Connor, *Biblical Hebrew Syntax*, §6.6c and the biblical texts cited by both.

[167] GKC §110k; cf. Judg 4:20; Isa 23:1; Mic 1:13; Zech 13:7.

[168] GKC §135o; cf., e.g., Gen 31:9; 32:16; 41:23, etc. The principle applies to the masculine suffixes in v. 2 as well. Contrast Andersen and Freedman, *Amos*, 421, who suggest that the mixture of gender references there is complementary, indicating that both halves of the population are addressed.

[169] See n. 12.

Line g contains another grammatical anomaly: the plural "lords" are addressed with a singular imperative. Some consider "lords" a plural of majesty referring to the king[170] or a single deity,[171] but the command for them to bring something for the women to drink argues for a less exalted status. The LXX, Syriac and Vulgate all render the imperative as plural, but modern commentators tend to take it as distributive, indicating the address of each female to her "lord."[172]

Although אָדוֹן here is commonly translated as "husband," the usual word is בַּעַל.[173] The use of אָדוֹן suggests some special significance for the word in this verse. In addition to the plural of majesty, mentioned above, foreigners,[174] the owners of concubines[175] and a plurality of pagan deities[176] have all been proposed. The first proposal is linked to Bič's view that the women are engaged in cultic prostitution during a Canaanite New Year's celebration, but there is no evidence that cultic prostitution was ever practiced in ancient Israel.[177] As for the last proposal, the subsequent command is as inappropriate directed to many gods as to one. This might also be the case for concubines addressing their paramours, although for my purpose the distinction between them and actual wives is minimal. Nonetheless, in light of the parallels between 4:1-3 and 6:1, 3-7,[178] where males are addressed with masculine plural participles, it is likely the females in 4:1 are the social equals of the "lords." In that case, the unusual term for "husband" may be intended to enhance the contrast with their true Lord, Yahweh, who speaks in v. 2,[179] or just to highlight their elite status.

---

[170] Harper, *Amos and Hosea*, 88; contrast his p. 86.

[171] Neher, *Amos*, 83, says it is Baʿal; Andersen and Freedman, *Amos*, 422, indicate it could refer to either Baʿal or Yahweh.

[172] E.g., Morgenstern, "Amos Studies IV," 324; Wolff, *Joel and Amos*, 203; Paul, *Amos*, 129; Wood, "Amos," 61n34. Cf. "each woman straight ahead" in v. 3 (Wood, p. 64).

[173] The only clear instance of אָדוֹן meaning "husband" is Gen 18:12.

[174] Bič, *Amos*, 85.

[175] G. J. Botterweck, "'Sie verkaufen den Unschuldigen um Geld.' Zur sozialen Kritik des Propheten Amos," *BibLeb* 12 (1971) 221, 222. Cf. Judg 19:26.

[176] J. D. W. Watts, "A Critical Analysis of Amos 4:1ff," *Society of Biblical Literature Annual Meeting Proceedings 2* (Missoula: Scholars Press, 1972) 496; Barstad, *Religious Polemics*, 41, 47.

[177] See the discussions of Barstad, *Religious Polemics*, 26-33; K. van der Toorn, "Prostitution [Heb *Zenût, Zenûnîm, Taznût*]: Cultic Prostitution," *ABD* 5.510-13, and the literature van der Toorn cites.

[178] See p. 109.

[179] Thus Bič, *Amos*, 86; Barstad, *Religious Polemics*, 41; Paul, *Amos*, 129.

## B. *Establishing the Unit*

One proposed deletion from Amos 4:1 must be considered. John D. W. Watts challenged the authenticity of lines c-e in v. 1, arguing that the original oracle consisted only of an address to "cows of Bashan, saying to their lords, // 'Come, let us drink.'"[180] This would remove the reference to "Mount Samaria" and the oppression of the poor as an indication of the social status of those being addressed. Since both indicate a connection between Amos 4:1 and 6:1, 3-7, and the addressees' elite status is a constitutive element of the *marzēaḥ*, Watts' proposal requires a response.

Watts deletes line c on the grounds that a Samaria speech is out of place between two Bethel speeches.[181] This argument depends upon the final form of the book of Amos for its relevance, but that form is the result of editorial arrangement; Amos 4:1 was not given its present location because it shared a common audience with the surrounding passages.[182] Watts also drops lines d and e as a later reinterpretation in terms of social justice. He notes that the verb עָשַׁק ("oppress") is not found elsewhere in Amos, while רָצַץ ("crush") only occurs at Amos 3:9 but is characteristic of later literature, and he claims, "The entire phrase is more stereotyped than the colorful language Amos usually employs to support attacks on privileged injustice."[183] But not only does this statement recognize that social justice is central to Amos' pronouncements, but Watts also notes that the terms דַּלִּים ("poor") and אֶבְיוֹנִים ("needy") occur together elsewhere in Amos' authentic speeches,[184] always in the context of such oppression by the elite. At the same time, while any characterization of a passage's "tenor" is necessarily subjective, I find the startling bovine metaphor with which the passage begins, as well as the sense of ongoing[185] and immediate action conveyed by the participial forms of the verbs to be "colourful." All of this argues in favour of the lines' authenticity, and suggests the common pairing of "oppress" and "crush" in later literature[186] may be dependent upon first being linked by Amos here.

[180] Watts, "Amos 4:1ff," 494.
[181] Watts, "Amos 4:1ff," 493. Bethel is named in Amos 3:14 and 4:4.
[182] See p. 109 above; cf. p. 118 below concerning Barstad.
[183] Watts, "Amos 4:1ff," 493-94.
[184] Watts, "Amos 4:1ff," 493. The terms occur together in Amos 2:6-7; 5:11-12 and 8:6; the latter is also found alone in Amos 8:4.
[185] Paul, *Amos*, 129.
[186] See the references in Watts, "Amos 4:1ff," 494n16.

## C. *Discussion*

Having established the textual integrity of Amos 4:1, it remains to consider whether it alludes to the *marzēaḥ*. As noted earlier, Barstad suggested it did on the basis of similarities with Amos 6:4-6, including wine, upper-class oppression of the poor and a religious context in both passages. These three points roughly correspond to the three consistent elements of a *marzēaḥ* established in Chapter 1.

Barstad finds a religious context for the verse in the phrase "cows of Bashan," which he considers an allusion to involvement with the Baʿal cult. He appeals to the use of פָּרָה ("cow") in Hos 4:16 and Jer 2:24 for Israelites worshipping other gods,[187] and notes the cow's mythological connections with fertility in the ancient near East.[188] Barstad's understanding of the phrase does not survive scrutiny, however. The general lack of polemic against other gods in Amos has already been noted,[189] and the same observation applies to this verse in particular. Secondly, in Hos 4:16 it is the adjective "stubborn" (סֹרֵרָה) that points to worship of other gods, not the noun פָּרָה.[190] Moreover, the adjective is absent from Jer 2:24, and the idea of rebelliousness is only present there if פֶּרֶא ("wild ass") is read.[191] In other words, the word "cow" is only connected with apostasy or syncretism in Hos 4:16, and there that connotation is conveyed by the adjective modifying the noun, not the noun itself. This does not justify a negative connotation to the phrase "cows of Bashan" in Amos 4:1. As for the mythological associations of cows, all of Barstad's examples deal with either a goddess represented by a cow (Hathor, Isis, Anat) or a god (Sîn, Baʿal, the Hurrian sun god) mating with one. But even if these divine associations can be legitimately applied to humans who are described metaphorically, nothing indicates that the

---

[187] Barstad, *Religious Polemics*, 43. In an earlier article he linked Amos 4:1 with cultic prostitution as part of the Baʿal cult, rather than a Baʿalistic *marzēaḥ*; see H. M. Barstad, "Die Basankühe in Amos 4:1," *VT* 25 (1975) 295. This verse had already been associated with the worship of Baʿal, but not the *marzēaḥ*, by Neher, *Amos*, 82-85; Vuilleumier-Bessard, *La Tradition Cultuelle*, 43; Bič, *Amos*, 82-84; Watts, "Amos 4:1ff," 496, 498.

[188] Barstad, *Religious Polemics*, 44-47.

[189] See pp. 105-06 above.

[190] Cf. the discussion of Hos 4:16-19 in Chapter 3.

[191] This alternative reading fits the context better, and is reflected in the vocalization as פֶּרֶה in the Leningrad Codex (*BHS*). It is also the reading of many Hebrew manuscripts, the Vulgate, Syriac, Targum, most English translations and the commentators.

prophet would have understood them negatively. Cultic issues do not appear in either the accusation (1d-g)[192] or the following announcement of punishment (vv. 2-3).

But despite the inadequacies of Barstad's interpretation, the phrase "cows of Bashan" does have religious connotations. Klaus Koch suggests the women, "imagined themselves to be the worshipers of the mighty bull of Samaria (Hos. 8.5f), a North Israelite manifestation of Yahweh."[193] Jacobs supports this by appealing to the Kuntillet ʿAjrûd inscription mentioning "Yahweh of Samaria and his *ʾšrh*" above two bovine figures.[194] This is suggestive, but since it is not certain that the inscription and the drawings are connected, inconclusive.[195] More probative is Yahweh's identification with El, including his assumption of El's bull imagery.[196] As a result, female wor-

---

[192] The erroneous interpretation of "their Lords" in 1f as a reference to foreign deities was dealt with above; see p. 112. On the form of Amos 4:1-3 see n. 206.

[193] Koch, *The Prophets I*, 46.

[194] P. E. Jacobs, "'Cows of Bashan'—A Note on the Interpretation of Amos 4:1," *JBL* 104 (1985) 109-110.

[195] On the Kuntillet ʿAjrûd texts, including the relationship between the inscription and the pictures as well as the proper understanding of the final word, see Z. Meshel, "Kuntillet ʿAjrud (M.R. 094954)," *ABD* 4.103-09; to the literature on Asherah cited there add: R. J. Pettey, *Asherah, Goddess of Israel* (American University Studies, Series 7: Theology and Religion 74; Frankfurt am Main/Bern/New York: Peter Lang, 1990); M. Dietrich and O. Loretz, *"Jahwe und seine Aschera": Anthropomorphes Kultbild in Mesopotamien, Ugarit und Israels: Das biblische Bilderverbot* (UBL; Ugarit-Verlag, 1992); S. A. Wiggins, *A Reassessment of "Asherah": A Study According to the Textual Sources of the First Two Millennia B.C.E.* (AOAT 235; Kevelaer: Verlag Butzon und Bercker; Neukirchen-Vluyn: Neukirchener Verlag, 1993); J. M. Hadley, "Yahweh and 'His Asherah': Archaeological and Textual Evidence for the Cult of the Goddess," *Ein Gott allein? JHWH-Verehrung und biblisher Monotheismus im Kontext der israelitischen und altorientalischen Religionsgeschichte* (OBO 139; eds. W. Dietrich and M. A. Klopfenstein; Göttingen: Vandenhoeck & Ruprecht; Freiburg: Universitätsverlag, 1994) 235-68; C. Frevel, *Aschera und der Ausschließlichkeitsanspruch YHWHs: Beiträge zu literarischen, religionsgeschichtlichen und ikonographischen Aspekten der Ascheradiskussion* (BBB 94; Weinheim: Beltz Athenäum, 1995); T. Binger, *Asherah: Goddess in Ugarit, Israel and the Old Testament* (JSOTSup 232; Sheffield: Sheffield Academic Press, 1997); J. A. Emerton, "'Yahweh and His Asherah': The Goddess or Her Symbol," *VT* 49 (1999) 315-37; J. Jeremias and F. Hartenstein, "'JHWH und seine Aschera,' 'Offizielle Religion,' und 'Volksreligion' zur Zeit der klassischen Propheten," *Religionsgeschichte Israels: Formale und materiale Aspekte* (VWGT 15; eds. B. Janowski and M. Köckert; Gütersloh: Christopher Kaiser Verlag/Gütersloher Verlagshaus, 1999) 79-138.

[196] See especially *CAT* 1.14.IV.168-69, where the human king Keret sacrifices to "Bull, his father El (*ṯr . abh . il*)"; see also "the bull (MT אֲבִיר) of Jacob" in Gen 49:24; Isa 49:26; 60:16; Ps 132:2, 5 (cf. Isa 1:24); cf. Jeroboam I's return to bull iconography at Dan and Bethel rather than the cherubim of the Jerusalem temple, on which see, conveniently, W. I. Toews, *Monarchy and Religious Institution*

shipers of Bull Yahweh could be considered "cows."

This religious interpretation of the "cows" is supported by religious associations for Bashan itself. In Ps 68:17, the "mountain of Bashan" is rebuked for its envy over Yahweh's chosen dwelling place, presumably Zion/Jerusalem. The reference to the *mountain* of Bashan, a region better known for its flat pasture land, is unique in the First Testament, and in the poem's mythological context suggests a connection with the mountain of the gods.[197] In light of this, its designation in the Psalm as הַר־אֱלֹהִים (v. 16; note the *maqqîp*) should be translated literally as "mountain of (the) gods" (cf. the *NJB*'s "A mountain of God"), rather than the *NRSV*'s "mighty mountain." As a result, both substantives in the phrase "the cows of Bashan" have religious connections, which establishes a necessary component of the *marzēaḥ* in v. 1.

The phrase also provides evidence of the upper-class status of the addressees. The feminine "cows," along with the subsequent feminine participles, indicate they are women, and in light of Bashan's reputation for fertile fields and sleek, well-fed cattle, most take them to be the upper-class ladies of the northern capital, Samaria.[198] There are only two dissenting opinions. A few suggest men are addressed as females in order to denigrate them,[199] but apart from whether or not the subtlety involved would be lost on Amos' audience, if that were the intention the feminine form should have been maintained throughout this and the next verse, even at the expense of violating the grammatical tendencies in the other direction noted earlier.

The second contrary proposal comes from Barstad, who views the phrase, "as including *all* inhabitants of the northern capital, rather

*in Israel Under Jeroboam I* (SBLMS 47; Atlanta: Scholars Press, 1993). The Masoretic pointing of אָבִיר without a *dagesh* in the second letter may reflect a later attempt to divorce the title from the bull imagery of the Northern Israelite cult and possible confusion with that of Baʿal.

[197] Cf. Ps 68:23 and the discussion of this Psalm in Barstad, *Religious Polemics*, 38.

[198] Whether it was meant as a compliment or an insult is tangential to my concerns, although the overwhelming majority consider it to be the former. On Bashan itself see J. C. Slayton, "Bashan (PLACE) [Heb *Bāshān*]," *ABD* 1.623-624. Salomon Speier sees a double-entendre ("ein üppig gebautes Mädchen") here on the basis of the Arabic *baṯne/baṯane*; see S. Speier, "Bermerkungen zu Amos," *VT* 3 (1953) 306-07, followed by Botterweck, "'Sie Verkaufen,'" 22.

[199] E.g., Neher, *Amos*, 82; Watts, "Amos 4:1ff," 496; Bovati and Meynet, *Amos*, 124, 128. Andersen and Freedman can't seem to decide if this is the point, but eventually indicate it is; cf. *Amos*, 416, 417 and 421. On p. 420 they suggest the issue may be women acting like men.

than referring to some separate group among them."[200] He supports this with five arguments: (1) the other biblical references to Bashan do not support taking Amos 4:1 as a "simile" [*sic*] for the looks or status of the Samarian female elite, (2) there are no biblical or ancient near-eastern parallels where women are compared with cows, (3) the rest of chapter 4 deals with the entire nation, (4) as do the surrounding chapters and (5) Amos 3:1; 4:1 and 5:1 all begin with "hear this word," and since 3:1 and 5:1 are addressed to the nation as a whole, then 4:1 should also be taken as an inclusive, gender-neutral address.[201]

A number of points can be made against Barstad's interpretation of the phrase. On a general level, it is at odds with his own view that the oppression of the poor and needy indicates that the addressees in Amos 4:1 are the elite.[202] His inclusive understanding of "the cows of Bashan" leads to the improbable conclusion that only the elite lived in the city. But more specifically, Barstad's individual arguments are not convincing. First, he himself acknowledges that 1b plays upon Bashan's status as "desirable,"[203] in which case Bashan does provide the basis for a metaphor conveying beauty and quality. Secondly, while it is true women are not compared to cows elsewhere, animal names were commonly used to refer to important members of society.[204] Bashan's bulls in particular were considered superior,[205] but to call the women "bulls" would suggest males, especially in light of the opening masculine imperative. As the female counterpart, "cows" would be more appropriate for the leading women of Samaria. Third, Amos 4:1-3 constitutes a self-contained unit separate from the rest of the chapter,[206] which owes its position to a later editor. Similarly, in his last two points Barstad improperly determines the addressees from the editorial arrangement

[200] Barstad, *Religious Polemics*, 40 (italics in the original).

[201] Ibid., 38-41.

[202] Ibid., 42.

[203] Ibid., 39.

[204] P. D. Miller, Jr., "Animal Names as Designations in Ugaritic and Hebrew," *UF* 2 (1970) 177-86.

[205] See Ezek 39:18; Ps 22:12; cf. Deut 32:14.

[206] Amos 4:1-3 is a classic example of the Judgment Against the Nation Speech (on the form in general see Westermann, *Basic Forms*, 169-76; for this passage see his p. 174). Verse 1 constitutes the call for attention (1a-c) and the accusation (1d-g), while vv. 2-3 contain the announcement of judgment. Amos 4:3 ends with "utterance of Yahweh," while v. 4 initiates a call to worship, setting what follows apart from 4:1-3 both formally and in terms of content.

of the prophet's sayings, which was done on grounds other than identical audiences.[207] Moreover, the introductions in 3:1 and 5:1 are not identical. The first addresses "*the people* of Israel" while the second is aimed at "*the house* of Israel," and the source of "this word" is different in each: Amos 3:1 says "which the Lord has spoken against you" while 5:1 has "which I have raised against you." In fact, these two similar but distinct formulas may have introduced independent sections at one point in the compositional history of the book.[208] Furthermore, unlike 3:1 and 5:1, in Amos 4:1 the source of "this word" is not indicated. As such, it has more in common with 6:1, with its initial cry of הוי followed immediately by the identification of a specific subset of the nation, also in the capital Samaria, than with the other two calls to "hear this word." Therefore, rather than the uniform addressees Barstad claims for chapters 3-5, the initial verses in each of chapters 3-6 alternate between a general and a specific audience. As part of this alteration, in Amos 4:1 certain women in the capital are called "cows of Bashan." The metaphor suggests quality and even superiority, which points to the female elite as the prophet's intended audience. Their social status is confirmed by their equality with the "lords"[209] and their ability to oppress the poor and crush the needy, while their gender is reinforced by the link with Amos 6. In short, Amos 4:1(-3) and 6:1, 3-7 are two sides of the same coin, describing the actions of the leading women and men of Samaria during a single banquet.[210]

The third constitutive element of the *marzēaḥ* is the consumption of large amounts of alcohol, often culminating in drunkenness. Barstad points to "the importance of the wine" in Amos 4:1,[211] but 1g doesn't actually mention wine, only drinking. However, this might be explained by the demands of the animal metaphor[212] as well as the need for poetic balance in terms of line length. The connections between 4:1-3 and 6:1, 3-7[213] suggest that is the case: since the same scene is described in both passages, the reference to drinking in 4:1g

---

[207] See p. 109 above.

[208] Jeremias, "Amos 3–6," 217-29.

[209] See p. 112 above.

[210] Rottzoll, *Studien*, 3, titles the two passages, "Gegen die Frauen Samarias" and "Gegen die Männer Samarias" respectively.

[211] Barstad, *Religious Polemics*, 42.

[212] I.e., cows don't normally drink wine; see Bovati and Meynet, *Amos*, 129.

[213] Again, see p. 109.

probably involves wine, as in Amos 6:6a. However, wine would have been part of most upper-class meals, so if Amos 4:1 reflects a *marzēaḥ*, there should be some indication that wine was consumed in large amounts. The use of participles suggest it was: the three feminine participles convey ongoing action, such that in 1f the women address their husbands more than once.[214] Thus, the command for their husbands to "bring, so that we can drink," was uttered, and presumably obeyed, a number of times during this banquet. Therefore, significant amounts were probably drunk, just as in Amos 6:6a. This probability is reinforced by the fact that only drinking is mentioned in 4:1g, but not the banquet where the drinking occurred,[215] thereby emphasizing the drinking aspect. Moreover, since this passage deals with the female participants in the *marzēaḥ* described in Amos 6:4-6, they may well have become as intoxicated as the "sprawlers" in Amos 6:4.

To summarize, the essential elements of a *marzēaḥ* are present in Amos 4:1, either explicitly or as illuminated by its companion piece in Amos 6, even if not in the way Barstad envisions. Amos 4:1 alludes to a religious celebration by the Samarian elite which included the consumption of large amounts of wine, probably to the point of drunkenness. The prophet does not call it a *marzēaḥ* because that is not his primary concern. Instead, he focuses on the injustice described in 4:1d-e which, as in Amos 6:3-6, created the economic conditions that gave them the luxury to participate in a *marzēaḥ* in the first place.

## D. *Dating the Text*

The relative date of Amos 4:1 is linked to that of its companion piece, Amos 6:1, 3-7, and requires little additional justification. As with the latter text, the allusion in Amos 4:1 to upper-class exploitation of the lower class in order to enjoy a luxurious lifestyle is consistent with the traditional date of the prophet Amos. Thus, this passage probably dates to ca. 760 BCE as well, which would also place it earlier than those to be considered in the following chapters.

[214] Paul, *Amos*, 129, calls them "nagging."

[215] Fosbroke, "Amos," 801, points out that the very word "feast" (מִשְׁתֶּה) is derived from the verb used here. Similarly, Harper, *Amos and Hosea*, 86, indicates the women's activity would have included eating as well as drinking.

## III. Amos 2:7c-8

The main proponent of the *marzēaḥ* in these verses is Hans Barstad once again, who notes similar content here and in Amos 4:1; 6:1, 3-7, and argues that the "girl" in 7c is a *marzēaḥ* hostess.[216] In order to evaluate his understanding of its content, the text itself must first be established. As with Amos 4:1, since Barstad only deals with Amos 2:7c-8 as a *marzēaḥ* allusion, the following discussion concentrates on those lines, but without ignoring the surrounding context.

### A. *The Text*

| | | | |
|---|---|---|---|
| וְאִישׁ וְאָבִיו יֵלְכוּ אֶל־הַנַּעֲרָה[217] | 7 | c | a man and his father "go to" the girl, |
| לְמַעַן חַלֵּל אֶת־שֵׁם קָדְשִׁי | | d | so that my holy name is profaned;[219] |
| וּבְגָדִים[218] חֲבֻלִים יַטּוּ | 8 | a | they stretch out seized garments[220] |
| אֵצֶל כָּל־מִזְבֵּחַ | | b | beside every altar,[221] |

---

[216] Barstad, *Religious Polemics*, 11-36, especially pp. 34-36. He is followed by Polley, *Amos and the Davidic Empire*, 89-90. The passage has also been connected with Amos 4:1 and/or 6:1, 3-7, primarily because of the shared reference to wine, but without necessarily linking it to a *marzēaḥ*, by Vuilleumier-Bessard, *La tradition cultuelle*, 44; Lang, *Monotheism*, 122; Wolff, *Joel and Amos*, 168; G. V. Smith, *Amos*, 86.

[217] Harper, *Amos and Hosea*, 51, 53, alters הַנַּעֲרָה to הַנֹּעָדָה and translates the line as, "a man and his judge deal according to the agreement," indicating the corruption of justice through bribery; a similar understanding of אָב (literally, "father") is suggested by Bovati and Meynet, *Amos*, 77. But this interpretation of אָב is not supported by the biblical texts Harper cites on p. 53: 2 Kgs 6:21 and 13:14 are addressed to Elisha as a spiritual father, Jer 17:10 is irrelevant and Gen 45:8 involves a high government official, not an ordinary judge (cf. Isa 22:20). Further, his appeal to the verbs הָלַךְ and יָעַד together in Amos 3:3 is beside the point, since they have no juridical significance there. The sexual connotations of יֵלְכוּ אֶל in this line (see n. 244) also argue against his emendation.

[218] Deleting (וְ)עַל־ at the beginning of the line with the LXX; see further below.

[219] This line is rejected as a priestly addition referring to cultic matters rather than social justice by Morgenstern, "Amos Studies IV," 315; Fendler, "Sozialkritik," 42n30; Fleischer, *Von Menschen verkaüfern*, 79; Rottzoll, *Studien*, 64-65. See, however, p. 122 below.

[220] Perhaps as an offering of some sort, or to display what they have seized.

[221] The references to cultic sites here and in 8d are deleted as additions that do not fit the context by Marti, *Dodekapropheton*, 168; Duhm, "Amos," 3; Würthwein, "Amos-Studien," 45n72; Fendler, "Sozialkritik," 35n6; Wolff, *Joel and Amos*, 134; Coote, *Amos Among the Prophets*, 71-72; Fleischer, *Von Menschen verkaüfern*, 43-44. But the interconnection of justice and proper worship builds upon 7d, and occurs elsewhere in Amos' prophecies (see Amos 4:4-5; 5:21-24, the previously examined *marzēaḥ* texts [4:1 and 6:1,3-7] and the expansion of 2:6-7 in 8:4-6). As such, the phrases are entirely appropriate here.

| | | |
|---|---|---|
| וְיֵין עֲנוּשִׁים יִשְׁתּוּ | c | and they drink exacted wine |
| בֵּית אֱלֹהֵיהֶם | d | in the house of their God.[222] |

The only divergence from the MT is the deletion of the preposition עַל at the beginning of 8a. The verbal form יַטּוּ at the end of the line is an *hiphil* of נָטָה; since the latter is always used transitively elsewhere, the preposition is anomalous. Some solve the problem by treating the verb as a reflexive,[223] others consider עַל here a conjunction meaning "because"[224] and many simply delete it.[225] The unlikelihood that the upper class would recline on the inferior garments of the poor[226] argues against the first suggestion. The second two yield the same sense, i.e., that they "spread out the garments" rather than lay themselves upon them, but the preposition is deleted by the LXX, producing a more balanced length in comparison with the parallel in 8c.

### B. *Establishing the Unit*

This passage is part of the Oracle against Israel in Amos 2:6-16,[227] in which vv. 6-8 comprise the initial accusation against Israel. However, Barstad separates vv. 6-7b and 7c-8 because of a perceived transition from social justice to religious polemics; this is based on his view that the phrase "to profane my holy name" in 7d is primarily cultic and refers only to 7c.[228] Yet 6-7b and 7c-8 are lexically linked by the repetition of יַטּוּ in 7b and 8a, which suggests the content of the two sections may be more closely connected than Barstad thinks.

---

[222] For the translation of אֱלֹהִים as a singular see n. 242.

[223] M. J. Dahood, "'To Pawn One's Cloak'," *Bib* 42 (1961) 364; Paul, *Amos*, 86.

[224] Harper, *Amos and Hosea*, 52; Andersen and Freedman, *Amos*, 319.

[225] Löhr, *Untersuchungen*, 6; E. Baumann, *Der Aufbau der Amosreden* (BZAW 7; Giessen: J. Ricker, 1903) 32; Marti, *Dodekapropheton*, 168; Nowack, *Propheten*, 127; Weiser, *Amos*, 92; Morgenstern, "Amos Studies IV," 316; Wolff, *Joel and Amos*, 134.

[226] Dahood, "'To Pawn One's Cloak,'" 364; Fendler, "Sozialkritik," 36; Andersen and Freedman, *Amos*, 320.

[227] It concludes the Oracles Against the Nations in Amos 1-2. For a recent survey of the form's history see Paul, *Amos*, 7-11, and the references cited there. On the oracles in Amos see especially J. Barton, *Amos' Oracles Against the Nations: A Study of Amos 1:3–2:5* (SOTSMS 6; Cambridge: Cambridge University Press, 1980).

[228] See Barstad, *Religious Polemics*, 16 and 19-21. In contrast, the phrase is linked to all of vv. 6-7 by Rudolph, *Joel–Amos*, 143; Paul, *Amos*, 83.

Since his cultic interpretation of 7c as referring to a *marzēaḥ* hostess is part of his identification of vv. 7c-8 as a *marzēaḥ* allusion, it will be considered in detail below. For now, I will only note that his view of "so that my holy name is profaned" is too restrictive. The phrase occurs in connection with social justice in Jer 34:16, when the Jerusalemites revoke the liberation of their slaves after a siege is lifted.[229] Although that text is later than Amos 2:7, it is roughly contemporary with, or perhaps a bit earlier than, the cultic uses in Ezekiel and Leviticus. The nuance of justice in Jer 34:16, contrary to the contemporary cultic one, suggests a precedence such as this Amos text.[230] In the context of the Oracle Against Israel, the actions described in Amos 2:6-7 are violations of covenantal bonds rooted in God's involvement in their history (vv. 9-13). As such, the exploitation of the poor and needy, who enjoy special protection from God, constitutes a rejection of the divine plan for their society, which could be considered a profanation of God's holy name.[231] Moreover, although v. 8 includes cultic references ("beside every altar" and "in the house of their God"), they are linked to exploitation, specifically, "seized garments" and "exacted wine."[232]

To summarize, the theme of social justice predominates throughout Amos 2:6-8 as the primary focus of the prophet's critique.[233] As such, vv. 7c-8 should not be interpreted in isolation from vv. 6-7b. But when the two sections are linked, Barstad's proposed *marzēaḥ* allusion in Amos 2:7c-8 appears uncertain.

## C. *Discussion*

Barstad's identification of a *marzēaḥ* allusion in Amos 2:7c-8 is based on two factors. First, he notes the combination of the upper class oppressing the poor and drinking wine at a religious feast, elements also found in the other two *marzēaḥ* texts in Amos (4:1 and 6:1, 3-

---

[229] See also Lev 19:20 where it is used of false oaths sworn in Yahweh's name.

[230] Cf. H. Gese, "Komposition bei Amos," *Congress Volume: Vienna* (VTSup 32; ed. J. Emerton; Leiden: E. J. Brill, 1981) 92n55.

[231] See further Harper, *Amos and Hosea*, 51; M. A. Beek, "The Religious Background of Amos ii 6-8," *OTS* 5 (1948) 137; Würthwein, "Amos-Studien," 45; Rudolph, *Joel–Amos*, 143-44; Paul, *Amos*, 83; W. Dommershausen, חלל *ḥll* I; חֹל *chōl*; חָלִיל *chālîl*, *TDOT* 4.410-12. Cf. Lev 22:32 where the phrase is linked to breaking God's commandments.

[232] See further on pp. 125-26 below.

[233] Cf. Beek, "Religious Background," 136-37.

7).[234] Second, he identifies the "girl" in 7c as a *marzēaḥ* hostess.[235] Upper-class drinking in a religious context approximates the basic elements of a *marzēaḥ*, but his second point has not yet been encountered in this study. As such it requires more substantial consideration, and I will consider it first.

Barstad's characterization of the female in Amos 2:7c as a *marzēaḥ* hostess is predicated on eliminating the usual proposals concerning her identity.[236] After surveying the usage of נַעֲרָה, Barstad identifies three nuances beyond its basic meaning of a young female: a virgin, a young married woman and a servant girl. Then, since he considers "a man and his father" a general description indicating a common occurrence[237] and thinks that ongoing violation of contemporary sexual mores concerning the first two types of females would not have been tolerated by Israelite society, he concludes the "girl" must be a servant. But since he only finds biblical opposition to sex with a servant if the servant belongs to someone else, he concludes the line is not concerned with a moral infraction. He finds confirmation for this in 7d, which according to his survey is used primarily in cultic contexts, and frequently in connection with non-Yahwistic cults and/or deities. He rules out a reference to cultic prostitution[238] on two grounds: the lack of evidence for such an in-

---

234 Barstad, *Religious Polemics*, 34-35.

235 Ibid., 35-36.

236 For the details of this paragraph, with supporting textual references, see Barstad, *Religious Polemics*, 17-36, especially pp. 17-21 and 33-36.

237 The phrase had already been placed on a par with going to a movie by N. H. Snaith, *Amos, Hosea and Micah* (Epworth Preacher's Commentaries; London: The Epworth Press, 1956) 19. איש is taken as distributive by Andersen and Freedman, *Amos*, 318; Bovati and Meynet, *Amos*, 76. Anderson and Freedman also consider the addition of "his father" as expressing distribution in time, such that the action had been going on for some time, as does Paul, *Amos*, 82.

238 *Contra* Driver, *Joel and Amos*, 153; E. A. Edghill, *The Book of Amos, with Notes* (Westminster Commentaries; 2nd ed.; ed. and introd. by G. A. Cooke; London: Methuen & Co. Ltd., 1926) 22; Weiser, *Amos*, 91-93; N. H. Snaith, *The Book of Amos* (London: The Epworth Press, 1945-46) 19; Weiser, *Propheten*, 141-42; Neher, *Amos*, 55, 76; T. H. Robinson, *Prophecy and the Prophets in Ancient Israel* (3rd ed.; London: Duckworth, 1953) 65; Cripps, *Amos*, 142; H.-J. Kraus, "Die prophetische Botschaft gegen das sociale Unrecht Israels," *EvT* 15 (1955) 298; Fosbroke, "Amos," 787; Dahood, "'To Pawn One's Cloak,'" 365; Wellhausen, *Propheten*, 72-73; Bič, *Amos*, 57; Ward, *Amos and Isaiah*, 135-37; Thorogood, *Amos*, 23; Soggin, *The Prophet Amos*, 87; King, *Amos, Hosea, Micah*, 101. Against them it should be noted that neither the word for a secular prostitute (זֹנָה) nor a so-called cultic prostitute (קְדֵשָׁה) is used here (Fosbroke explains the absence of the latter as an attempt to strip the prostitution of any religious significance).

stitution in ancient Israel[239] and his view that יֵלְכוּ אֶל in Amos 2:7c does not refer to sexual activity.[240] As a result, the men's involvement with the woman must be non-sexual cultic activity, which, when linked with the other elements in v. 8 suggests a *marzēaḥ*. So Barstad hypothesizes that she is the hostess at such an event.[241]

However, a female *marzēaḥ* hostess is unattested for the *marzēaḥ* elsewhere. The closest parallel would be the *marzēaḥ* leader (*rb mrzḥ*) mentioned at Ugarit, Nabatea and Palmyra, but in the extant references that position is always held by a male. Amos 2:7c *might* indicate an otherwise unknown aspect of the *marzēaḥ*, or even an innovation originating around the time of Amos, although the complete silence on the matter elsewhere would require some explanation. On the other hand, problems with much of Barstad's argument call his conclusion into question.

In the first place, he thinks the prophet objects to a *marzēaḥ* here because it is a Canaanite, non-Yahwistic feast.[242] But non-Yahwistic polemics are not characteristic of Amos, and there is no indication he considered the *marzēaḥ* itself incompatible with Yahweh.[243] Secondly, Barstad's rejection of any sexual connotation for the phrase יֵלְכוּ אֶל in Amos 2:7c must now be reconsidered in light of Akkadian and Aramaic examples where the cognate expressions mean exactly that.[244] Since Barstad is correct in his assessment of cultic pros-

---

[239] Cf. n. 177 above.

[240] Contrast n. 244 below.

[241] Barstad, *Religious Polemics*, 35-36. He is followed by Bohlen, "Sozialkritik," 287. Coote, *Amos Among the Prophets*, 35-36, suggests she is an alewife who functions as a pawnbroker and also links the passage to the *marzēaḥ*; he is followed with respect to her occupation, but without explicitly connecting this to the *marzēaḥ*, by M. Silver, *Prophets and Markets: The Political Economy of Ancient Israel* (Social Dimensions of Economics; Boston/The Hague/London: Kluwer-Nijhoff Publishing, 1983) 66; Jaruzelska, "Social Structure," 96.

[242] Barstad, *Religious Polemics*, 35, 36; cf. his p. 15n18. This in keeping with the thrust of his entire monograph. אֱלֹהֵיהֶם in 8d is also translated "their gods" in reference to foreign deities by Harper, *Amos and Hosea*, 50; Edghill, *Amos*, 22; Neher, *Amos*, 55; Hammershaimb, *Amos*, 49; Polley, *Amos and the Davidic Empire*, 94. But the plural אֱלֹהִים is commonly used of Yahweh as a *de facto* singular, and in the absence of religious polemic in the book of Amos, there is no reason the phrase cannot be translated in the singular as "their God." Andersen and Freedman, *Amos*, 318, 321, take "*the* girl" in 7c to be their god, whom they identify as Ashima from Amos 8:14. Lang, *Monotheism*, 122, proposes the clan's patron deity, who may or may not be Yahweh.

[243] See pp. 105-07.

[244] S. M. Paul, "Two Cognate Semitic Terms for Mating and Copulation," *VT* 32 (1982) 492-94; Paul, *Amos*, 82. A similar interpretation is held, of necessity,

titution in ancient Israel, the "girl" must be one of the three nuances of נַעֲרָה he identifies. His rejection of either a virgin or a married woman is dependent on the men's action being common yet unobjectionable, but the two do not necessarily coincide. The very fact that laws against adultery and deflowering virgins existed indicates they were not isolated actions. But be that as it may, most take the girl to be a servant and refer to Exod 21:7-11, which directs a man who designates a slave for his son to treat her as his daughter-in-law.[245] However, the term there is אָמָה, not נַעֲרָה, which leads Wolff to postulate a scenario in which a young man has impregnated a "marriageable girl" and become engaged, after which his father has sex with her, in effect violating the laws of consanguinity in Lev 18:15; 20:12.[246]

But the surrounding verses all deal with social and economic justice. This is clear in vv. 6-7b, but requires some elaboration for v. 8. The passive participle חֲבֻלִים, modifying בְּגָדִים in 8a, is generally understood as something pledged in surety for a loan, but biblical and extra-biblical evidence indicates the root word actually refers to the seizure of items when loans were defaulted.[247] Similarly, עֲנוּשִׁים in 8c often refers to compensation for an injury, either physical or to one's reputation,[248] but in 2 Kgs 23:33 it is used of tribute

by all those who view 7c as referring either to cultic prostitution (see n. 238) or abuse of a servant (see notes 245 and 252). The usual idiom is בּוֹא אֶל, which suggests that the alternative formulation was chosen to indicate something of significance. Paul, *Amos*, 82, suggests this was to echo הָלְכוּ אֲבוֹתָם ("their fathers went") in Amos 2:4 while Fleischer, *Von Menschen verkaüfern*, 68-69, argues that בּוֹא אֶל applies to permissable sex (as defined by that society) whereas הָלַךְ אֶל indicates illegitimate sexual actions.

[245] See, e.g., Beek, "Religious Background," 135-37; Würthwein, "Amos-Studien," 45-46; R. Bach, "Gottesrecht und weltliches Recht in der Verkündigung des Propheten Amos," *Festschrift für Günther Dehn* (ed. W. Schneemelcher; Neukirchen-Vluyn: Kreis Moers, 1957) 30-33; Rudolph, *Joel–Amos*, 142-43; Vesco, "Amos de Téqoa," 491-92; Martin-Achard and Re'emi, *God's People in Crisis*, 22; J. A. Dearman, *Property Rights in the Eighth-Century Prophets: The Conflict and Its Background* (SBLDS 106; Atlanta: Scholars Press, 1988) 23.

[246] H. W. Wolff, *Die Stunde des Amos: Prophetie und Protest* (München: Christopher Kaiser Verlag, 1969) 61; *idem*, *Joel and Amos*, 167.

[247] J. Milgrom, "The Missing Thief in Leviticus 5:20ff," *RIDA*$^3$ 22 (1975) 77-81. See also the discussion in Paul, *Amos*, 83-86, and the literature he cites.

[248] E.g., Exod 21:22; Deut 22:19. The compensation was paid to the offended party, however that was defined (e.g., in Deut 22:19 compensation for slandering a virgin goes to her father as the offended party, in keeping with that society's patriarchal orientation), and some think the indictment here is because such funds were misdirected; see Driver, *Joel and Amos*, 154; Wolff, *Die Stunde Des Amos*, 61;

exacted by Pharoah, and a similar nuance of tribute or taxation underlies the LXX and Targum at 1 Kings 10:15 and is reflected in the cognate usage.[249] This provides a better parallel with "seized garment" than "compensation."[250] Thus, since the surrounding verses all deal with the exploitation of the lower class, 7c should be interpreted in terms of the girl's subservient status rather than her marital eligibility.[251] But she is not designated a "slave," and the best interpretation is Fleischer's, who identifies her as a free servant forced into sexual actions in addition to her designated household duties.[252] As a result, Barstad's identification of the girl as a *marzēaḥ* hostess can not be sustained. The "girl" can be explained in terms consistent with the term's normal meaning and its immediate context, so hypothesizing an unprecedented role is not necessary.

But that does not automatically rule out an allusion to a *marzēaḥ* in these verses, especially v. 8. As noted earlier, the main elements of that banquet *appear* to be present, but in reality one is missing. The oppression of the poor points to the upper-class,[253] and the reference to the "needy" (אֶבְיוֹן) and "poor" (דַּלִּים) in Amos 2:6e-7a, in the reverse order from Amos 4:1, is also suggestive. But while it may indicate that the same social class is exploited in both cases, it does not guarantee this was done by the exact same group in the same context. In particular, the cultic sites in 8b and d may indicate temple functionaries, a specific subset of the elite, are involved,[254] which

---

*idem*, *Joel and Amos*, 168; Rudolph, *Joel–Amos*, 145; Hayes, *Amos*, 114; Paul, *Amos*, 86-88; Wood, "Amos," 49. Rudolph, *Joel–Amos*, 139, also considers the word an abstract noun, referring to those who have been fined; cf. Beek, "Religious Background," 134: "the wine of those condemned."

[249] For the pre-biblical parallels see Barstad, *Religious Polemics*, 15n19; for later Phoenician tariffs see R. S. Tomback, *A Comparative Semitic Lexicon of the Phoenician and Punic Languages* (SBLDS 32; Missoula: Scholars Press, 1978) 253; a Palmyrene parallel is presented in D. R. Hillers, "Palmyrene Aramaic Inscriptions and the Old Testament, Especially Amos 2:8," *ZAH* 8 (1995) 60-61.

[250] Regardless of whether the "exacted wine" refers to wine bought with such funds, as suggested by Dearman, *Property Rights*, 24, or to payment in kind (thus Mays, *Amos*, 47; Hayes, *Amos*, 114. Rosenbaum, *Amos of Israel*, 56n23, 65, points to the frequent mention of wine in the Samaria Ostraca). Amos 5:11 supports the latter interpretation.

[251] Fleischer, *Von Menschen verkaüfern*, 68; Paul, *Amos*, 82-83.

[252] For a full discussion see Fleischer, *Von Menschen verkaüfern*, 61-69. See also Vawter, *Amos, Hosea, Micah*, 41-42; G. V. Smith, *Amos*, 85.

[253] But contrast the reservations concerning the high social standing of the oppressors in Fendler, "Sozialkritik," 49-52.

[254] Suggested to me by John S. Kloppenborg Verbin. Barstad, *Religious Polemics*, 34, argues that the altars are private shrines, but the singular "house of their God" indicates a specific temple.

would distinguish this group from the Samarian women of Amos 4:1. These sites also establish a clear religious context for the activity, which included wine (8c). But unlike Amos 4:1 and 6:1, 3-7 there is no indication the drinking here was in any way excessive.[255] Without some evidence that they drink substantial amounts in Amos 2:8, as is characteristic of the *marzēaḥ*, that verse cannot be confidently classified as alluding to a *marzēaḥ*.

## IV. Summary

Amos 6:7 is the earliest biblical reference to the *marzēaḥ*. The preceding verses (Amos 6:1, 3-6) show that the *marzēaḥ* Amos knew was comparable to those encountered elsewhere. Samaria's upper class celebrated a religious feast that was characterized by, among other things, drunkenness, but with no evidence of any funerary associations. At the same time, in that passage Amos does not oppose the *marzēaḥ* itself but rather the attitude to which it gave expression, one in which the members "are not grieved by the ruin of Joseph." In other words, the prophet denounces the social inequities of Israel, and to the extent the *marzēaḥ* practices such injustice it too is condemned to exile. What Amos would have thought about it in a more egalitarian society, if it could even exist in such a context, is unknown.

Amos 4:1 alludes to the Samarian *marzēaḥ* without using the term. The verse is part of a three-verse unit which was paralleled with 6:1(2)3-7 in the final editorial structure of the book because of internal similarities of both form and content between the two passages. The offenses for which the female and male audiences are condemned are expressed in both passages through participles and in each case the punishment they receive is exile. Furthermore, both describe extensive wine consumption by the elite in a religious context. Thus the two passages address the members of a single *marzēaḥ* according to their gender.

In contrast, although there are points of contact with those two *marzēaḥ* texts, Amos 2:7c-8 does not meet all of the criteria for a

[255] *Contra* Hammershaimb, *Amos*, 49; Coote, *Amos Among the Prophets*, 38, neither of whom provides any arguments in support of their assertion (although Coote specifies it is drinking at a *marzēaḥ*). Paul, *Amos*, 79, claims the imperfect verbs in vv. 7-8 indicate ongoing actions (see also Fleischer, *Von Menschen verkaüfern*, 72), but as evidence of duration over time, not intensity at a specific time. Contrast the use of participles in Amos 4:1 and 6:6.

*marzēaḥ* allusion. Although Barstad's identification of the girl in 7c as a *marzēaḥ* hostess was rejected, two of the elements of the *marzēaḥ* were present: members of the upper class drink wine in a religious context. But it is not certain that large amounts of wine were consumed, so Amos 2:7c-8 cannot be confidently accepted as a *marzēaḥ* allusion.

CHAPTER THREE

# THE *MARZĒAḤ* IN HOSEA?

The prophet Hosea is commonly thought to have preached in the northern kingdom of Israel during the years prior to the Assyrian conquest in 722/721 BCE. As Amos' younger contemporary, preaching in the same geographic area, it would not be surprising to find the *marzēaḥ* reflected in Hosea's oracles as well. However, the word does not occur in the book of Hosea, which therefore did not figure in Bryan's dissertation. Nor has it received much attention as a source of possible *marzēaḥ* allusions. Prior to 1995, two proposals were advanced, both very much in passing. Brian Peckham listed possible *marzēaḥ* elements in Hos 9:1-6,[1] and Andersen and Freedman mentioned Hos 7:3-7 as a text "which may be placed alongside" Amos 6:4-6.[2] Then, in a 1995 article, Frédéric Gangloff and Jean-Claude Haelewyck argued that Hos 4:17-19 deals with a *marzēaḥ* in honour of the goddess Anat.[3]

Of these proposals, only the first and third will be treated in this chapter. Andersen and Freedman did not elaborate on their suggestion, but one can easily see that Hos 7:3-7 is not germane to the topic at hand. It consists of a series of metaphors describing the king's assassination by poison wine, but there is no indication more than one drink was involved, or that this occurred during a *religious* drinking feast of the elite. Therefore, that text can be excluded from further

---

[1] B. Peckham, "Phoenicia and the Religion of Israel: The Epigraphic Evidence," *Ancient Israelite Religion: Essays in Honor of Frank Moore Cross* (eds. P. D. Miller, P. D. Hanson and D. S. McBride; Philadelphia: Fortress Press, 1987) 95n59.

[2] F. I. Andersen and D. N. Freedman, *Amos: A New Translation with Introduction and Commentary* (AB 24A; New York/London/Toronto: Doubleday, 1989) 562; cf. D. N. Freedman, "But Did King David Invent Musical Instruments?" *BRev* 1/2 (1985) 51. There is no mention of this in their earlier Hosea commentary: F. I. Andersen and D. N. Freedman, *Hosea: A New Translation with Introduction and Commentary* (AB 24; New York/London/Toronto: Doubleday, 1980).

[3] F. Gangloff and J.-C. Haelewyck, "Osée 4,17-19: un marzeah en l'honneur de la déesse 'Anat" *ETL* 71 (1995) 470-82. Grace Emmerson had earlier suggested an unidentified fertility goddess as the background to this passage, but without the *marzēaḥ* connection; see G. I. Emmerson, "A Fertility Goddess in Hosea IV 17-19?" *VT* 24 (1974) 492-97.

consideration. I will consider the two remaining texts according to their location in the prophetic book.

## I. Hos 4:16-19

Although others had already linked Hos 4:16-19 with Isaiah 28, which contains possible allusions to the *marzēaḥ*,[4] Gangloff and Haelewyck were the first to suggest a direct connection between the Hosea text and a *marzēaḥ*. However, they simply note "les trois termes qui évoquent un cercle restreint d'individus (cf. חבור) étendus (cf. הנח־לו) et s'adonnant à une sorte de banquet (cf. סבאם)," followed by a survey of extra-biblical and biblical *marzēaḥ* references.[5] They do not directly correlate this text with features of particular *marzēaḥ*s or establish even some minimal correspondence with the *marzēaḥ* in general, but simply assert that Hos 4:17-19 alludes to a *marzēaḥ*. In what follows, I will rectify that shortcoming by establishing that the basic elements of the *marzēaḥ* identified in Chapter 1 are present here as well. But since I think their identification of a specific group reclining is incorrect it is first necessary to establish the text's wording as well as its context.

### A. *The Text*

| | | | |
|---|---|---|---|
| כִּי כְּפָרָה סֹרֵרָה | 16 | a | Truly, like a stubborn heifer, |
| סָרַר יִשְׂרָאֵל | | b | Israel is stubborn. |
| עַתָּה יִרְעֵם יהוה | | c | Can Yahweh now feed them |
| כְּכֶבֶשׂ בַּמֶּרְחָב | | d | like a lamb in a broad pasture?[7] |
| חֲבוּר עֲצַבִּים אֶפְרָיִם | 17 | a | Ephraim is a companion of idols, |
| הִנִּחַ־לוֹ[6] | | b | he has set up[8] for himself . . . .[9] |

[4] See H. McKeating, *The Books of Amos, Hosea and Micah* (CBC; Cambridge: Cambridge University Press, 1971) 102; Andersen and Freedman, *Hosea*, 378. Neither explicitly identify the latter as a *marzēaḥ*. Isaiah 28 will be considered in the next chapter.

[5] Gangloff and Haelewyck, "Osée 4,17-19," 375-78; the quotation is from p. 375. They point 17b as הָנִּחַ־לוֹ (p. 374), an *hiphil* I of נוּחַ, with the sense "he rests himself." I point the verb as an *hiphil* II (see n. 8 and pp. 131-32). They omit v. 16, but see pp. 133-34 below.

[6] The MT vocalizes as הַנַּח־לוֹ; see further below.

[7] For 16c-d as a question see n. 36.

[8] The LXX's ἔθηκαν suggests this nuance for *hiphil* II of נוּחַ here. It is used for the erection of shrines to foreign gods in 2 Kgs 17:29, where the LXX also

| | | | |
|---|---|---|---|
| סָר סָבְאָם הַזְנֵה הִזְנוּ | 18 | a | When[11] their liquor is gone,[12] they fornicate greatly; |
| אָהֹב אָהֲבוּ[10] קָלוֹן מָגִנֶּיהָ | | b | they deeply love the dishonour of her shields. |
| צָרַר רוּחַ אוֹתָהּ בִּכְנָפֶיהָ | 19 | a | A wind will enclose her in her wings, |
| וְיֵבֹשׁוּ מִזִּבְחוֹתָם | | b | and they shall be ashamed of their sacrifices. |

These verses have been the object of numerous contradictory and mutually exclusive emendations. Gangloff and Haelewyck survey more than eighty proposed "corrections" to the eighteen Hebrew words of vv. 17-19,[13] but for Andersen and Freedman, the emendations, "are a tribute to scholarly ingenuity but leave serious questions about the validity of the changes and the intention of the original author."[14] Few of the proposed changes directly affect the issue of a *marzēaḥ* allusion in this text, but the relevant ones will be noted as the discussion progresses.

The text above preserves the MT in all but two places, only one of which alters the consonantal text. The Masoretes pointed 17b as an *hiphil* II imperative (הַנַּח־לוֹ), which in itself is acceptable Hebrew, but "leave him alone" is problematic here on two points. First, all other instances of this construction occur in the context of direct

translates ἔθηκαν; see Emmerson, "Fertility Goddess?" 497. The *hiphil* of the verb is used in connection with the Ark of Yahweh in 1 Sam 6:18 and of items to be deposited in the temple in Exod 16:33, 34; Lev 16:23; 1 Kgs 8:9; Ezek 42:13; see also Josh 4:3, 8.

[9] Emmerson, "Fertility Goddess?" 496-97, suggests on the basis of the LXX that a reference to a deity or idol has dropped out of the MT at this point. Cf. n. 38 and p. 140 below.

[10] The MT reads אָהֲבוּ הֵבוּ; see further below.

[11] This line's verbs are considered sequential by W. R. Harper, *A Critical and Exegetical Commentary on the Books of Amos and Hosea* (ICC 18; Edinburgh: T. & T. Clark, 1912) 265; H. W. Wolff, *Hosea: A Commentary on the Book of the Prophet Hosea* (Hermeneia; trans. G. Stansell; Philadelphia: Fortress Press, 1974) 91; Emmerson, "Fertility Goddess?" 497; G. I. Davies, *Hosea* (NCBC; Grand Rapids: Wm. B. Eerdmans Publishing Co., 1992) 132; A. A. Macintosh, *A Critical and Exegetical Commentary on Hosea* (ICC; Edinburgh: T. & T. Clark, 1997) 169. Cf. GKC §164b.

[12] For this meaning of סָר see Amos 6:7.

[13] Gangloff and Haelewyck, "Osée 4,17-19," 371-74; this does not include possible deletions. See also the discussion in D. Barthélemy, *Critique textuelle de l'Ancien Testament. 3. Ezéchiel, Daniel et les Douze Prophètes* (OBO 50; Fribourg: Editions Universitaires; Göttingen: Vandenhoeck & Ruprecht, 1992) 512-17. Most of the emendations are also considered, and at points adopted, by Macintosh, *Hosea*, 167-74.

[14] Andersen and Freedman, *Hosea*, 373.

speech,[15] but here it would be the only imperative in a succession of indicative verbs. Second, there is no indication in the passage of any addressee for an imperative.[16] Gangloff and Haelewyck vocalize as הָנַח־לוֹ, an *hiphil* I perfect of נוּחַ, with the sense, "he rests himself,"[17] but contrary to their assertion, their understanding of the line has no bearing on whether the passage alludes to a *marzēaḥ*. For them, in 17b the text "passe à l'idée de repos,"[18] which they consider one of three indicators of a *marzēaḥ* here, but the posture of those involved is irrelevant. Granted, some *marzēaḥ* references indicate people sat, reclined or even sprawled, but they do the same at other gatherings as well. Therefore, rejecting their vocalization does not affect the possibility of a *marzēaḥ* in this passage. Instead, I repoint the verb as an *hiphil* II perfect of נוּחַ, with the LXX and most commentators.[19] Even in its possibly truncated form in the MT[20] this provides a better parallel with 17a, in terms of both grammar and content, and lends support to the necessary religious aspect of a *marzēaḥ*.[21]

In 18b, the MT reads אָהֲבוּ הֵבוּ, but the second word's meaning is problematic.[22] Since it is not represented in the LXX or Peshitta some simply delete it.[23] Others combine it with the preceding word

---

[15] See Exod 32:10; 2 Sam 16:11; 2 Kgs 23:18.

[16] The proposed audiences are all hypothetical. Wolff, *Hosea*, 91, suggests the prophet turned to his disciples, but the imperative is in the singular not the plural (a "corporate personality" is proposed by H. Balz-Cochois, *Gomer: Der Höhenkult Israels im Selbstverständnis der Volksfrömmigkeit. Untersuchungen zu Hosea 4,1-5,7* [Europäische Hochschulschriften Reihe XXIII: Theologie 191; Frankfurt am Main/Bern: Peter Lang, 1982] 34), and Hosea's disciples are not mentioned elsewhere in the entire chapter. Jerome, K. Marti, *Das Dodekapropheton erklärt* (KHAT 13; Tübingen: J. C. B. Mohr [Paul Siebeck], 1904) 45; J. M. Ward, *Hosea: A Theological Commentary* (New York: Harper & Row, 1966) 80, all think the command is addressed to Judah, but v. 15 is separate from this passage (see p. 134 below).

[17] Gangloff and Haelewyck, "Osée 4,17-19," 374

[18] Ibid., 375.

[19] See those listed in Gangloff and Haelewyck, "Osée 4,17-19," 371n12; other emendations are listed in their notes 13-20; concerning their vocalization, cf. n. 5 above. For the pointing without the medial *yod* see 1 Kgs 8:9.

[20] See n. 9.

[21] Cf. p. 140 below.

[22] W. Rudolph, *Hosea* (KAT 13; Gütersloh: Güterslohcr Verlagshaus/Gerd Mohn, 1966) 108, takes it as a masculine plural imperative of יָהַב and renders, "sie lieben das 'her damit'" ("They love, [the command] 'give!'"). He appeals to the Vulgate and the *KJV* (". . . do love, Give ye"), but the former's *dilexerunt adferre (ignominiam)* ("they love to bring [disgrace]") does not support his proposal, which produces a strained meaning for the entire line.

[23] Thus GKC §55e; Harper, *Amos and Hosea*, 263; I. Willi-Plein, *Vorformen der Schriftexegese innerhalb des Alten Testaments: Untersuchungen zum literarischen Werden der*

as a *peʿalal* form, with an intensive meaning.[24] However, the preceding הַזְנֵה הִזְנוּ and Symmachus' ἠγάπησαν ἀγάπην suggests the emendation to אָהֹב אָהֲבוּ.[25] The resulting infinitive absolute plus finite verb of the same root has a "strengthening"[26] effect in both lines of v. 18.

## B. *Establishing the Unit*

I also disagree with Gangloff and Haelewyck concerning the extent of the passage, while they say nothing of its larger context. There is virtually unanimous scholarly agreement that the unit ends at v. 19, since Hos 5:1 initiates a new section with a direct address to the priests, in contrast to the third person description of the entire nation (Israel/Ephraim) in the preceding verses. Gangloff and Haelewyck begin the unit at v. 17, dismissing the wordplay among סֹרֵרָה, סָרַר (v. 16), סָר (v. 18) and צָרַר (v. 19) as nothing more than the reason why v. 16 was redactionally linked to vv. 17-19.[27] But this creates a problem as to v. 16's original context, since it is separate from the preceding verses (see below). Moreover, they fail to recognize the consonantal paranomasia between מרחב and חבור, linking vv. 16 and

---

*auf Amos, Hosea und Micha zurückgehenden Bücher im hebräischen Zwölfprophetenbuch* (BZAW 123; Berlin: Walter de Gruyter, 1971) 138.

[24] I.e. אֲהַבְהֵבוּ; see, e.g., Marti, *Dodekapropheton*, 45; H. S. Nyberg, *Studien zum Hoseabuche. Zugleich ein Beitrag zur Klärung des Problems der alttestamentlichen Textkritik* (UUÅ 6; Uppsala: Almqvist & Wiksell, 1935) 35; Andersen and Freedman, *Hosea*, 379; M. Nissinen, *Prophetie, Redaktion und Fortschreibung im Hoseabuch: Studien zum Werdegang eines Prophetenbuches im Lichte von Hos 4 und 11* (AOAT 231; Neukirchen-Vluyn: Neukirchener Verlag, 1991) 124; M.-T. Wacker, *Figurationen des weiblichen im Hosea-Buch* (HBS 8; Freiburg: Herder, 1996) 265; Macintosh, *Hosea*, 169.

[25] Following M. T. Houtsma, "Bijdrage tot de kritiek en verklaring van Hosea," *ThT* 9 (1875) 59; Marti, *Dodekapropheton*, 45; B. Duhm, "Anmerkungen zu den Zwölf Propheten II: Buch Hosea," *ZAW* 31 (1911) 22; A. Weiser, *Das Buch der zwölf Kleinen Propheten* (ATD 24; Göttingen: Vandenhoeck & Ruprecht, 1949) 49; Wolff, *Hosea*, 73; J. L. Mays, *Hosea: A Commentary* (OTL; Philadelphia: Westminster Press, 1969) 76; Emmerson, "Fertility Goddess?" 494; Balz-Cochois, *Gomer*, 35; J. Jeremias, *Der Prophet Hosea* (ATD 24; Göttingen: Vandenhoeck & Ruprecht, 1983) 64; Davies, *Hosea*, 133.

[26] See GKC §§113l-r; R. J. Williams, *Hebrew Syntax: An Outline* (2nd ed.; Toronto: University of Toronto Press, 1976) §205; B. K. Waltke and M. O'Connor, *An Introduction to Biblical Hebrew Syntax* (Winona Lake: Eisenbrauns, 1990) §§35.21a, 35.3.1b.

[27] Gangloff and Haelewyck, "Osée 4,17-19," 370n3. The same demarcation is apparently held by Emmerson, "Fertility Goddess?" 492-97.

17, and ignore the *inclusio* effected by סָרַר and צָרַר. Therefore, v. 16 should be included as part of the unit.

Some scholars extend the starting point to v. 15,[28] but the reference to Judah and the similarity to Amos 5:5 cause others to consider that verse secondary.[29] More importantly, even if v. 15 does stem from Hosea, it is formulated as direct, divine speech like the preceding verses, whereas v. 16 switches to third-person description.[30] The latter continues to the end of v. 19, leading most commentators to consider vv. 16 and 19 the outer limits of a prophetic oration.[31] This is confirmed by the paranomastic inclusion of סָרַר and צָרַר.

Within those limits, various parts of the passage have been deleted as redactional insertions by different scholars. The most extreme proposal is by Gale Yee, for whom the only parts of the entire chapter stemming from Hosea are vv. 4 (minus כֹּהֵן), 5b, 12bA, קָלוֹן מָגִנֶּיהָ from 18b, and 19a; the rest is attributed to one of two redactors.[32] But even those who only delete portions of Hos 4:16-19 do not agree with either Yee or each other.[33] On the other hand, most scholars

---

[28] E.g., E. Sellin, *Das Zwölfprophetenbuch übersetzt und erklärt* (KAT 12; 2nd ed.; Leipzig: Deichert, 1929) 60; W. Rudolph, "Hosea 4,15-19," *Gottes Wort und Gottes Land: Hans-Wilhelm Hertzberg zum 70. Geburtstag am 16. Januar 1965 dargebracht von Kollegen, Freunden und Schülern* (ed. H. G. Reventlow; Göttingen: Vandenhoeck & Ruprecht, 1965) 193, 197; *idem*, *Hosea*, 112; Ward, *Hosea*, 80; Mays, *Hosea*, 76-77; B. C. Birch, *Hosea, Joel, and Amos* (Westminster Bible Companion; Louisville: Westminster/John Knox Press, 1997) 15-19. Good begins a new poem at 14e; see E. M. Good, "The Composition of Hosea," *SEÅ* 31 (1966) 35.

[29] E.g., Marti, *Dodekapropheton*, 44; Duhm, "Hosea," 21; Harper, *Amos and Hosea*, 262; K. Budde, "Zu Text und Auslegung des Buches Hosea," *JBL* 45 (1926) 289; Jeremias, *Hosea*, 71; G. A. Yee, *Composition and Tradition in the Book of Hosea: A Redactional Critical Investigation* (SBLDS 102; Atlanta: Scholars Press, 1987) 270 and, most recently, Macintosh, *Hosea*, 162.

[30] Wolff, *Hosea*, 90, accounts for the transition by postulating an intervening objection by the people, but this lacks textual support.

[31] Thus, Marti, *Dodekapropheton*, 45; Duhm, "Hosea," 21; Wolff, *Hosea*, 90; C. Hauret, *Amos et Osée* (Verbum Salutis, Ancien Testament 5; Paris: Beauchesne, 1970) 180-82; Willi-Plein, *Vorformen*, 136; Andersen and Freedman, *Hosea*, 373; E. Jacob, "Osée," *Osée Joël Amos Abdias Jonas* (CAT 11a; 2nd ed.; Genève: Labor et Fides, 1982) 44; Jeremias, *Hosea*, 71; Nissinen, *Prophetie*, 118; Davies, *Hosea*, 131; Wacker, *Figurationen*, 264-68; Macintosh, *Hosea*, 166.

[32] Yee, *Composition and Tradition*, 160-69, 262-72. She dates these redactors to the reign of Josiah and the exilic period respectively.

[33] For example, even prior to Yee's monograph, 16b was considered a gloss by both Marti and Willi-Plein, but Marti considered 17a secondary and 17b original while the reverse was held by Willi-Plein (see Marti, *Dodekapropheton*, 45; Willi-Plein, *Vorformen*, 137); Yee disagrees with both concerning v. 17, which she attributes to her two different redactors (see below). In contrast to all three of them, Nis-

consider the entire passage to be Hosea's own composition. Such disagreements make consensus on the matter unlikely, especially since the same textual data can be used to support contradictory conclusions. For instance, Andersen and Freedman see the interplay of consonants between מרחב and חבור as an indication 16d and 17a come from the same author, while for Yee it is evidence her 2nd redactor has artificially linked his composition (16d) to the text he inherited (17a).[34] Similarly, different interpretations are put on the same material. For instance, to some the positive tone of Hos 4:16c-d is a clear indication those lines are a later addition proclaiming that the situation of the preceding lines has changed.[35] Most, however, view the lines as a question calling for a negative answer, reinforcing the negative evaluation of Israel in 16a-b.[36]

Despite such divergent opinions, the passage is consistent with Hosea's authentic message. Wolff dates the motif of harlotry as a metaphor for Israel's involvement with other gods to the early period of Hosea's ministry, and notes that the political upheaval following the death of Jeroboam II is not reflected in this text, which also supports a date early in Hosea's prophetic career.[37] Putting the matter negatively, nothing in these verses requires a date after the time of Hosea,[38] so the passage can be retained intact.

---

sinen, *Prophetie*, 118-28, 228, considers vv. 16 and 19 to be the original text, with vv. 17-18 a later insertion explaining the chronologically earlier verses.

[34] Cf. Andersen and Freedman, *Hosea*, 374; Yee, *Composition and Tradition*, 169. Yee attributes 17a to her first redactor.

[35] Marti, *Dodekaprophetom*, 45; Willi-Plein, *Vorformen*, 137; Yee, *Composition and Tradition*, 168.

[36] Among older commentators this view is represented by Duhm, "Hosea," 21; Harper, *Amos and Hosea*, 264; Sellin, *Zwölfprophetenbuch*$^2$, 61; J. Wellhausen, *Die Kleinen Propheten übersetzt und erklärt* (4th ed.; Berlin: Walter de Gruyter, 1963) 112. It continues to dominate in more recent scholarship, as evidenced by Wolff, *Hosea*, 91; Rudolph, *Hosea*, 107; Mays, *Hosea*, 76; Jeremias, *Hosea*, 72; Davies, *Hosea*, 131; G. Eidevall, *Grapes in the Desert: Metaphors, Models and Themes in Hosea 4-14* (ConBOT 43; Stockholm: Almqvist & Wiksell, 1996) 64; Macintosh, *Hosea*, 165, 166. At first glance the construction עַתָּה . . . כִּי might suggest cause and effect ("because . . . now"), but a statement that Yahweh will care for Israel *because* it is stubborn is highly unlikely. For the indication of a question by "the natural emphasis upon the words," rather than a distinct interrogative marker, see GKC §150a (Hos 4:16 is listed as an example); Williams, *Hebrew Syntax*, §542; see also Waltke and O'Connor, *Biblical Hebrew Syntax*, §31.4f. None of this requires accepting Wolff's claim that "when this was first written down, there was still knowledge of the speech's inflection" (Wolff, *Hosea*, 91).

[37] Wolff, *Hosea*, 76.

[38] The issue of 16c-d has already been dealt with. Willi-Plein and Yee also take

At the same time, although Hos 4:16-19 is a self-contained unit, its relationship to the rest of the chapter should not be ignored. A number of links, both thematic and lexical, support interpreting the former in conjunction with the latter. The image of idolatry as harlotry dominates the chapter, the motif of drunkenness occurs in vv. 11 and 18 and the reference to idols in v. 17 echoes v. 12. In addition to these general parallels, a number of words from the first part of the chapter are repeated in vv. 16-19: קָלוֹן is found in both vv. 7 and 18, the root זנה occurs 8 times in vv. 10-15 and twice in v. 18, רוּחַ is found in vv. 12 and 19 and the root זבח appears in vv. 13, 14 and 19. The frequent and often abrupt changes in speaker and addressee indicate the chapter is not a single, unified composition, but rather a collection of separate oracles. Nonetheless, the majority of recent scholars agree that they reflect Hosea's authentic message, even if not a verbatim report of his actual words.[39]

The chapter has a unifying organizational principle as well. Running through individual sections and the chapter as a whole is the idea that the actions and fates of the priests[40] and the people are

v. 17b as a later addition meant to soften the harshness of the surrounding lines (Willi-Plein, *Vorformen*, 137; Yee, *Composition and Tradition*, 168; Yee translates as "but he [Yahweh] will provide rest for him"). This derives the verb from *hiphil* I of נוּחַ rather than *hiphil* II, as is usually done. The LXX's ἔθηκεν supports the latter (see also n. 8), as does the Masoretes' (incorrect) pointing as an imperative from *hiphil* II.

The reference to a "broad space" (16d) and the supposed cessation of sacrifice (19b) are seen by Nissinen, *Prophetie*, 119, 223, as evidence of deportation after the Assyrian conquest. Also, the wind in 19a is taken as a symbol for foreign conquerors by Jeremias, *Hosea*, 73; Nissinen, *Prophetie*, 119; Eidevall, *Grapes in the Desert*, 67. However, מֶרְחָב always has a positive connotation (Rudolph, *Hosea*, 107). Moreover, 19b speaks of the nation being ashamed of their sacrifices, not the latter's termination, and in 19a the wind affects "her," not "them."

[39] See especially the discussions in Mays, *Hosea*, 15-17; Wolff, *Hosea*, 74-76; Andersen and Freedman, *Hosea*, 57-65; Davies, *Hosea*, 110-13 and most recently Macintosh, *Hosea*, lxxii: "[Hosea's] words are reflected predominantly in chapters 4 and 5:1-7 . . . ." The extreme skepticism concerning the chapter's authenticity expressed by Yee, *Composition and Tradition*, *passim*, is only shared by a minority of contemporary scholars.

[40] A single priest is addressed in v. 4. Most consider him to be a chief priest, if not the High Priest, but the vocative is taken as a collective by Macintosh, *Hosea*, 135; the basic point is unaffected. Verse 7 switches to third person plurals, indicating the larger priestly class. On the basis of v. 6, Andersen and Freedman, *Hosea*, 342-44, think this indicates the High Priest's actual children, but בָּנֶיךָ there is better understood as indicating members of a guild (cf. the "sons of the prophets in 1 Kgs 20:35; 2 Kgs 2:3, 5, 7, 15; etc.) rather than biological descendants. The priests are in view until v. 12, when "my [Yahweh's] people" are introduced.

intertwined. This principle is succinctly articulated in v. 9: "like people, like priest." Thus, in v. 6 the people's lack of knowledge is blamed on the priest's own rejection of knowledge, and both priests and people lack understanding in vv. 11 and 14. Similarly, the priests and the people fornicate, forsaking Yahweh/their God (vv. 10 and 12). The correlation between priests and people is also in effect between the earlier verses and vv. 16-19. For instance, the people's fornication in v. 18 echoes that of the priests from v. 10 and their drinking in v. 18 also reflects the priests' actions in v. 11.

To summarize, the connections among the parts, combined with the chapter's organizational principle, suggests that these oracles, although delivered individually, stem from the same approximate time.[41] As such, the rest of Hosea 4 provides the larger context for analyzing vv. 16-19 as a *marzēaḥ* allusion.

## C. *Discussion*

Gangloff and Haelewyck identify Hos 4:17-19 as a *marzēaḥ* allusion on the basis of references to a specific group of individuals reclining at a banquet.[42] This is inadequate grounds for a *marzēaḥ* allusion, however. Their understanding of v. 17b in terms of "reclining" has already been rejected, and in any case is irrelevant to the essential characteristics of the *marzēaḥ*.[43] More importantly, the passage does not refer to a specific group of people, but rather the entire nation of Israel/Ephraim. This only leaves the reference to drinking, which is insufficient by itself to establish an allusion to the *marzēaḥ*. Nonetheless, the passage does reflect the three constitutive elements of a *marzēaḥ* established in Chapter 1. Drinking in a religious context is easily identified in the text, and the reference to the whole nation can be explained in a manner consistent with the *marzēaḥ*'s usually restricted upper-class membership.

The religious element is immediately evident in the references to "idols" (עֲצַבִּים) in 17a and "their sacrifices" in 19b.[44] In addition,

[41] Argued most strongly by Wolff, *Hosea*, 75-76. See also Balz-Cochois, *Gomer*, 40, 45, 68-69; Davies, *Hosea*, 111-12.

[42] See p. 130 above.

[43] See p. 132.

[44] A feminine plural of זֶבַח does not occur elsewhere, and most commentators emend it to מִמִּזְבְּחוֹתָם ("of their altars") on the basis of haplography of the initial מ, following Wellhausen, *Propheten*, 112, (the 1st ed. appeared in 1892) and the LXX,

Emmerson has argued that the 3rd feminine singular suffixes in vv. 18b-19a refer to an unspecified goddess, whom Gangloff and Haelewyck subsequently identified as Anat.[45] The suffix occurs in references to "her shields" (מָגִנֶּיהָ), "her" (אוֹתָהּ) and "her/its wings" (כְּנָפֶיהָ). At first glance these are problematic, since there is no appropriate antecedent in the immediate passage or the chapter as a whole. The only feminine noun in the passage is the metaphorical description of Israel as a "stubborn heifer" (פָּרָה, v. 16a), and some have proposed that as the pronouns' referent.[46] Others look beyond the chapter and refer the suffixes to the adulterous woman of Hosea 1-3 as a symbol of the nation.[47] But both proposals ignore the many intervening masculine forms (both verbs and suffixes), for Israel/Ephraim,[48] and do not explain why either a cow or an adulteress would have a shield or wings.[49]

In the absence of a clear antecedent for the feminine suffixes, the best way to clarify their point of reference is by examining the words to which they are attached, with the expectation that whatever or whoever they refer to is consistent with the words they modify. The 3rd feminine suffix first appears in מָגִנֶּיהָ ("her shields," 18a), but is often changed to a 3rd masculine plural, while the root word is emended to מִגְּאֹן. The line then reads, "They love dishonour more than their pride," with "pride" refering to Yahweh. But although the root's emendation can be supported from the LXX's ἐκ φρυάγματος, this alteration should not be accepted too quickly.

---

Syriac and Targum. The MT is supported by the Vulgate's *a sacrificiis suis* and is explained as a northern dialectical variant by Nyberg, *Studien*, 35; Rudolph, *Hosea*, 109; Mays, *Hosea*, 78; Davies, *Hosea*, 135; Macintosh, *Hosea*, 173. Either reading entails a religious connection, but "sacrificial meals" are more consistent with a *marzēaḥ* than "altars."

[45] Emmerson, "Fertility Goddess?" 492-97; Gangloff and Haelewyck, "Osée 4,17-19," 378-80.

[46] J. M. Ward, "The Message of Hosea," *Int* 23 (1969) 81; Willi-Plein, *Vorformen*, 139; Nissinen, *Prophetie*, 118. The feminine suffixes are considered collectives referring to Israel by Wacker, *Figurationen*, 266; Macintosh, *Hosea*, 170, 173; for the feminine singular suffix as a collective see GKC §135p. They are given a "neutral" meaning by Rudolph, *Hosea*, 108.

[47] Thus Budde, "Hosea," 295; Yee, *Composition and Tradition*, 265; Yee identifies this image in Hos 4:12 as well. Balz-Cochois, *Gomer*, 26, debates whether the suffixes refer to "the whore" Israel, but in the end emends them to masculine plurals. Budde, "Hosea," 295, 296, also relates them to 17b, which he emends to נַחֲלָתוֹ ("his inheritance").

[48] Emmerson, "Fertility Goddess?" 493.

[49] This is usually resolved by emending the problem away; see further below.

Wellhausen argues that "glory" (כָּבוֹד) is a better antonym to "dishonour" (קָלוֹן) than "pride,"[50] and it is certainly a more appropriate term for Yahweh, the proposed antithesis to "dishonour" in the sentence. Moreover, the feminine suffix remains in the best LXX manuscripts,[51] and is confirmed by אוֹתָהּ in 19a. The latter is itself often emended to אוֹתָם, but in the absence of manuscript support and against much of the versional evidence.[52] Moreover, a correlation between a female and military gear ("her shields") constitutes a more difficult reading than "her glory," so if such a connection can be established the MT should be retained. In short, it is preferable to retain these two feminine suffixes.[53] This leaves the third instance of the suffix: "her/its wings" (כְּנָפֶיהָ) in v. 19a. The pronoun's antecedent there is often thought to be the feminine "wind"[54] at the beginning of the line, but unless "her" (אוֹתָהּ) in the middle of 19a is changed to "them," which is problematic,[55] "she" remains unidentified.

In light of these difficulties, it is simpler to refer all of the suffixes to a single female antecedent who has a shield and wings, and these features, combined with the reference to idols earlier in the text, suggest the female is a deity. This leads to the question whether there is a winged semitic goddess associated with warfare, and Anat fits

---

[50] Wellhausen, *Propheten*, 112, followed by Marti, *Dodekapropheton*, 45; Willi-Plein, *Vorformen*, 139. Cf. Hos 4:7.

[51] The phrase is qualified by αὐτῶν ("their") in A Q*, whereas B Q[A] reads αὐτῆς; as both the older (B) and more difficult reading, the latter is to be preferred.

[52] E.g., Aquila reads "her" (αὐτῆς) while the LXX's σὺ εἶ (= אַתָּה) confirms the MT's final ה and the consonants of the direct object marker, minus the vowel letter. Note also *eam* in the Vulgate.

[53] Note the comment by Emmerson, "Fertility Goddess?" 493: "there is the difficulty of explaining how two plural forms consistent with the context, and only two, were corrupted to the difficult feminine singular apart from the influence of another such form in the immediate context."

[54] רוּחַ can be either masculine or feminine; although the latter predominates, the masculine verb צָרַר might suggest otherwise here. But if רוּחַ is understood as masculine, then the feminine suffix on "wings" cannot refer to the wind. However, a feminine subject can take a masculine verb when the verb precedes the subject (see GKC §145o-p; Waltke and O'Connor, *Biblical Hebrew Syntax*, §6.6c and the references cited by both). As such, the issue of emendation does not arise for most scholars in this instance. For the few exceptions see the references in Gangloff and Haelewyck, "Osée 4,17-19," 374nn77-81; of the five changes listed, only one involves a third masculine singular referring to a masculine "wind."

[55] See n. 52.

the description well. In the Ugaritic tablets,[56] Anat is the goddess most frequently connected with warfare,[57] she is the only ancient semitic female deity depicted with a shield,[58] and the only winged female deity in the semitic pantheon.[59] Nonetheless, Eidevall objects to relating the feminine suffixes to any goddess because there is no explicit reference to one in the passage.[60] It is questionable whether an explicit mention is necessary, however: people devoted to a winged goddess equipped with a shield would surely recognize an allusion to her. Moreover, the LXX may contain a trace of such an antecedent in 17b. The Greek reads ἔθηκεν ἑαυτῷ σκάνδαλα, and Emmerson suggests that the final word may be an interpretive substitute for a goddess' name or epithet, with the latter now lost from the MT.[61] She admits that the LXX may only reflect the translator's attempt to make sense of a difficult line, but the restoration of another word would provide better balance with the preceding line, in terms of both length and semantic parallelism.[62]

Furthermore, a goddess, named or otherwise, is a preferable an-

---

[56] Although they antedate Hosea by over five centuries, the Ugarit tablets provide the geographically closest antecedent semitic mythological texts, and as such are an appropriate place to look for a deity alluded to in Israel. For a detailed discussion of Anat herself see N. H. Walls, *The Goddess Anat in Ugaritic Myth* (SBLDS 135; Atlanta: Scholars Press, 1992). See also W. A. Maier, III, "Anath (DIETY) [Heb *ʿănāt* עֲנָת]," *ABD* 225-27; P. L. Day, "Anat ענת," *DDD* 36-43; E. Lipiński, *Studia Phoenicia XIV: Dieux et déesses de l'univers phénicien et punique* (OLA 64; Leuven: Peeters, 1995) 309-13.

[57] The most (in)famous text describes her wading through the blood of battle up to her thighs, with the heads and hands of her enemies strapped to her waist; see *CAT* 1.3.II.3-III.2.

[58] Gangloff and Haelewyck, "Osée 4,17-19," 378-79. See also Andersen and Freedman, *Hosea*, 376.

[59] See Gangloff and Haelewyck, "Osée 4,17-19," 379-80. At Ugarit she is described as winged (*CAT* 1.10.II.10-11) and as flying, usually with falcons (*CAT* 1.10.II.11; 1.13.8; 1.18.IV.21,31-32), and once is identified as a bird (*CAT* 1.108.8-9). She is also depicted as winged on a stele (RS 2.038), on which see M. Yon, "Les stèles en pierre," *Arts et industries de la pierre* (RSO VI; ed. M. Yon; Paris: Éditions Recherche sur les Civilisations, 1991) 278-79, 291-93, 329 fig. 9c; *idem*, "L'archéologie d'Ougarit," *Ugarit—ein ostmediterranes Kulturzentrum im Alten Orient: Ergebnisse und Perspecktiven der Forschung, Band 1—Ugarit und seine altorientalische Umwelt* (ALASPM 7; eds. M. Dietrich and O. Loretz; Münster: Ugarit-Verlag, 1995) 270-71. Andersen and Freedman, *Hosea*, 376, combine lines 18b-19a as "her shielding wings."

[60] Eidevall, *Grapes in the Desert*, 66.

[61] Emmerson, "Fertility Goddess?" 496-97.

[62] Since it is not essential to either the line or the passage, the English translation presented earlier simply indicates the possibility that something is missing from the line.

tecedent for the three feminine suffixes in 18b-19a for four reasons. First, this removes the perceived need to change the suffixes. Second, it renders unnecessary all emendations and alternative meanings for the consonants מגן in 18b, most of which were prompted by the need to produce something more consistent with the altered suffixes.[63] Third, a winged goddess yields a better sense than if the wings belonged to the wind. Rendering the line as "The wind will enclose her in her (own) wings" more clearly connotes a sense of confinement, indicating she has been made powerless by restricting her means of locomotion.[64] Fourth, this establishes a unifying rhe-

[63] The emendation to מִגְּאוֹן was considered above. Nyberg, *Studien*, 32-35, revocalized מָגִנֶּיהָ as מִגַּנֶּיהָ ("from her gardens") and read אוֹתָהּ as "her sign"; this suggests Asherah's frequent association with trees and gardens; see also Hos 4:13. The connection had already been raised, but with the suffix emended to a masculine plural, by H. Torczyner, "Dunkle Bibelstellen," *Vom Alten Testament. Karl Marti zum siebzigsten Geburtstage gewidmet von Freunden, Fachgenossen und Schülern* (BZAW 41; ed. K. Budde; Giessen: Alfred Töpelmann, 1925) 277; see also Marti, *Dodekapropheton*, 46; for 19th Century proponents see Gangloff and Haelewyck, "Osée 4,17-19," 373nn52-53 and 55.

Three alternative meanings for מָגֵן ("shield") have been proposed. First, since the underlying verb גָּנַן means "cover, surround, protect" (BDB 171), Nissinen, *Prophetie*, 127, opts for a literal "cover," and Macintosh, *Hosea*, 170-71, following Morag, relates it to the marriage canopy (חֻפָּה). The word was understood figuratively of the leaders by the Targum, the Vulgate and by Harper, *Amos and Hosea*, 265; Jacob, "Osée," 44n1; cf. Ps 47:10; 84:10 89:19 ("Shield" can serve as an epithet of Yahweh [see Ps 3:4; 18:2, 31, 36; etc., and especially Gen 15:1], but such a nuance would be incomprehensible here). Second, relying on the Arabic adjective *māğin*, G. R. Driver proposed the meaning, "shameless, insolent"; see G. R. Driver, "Studies in the Vocabulary of the Old Testament VI," *JTS* 34 (1933) 383-84. This is adopted by, e.g., Wolff, *Hosea*, 73, 91; Ward, *Hosea*, 81; Mays, *Hosea*, 78; Balz-Cochois, *Gomer*, 36; Davies, *Hosea*, 134. Similarly, an abstract noun meaning "insolence, wantonness" is proposed by J. J. Glück, "Some Semantic Complexities in the Book of Hosea," *Die O.T. Werkgemeenskap in Suid-Afrika: Studies on the Books of Hosea and Amos* (Pretoria: Potchefstroom Herald, 1966) 57; he is followed by Emmerson, "Fertility Goddess?" 495. Third, Rudolph, *Hosea*, 108, following Rabin, proposes the meaning, "gift."

While each of these suggestions has some merit, it is preferable to adopt the plain meaning of the text rather than an emended text or a secondary or derived meaning.

[64] Andersen and Freedman repoint אוֹתָהּ as אִוְּתָה, take Yahweh as the subject of the verb, and translate the line as, "He has restrained the spirit of [her] appetites in [her] wings"; see Andersen and Freedman, *Hosea*, 376; followed by Yee, *Composition and Tradition*, 265. A masculine subject for צָרַר is unnecessary (see n. 54), but it is worth noting that they too envision a winged goddess here.

כָּנָף can be used metaphorically for the skirt of a garment (BDB 489; cf. Deut 23:1; Ruth 3:9; Ezek 16:8, etc.). In light of Syrian representations of a goddess holding her skirt open, Emmerson, "Fertility Goddess?" 496, takes the line as "an ironic reversal of the seductive enticements of the goddess" (for the Syrian

torical structure in vv. 18-19. Verse 18a deals with the people's actions while 19b describes their future attitude. Similarly, in 18b "her shields" are the object of their love while in 19a "her wings" receive the effect of the wind's efforts. In other words, the two verses create a mirror pattern in which v. 18 describes the people's actions in connection with the goddess, while v. 19 describes her future fate first and then the people's reaction.[65]

To summarize, since the feminine suffixes in 18b-19a should be retained, they are best interpreted as alluding to a goddess, and the evidence supports identifying her as Anat.[66] As a result, if this passage alludes to a *marzēaḥ*, she should be understood as its patron.[67] However, for this passage to be a *marzēaḥ* allusion, it must show evidence of a definable upper-class group consuming large amounts of alcohol.

The latter is easily seen in the phrase סָר סָבְאָם ("their liquor is gone") in 18a.[68] The noun denotes strong drink, and the cognate verb refers to drinking in excess.[69] Most relevant to this text is the use of

---

representations see the references in her n. 5). Gangloff and Haelewyck, "Osée 4,17-19," 379-80, consider either interpretation of "wings" possible. I prefer the literal meaning, with a secondary metaphorical allusion possible in light of the sexual content of v. 18.

[65] See Emmerson, "Fertility Goddess?" 495.

[66] Thus Andersen and Freedman, *Hosea*, 325-26, 376; Gangloff and Haelewyck, "Osée 4,17-19," 378-80. Emmerson suggested an unidentified fertility goddess and Davies proposes Asherah (Emmerson, "Fertility Goddess?" 496-97; Davies, *Hosea*, 133; see also Nyberg, *Studien*, 32-35). Although Asherah is mostly commonly associated with fertility motifs, that realm (vs. simple sexual license) is not completely foreign to Anat; see Walls, *Anat*, 166-74.

[67] This would not be an innovation, since she is probably linked with a *marzēaḥ* at Ugarit; see the discussion of *CAT* 4.642 in Chapter 1. This establishes a precedent, not a direct connection.

[68] The popularity of Houtsma's emendation to סֹד סֹבְאִים ("a band of drunkards"; see Houtsma, "Bijdrage," 60; Wellhausen, *Propheten*, 112; Marti, *Dodekapropheton*, 45; Harper, *Amos and Hosea*, 262; Duhm, "Hosea," 21; Budde, "Hosea," 295; Sellin, *Zwölfprophetenbuch*$^2$, 61; Ward, *Hosea*, 81; *BHS*; the *RSV* [contrast the *NRSV*]; the *NEB*; the *JB*; for other emendations see Gangloff and Haelewyck, "Osée 4,17-19," 371nn22-29), has waned in recent years. Although the change is consistent with a *marzēaḥ*, the MT's *ר in the first word is confirmed by the versions, Symmachus and Aquila (see below); keeping the MT also preserves the paranomasia with סָרַר סֹרֵרָה (v. 16), and צָרַר (v. 19). The MT is retained by, *inter alia*, Nyberg, *Studien*, 33-34; Rudolph, *Hosea*, 108; Wolff, *Hosea*, 91; Andersen and Freedman, *Hosea*, 378-79; Nissinen, *Prophetie*, 124-26; Balz-Cochois, *Gomer*, 34-35; Davies, *Hosea*, 132-33; Wacker, *Figurationen*, 265; the *NRSV*; the *NAB*; cf. Willi-Plein, *Vorformen*, 138. For I. Zolli, "Hosea 4 17-18," *ZAW* 15 (1938) 175, סר means "putrid."

[69] See BDB 684-85; cf. Isa 56:12.

the participle סֹבֵא for habitual drinkers at Prov 23:20, 21 and at Deut 21:20, where parents label their drunkard son "stubborn" (סוֹרֵר).[70] By emphasizing that their drink is now gone, the verb סָר[71] suggests that significant amounts were consumed, and the connotations of the root סבא noted above suggest that the result was drunkenness (cf. v. 11).

However, this passage does not deal with a specific portion of the upper class. Despite the assertion by Gangloff and Haelewyck that this was "une association regroupant l'élite d'Ephraïm,"[72] the text addresses Ephraim as a whole (17a), and the earlier reference to Israel (16b) confirms that the entire nation is meant.[73] But if the whole nation was involved, the passage lacks the restricted membership characteristic of the extra-biblical *marzēaḥ*.

Nonetheless, two points suggest that a connection with the *marzēaḥ* association should not be discounted too hastily. The first is in 17a, where Ephraim is called a "companion (חֲבוּר) of idols."[74] This is an unusual construction: when humans are the subject of the root consonants חבר, it almost always refers to association with other people.[75] Moreover, since Ephraim is a designation for the entire nation, חֲבוּר

[70] The adjective also appears in Hos 4:16; the participle denotes drunkards at Ezek 23:42 and Nah 1:10 as well.

[71] Although סָר occurs with the same nuance in Amos 6:7, I am not convinced a direct correlation can be drawn between the cessation of the *marzēaḥ* there and the end of their alcohol here (*pace* Nissinen, *Prophetie*, 125; see also C. Maier and E. M. Dörrfuß, "'Um mit ihnen zu sitzen, zu essen und zu trinken': Am 6,7; Jer 16,5 und die Bedeutung von *marzeaḥ*," *ZAW* 111 (1999) 48). In Amos the verb is connected to the future exile of the *marzēaḥ* members, whereas here it simply indicates their current liquor supply is exhausted. Nonetheless, the fact the verb only has this meaning in these two places is suggestive.

[72] Gangloff and Haelewyck, "Osée 4,17-19," 380.

[73] In Hosea, especially when the two terms are paralleled, "Ephraim" tends to serve as a geographic designation for the northern kingdom while "Israel" indicates the people, especially in relationship to Yahweh. See Wolff, *Hosea*, 164; Jacob, "Osée," 67; Macintosh, *Hosea*, 338 and the texts they cite.

[74] The verb חָבַר means "to unit, join," and the *qal* passive participle (construct) here means "one united/joined with," i.e., a companion. It is altered to either חֶבֶר or חָבֵר by Duhm, "Hosea," 21; Harper, *Amos and Hosea*, 264; Budde, "Hosea," 294; Wellhausen, *Propheten*, 112; cf. Andersen and Freedman, *Hosea*, 377-78. Since this does not change the essential meaning, I retain the MT with, *inter alia*, Marti, *Dodekapropheton*, 45; Sellin, *Zwölfprophetenbuch*², 61; Wolff, *Hosea*, 72; Nissinen, *Prophetie*, 122; Davies, *Hosea*, 132; Wacker, *Figurationen*, 264.

[75] By way of contrast, it denotes those who cast (combine?) spells in Deut 18:11 (see also Isa 47:9, 11) and snake charmers in Ps 58:6. The only other exception is Isa 44:11, where "[an idol's] companions" may have the same nuance I am proposing here.

has the force of a collective here, i.e., "companions" or "a company." If the combined phrase is an elliptical reference to Ephraim as "a company (associated with) idols,"[76] it points to an identifiable group. In light of the drinking mentioned elsewhere in the passage, this might reflect "the men of the *marzēaḥ*" known from the extra-biblical references. That possibility is strengthened by the later use of חבר in reference to the "companions" of Obaidu who comprise a *marzēaḥ* at Petra.[77] Hos 4:17a may even represent the first use of the root in connection with a *marzēaḥ*.

The second factor to consider is the treatment of סָר סָבְאָם by ancient translators. The Targum and Vulgate both rendered the second word as "feast."[78] More importantly, both Aquila and Symmachus identified it as a "symposium," which is the Greek term used to render *marzēaḥ* in bilingual inscriptions from Palmyra. Aquila, apparently reading שׂר rather than סר (as did the Targum), even translated the resulting phrase as ἄρχων συμποσίου αὐτῶν ("leaders of their symposium"); the first two words are the plural equivalent of συμποσίαρχος, used to translate רב מרזחא ("*marzēaḥ* leader") at Palmyra.[79]

Since a basic principle of this study has been that information from later *marzēaḥ*s should not be read into earlier ones, I do not claim these parallels are decisive. But the later connotations of חבור are suggestive, and Aquila's and Symmachus' translations show that they saw the contemporary Greek equivalent of a *marzēaḥ* in the word סָבְאָם. If they could, so too might Hosea and his audience recognize their own contemporary *marzēaḥ* here. The passage does refer to

---

[76] Cf. Nissinen, *Prophetie*, 122 ("[Eine] Gemeinschaft mit den Götzenbilden") and Rudolph, *Hosea*, 106 ("In der Gesellschaft von Götzen ist Israel [*sic*]").

[77] See the discussion of the Nabatean *marzēaḥ* in Chapter 1 and O'Connor's suggestion that the word was a *terminus technicus* for a *marzēaḥ* member (M. O'Connor, "Northwest Semitic Designations for Elective Social Affinities," *JANES* 18 [1986] 72-80).

[78] שירויאן and *convivium* respectively. It is absent from the Peshitta and the LXX reads ᾑρέτισεν Χαναναίους ("he has chosen the Canaanites"). The verb may be a corruption of ἠρέθισε, which points to the adjective סַר, derived from סָרַר rather than the MT's perfect from סוּר; cf. Jerome's *provocavit* and Harper, *Amos and Hosea*, 262. As for the noun, Zolli suggests the translator read סֹבְאִם ("drunkards") and connected this with an understanding of the Canaanites (כְּנַעֲנִי) as those who "stagger" (נוּעַ) or are "subdued" (cf. כָּנַע) by drink; see Zolli, "Hosea 4 17-18," 175. William Irwin has suggested to me that the LXX may have understood the Hebrew to mean Ephraim had "turned aside" through their banquets, which was expressed as choosing the Canaanites (and their form of feasting).

[79] See in Chapter 1.

drinking in a religious context, so the only major characteristic missing is the restriction of the participants to a definable portion of the elite. The points noted in the preceding paragraphs do not negate that fact, but they raise the possibility Hosea may have had the *marzēaḥ* in mind when formulating the oracle.

In fact, when Hos 4:16-19 is read in the context of the entire chapter, the nation's involvement in a *marzēaḥ* could be seen as an imitation of their leader's *marzēaḥ*. I argued earlier that although Hosea 4 comprises separate oracles, they were delivered around the same time, and that the chapter draws significant parallels between the actions of the priests in the first part and those of the people in the second half.[80] In the words of Francis Landy, "Priest and people are mirror images of each other."[81] It is unlikely the entire nation, to a person, engaged in the deeds described in vv. 17-18, but in keeping with the principle of "like people, like priest" Hosea speaks as if they did. The priests have fornicated, numbed themselves with drink, and turned away from Yahweh towards dishonour. In imitation, the people dishonour themselves by forming a group dedicated to the goddess Anat and marked by copious, and probably excessive, drinking. While the large number of participants means this is not a *marzēaḥ* in the precise sense, the prophet has described the people's actions in terms of one. They are imitating the priests, who formed part of the Samarian elite, and some of whom may even have participated in the northern *marzēaḥ* Amos condemned.[82] In the prophet's mind, the actions of a significant part of the population is no different from that of a smaller part of the upper class, and it seems that he used features of a *marzēaḥ* to convey that point.

On the other hand, this passage contains an element not present in other instances of the *marzēaḥ*, namely, sexual license.[83] Gangloff and Haelewyck think this reflects later deuteronomistic influence,[84] but it is integral to the entire chapter. As such, it might provide evidence of a libidinous element to the specific *marzēaḥ* Hosea encoun-

---

[80] See pp. 136-37.

[81] F. Landy, *Hosea* (Readings: A New Biblical Commentary; Sheffield: JSOT Press, 1995) 66. See also Balz-Cochois, *Gomer*, 68-69; Jeremias, *Hosea*, 72.

[82] See especially the discussion of Amos 6:1, 3-7 in chapter 2.

[83] Pope, *Song of Songs*, 210-19, considers this to be a basic part of the *marzēaḥ*, but his evidence is from later sources not directly related to the *marzēaḥ*.

[84] Gangloff and Haelewyck, "Osée 4,17-19," 380. They also attribute the "idols" motif to the same source, but it in fact reflects the opinion of the prophet (see below).

tered, but it is not certain the sexual license occurs during the *marzēaḥ* itself. With many scholars, I take the verbs in v. 18a as sequential,[85] but even if they are concurrent, and the sex occurs simultaneously with the cessation of liquor, the fact remains that fornication only occurs after the drinking has ended. Since a primary aspect of the *marzēaḥ* elsewhere is drinking, and sexual license is unattested in connection with any other *marzēaḥ*, it seems best to separate the two.

Two remaining points can be treated briefly, namely the prophet's attitude toward this *marzēaḥ*, and the reason for it. It is obvious from the passage that Hosea does not approve of it, but unlike in Amos 6, this opposition is not provoked by the injustice reflected in the Samarian *marzēaḥ*. That is not to say the situation had changed significantly since Amos' condemnation, only that Hosea's main concern lies elsewhere. His primary objection is to this *marzēaḥ*'s connection with deities other than Yahweh, in keeping with his general attitude towards what he considers idolatry.[86]

## II. Hosea 9:1-6

The second text to consider is Hos 9:1-6, which Brian Peckham identifies as a "symposium" (= *marzēaḥ*) comparable to that described in Amos 6:4-7. In his words, "Hosea describes a festival of mourning for the dead that features drinking wine (Hos 9:1-4). It is a day of Yahweh (Hos 9:5), a time of death and burial (Hos 9:6) that money cannot divert (Hos 9:6)."[87] This statement will be examined in light of the biblical text and the criteria established from extra-biblical *marzēaḥ*s. A Hebrew text with English translation is presented first to facilitate the analysis.

### A. *The Text*

| | | | |
|---|---|---|---|
| אַל־תִּשְׂמַח יִשְׂרָאֵל | 1 | a | Do not rejoice, O Israel! |
| אַל־תָּגֵל[88] כָּעַמִּים | | b | Do not exult like the peoples! |

---

[85] See n. 11.

[86] For Hosea as an initiator of the "Yahweh-alone" movement see M. Smith, *Palestinian Parties and Politics That Shaped the Old Testament* (2nd ed.; London: SCM Press, 1987) 31-32; B. Lang, *Monotheism and the Prophetic Minority* (SWBA 1; Sheffield: The Almond Press, 1983) 30-33. On the movement in general see Smith, pp. 11-42; Lang, pp. 13-59.

[87] Peckham, "Phoenicia," 95n59.

[88] In place of the MT's אֶל־גִּיל.

| | | | |
|---|---|---|---|
| כִּי זָנִיתָ מֵעַל אֱלֹהֶיךָ | | c | For you have fornicated against your God,[90] |
| אָהַבְתָּ אֶתְנָן | | d | you have loved a prostitute's pay |
| עַל כָּל־גָּרְנוֹת דָּגָן | | e | on all the threshing floors of grain. |
| גֹּרֶן וָיֶקֶב לֹא יִרְעֵם | 2 | a | Threshing floor and vat will not befriend them,[91] |
| וְתִירוֹשׁ יְכַחֶשׁ בָּהּ | | b | and new wine will fail her.[92] |
| לֹא יֵשְׁבוּ בְּאֶרֶץ יהוה | 3 | a | They will not dwell in the land of Yahweh. |
| וְשָׁב אֶפְרַיִם מִצְרַיִם | | b | Ephraim will return to Egypt, |
| וּבְאַשּׁוּר טָמֵא יֹאכֵלוּ | | c | and in Assyria they will eat unclean food. |
| לֹא־יִסְּכוּ לְיהוה יַיִן | 4 | a | They will not pour out wine to Yahweh |
| וְלֹא יַעַרְבוּ־לוֹ[89] זִבְחֵיהֶם | | b | and they will not bring their sacrifices to him. |
| כְּלֶחֶם אוֹנִים לָהֶם | | c | (They will be)[93] like mourners' bread for them: |
| כָּל־אֹכְלָיו יִטַּמָּאוּ | | d | all who eat it will be defiled, |
| כִּי־לַחְמָם לְנַפְשָׁם | | e | for their bread will be for their (own) throats; |
| לֹא יָבוֹא בֵּית יהוה | | f | it will not come to the house of Yahweh. |
| מַה־תַּעֲשׂוּ לְיוֹם מוֹעֵד | 5 | a | What will you do on the day of assembly, |

[89] The verb is vocalized יֶעֶרְבוּ in the MT.

[90] The sense is that their fornication leads them away from God.

[91] יִרְעֵם derives from רָעָה II ("associate with, befriend"); cf. Nyberg, *Studien*, 68; Wolff, *Hosea*, 149; H. Utzschneider, *Hosea, Prophet vor dem Ende: Zum Verhältnis von Geschichte und Institution in der alttestamentlichen Prophetie* (OBO 31; Freiburg: Universitätsverlag; Göttingen: Vandenhoeck & Ruprecht, 1980) 155; Jeremias, *Hosea*, 112; Eidevall, *Grapes in the Desert*, 141. The LXX (οὐκ ἔγνω αὐτούς) apparently read the verb יָדַע ("know"); it is followed by Marti, *Dodekapropheton*, 70; Duhm, "Hosea," 29; Sellin, *Zwölfprophetenbuch*², 91; Wellhausen, *Propheten*, 122; Rudolph, *Hosea*, 170; Willi-Plein, *Vorformen*, 172. The Targum, Peshitta and Vulgate all reflect רָעָה II ("graze, feed"), while Macintosh, *Hosea*, 340, suggests רָעָה III ("attend to"). However, רָעָה II fits the context best: "associate with" provides a better parallel with זָנָה and אָהַב in v. 1 (Utzschneider, *Hosea*, 155), and negated, it constitutes a more appropriate contrast with those verbs and a better parallel with the following line. In any case, none of the proposed nuances affect the issue of a *marzēaḥ* allusion in the passage.

[92] "Her" refers to the harlotrous nation.

[93] Taking "their sacrifices" (זִבְחֵיהֶם) as doing double-duty in lines b and c, with Wacker, *Figurationen*, 162.

| | | | |
|---|---|---|---|
| וּלְיוֹם חַג־יהוה | | b | and on the day of the festival of Yahweh? |
| כִּי־הִנֵּה הָלְכוּ מִשֹּׁד | 6 | a | For even if[95] they escape destruction, |
| מִצְרַיִם תְּקַבְּצֵם | | b | Egypt will gather them,[96] |
| מֹף תְּקַבְּרֵם | | c | Memphis will bury them. |
| מַחְמַד לְכַסְפָּם[94] | | d | The best of their "silver"[97]— |
| קִמּוֹשׂ יִירָשֵׁם | | e | Nettles will dispossess them, |
| חוֹחַ בְּאָהֳלֵיהֶם | | f | thorns will be in their tents. |

The text above diverges from the MT twicc. In line 1b, rather than the MT's אֶל־גִּיל ("to exultation") I emend to אַל־תָּגֵל with the LXX,

[94] This line has been the object of numerous emendations. מַחֲמַדֵּי כַסְפָּם ("their precious things of silver") is proposed by Wellhausen, *Propheten*, 123; Harper, *Amos and Hosea*, 326. Following the LXX's Μαχμάς, Duhm, "Hosea," 29, emends the first word to מכמס ("Aufbewahrungsort"), which yields "depository for their silver." The same word is changed to מעמד ("pedestal"), and "silver" is identified as "idols" (cf. n. 97 below) by Ward, *Hosea*, 157, 160. Marti, *Dodekapropheton*, 71-72 and Sellin, *Zwölfprophetenbuch*[2], 91, 94 alter the first word to מַחֲמַדֵּיהֶם and delete the second as a gloss; Marti translates the word as "their valuables/jewelry" ("ihre Kostbarkeiten/Kleinodien") while Sellin prefers "their sanctuaries" ("ihre Heiligtümer"; cf. Lam 1:10; Ezek 24:21; Joel 4:5; Hag 2:17; 2 Chr 36:19). For discussion of these and even more extensive emendations, plus the versional evidence, see Barthélemy, *Critique Textuelle 3*, 563-64; for the versions see also Macintosh, *Hosea*, 350-51. See further n. 97 below.

[95] For הִנֵּה initiating conditional statements see BDB 244; Williams, *Hebrew Syntax*, §513; cf. Waltke and O'Connor, *Biblical Hebrew Syntax*, §40.2.1.d. The conditional nature of this line is not clarified until 6c; cf. n. 96.

[96] By itself, this line seems to indicate protection, but 6c shows it is the reverse: Egypt will "gather them" to their ancestors.

[97] The Hebrew in this line is obscure; for various emendations see n. 94. Rudolph, *Hosea*, 170, 172, on the basis of G. R. Driver, "Babylonian and Hebrew Notes," *WO* 2 (1954) 26, gives the meaning "shame, disillusionment" for the root כסף here (cf. Zeph 2:1), and translates "Was sie begehrten, wird ihnen zur Enttäuschung werden" (the "desired thing" is Egypt); see also Mays, *Hosea*, 125; Davies, *Hosea*, 219-20. According to Barthélemy, *Critique Textuelle 3*, 564, Driver was anticipated by Michaelis. Macintosh, *Hosea*, 348, 350, renders the phrase as "the proud glory pertaining to their silver," which he interprets as Israel's trust in tribute paid to Egypt. However, since all but one reference to silver in Hosea is directly connected to idols (Hos 2:10; 8:4; 13:2; the only other instance of the word is Hos 3:2, where Hosea buys an adulteress [Gomer?], for fifteen silver shekels, but even this is related to worship of other gods), the line should be interpreted accordingly; see Wolff, *Hosea*, 156; Andersen and Freedman, *Hosea*, 531; Barthélemy, *Critique Textuelle 3*, 564. Thus, I take the line as a periphrastic genitive with *lamed* (cf. GKC §130a; Waltke and O'Connor, *Biblical Hebrew Syntax*, §9.7a-b) and interpret it as a superlative, following Andersen and Freedman, *Hosea*, 514. This results in a balance between the two halves of v. 6: lines a-c deal with the peoples' death and d-f with their idols' gradual "eviction."

Targum, Syriac, Vulgate, and the majority of scholars.[98] The change creates a better parallel with line a, and is more consistent with the verbs שָׂמַח and גִּיל as a fixed pair.[99] The result does not significantly alter the meaning. Secondly, in 4b the verb was pointed as יֶעֶרְבוּ by the Masoretes, who understood עָרַב III ("be pleasing"), as did the versions. While this provides an acceptable meaning, the cognate languages give evidence of the meaning "to enter" for this root as well.[100] Pointing it as a (negated) *hiphil* yields "they will not bring (their sacrifices)," which is a more precise parallel to the preceding "they will not pour out wine."[101] In either case the reference to "sacrifices" remains.

## B. *Establishing the Unit*

There is general agreement that the larger unit for this passage comprises Hos 9:1-9.[102] Although there are redactional links between those verses and the surrounding material, Hosea 8 and 9:10ff constitute divine speech, whereas Hos 9:1-9 is prophetic speech referring to God in the third person. But at the same time, vv. 1-6 deal with the prophet's announcement concerning the fall harvest festival while vv. 7-9 reflect his interaction with the people on the basis of that message. Since vv. 1-6 contain the proposed allusions to the *marzēaḥ*, only they have been reproduced above, and the following discussion will be restricted to those verses.

---

[98] Macintosh, *Hosea*, 337, is a rare exception; cf. the ambivalence of Jacob, "Osée," 66. Harper, *Amos and Hosea*, 325, deletes the phrase as a gloss on 1a; Rudolph, *Hosea*, 171, deletes אֶל.

[99] See P. Humbert, "Laetari et exultare dans le vocabulaire religieux de l'Ancien Testament," *RHPR* 22 (1942) 185-214. For their pairing in Ugaritic see W. Kuhnigk, *Nordwestsemitische Studien zum Hoseabuch* (BibOr 27; Rome: Biblical Institute Press, 1974) 110.

[100] For discussion and examples see G. R. Driver, "Linguistic and Textual Problems: Minor Prophets I," *JTS* 39 (1939) 158-59; *idem*, *Studies in Old Testament Prophecy* (ed. H. H. Rowley; Edinburgh: T. & T. Clark, 1950) 64-65; M. J. Dahood, *Psalms III: 101-150. A New Translation with Introduction and Commentary* (AB 17A; New York: Doubleday, 1970) 47; Kuhnigk, *Hoseabuch*, 115; Andersen and Freedman, *Hosea*, 526.

[101] In addition to those mentioned (minus Dahood) in n. 100, this change is adopted by J. Mauchline, "The Book of Hosea," *IB* 6.657; Rudolph, *Hosea*, 172; Mays, *Hosea*, 124; Willi-Plein, *Vorformen*, 172; Jeremias, *Hosea*, 112. The emendation to יַעַרְכוּ by older scholars such as Wellhausen, *Propheten*, 123; Marti, *Dodekapropheton*, 71; Harper, *Amos and Hosea*, 328, is not necessary.

[102] See the commentaries.

Within those limits, vv. 4-5 are often taken as a later addition reflecting cultic centralization under Josiah.[103] However, "Yahweh's house" in Hos 8:1 and 9:15 cannot mean the Jerusalem temple, and the parallel with 9:3a suggests the phrase in 9:4f refers to the land,[104] and thus is to be retained.

## C. *Discussion*

Peckham's characterization of this text as a *marzēaḥ* (symposium) is linked to his understanding of the *marzēaḥ* as a funerary banquet.[105] For Peckham, it alludes to the *marzēaḥ* because v. 6 is "a time of death and burial" and vv. 1-4 describe "a festival of mourning for the dead."[106] However, there is no evidence of a funerary connection for earlier *marzēaḥs*, and minimal links afterwards.[107] This does not mean such a connection is impossible here *a priori*, but in any case the practices Peckham names are not contemporary with Hosea. Granted, v. 4c begins with the phrase, "like mourners' bread" (כְּלֶחֶם אוֹנִים)[108] and v. 6 mentions burial, but Hos 9:1-6 reflects the Judgment Against the Nation form:[109] v. 1 contains a call to attention

---

[103] Marti, *Dodekapropheton*, 71; Sellin, *Zwölfprophetenbuch*², 93; Rudolph, *Hosea*, 176; Wolff, *Hosea*, 150; Mays, *Hosea*, 127; Willi-Plein, *Vorformen*, 172; Jeremias, *Hosea*, 116n13; Yee, *Composition and Tradition*, 199; T. Naumann, *Hoseas Erben: Strukturen der Nachinterpretation im Buch Hosea* (BWANT 131; Stuttgart/Berlin/Cologne: Kohlhammer, 1991) 81-83; Wacker, *Figurationen*, 162; Macintosh, *Hosea*, 345.

[104] Andersen and Freedman, *Hosea*, 528, note the phrase נְוַת בַּיִת ("sheep fold of the house") in Ps 68:13 and the Akkadian reference to rural temple land as *bît-ilanī* (*CAD* B:287). Wellhausen and Harper take it as a reference to any "temple" or "place" (respectively) dedicated to Yahweh (Wellhausen, *Propheten*, 123; Harper, *Amos and Hosea*, 329). Ward, *Hosea*, 164, identifies the phrase with Yahweh's people and also retains it.

[105] Peckham, "Phoenicia," 83.

[106] Ibid., 95n59.

[107] See chapters 1 and 2, *passim*. Hos 4:16-19 does not reflect mourning practices either.

[108] Andersen and Freedman consider the MT's initial preposition an asseverative כִּי and take אוֹנִים as the plural of אָוֶן ("wickedness); understanding the latter as "idols," they translate, "Indeed, the food of idols is theirs"; see Andersen and Freedman, *Hosea*, 514, 526-27. However, vv. 3-5 do not contrast the worship of Yahweh and other deities, but describe the cessation of Yahwistic worship when the people are in foreign lands (cf. further in n. 110). The preservation of the MT and the traditional rendering of the phrase is more fitting in this context.

[109] On the form see C. Westermann, *Basic Forms of Prophetic Speech* (trans. H. C. White, foreword by G. M. Tucker; 1967; rpt. Cambridge: The Lutterworth Press; Louisville: Westminster/John Knox Press, 1991) 169-76.

plus the accusation, while the rest of the passage constitutes the punishment which will follow. As such, only v. 1 reflects the situation at the time the oracle was delivered, while vv. 2-6 indicate the future fate of the nation. Moreover, v. 4c is not even a statement of reality, but rather a simile comparing their future sacrifices with mourners' food. Because they will be separated from "the land of Yahweh" they will not be able to offer sacrifice to Yahweh and, devoid of cultic significance, their sacrifices will serve only to satisfy their hunger, just like food rendered impure by proximity to death.[110] In short, there is only one reference to death in this passage (v. 6), and that is linked to Israel's future punishment, not the practice of Hosea's contemporaries.[111]

Nevertheless, the lack of a funerary connection does not automatically rule out a *marzēaḥ* allusion here. However, in order to determine whether a non-funerary *marzēaḥ* constitutes the background to this passage the criteria established in the first chapter must be applied. In other words, does this text reflect extensive alcohol consumption by the elite within a religious context? But before that question can be answered, the situation Hosea addressed in this text must be reconstructed. That can be done in two ways, on the basis of the form-critical considerations noted above. First, the call to attention and the accusation in v. 1 give direct evidence of the nation's activity. Secondly, this can be supplemented by the pronouncement of judgment in vv. 2-6. Specifically, if certain actions are eliminated as part of the future punishment, it is likely they were practiced by Hosea's contemporaries.

On this basis, only one of the criteria for a *marzēaḥ* allusion is present here, namely the religious connection. The verbs שָׂמַח and גִּיל in v. 1 are cultic terms,[112] while the judgment section speaks of wine libations (4a), sacrifices (4b), the "day of assembly" (5a) and the "festival of Yahweh" (5b).[113] There is some indication of non-yah-

[110] Cf. Deut 26:14. Hos 9:3-5 reflects the early notion that Yahweh is linked with the land of Israel, and cannot be properly worshipped outside of it. Cf. 1 Sam 26:19; 2 Kgs 5:17; Ps 137:4.

[111] Hos 9:4c lacks a verb, but the surrounding lines establish a future orientation.

[112] Humbert, "Laetari et Exultare," 185-214.

[113] Probably the fall harvest festival of Sukkoth; it is given this designation at Lev. 23:39; Judg 21:19. This is consistent with the harvest imagery in vv. 1d-2b (understanding the "prostitute's pay" as the harvest, which they have not attributed to Yahweh, thus leading to the harlotry motif).

wistic elements in this worship, such as the harlotry motif Hosea uses for unacceptable worship and the associations of גִּיל with Canaanite practices.[114] But on the other hand, Yahweh is mentioned four times in vv. 3-5, while "Israel" in v. 1 is associated with Yahweh's cultic community.[115] It seems, therefore, that the passage describes a form of yahwistic worship that includes aspects unacceptable to Hosea.

Nevertheless, there is insufficient evidence in the passage of extensive drinking by a specific portion of the upper class. "New wine" is mentioned in 2b and libations of wine in 4a, but there is no indication of excess. More importantly, the text deals with the entire nation, identified as Israel in v. 1a and Ephraim in 3b. But unlike Hos 4:16-19, the context does not reflect the principle of "like priest, like people." Rather than the nation imitating the activities of the leaders, as in the earlier passage, this text deals with the fall harvest festival, which would have normally included the majority of the people. Moreover, the two passages stem from different points in Hosea's ministry,[116] so without something in Hos 9:1-6 to show that the prophet was thinking in those terms, the restrictive nature of the *marzēaḥ* is neither present nor imitated.

Since the two points covered in the preceding paragraph are constitutive elements of the *marzēaḥ* throughout its history, their absence here is decisive. Without any indication that large amounts of alcohol were consumed by a recognizable and restricted group, Hos 9:1-6 must be rejected as an allusion to the *marzēaḥ*.

---

[114] On the latter see Humbert, "Laetari et Exultare," 185-214; D. W. Harvey, "Rejoice Not, O Israel," *Israel's Prophetic Heritage: Essays in Honor of James Muilenburg* (eds. B. W. Anderson and W. Harrelson; New York: Harper & Brothers, 1962) 115-27. Cf. Hos 10:5 and Rudolph, *Hosea*, 171; Wolff, *Hosea*, 153; Utzschneider, *Hosea*, 178; Andersen and Freedman, *Hosea*, 522; Jeremias, *Hosea*, 115; Landy, *Hosea*, 112; Macintosh, *Hosea*, 337. Some see a reference to Dagon, the god of grain, in 1e (e.g., Ward, *Hosea*, 159, 163; Kuhnigk, *Hoseabuch*, 112); Kuhnigk also takes Tirosh as a divine name and emends 2a to read "Victor" and "Thunder," Ugaritic titles for Baʿal.

[115] See n. 73.

[116] Hos 4:16-19 is generally dated to late in the reign of Jeroboam II, while 9:1-6 post-dates the Assyrian invasion of 733 BCE. See, for example, the discussions of Wolff, *Hosea*, 75-76 and 153; *Davies*, Hosea, 112 and 211-12.

## III. Summary

In this chapter, Hos 4:16-19 and 9:1-6 were considered as possible allusions to the *marzēaḥ*. The first provided clear evidence of drinking within an explicitly religious context, and the connotations associated with the root סבא suggest this was to the point of drunkenness. Although this was done by the entire nation, Hosea's interpretive principle in the chapter indicates he envisioned their actions as an imitation of the priests, who constitute a recognizable group among the elite. After the alcohol was consumed they engaged in promiscuous sex, but this was not so much a part of their *marzēaḥ*-like actions as supplemental to them. Attributing the passage to Hosea himself[117] would date this *marzēaḥ* allusion slightly after Amos 4:1 and 6:1, 3-7.

In contrast, the only thing Hos 9:1-6 has in common with a *marzēaḥ* is the religious references. The passage deals with the entire nation engaged in an activity proper to it rather than to a small portion thereof. Thus, this is not a case of the general populace imitating their leaders. In addition, the element of abundant drinking cannot be established from the text. Therefore, Hos 9:1-6 does not meet the minimum criteria for a *marzēaḥ* allusion.

---

[117] See p. 135 and n. 116.

CHAPTER FOUR

# THE *MARZĒAḤ* IN ISAIAH?

Four Isaiah texts have been proposed as *marzēaḥ* allusions: Isa 5:11-13; 28:1-4; 28:7-8 and 56:9-57:3.[1] All deal with drunkenness, the similarity to Amos 6:1, 3-7 is often noted, and other arguments are presented for each Isaiah passage as well. No one has explicitly identified Isa 5:11-13 as a *marzēaḥ* allusion, but Reinhard Fey has argued that Isaiah relied on the Amos passage in composing Isa 5:11-13.[2] Bernhard A. Asen connects Isa 28:1-4 with a *marzēaḥ* on the basis of the references to drunkenness, flowers and oil.[3] Some scholars find parallels between Isa 28:7-8 and El's *marzēaḥ* at Ugarit,[4] with a few also noting funerary elements in the surrounding context.[5] Finally, Jared Jackson points to the beds in both Amos 6:4 and Isa 57:7-8.[6]

---

[1] Since the word *marzēaḥ* does not appear in the book of Isaiah, the latter was not considered in Bryan's dissertation. Heider implies that Isa 65:4 describes a *marzēaḥ* feast (G. C. Heider, *The Cult of Molek: A Reassessment* [JSOTSup 43; Sheffield: JSOT Press, 1985] 389), but there is no mention of alcohol in the text and, as Heider notes, it describes a "nation" and a "people," not just the elite. For these reasons, Isa 65:4 can be excluded from future consideration.

[2] R. Fey, *Amos und Jesaja: Abhängigkeit und Eigenständigkeit des Jesaja* (WMANT 12; Neukirchen-Vluyn: Neukirchener Verlag, 1963) 10-22.

[3] B. A. Asen, "The Garlands of Ephraim: Isaiah 28:1-6 and the *marzēaḥ*," *JSOT* 71 (September 1996) 73-87. Isa 28:1-4 are also called a *marzēaḥ* by J. J. Jackson, "Style in Isaiah 28 and a Drinking Bout of the Gods (RS 24.258)," *Rhetorical Criticism: Essays in Honor of James Muilenburg* (PTMS 1; eds. J. J. Jackson and M. Kessler; Pittsburgh: Pickwick, 1974) 97. He too mentions the garland, but provides no arguments for his designation or a connection between flowers and the *marzēaḥ*.

[4] M. H. Pope, "A Divine Banquet at Ugarit," *The Use of the Old Testament in the New and Other Essays: Studies in Honor of W. F. Stinespring* (ed. J. M. Efird; Durham: Duke University Press, 1972) 196; *idem*, *Song of Songs: A New Translation with Introduction and Commentary* (AB 7C; Garden City: Doubleday, 1977) 217; *idem*, "The Cult of the Dead at Ugarit," *Ugarit in Retrospect* (ed. G. D. Young; Winona Lake: Eisenbrauns, 1981) 178; Jackson, "Style," 94-95; R. B. Coote, *Amos Among the Prophets: Composition and Theology* (Philadelphia: Fortress Press, 1981) 38; B. Halpern, "'The Excremental Vision': The Doomed Priests of Doom in Isaiah 28," *HAR* 10 (1987) 118; Asen, "Garlands," 76.

[5] Halpern, "'The Excremental Vision,'" 118-19; K. van der Toorn, "Echoes of Judaean Necromancy in Isaiah 28:7-22," *ZAW* 100 (1988) 213; M. A. Sweeney, *Isaiah 1-39, with an Introduction to Prophetic Literature* (FOTL 16; Grand Rapids: Wm. B. Eerdmans Publishing Co., 1996) 367, 369, 371.

Each passage and the accompanying arguments will be considered in turn.

## I. Isa 5:11-13

Although most critics note similar content here and in various portions of Amos 6:1, 3-7 (one of the two explicit *marzēaḥ* texts in the Bible) no one has directly identified Isa 5:11-13 as a *marzēaḥ* allusion. However, if Fey is correct concerning the latter's literary dependence on the Amos passage, it may be addressing the same situation, namely a *marzēaḥ*. Since Fey's proposal is built upon lexical and structural aspects of the two texts, it is important to establish the wording and extent of the Isaiah passage[7] before considering the details of his argument and its relevance for a *marzēaḥ* allusion in Isa 5:11-13.

### A. *The Text*

| | | | |
|---|---|---|---|
| הוֹי מַשְׁכִּימֵי בַבֹּקֶר | 11 | a | Alas, you who rise early in the morning |
| שֵׁכָר יִרְדֹּפוּ | | b | in pursuit of strong drink, |
| מְאַחֲרֵי[8] בַנֶּשֶׁף | | c | who linger in the evening, |
| יַיִן יַדְלִיקֵם[9] | | d | (with) wine inflaming them. |
| וְהָיָה[10] כִנּוֹר וָנֶבֶל | 12 | a | Whose feast[11] consists of lyre and lute, |

---

[6] Jackson, "Style," 96.

[7] Amos 6:1, 3-7 has already been presented in Chapter 2.

[8] The addition of הוֹי at the beginning of this line by O. Procksch, *Jesaia I übersetzt und erklärt* (KAT 9; Leipzig: Deichert, 1930) 91, is without textual or versional support, and unnecessary, since the הוֹי at the beginning of v. 11 governs the succeeding lines.

[9] This is emended to יִדְלִיקוּן by Kissane, who translates "they pursue"; see E. J. Kissane, *The Book of Isaiah: Translated from a Critically Revised Hebrew Text with Commentary* (Rev. ed.; Dublin: Richview, 1960) 54, 55, 57. However, the *hiphil* of דָּלַק does not bear this meaning (H. Wildberger, *Isaiah 1-12: A Commentary* [Continental Commentaries; trans. T. H. Trapp; Minneapolis: Fortress Press, 1991] 190); H. L. Ginsberg, "Some Emendations in Isaiah," *JBL* 69 (1950) 52-53, avoids this objection by emending to יִדְלָקוּן. Although the meaning fits the parallelism, the MT prepares for the lack of comprehension in 12c-d; see J. N. Oswalt, *The Book of Isaiah, Chapters 1-39* (NICOT; Grand Rapids: Wm. B. Eerdmans Publishing Co., 1986) 155n3.

| | | | |
|---|---|---|---|
| תֹּף וְחָלִיל וָיַיִן[12] מִשְׁתֵּיהֶם[13] | | b | tambourine and flute, and wine, |
| וְאֵת פֹּעַל יהוה לֹא יַבִּיטוּ | | c | but who do not consider the deeds of Yahweh, |
| וּמַעֲשֵׂה יָדָיו לֹא רָאוּ | | d | or see the work of his hands! |
| לָכֵן גָּלָה עַמִּי מִבְּלִי־דָעַת | 13 | a | Therefore my people are exiled without knowledge; |
| וּכְבוֹדוֹ מֵתֵי[14] רָעָב | | b | its nobles[15] are dying of hunger, |
| וַהֲמוֹנוֹ צִחֵה צָמָא | | c | and its multitude is parched with thirst. |

Apart from a minor revocalization in 13b, this text duplicates the MT. The Masoretic pointing as מְתֵי רָעָב ("men of hunger") gives an acceptable meaning, but is not a good parallel to 13c, where the word "parched" (צִחֵה) indicates the deprivation's effect. The first word is often emended to מְזֵי ("exhausted [from hunger]"),[16] but although this provides a better parallel, it is without manuscript or versional

---

[10] Emended to הוֹי by R. B. Y. Scott, "Isaiah Chapters 1-39: Introduction and Exegesis," *IB* 200. This incorrectly shifts the lament's address from the individuals to their actions. See also n. 8.

[11] For the singular with a ' (in line b of the Hebrew) see GKC §93ss; F. Delitzsch, *Biblical Commentary on the Prophecies of Isaiah* (4th ed.; Edinburgh: T. & T. Clark, 1890) 126-27; K. Marti, *Das Buch Jesaja erklärt* (KHAT 10; Tübingen: J. C. B. Mohr [Paul Siebeck], 1900) 56; G. B. Gray, *A Critical and Exegetical Commentary on the Book of Isaiah. Vol. I: Introduction and Commentary on I-XXVII* (ICC; Edinburgh: T. & T. Clark, 1912) 93; E. J. Young, *The Book of Isaiah: The English Text, with Introduction, Exposition, and Notes* (NICOT; Grand Rapids: Wm. B. Eerdmans, 1965) 209n13.

[12] This is changed to בֵּין ("during [their feast]") by W. Caspari, "Hebräisch בין temporal," *OLZ* 16 (1913) 337-341. He is followed by E. Jacob, *Esaïe 1-12* (CAT 8a; Genève: Labor et Fides, 1987) 85; Wildberger, *Isaiah 1-12*, 191. However, a reference to wine is consistent with the enumeration of a banquet's elements (cf. Isa 24:7-9; Amos 6:4-6).

[13] Emendation to either משעתם ("their interests") with Ginsberg, "Some Emendations," 52, or מְזִמָּתָם ("their scheming") with G. Fohrer, *Das Buch Jesaja Bd. 1: Kap. 1-23* (Zürcher Bibelkommentare; 2nd ed.; Zürich/Stuttgart: Zwingli Verlag, 1966) 81, is unnecessary, since the MT makes perfect sense and neither change has textual or versional support.

[14] In place of the MT's מְתֵי; see immediately below.

[15] A case of the abstract (literally, "its nobility") for the concrete.

[16] E.g., by T. K. Cheyne, *The Prophecies of Isaiah: A New Translation with Commentary and Appendices* (4th ed., rev.; New York: Thomas Whittaker, 1886) 1.32, 2.138; Marti, *Jesaja*, 57; B. Duhm, *Das Buch Jesaia übersetzt und erklärt* (HAT 3; 4th ed.; Göttingen: Vandenhoeck & Ruprecht, 1922) 58; Fohrer, *Jesaja 1*, 81; O. Kaiser, *Isaiah 1-12: A Commentary* (OTL; 2nd ed., revised and completely rewritten; trans. J. Bowden; Philadelphia: Westminster Press, 1983) 94n7; J. D. W. Watts, *Isaiah 1-33* (WBC 24; Waco: Word Books, 1985) 59; Wildberger, *Isaiah 1-12*, 191. The proposal can be traced to F. Hitzig, *Der Prophet Jesaja, übersetzt und ausgelegt* (Heidelberg: C. F. Winter, 1833).

support. The adopted reading (a construct plural participle from מות) enjoys both.[17] It also indicates the effect of the hunger, while the reduced intensity in the next line highlights the shift from the nobles (the principle recipients of the punishment) to the general populace.[18] The repointing does not affect the essential meaning of the line or the issue of a *marzēaḥ* allusion in the passage.

### B. *Establishing the Unit*

The opening cry of "alas" (הוֹי) marks the unit's starting point. Since the same word occurs in v. 18, a few consider vv. 11-17 as the basic unit.[19] There are problems with that delineation, however. The word "therefore" (לָכֵן) occurs in both vv. 13 and 14,[20] corresponding to a switch from masculine addressees in vv. 11-13 to 3rd feminine singular pronouns in v. 14.[21] A double announcement of judgment is not impossible, but the switch from the city's inhabitants to the city itself indicates that vv. 11-13 and 14-17 should be separated. Structural features support this conclusion. The judgment in v. 13 is an ironic reversal of the failings described in vv. 11-12, which creates a mirror structure: their carousing (11-12b) and unawareness of God's

[17] It is found in two manuscripts (see *BHS*) and was read by the LXX, Targum, Vulgate and Syriac. This reading is adopted by Gray, *Isaiah I*, 92, 93; Kissane, *Isaiah*, 54, 55; Jacob, *Esaïe 1-12*, 83 and most modern English translations. The MT is retained by Delitzsch, *Isaiah*, 127; Young, *Isaiah*, 205; D. Barthélemy, *Critique textuelle de l'Ancien Testament. 2. Isaïe, Jérémie, Lamentations* (OBO 50; Fribourg: Editions Universitaires; Göttingen: Vandenhoeck & Ruprecht, 1986) 33-34; Oswalt, *Isaiah 1-39*, 156.

[18] See also on p. 162.

[19] Thus, e.g., Young, *Isaiah*, 205; Watts, *Isaiah 1-33*, 61. Verses 8-17 are combined by Oswalt, *Isaiah 1-39*, 155-62; Sweeney, *Isaiah 1-39*, 124-25. Isa 5:11-30 + 10:1-6 (minus 5:24c-25 and 10:4b) are considered a (probably) Isaianic exposition of the Vineyard Song in 5:1-7 by M. C. A. Korpel, "Structural Analysis as a Tool for Redaction Criticism: The Example of Isaiah 5 and 10.1-6," *JSOT* 69 (March 1996) 53-71. See also C. E. L'Heureux, "The Redactional History of Isaiah 5:1–10:4," *In the Shelter of Elyon: Essays on Ancient Palestinian Life and Literature in Honor of G. W. Ahlström* (JSOTSup 31; eds. W. B. Barrick and J. R. Spencer; Sheffield: JSOT Press, 1984) 99-119.

[20] The second is absent from the LXX, but confirmed by the Vulgate and Syriac. A missing verse, introduced by הוֹי, to which the second "therefore" would respond, is proposed by Gray, *Isaiah I*, 92; Procksch, *Jesaia I*, 91, 94.

[21] Verses 11-12 contain masculine plural participles and finite verbs; v. 13 contains 3rd masculine singular pronouns, referring to the collective "my people." The feminine pronouns in v. 14a-b refer to Sheol, but those in 14c-d are generally understood to indicate the city Jerusalem.

activity (12c-d) results in exile "without knowledge" (13a) and the negation of their carousing (13b-c).[22] This pattern turns the verses in upon themselves, and is duplicated in vv. 14-17.[23] Thus, the majority of critics consider vv. 14-17 an expansion of the primary proclamation of judgment in v. 13.[24]

Within the boundaries of Isa 5:11-13, a few deletions have been proposed. Various portions of line 12 have been deleted for reasons of metre,[25] but all parts of the line are normal components of an ancient feast.[26] More significantly, Otto Kaiser would remove v. 12 as a "later eschatological interpretation" and v. 13 as an "historicizing" one.[27] Since Fey relies on both verses in establishing dependence on Amos, their deletion would negate some of his arguments. However, both are intricately linked with v. 11 in the mirror pattern as an ironic reversal of the condemned action. At the same time, the basic structure of a Judgment Oracle in terms of a condemnation and announcement of judgment[28] supports the retention of vv. 12 and 13 as original parts of the oracle.

---

[22] R. B. Chisholm, Jr., "Structure, Style, and the Prophetic Message: An Analysis of Isaiah 5:8-30," *BSac* 143 (1986) 52. This feature's importance is highlighted by comparison with Amos 6:1, 3-7, where the judgment section is also an ironic reversal of their situation, but without a mirror pattern.

[23] Sheol eats (v. 14), the self-exalted are humbled (v. 15), Yahweh is exalted (v. 16), sheep eat (v. 17); see Chisholm, "Isaiah 5:8-30," 52.

[24] There are exceptions: in addition to the views presented in n. 19 above, Kissane, *Isaiah*, 56-57, links vv. 13-14 while transposing vv. 15-17 after v. 10; vv. 13-14 are considered a subunit by Korpel, "Structural Analysis," 58; R. B. Y. Scott, "Isaiah 1-39," 200-201, considers vv. 14-16 "out of place," with v. 17 as the completion of v. 13; and Hayes and Irvine think vv. 13-17 "expound upon and develop the claim of verse 12*b*," although the content shifts from exile in v. 13 to an earthquake in vv. 14-17 (J. H. Hayes and S. A. Irvine, *Isaiah the Eighth-Century Prophet: His Times and His Preaching* [Nashville: Abingdon Press, 1987] 104). Vv. 14 and 17 (with vv. 15-16 a later addition) are considered the original conclusion to vv. 11-12 by R. Porath, *Die Sozialkritik im Jesajabuch: Redaktionsgeschichtliche Analyse* (Europäische Hochschulschriften Reihe XXIII: Theologie 503; Frankfurt am Main: Peter Lang, 1994) 113-16.

[25] E.g., "tambourine and flute" is rejected by Duhm, *Jesaia*, 58, "and wine" is omitted by Ginsberg, "Some Emendations," 52 and Procksch, *Jesaia I*, 91, drops "and wine (is) their feast."

[26] Cf. Isa 24:7-9; Amos 6:4-6.

[27] See Kaiser, *Isaiah 1-12*, 97, 98, 104, 106, 108-09; he dates both redactions to the exilic period or later. Verse 13 (only) is also considered later by Porath, *Sozialkritik*, 113-16, 137.

[28] C. Westermann, *Basic Forms of Prophetic Speech* (trans. H. C. White, foreword by G. M. Tucker; 1967; rpt. Cambridge: The Lutterworth Press; Louisville: Westminster/John Knox Press, 1991) 169-76.

## C. *Discussion*

As a woe oracle,[29] Isa 5:11-13 laments the inescapable death of drunken banqueters. Their geographical location is not specified, but they are generally considered Judahites. An exception is Marvin Sweeney, who thinks the prophet is addressing the south but describing the inhabitants of the north.[30] Their identity is important because of the reference to a northern *marzēaḥ* in Amos 6:7, and the allusion to one at the time of Hosea (Hos 4:16-19). If Isaiah is describing a scene in northern Israel, this increases the possibility that he is alluding to the same situation as his predecessors.[31] Sweeney's proposal is tenuous, however. Since participles within a woe oracle function as vocatives,[32] Isaiah is directing the lament at the feast's participants, and while he could have addressed northern drinkers from a distance, the text does not demand that conclusion.[33] Since Sweeney admits the text is ambiguous,[34] judgment should be withheld, and any allusion to a *marzēaḥ* established on grounds other than an uncertain geographical location.

Although not in itself conclusive, Fey's proposal that Isa 5:11-13 is based upon Amos 6 would support a *marzēaḥ* allusion in this text.[35] Both passages contain an accusation, introduced by הוֹי ("alas"), which is followed by a relatively shorter announcement of judgment, introduced by לָכֵן ("therefore"). In both instances the accusation alternates between participial and finite verb forms, and is formulated with a lengthy description of what they have done (Amos 6:1, 3-6b; Isa 5:11-12b) followed by brief statement of what they have not done (Amos 6:6c; Isa 5:12c-d). Finally, in both, the threat of exile constitutes an ironic reversal of their situation: in Amos the "first of the nations" will be the first exiles, while in Isaiah those who drink at feasts will suffer hunger and thirst.

---

[29] See the discussion of this form in Chapter 2.

[30] Sweeney, *Isaiah 1-39*, 130-31.

[31] Especially in light of the probable dependence of Isa 5:11-13 on Amos 6:1, 3-7 (see further below).

[32] See the discussion in chapter 2.

[33] *Contra* Sweeney's claim that the kind of land-grabbing described in the companion woe of Isa 5:8-10 was not practiced in Judah at this time, see H. Bardtke, "Die Latifundien in Juda während der zweiten Hälfte des achten Jahrhunderts v. Chr. (zum Verständnis von Jes 5, 8-10)," *Hommages à André Dupont-Sommer* (ed. A. Caquot; Paris: Librairie Adrien Maisonneuve, 1971) 235-54.

[34] Sweeney, *Isaiah 1-39*, 131.

[35] For a detailed presentation of the following, see Fey, *Amos und Jesaja*, 10-22.

The only significant objection to Fey's proposal is advanced by Eryl W. Davies,[36] who attributes the similar form and content to the shared use of the Woe form in addressing a similar cultural, social and religious situation. He also discounts the threat of exile as too common in the prophets to be significant, and notes that "my people" (עַמִּי) and "without knowledge" (מִבְּלִי־דָעַת) are absent from the Amos text.[37] Davies is correct that the basic structure and the verb forms are due to the Woe form, and that the common general content might reflect a similar situation encountered by both prophets, but the detailed structure and shared vocabulary cannot be as easily dismissed. The extreme imbalance in length between the accusation and the judgment sections of Amos 6:1, 3-7 and Isa 5:11-13 is unparalleled in other woe oracles.[38] The formulation of the accusation as a long statement of their actions plus a short statement of their inaction is also rare in the prophetic woes,[39] and judgment as an ironic reversal is not a necessary feature either.[40] As for vocabulary, although exile is a frequent threat in the prophetic literature, Fey's point is that Isaiah only uses the verb גָּלָה in the *qal*, as in Amos 6:7, here in v. 13.[41] Finally, Fey acknowledges that both "my people" and "without knowledge" are not paralleled in Amos 6:1, 3-7, but takes this as evidence of development by Isaiah, similar to the latter's elaboration of Amos' "instruments of music" (5b) as "lyre and lute, tambourine and flute."[42]

[36] See E. W. Davies, *Prophecy and Ethics: Isaiah and the Ethical Traditions of Israel* (JSOTSup 16; Sheffield: JSOT Press, 1981) 38.

[37] Although they occur together in Hos 4:6 as part of the larger context for the *marzēaḥ* allusion in Hos 4:16-19, in the absence of other lexical contacts between the latter and Isa 5:11-13 dependence in either direction cannot be established.

[38] The elements are not clearly defined in Amos 5:18-20, but the accusation appears to encompass v. 18a-b with vv. 18c-20 comprising the judgment section. In the woe series of Habakkuk 2, the judgment portion is always longer: cf. Hab 2:6 and 7-8, 9 and 10-11, 12 and 13-14, 15 and 16-17. In Isaiah, a cry of woe plus an accusation is found without a subsequent pronouncement of judgment at Isa 5:18-19, 20 and 21; apart from Isa 5:11-13, elsewhere in the book the accusation section is either shorter (see Isa 5:8 and 9-10; 28:1 and 2-4; 29:1 and 2-4; 31:1 and 2-3) or roughly equal to the judgment proclamation (see Isa 5:22-23 and 24; 10:1-2 and 3-4 and 29:15-16, 20-21 and 17-19).

[39] Of all the examples listed in n. 38, it occurs only at Isa 30:1-2 and 31:1.

[40] It is absent from Isa 5:22-24; 29:1-4; 31:1-3; Hab 2:12-14, and only minimally present in Isa 29:15-21.

[41] Fey, *Amos und Jesaja*, 15. It does occur in the *qal* at Isa 24:11 and 49:24, but neither is from Isaiah himself.

[42] Fey, *Amos und Jesaja*, 14-16.

Thus, Davies' objections are not conclusive, and Isa 5:11-13 may indeed be dependent on Amos 6:1, 3-7.[43] But that does not necessarily mean Isaiah was addressing members of a *marzēaḥ*; he could have adapted his predecessor's message to a similar yet distinct context. Therefore, whether this passage alludes to a *marzēaḥ* must be established on the basis of the *marzēaḥ* elements identified in Chapter 1.

One of those three constitutive components is unquestionably present in Isa 5:11-13. Both "wine" (יַיִן; 11d, 12b) and strong drink (שֵׁכָר; 11b) are mentioned, with a clear indication they are consumed in large quantities: their imbibing "inflames" them (11d), making them unaware of divine action (12c-d; cf. 13a). Moreover, the references to "morning" and "evening" (11a and c) are the poles of a *merismus* encompassing the intervening time as well. As such, v. 11 describes an all-day drinking feast, during which the participants drink enough to cloud their senses.

A second *marzēaḥ* component is the involvement of a definable, upper-class group. The announcement of punishment against the "nobles" in 13b is suggestive in this regard, but its probative value is limited by the surrounding lines. They indicate that the punishment will be experienced by God's people (13a), of which the nobles are one part and "its multitude" (הֲמוֹנוֹ; 13c) is another.[44] Since the judg-

[43] The wisdom tradition has also been suggested as a source for Isa 5:11; see Marti, *Jesaja*, 56; J. Fichtner, "Isaiah Among the Wise," *Studies in Ancient Israelite Wisdom* (ed. J. L. Crenshaw; New York: Ktav Publishing House, 1976) 429-39; J. W. Whedbee, *Isaiah and Wisdom* (Nashville: Abingdon Press, 1971) 98-100; Kaiser, *Isaiah 1-12*, 101; J. Jensen, *Isaiah 1-39* (OTMS 8; Wilmington: Michael Glazier, 1984) 80; Watts, *Isaiah 1-33*, 61; Wildberger, *Isaiah 1-12*, 201; Porath, *Sozialkritik*, 129. Prov 23:29-35 reflects on the negative effects of wine, and Qoh 10:16-17 specifically laments early morning feasts by the rulers. Other wisdom texts which view alcohol negatively, or at least with reserve, include Prov. 20:1; 21:17; 31:4-5; Sir 18:33; 19:2; 31:25-30. Some influence is likely (note especially the parallel between "those who linger after wine" in Prov. 23:30 and Isa 5:11c-d, as well as the vocal similarity between אוֹי in Prov 23:29 and the opening הוֹי in Isa 5:11 [but for the distinction between the two terms see G. Wanke, "אוי und הוי," *ZAW* 78 (1966) 215-18]), yet this is not a simple case of copying. By presenting the ideas in a divine speech with a pronouncement of judgment, rather than a riddle followed by an appeal to common sense as in Proverbs 23, Isaiah has transformed the wisdom *topos* (see further Fey, *Amos und Jesaja*, 10; Fohrer, *Jesaja 1*, 82). Ultimately, only Isa 5:11 can be linked to the wisdom tradition, and that verse only in a radically altered form. As such, the formulation and content of Isa 5:11-13 as a whole owe more to Amos than to wisdom precursors.

[44] In contrast to virtually all other commentators, Gerald T. Sheppard takes lines b and c as roughly synonymous, and interprets "its nobility" as a reference

ment in v. 13 is a reversal of the actions in vv. 11-12, its application to the entire population seems to argue against the restriction of vv. 11-12 to the nobles. Nonetheless, the content of vv. 11-12 suggests the nobles are, in fact, the agents there. Many scholars think this woe continues the address in Isa 5:8-10,[45] in which the wealthy are condemned for their land-grabbing practices. That cannot be proven, but even if vv. 11-13 stem from a different time,[46] a comparable group with both the resources and the leisure to engage in all-day drinking bouts is envisioned. It would seem, therefore, that Isaiah has expanded the judgment section to indicate the true impact of conquest and exile: the reality is that, in the language of modern military obscurantism, there will be "collateral damage." In the theatre of human affairs not even God can limit punishment to a "surgical strike" against the leaders.

But even though the passage describes members of the upper-class consuming large amounts of alcohol, there is no indication of the third component, i.e., a religious context for their actions.[47] Granted, wine can be used in religious situations,[48] but that is not its exclusive setting. Thus, although the religious and secular spheres of life were not separate in the ancient world, without evidence to the contrary it is best to consider this passage as describing a primarily non-religious feast. That would explain why the prophet did not duplicate the word *marzēaḥ* from Amos 6:7. Since he was not describing a true *marzēaḥ* he substituted the general term "feast" (מִשְׁתֶּה) in v. 12b.

---

to the lowly, "who should be held in high esteem"; see G. T. Sheppard, "Isaiah 1-39," *Harper's Bible Commentary* (ed. J. L. Mays, *et al.*; San Francisco: Harper, 1988) 553. However, the surrounding verses and parallel woes in this chapter all deal with the upper class, which makes his reading unlikely.

[45] Cf., e.g., the discussions of Marti, *Jesaja*, 56; Kissane, *Isaiah*, 53; J. Mauchline, *Isaiah 1-39: Confidence in God* (Torch Bible Commentaries; London: SCM Press, 1962) 83; Jensen, *Isaiah 1-39*, 76; Oswalt, *Isaiah 1-39*, 159; Chisholm, "Isaiah 5:8-30," 51; Jacob, *Esaïe 1-12*, 88; Sweeney, *Isaiah 1-39*, 124-25. In the Targum there is a link between the "field of oppression" in v. 8 and the "wine of oppression" in v. 11.

[46] Korpel, "Structural Analysis," 56-57, attributes the location of vv. 8-10 to a redactor, but thinks they are probably Isaian nonetheless.

[47] The reference to the lute (for its cultic associations see P. J. King, *Amos, Hosea, Micah—An Archaeological Commentary* [Philadelphia: Westminster Press, 1988] 154), is not enough to establish this as a religious feast, unlike in Amos 6:5a where it is in sequence with other religious items and actions.

[48] See Jacob, *Esaïe 1-12*, 88; Wildberger, *Isaiah 1-12*, 200 and the biblical and Ugaritic (respectively) texts they cite. Note that both reject any religious connection for this passage.

## II. Isa 28:1-4

A second possible *marzēaḥ* allusion is Isa 28:1-4. Not only does it share a concern for drunkenness with Amos 6:1, 3-7, but Asen has claimed the references to flowers and oil in connection with this drunkenness are indicative of a *marzēaḥ*. Once the text has been established, his evaluation of its content can be examined.

### A. *The Text*

| | | | |
|---|---|---|---|
| הוֹי עֲטֶרֶת גֵּאוּת שִׁכֹּרֵי אֶפְרַיִם | 1 | a | Alas, proud crown of the drunkards of Ephraim, |
| וְצִיץ נֹבֵל צְבִי תִפְאַרְתּוֹ | | b | and the fading garland,[51] the beauty of its glory, |
| אֲשֶׁר עַל־רֹאשׁ גֵּיא[49]־שְׁמָנִים | | c | which is on the head of the fertile valley, |
| הֲלוּמֵי יָיִן | | d | of those overcome with wine![52] |
| הִנֵּה חָזָק וְאַמִּץ לַיהוה[50] | 2 | a | See, Yahweh has one who is mighty and strong; |

[49] This is emended to גֵּאֵי ("proud [of fat things]") by J. Halévy, *RevSém* 21 (1913) 5; L. Rost, "Zu Jesaja 28:1ff," *ZAW* 12 (1935) 292; cf. now 1QIs[a]. Driver accepts the emendation, but renders as "streaming with oils"; see G. R. Driver, "'Another Little Drink'—Isaiah 28:1-22," *Words and Meanings: Essays Presented to David Winton Thomas on His Retirement from the Regius Professorship of Hebrew in the University of Cambridge, 1968* (eds. P. R. Ackroyd and B. Lindars; Cambridge: Cambridge University Press, 1968) 48-49. In support of the MT, Irwin argues that lines b-d each develop a phrase from line a. Thus, 1b elaborates "proud crown," 1c refers to Samaria as the capital of "Ephraim," and 1d expands upon "drunkards." For a full discussion see W. H. Irwin, *Isaiah 28-33: Translation with Philological Notes* (BibOr 30; Rome: Biblical Institute Press, 1977) 6; see also the discussion of this word in Barthélemy, *Critique Textuelle 2*, 196-98. Asen's acceptance of Driver's interpretation (see Asen, "Garlands," 82-83) weakens, but does not completely invalidate, his proposed *marzēaḥ* allusion in this text.

[50] In place of the MT's לַאדֹנָי; see below.

[51] The parallel "crown" in 1a suggests צִיץ may be a diadem comparable to the gold object in the front of the high priest's turban (see Exod 28:36; 39:30; Lev 8:9), but the phrase נָבֵל צִיץ ("the flower fades") in Isa 40:7,8 points to flora here as well; nonetheless, the parallel suggests the nuance "garland" (Irwin, *Isaiah 28–33*, 4). This vegetative imagery anticipates the fertile valley in the next line, and a wilting flower is an even better metaphor for impermanence than tarnished metal; it also sets up the ironic reversal of 4c-e (for the garland and the fig in v. 4c as images of transitoriness see W. H. Irwin, "Isaiah 24-39," *NJBC* 245). This argues against the meaning "young shoot, sprig" for the consonants נבל, proposed on the basis of Akkadian, Aramaic and Arabic cognates by Driver, "'Another Little Drink,'" 48; see also the criticism of Driver by Irwin, *Isaiah 28–33*, 4n2.

[52] This line's apparent grammatical dependence on גֵּיא־שְׁמָנִים, which is in the

| | | | |
|---|---|---|---|
| כְּזֶרֶם בָּרָד שַׂעַר קָטֶב | | b | like a storm of hail, a devastating[56] tempest, |
| כְּזֶרֶם מַיִם כַּבִּירִים שֹׁטְפִים | | c | like a storm of mighty, overflowing waters; |
| הִנִּיחַ לָאָרֶץ בְּיָד | | d | he will hurl to the earth with his hand. |
| בְּרַגְלַיִם תְּרָמַסְנָה[53] | 3 | a | Trampled under foot will be |
| עֲטֶרֶת גֵּאוּת שִׁכּוֹרֵי אֶפְרָיִם | | b | the proud garland of the drunkards of Ephraim. |
| וְהָיְתָה צִיצַת נֹבֵל צְבִי תִפְאַרְתּוֹ | 4 | a | And the fading flower, the beauty of its glory, |
| אֲשֶׁר עַל־רֹאשׁ גֵּיא שְׁמָנִים | | b | which is on the head of the fertile valley, |
| כְּבִכּוּרָה[54] בְּטֶרֶם קַיִץ | | c | will be like a first-ripe fig before the summer: |
| אֲשֶׁר יִרְאֶה[55] הָרֹאֶה אוֹתָהּ | | d | when the observer sees it, |

absolute state, has long been considered problematic. The LXX reads the line as a vocative, it is moved to after 1a by Kissane, *Isaiah*, 303 and R. B. Y. Scott, "Isaiah 1-39," 314, and is deleted as a gloss by E. Vogt, "Das Prophetenwort Jes 28,1-4 und das Ende der Königsstadt Samaria," *Homenaje a Juan Prado: Miscelanea de Estudios Biblicos y Hebraicos* (eds. L. A. Verdes and E. J. A. Hernandez; Madrid: Consejo Superior de Investigaciones Cientificas, 1975) 114. Procksch, *Jesaia I*, 347, inserts כַּעֲטֶרֶת ("like a crown . . .)" at the beginning of 1d while "the fertile valley" is deleted by G. Fohrer, *Das Buch Jesaja, Bd. 2: Kap. 24-39* (Zürcher Bibelkommentare; 2nd ed.; Zürich/Stuttgart: Zwingli Verlag, 1967) 43; O. Kaiser, *Isaiah 13-39: A Commentary* (OTL; trans. R. A. Wilson; Philadelphia: Westminster Press, 1974) 236 note a; H. Wildberger, *Jesaja 28-39: das Buch, der Prophet und seine Botschaft* (BKAT 10; Neukirchen-Vluyn: Neukirchener Verlag, 1982) 1042. None of the modern proposals has textual or versional support. The deletions can be rejected on the basis of the integrity of each line to the verse as a whole (see n. 49). Moreover, the syntax is not impossible. Similar constructions are listed in Delitzsch, *Isaiah*, 436; Young, *Isaiah*, 264n2 (but cf. GKC §128c), while a construct form (שְׁמָנֵי) plus an enclitic *mem* is proposed by H. D. Hummel, "Enclitic *Mem* in Early Northwest Semitic, Especially Hebrew," *JBL* 76 (1957) 98. Oswalt, *Isaiah 1-39*, 507, takes "which is upon the head of . . ." from 1c as doing double-duty for this line as well. This preserves the dual adornments of the city and its leaders from 1a-b (although his appeal to GKC §128a [his n. 25] is not to the point, since GKC deals with a series of true genitives).

[53] The MT reads תֵּרָמַסְנָה; see below.

[54] The MT reads כְּבִכּוּרָהּ; see below.

[55] Changed to יֶאֱרֶה ("he plucks") by Kissane, *Isaiah*, 303; Driver, "'Another Little Drink,'" 50; R. E. Clements, *Isaiah 1-39* (NCBC; Grand Rapids: Wm. B. Eerdmans Publishing Co., 1980); Driver appeals to the LXX and Houbigant (unavailable to me). The MT yields a greater sense of immediacy appropriate to the threatened punishment.

[56] Fohrer, *Jesaja 2*, 43; Irwin, *Isaiah 28–33*, 8, see the demon Qeteb here (cf. Deut 32:24; Hos 13:14; Ps 91:6); the latter understands it as a superlative (see his n. 16 for literature).

| | | |
|---|---|---|
| בְּעוֹדָהּ בְּכַפּוֹ[57] יִבְלָעֶנָּה[58] | e | as soon as it is in his hand, he swallows it |

This text departs from the MT at three points, none of which affects the basic meaning or the issue of a *marzēaḥ* allusion in the passage. First, since it is more likely that a circumlocution was substituted for the divine name than the reverse, לַיהוה is read at the end of 2a with 1QIs[a], against the MT's לַאדֹנָי.[59] Second, the MT's תֵּרָמַסְנָה in 3a is a 3rd feminine plural *niphal*, while the subject (in the next line) is singular. Pointing it as a singular with an energic ending was proposed at least as early as Delitzsch and is followed by most scholars.[60] Third, the MT has a *mappîq* in the final consonant of כְּבִכּוּרָהּ (thus, "its early fig") but a simple ה is read by Aquila, Theodotion, the Vulgate, the Targum, the Peshitta and most modern authors and translations.

## B. *Establishing the Unit*

The unit's starting point is indicated by the initial הוֹי, but the end is not as immediately obvious. Since a new geographical location, namely Jerusalem, is not mentioned until v. 14, some treat vv. 1-13 as a unity dealing with Samaria,[61] but this view can be rejected on

---

[57] Vogt, followed by Loretz, emends to בְּכִפָּה ("on a branch"); see Vogt, "Jes 28,1-4," 119; O. Loretz, "Das Prophetenwort über das Ende der Königsstadt Samaria (Jes 28,1-4)," *UF* 9 (1977) 363. While Vogt is correct that eating directly from the tree is a more immediate image, it detracts from both the emphasis on the agent found elsewhere in 4d-e (cf. n. 58) and the semantic interplay with יָד in v. 2d (on which see D. L. Petersen, "Isaiah 28: A Redaction Critical Study," *SBLSP* 17 [1979] 106).

[58] Divided as יִבֹּל עֵינָהּ ("its bloom will wither") by Driver, "'Another Little Drink,'" 50; he cites M. Scott, *Textual Discoveries in Proverbs, Psalms and Isaiah* (London: S.P.C.K., 1927) 197-98. However, the MT's image of active rather than passive consumption fits better with the context of judgment by the divine agent initiated in v. 2. See also n. 55 above.

[59] The latter may have been substituted in order to enhance the alliteration in the line.

[60] See Delitzsch, *Isaiah*, 436-47. In contrast, Kissane, *Isaiah*, 303, changes the בּ on the preceding word to an article and points the verb as a 3rd feminine plural *qal* (but cf. his p. 304). Oswalt, *Isaiah 1-39*, 502n3, takes the following line as a collective. Vogt, followed by Loretz, emends to a 3rd masculine (prophetic) perfect, with v. 2 providing the subject; see Vogt, "Jes 28,1-4," 116, 118; Loretz, "Jes 28,1-4," 362.

[61] See Watts, *Isaiah 1-33*, 362; Oswalt, *Isaiah 1-39*, 506; Hayes and Irvine, *Isaiah*, 322; Sweeney, *Isaiah 1-39*, 367-68. Francis Landy ends the unit with v. 8; see

a number grounds. To begin with, Isa 28:5-6 should be separated from the surrounding verses. "In that day" suggests a new unit, and despite some shared vocabulary with vv. 1-4 (עֲטֶרֶת, צְבִי and תִּפְאָרָה) the point of reference is completely different. The "crown," "garland" and "glory" are related to the capital of Ephraim and its leaders in vv. 1-4 while they describe Yahweh in vv. 5-6. Further, the latter deal with his relationship with "his people," who are never mentioned in the earlier verses. At the same time, there are no lexical links between vv. 5-6 and what follows, and the ideas of justice and battle introduced in v. 6 do not carry over into the following verses either. Finally, the tone and content shift from the condemnation of drunkenness in vv. 1-4 and 7-8 to Yahweh's future presence in vv. 5-6. In short, vv. 5-6 are intrusive between vv. 4 and 7, and are rejected as a later addition by the majority of critics.[62]

At the same time, vv. 7-13 should be disassociated from vv. 1-4, despite the shared drunkenness motif and the apparent link created by "these also" at the beginning of v. 7. Only four terms from vv. 1-4 are repeated in the later verses, with three of them clustered in v. 7, and not all are as significant as first appears. The verb נוּחַ occurs in vv. 2 and 12, but the sentiments are completely opposite: "he will cast down" vs. "give rest" respectively. The verb "swallow" (בָּלַע) occurs in vv. 4 and 7, but the objects are different (a first-ripe fig and the drinkers). The repetition of the consonants שׁכר in "drunkards" (vv. 1, 3) and "strong drink" (v. 7 [3x]) is closer, but only "wine" is used identically in vv. 1 and 7 [2x]. In short, the shared vocabulary operates more on the level of catch-word association than as part of an organic unity. As such, "these also" is most likely a redactional link.[63] Form-critical considerations support this conclusion. The opening הוֹי marks what follows as a "woe-oracle," with v.

---

F. Landy, "Tracing the Voice of the Other: Isaiah 28 and the Covenant with Death," *The New Literary Criticism and the Hebrew Bible* (JSOTSup 143; eds. J. C. Exum and D. J. A. Clines; Sheffield: JSOT Press, 1994) 149n25. Although they accept a shift from Ephraim to Jerusalem at v. 7, the entire chapter is treated as a single poem from Isaiah by Kissane, *Isaiah*, 298-309; Young, *Isaiah*, 262-94.

62 With the exception of those listed in n. 61.

63 Again, the exceptions to this consensus view are listed in n. 61. Fohrer, *Jesaja 2*, 44-45, thinks Isa 28:1-4 was originally part of the Oracles Against the Nations collection (Isaiah 13-23) but moved here because of the drunkenness motif in 28:7-8; he is followed by Wildberger, *Jesaja 28-39*, 1046; see also Halpern, "'The Excremental Vision,'" 112, 114. This does not rule out the connection having been made by Isaiah himself, as suggested by Procksch, *Jesaia I*, 353; W. L. Holladay, *Isaiah: Scroll of a Prophetic Heritage* (New York: Pilgrim Press, 1978) 59.

1 constituting the accusation and vv. 2-4 announcing punishment. While not impossible, the addition of a salvation oracle (vv. 5-6) and/or the resumption of the accusation (7-8) would be unusual. It is simpler to take Isa 28:1-4 as a self contained unit.

Numerous deletions from those verses have been proposed, but only those relevant to whether the passage is a *marzēaḥ* allusion will be considered here. The portions of the text which bear directly on that issue are the references to being "overcome with wine" in 1d, and the double mention of "drunkards" in 1a and 3b and flowers in 1b and 4a. All of these have been challenged as secondary by one scholar or another. For instance, Vogt considers 1d a gloss on 1a,[64] while Kissane and Loretz omit 1b-c.[65] However, the integrity of the entire verse has already been established, ruling out deletion of these lines.[66] Similarly, v. 3b is considered a gloss on 3a by Loretz,[67] and 4a (and b) is deleted by Vogt and Loretz,[68] but both 3b and 4a(-b) are essential to the ironic reversal of the situation lamented in the accusation:[69] the "proud crown" (1a) will be trampled underfoot (3a-b) while the fading garland (1b) will be consumed as greedily as a first-ripe fruit (4c-e). Thus, the questioned lines should be retained. It remains to be seen whether they allude to a *marzēaḥ*.

## C. *Discussion*

The similar content in Isa 28:1-4 and Amos 6:1,3-7 is often noted, and Fey also considers Isa 28:1-4 dependent on the Amos text.[70] His

Cf. Jackson, "Style," 90, who takes the phrase as anticipatory rather than reflective.

[64] Vogt, "Jes 28,1-4," 114.

[65] Kissane, *Isaiah*, 304; Loretz, "Jes 28,1-4," 362. The former considers them an interpolation from 4a-b while Loretz thinks they are a gloss on "proud crown" in 1a. He also deletes 4a-b (see n. 68 below).

[66] See n. 49 above.

[67] Loretz, "Jes 28,1-4," 363.

[68] Vogt, "Jes 28,1-4," 117-18; Loretz, "Jes 28,1-4," 363. Vogt retains the supposed "doublet" in 1a and 3b. Only Loretz omits both instances of a repeated phrase, i.e., 1b-c and 4a-b.

[69] That this was done by repeating phrases verbatim may just as easily be evidence of pedestrian style as of editorial activity. In any case, at least one of 1b or 4a is retained by all commentators except Loretz, who never explains why 4a-b, a supposed gloss on 3b, exactly reproduces 1b-c, which he considers a separate gloss on part of 1a.

[70] Fey, *Amos und Jesaja*, 82.

case for direct use by Isaiah is not as strong as in the earlier text,[71] but Amos 6:1, 3-7 and Isa 28:1-4 are both woe oracles aimed at Samarian drinkers. Yet, as with Isa 5:11-13, that does not mean this passage describes a *marzēaḥ* rather than a "secular" drinking party. A firmer basis than this shared concern about drinking is required.

Asen has sought to establish just such a firm connection between Isa 28:1-4 and the *marzēaḥ*, based on the combination of drunkenness, flowers and oil.[72] However, there are serious problems with Asen's proposal. In the first place, his discussion of oil in this text is dependent on Driver's emendation and interpretation of 1c and 4b, which was rejected above.[73] As a result, only the association of flowers and drunkenness remains as a possible indicator of a *marzēaḥ* in this text. Drinking is an essential component of any *marzēaḥ*, and intoxication is indicated here by the designations "drunkards of Ephraim" (שִׁכֹּרֵי אֶפְרַיִם; 1a, 3b) and "those overcome by wine" (1d). Similarly, flowers are mentioned in 1b and 4a, and vegetative imagery is also present in 4c. But the presence of flowers at a drinking party does not make it a *marzēaḥ*. Much of Asen's article is devoted to establishing a connection between flowers and the *marzēaḥ*, but in my opinion that attempt is unsuccessful. He surveys the widespread association of flowers and banquets in the ancient world,[74] but with the possible exception of the Greek *symposium* nothing connects those

---

[71] He compares the Samarians' self-importance in Amos 6:1 ("the notables of the first of the nations") with the "proud crown" in Isa 28:1a and 3b, as well as the antithetical parallelism of Amos 6:3 ("O you who put far away the evil day // but bring near the reign of violence") with Isa 28:1-2, but these are general parallels that do not require dependence. Fey also notes the similarity between רֵאשִׁית שְׁמָנִים in Amos 6:6b and עַל־רֹאשׁ גֵּיא־שְׁמָנִים in Isa 28:1c, 4b; at first glance this does seem indicative of literary dependence, but the similarity is more apparent than real. In Amos 6:6b רֵאשִׁית is used abstractly in the sense of "finest" and שְׁמָנִים refers to real oil, whereas in Isa 28:1c, 4b the former is used concretely (albeit metaphorically) of the city that sits above the valley and the latter is used abstractly with the sense of "fatness" and thus "fertility." Moreover, significant structural patterns in Amos 6:1, 3-7 and Isa 5:11-13 are either reversed or absent from Isa 28:1-4. For instance, rather than a lengthy accusation followed by a short announcement of judgment (Amos 6:1, 3-6; Isa 5:11-12), the opposite is found in Isa 28:1 and 2-4 respectively. In addition, the accusation's formulation as a lengthy statement of their actions plus a short statement of their inaction (Amos 6:1, 3-6b and 6c; Isa 5:11-12b and 12c-d), as well as the formulaic "therefore" introducing the judgment section, are both missing from Isa 28:1-4. On the uniqueness of these features see notes 38-40.

[72] See n. 3 above.

[73] See n. 49 and cf. Asen, "Garlands," 82-84.

[74] Asen, "Garlands," 74-79.

banquets with a *marzēaḥ*.[75] In short, the combination of flowers and drunkenness does not indicate a *marzēaḥ*: ultimately, Asen is only able to show that flowers were a common feature of ancient banquets in general, especially upper-class ones. Granted, some of those feasts involved drunkenness, but no one would claim the *marzēaḥ* is the only ancient gathering at which the participants got drunk. Furthermore, if neither flowers nor drunkenness alone is sufficient indication of a *marzēaḥ*, neither is their combination.

Thus, it is necessary to employ the criteria for a *marzēaḥ* allusion used earlier: heavy upper-class drinking within a religious connection. This can be done quite quickly. Their intoxication has been considered above, and there are indications that the "drunkards" are members of the top stratum of society. In addition to the financial resources necessary for ongoing and/or recurrent intoxication,[76] flower garlands were a luxury not commonly worn by the poor.[77] However, there is no indication of a religious context for this activity,[78] and without a religious link for these verses, the text cannot be considered a *marzēaḥ* allusion with any certainty. Put succinctly, there is nothing in Isa 28:1-4 to distinguish it from upper-class drunkenness in general, and therefore nothing to mark it as describing a *marzēaḥ*.

## A. Isa 28:7-8

The third Isaiah text to consider is Isa 28:7-8. Although they are part of a larger unit encompassing vv. 7-22, because the reference to drinking in vv. 7-8 is the primary basis for a possible *marzēaḥ* allusion, the discussion will focus on those two verses. Drunkenness, combined with perceived similarities to the Ugaritic description of

---

[75] Asen, "Garlands," 76, even admits that El's *marzēaḥ* (*CAT* 1.114) does not mention flowers. His appeal to a relief described by Pope, "Divine Banquet," 189, fig. 4; *idem*, *Song of Songs*, 215, fig. 4, is invalid because the image derives from Corinth not Ugarit, and there is nothing to link it to the *marzēaḥ* in any case.

[76] As indicated by the use of participles in 1a and 1d.

[77] See J. Goody, *The Culture of Flowers* (Cambridge: Cambridge University Press, 1993) 10, cited in Asen, "Garlands," 75.

[78] A point acknowledged by Asen, "Garlands," 82. Although various links have been proposed, they are only possibilities at best and conjectures at worst. A possible allusion to the high priest's head gear has already been ruled out (cf. n. 51); A. S. Herbert, *The Book of the Prophet Isaiah: Chapters 1-39* (CBC; Cambridge: Cambridge University Press, 1973) 162, suggests the garland alludes to a fertility deity's devotees, but such an association is not developed in the passage.

El's *marzēaḥ* and possible connections with the cult of the dead, are the main reasons this text has been identified as a *marzēaḥ* allusion. As a point of reference, a Hebrew text and English translation will be presented first.

## A. *The Text*

| | | |
|---|---|---|
| בַּיַּיִן שָׁגוּ | 7 a | With wine they reel,[80] |
| וּבַשֵּׁכָר תָּעוּ | b | with strong drink they stagger;[81] |
| כֹּהֵן וְנָבִיא שָׁגוּ בַשֵּׁכָר[79] | c | priest and prophet[82] reel with strong drink, |
| נִבְלְעוּ מִן־הַיַּיִן | d | they are swallowed up[83] by wine, |
| תָּעוּ מִן־הַשֵּׁכָר | e | they stagger with strong drink; |
| שָׁגוּ בָּרֹאֶה | f | they reel while seeing,[84] |

[79] Deleted by Procksch, Jesaia I, 352, with the LXX. The word is part of a mirror pattern in 7a-d (wine:strong drink::strong drink:wine) and should be retained.

[80] Appealing to the Arabic *sajâ* I, Driver, "'Another Little Drink,'" 51, proposes the meaning, "was wrapped up in, addicted to," for the verb שָׁגָה here and in lines c and f. Yet the traditional meaning "go astray" is quite acceptable here; that it results from intoxication suggests the rendering "reel." See further in n. 81.

[81] The meaning "cackled, croaked, guffawed" is proposed by Driver, "'Another Little Drink,'" 51-52, 62, on the basis of the Arabic *tagiya*; he translates "bawl" here and in 7e. Yet he acknowledges that תָּעָה is used of drunkenness at Isa 19:13,14 (p. 52; in addition, Job 12:24-25; Hos 4:11-12 are noted by Irwin, *Isaiah 28—33*, 15), and the nuance "stagger" is most appropriate for the effects of intoxication. Also, Irwin points out that Driver's proposal yields divergent meanings for שָׁגָה (see n. 80 above) and תָּעָה, which elsewhere are synonymous; see Irwin, *Isaiah 28–33*, 16.

[82] Despite the singular nouns many translate in the plural without comment. The plural verbs, especially in reference to the separate roles of prophet and priest (lines f and g) confirm that the verse as a whole is concerned with more than one of each. The single priest and prophet are best understood as representative members of their respective religious guilds.

[83] Driver, "'Another Little Drink,'" 52, claims this phrase "means nothing," and proposes "overcome" on the basis of the Arabic *balaga* and the Syriac *blaʿ*. Most modern English versions translate as "confused" or something similar, from בָּלַע II. But "swallowed by" is an ironically appropriate way of indicating the alcohol's effect here: what they swallowed has in fact swallowed them; cf. Irwin, *Isaiah 28–33*, 16; J. C. Exum, "'Whom Will He Teach Knowledge?' A Literary Approach to Isaiah 28," *Art and Meaning: Rhetoric in Biblical Literature* (JSOTSup 19; eds. D. J. A. Clines, D. M. Gunn and A. J. Hauser; Sheffield: JSOT Press, 1982) 119; Oswalt, *Isaiah 1-39*, 510; P. D. Miscall, *Isaiah* (Readings: A New Biblical Commentary; Sheffield: JSOT Press, 1993) 74.

[84] Driver considers the verb "to see" inappropriate in the context of drinking, and explains the consonants as a substantive derived from the verb רָוָה, "drink

| | | |
|---|---|---|
| פָּקוּ פְּלִילִיָּה | g | they stumble[86] while[87] giving judgment.[88] |
| כִּי כָּל־שֻׁלְחָנוֹת מָלְאוּ קִיא | 8 a | Indeed, every table is full of vomit; |
| צֹאָה[85] בְּלִי מָקוֹם | b | excrement, with no (clean) place. |

---

one's fill"; see G. R. Driver, "Studies in the Vocabulary of the Old Testament VII," *JTS* 35 (1935) 151-53; *idem*, "'Another Little Drink,'" 52; see also Irwin, *Isaiah 28–33*, 18; on that root see C. S. Rodd, "Modern Issues in Biblical Study: Rediscovered Hebrew Meanings," *ExpTim* 71 (1959-1960) 131; D. W. Thomas, "A Consideration of Isaiah LIII in the Light of Recent Textual and Philological Study," *ETL* 44 (1968) 85-86; M. J. Dahood, *Proverbs and Northwest Semitic Philology* (Rome: Biblical Institute Press, 1963) 23; *idem*, *Psalms I: 1-50. A New Translation with Introduction and Commentary* (AB 17; New York: Doubleday, 1968) 206; *idem*, *Psalms II: 51-100. A New Translation with Introduction and Commentary* (AB 17; 3rd ed.; New York: Doubleday, 1968) 78. However, a vision is an appropriate experience for the prophet mentioned in 7b (thus Petersen, "Isaiah 28," 120n21). It also provides a good parallel to the priest's "judgment" in the next line (see further in n. 88) and anticipates the "message" in 9b (on the oracular nuance of שְׁמוּעָה see van der Toorn, "Judaean Necromancy," 213-15). The prophet (נָבִיא) and the seer (רֹאֶה) are equated in 1 Sam 9:9.

85 The MT accent includes צֹאָה with the preceding line, but its shift to this line creates a more balanced line and better parallelism. The modern English translations and most critics make this change; exceptions include Oswalt, *Isaiah 1-39*, 503n11, who retains the MT stichometry and translates "filthy vomit," and Marvin Pope, who moves קִיא here as well; see Pope, "Divine Banquet," 196; *idem*, *Song of Songs*, 217; *idem*, "The Cult of the Dead," 178. *Pace* both, the separation of the two terms establishes a chiasm in the two lines: a location is followed by something expelled from the body in 8a, while the reverse order occurs in 8b.

86 Driver, "'Another Little Drink,'" 53, rejects this meaning for the root פּוּק, arguing on the basis of cognate languages for the nuance "hiccoughed." This provides a poor parallel with "reel" in the preceding line, however, as does Irwin's "brim over," derived from a root meaning "to flow" (see Irwin, *Isaiah 28–33*, 18-19). Both proposals are also dependent on accepting non-traditional meanings for פְּלִילִיָּה; see further in n. 88.

87 The temporal preposition from בָּרֹאֶה in the preceding line does double-duty here.

88 In light of the Arabic *falla*, Driver, "'Another Little Drink,'" 53, argues for the meaning "frenzy," while Irwin, *Isaiah 28–33*, 19-20, derives the word from a root פָּלַל cognate with Arabic *bll* ("soak, moisten") and translates as "booze." Both proposals are intrinsically linked to their proponents' different understandings of the preceding verb, which were rejected in n. 86. As with the preceding line, the traditional translation as "judgment" is consistent with priestly activity (cf. n. 84) and anticipates the phrase, "teach knowledge" in 9a (for the revelatory character of this knowledge see Irwin, *Isaiah 28–33*, 21; *idem*, "Isaiah 24-39," 245; Halpern, "'The Excremental Vision,'" 114n9; "teaching/instruction" and "knowledge" are considered priestly prerogatives in, e.g., Jer 18:18; Hos 4:6; Mal 2:7). The result is a mirror pattern in which the functionaries mentioned in 7c are followed by their actual functions in the reverse order in 7f-g, i.e., priest:prophet ::seeing:judgment; see G. Stansell, *Micah and Isaiah: A Form and Tradition Historical Comparison* (SBLDS 85; Atlanta: Scholars Press, 1988) 86n77.

Except for the deletion of the redactional "these also" at the beginning of v. 7,[89] this duplicates the MT exactly. Although a number of variant translations have been proposed for this text, they have all been rejected in favour of the more traditional understanding of the words.[90]

## B. *Establishing The Unit*

As mentioned above, Isa 28:7-8 is part of a larger unit. Since the latter provides important context for interpreting those two verses, the extent of that context must be determined. The disjuncture with the preceding verses[91] establishes v. 7 as the starting point, but opinions differ as to where the unit ends. The parable of the farmer in vv. 23-29 is formally distinct from what precedes it, but not all treat vv. 7-22 as a single unit. Francis Landy, for instance, emphasizes the syntactical break between vv. 8 and 9, and does not see any thematic or lexical links between vv. 7-8 and 9-13.[92] Verse 8 does coincide with the end of a sentence, but this is not sufficient grounds for a complete break with what follows, especially since Landy is incorrect concerning the absence of links between vv. 7-8 and the following verses. The connection between the prophetic and priestly functions in 7f-g and "knowledge" and "message" in 9a-b has already been noted,[93] while the repeated consonants צ and ק in v. 10 echo in reverse order the initial letters of קִיא ("vomit") and צֹאָה ("excrement") from v. 8.[94] Nor is the transition between vv. 8 and 9 as abrupt as Landy suggests. Granted, vv. 7-8 describe a specific scene, the de-

[89] See p. 166 above.

[90] See the preceding footnotes.

[91] See p. 166 above.

[92] Landy, "Isaiah 28," 149n25; cf. A. van Selms, "Isaiah 28:9-13: An Attempt to Give a New Interpretation," *ZAW* 85 (1973) 332. That Landy incorrectly, in my view, considers vv. 1-8 a unit does not automatically rule out a break after v. 8. The result would be a unit consisting simply of vv. 7-8; Marti and Duhm consider those verses an introduction added later by Isaiah to link vv. 1-4 and 9-13; see Marti, *Jesaja*, 204; Duhm, *Jesaia*, 197.

[93] See notes 84 and 88.

[94] R. H. Kennett, *Ancient Hebrew Social Life and Custom as Indicated in Law, Narrative and Metaphor* (The Schweich Lectures on Biblical Archaeology, 1931; London: Oxford University Press, 1931) 12; Driver, "'Another Little Drink,'" 55; Driver does not seem to know of Kennett's work. The significance of v. 10 will be considered further below.

tails of which are not repeated in what follows, but there is no indication of a new speaker or addressees in v. 9.[95]

Since there is little basis for a sharp break after v. 8, most scholars continue the unit to at least v. 13. At first glance, the second "therefore," at the beginning of v. 14, coming after the same word in v. 13, seems to coincide with a shift from the priests and prophets to the "rulers of this people in Jerusalem" (14b). However, the parallel term "scoffers" (אַנְשֵׁי לָצוֹן) points to a nuance of speech rather than governance for מֹשְׁלֵי,[96] echoing the verbal associations of the words "teach" and "instruct" in 9a-b. As such, v. 14 may not constitute as clear a shift in addressees as is often thought. To begin with, nothing in vv. 14-22 requires a political interpretation, and therefore an address to rulers. For instance, although the "covenant with Death/Sheol" in vv. 15 and 18 is often interpreted as an alliance with Egypt,[97] the surrounding verses do not support that view. The use of the term "Zion" for Jerusalem in v. 16 suggests a concern with religious matters in this section, and many commentators think vv. 15 and 18 deal with the worship of Mot, the Canaanite god of death,[98] which in turn points to the priests' and prophets' sphere of

[95] Verse 9 is often considered the words of Isaiah's opponents, but the usual indicators of a quotation are lacking. Against starting an oracle with a quotation see R. F. Melugin, "The Conventional and the Creative in Isaiah's Judgement Oracles," *CBQ* 36 (1974) 305; J. Vermeylen, *Du prophète Isaïe à l'apocalyptique: Isaïe I-XXXV, miroir d'un demi-millénaire d'expérience religieuse en Israël* (EBib; Paris: J. Gabalda, 1978) 390n1.

[96] A. B. Ehrlich, *Randglossen zur Hebräischen Bibel* (Leipzig: J. C. Hinrichs, 1912) 4.100, translates it as "epigrammatists" and Kaiser, *Isaiah 13-39*, 248, renders "proverb-makers"; see also Procksch, *Jesaia I*, 360; Vermeylen, *Du Prophète Isaïe*, 391; Wildberger, *Jesaja 28-39*, 1064; A. C. Stewart, "The Covenant with Death in Isaiah 28," *ExpTim* 100 (1989) 376. A play on both meanings is suggested by Irwin, *Isaiah 28–33*, 25; Exum, "Isaiah 28," 124. Van der Toorn, "Judaean Necromancy," 200-201, retains the meaning "rulers" but relates it to the influence of priests and prophets rather than political leaders. They are considered royal advisers by J. P. Floß, "Biblische Theologie als Sprecherin der 'Gefährlichen Erinnerung' dargestellt an Jes 28,7-12," *BN* 54 (1990) 72.

[97] Thus, e.g., Delitzsch, *Isaiah*, 442; Marti, *Jesaja*, 207; Exum, "Isaiah 28," 125; Jensen, *Isaiah 1-39*, 219; Watts, *Isaiah 1-33*, 369; Irwin, "Isaiah 24-39," 246; Sweeney, *Isaiah 1-39*, 366-67. The treaty partner is identified as Assyria by B. B. Schmidt, *Israel's Beneficent Dead: Ancestor Cult and Necromancy in Ancient Israelite Religion and Tradition* (Winona Lake: Eisenbrauns, 1996) 160. Hayes and Irvine, *Isaiah*, 326, interpret the phrase in terms of Judah's support for Israel against Assyria.

[98] See Procksch, *Jesaia I*, 360; R. B. Y. Scott, "Isaiah 1-39," 317; Driver, "'Another Little Drink,'" 57; Herbert, *Isaiah*, 163; Jackson, "Style," 97-98; Irwin, *Isaiah*

activity rather than political leaders. Thus, the general content of vv. 14-22 indicates a connection between them and vv. 7-13. Secondly, this is supported by lexical, structural and developmental links between the two passages. Although "this people" in vv. 11 and 14 and קָו in vv. 10, 13 and 17 might be attributed to catch-word linking, other repeated vocabulary cannot be as easily dismissed. For instance, שְׁמוּעָה is used of a revelatory message and preceded by a *hiphil* form of בִּין in vv. 9 and 19, while חָזוּת/חֹזֶה[99] in vv. 15 and 18 semantically echoes רֹאֶה ("seeing") from v. 7f. Such terminology also points to the religious realm, and therefore to the priests and prophets of vv. 7-13. Thirdly, the preceding points are reinforced by the organizational structure of vv. 7-22, which Jared Jackson has shown to be a mirror pattern hinging upon vv. 13 and 14,[100] as well as the passage's developmental structure, which builds upon the gradual

*28–33*, 26; Wildberger, *Jesaja 28-39*, 1064; Halpern, "'The Excremental Vision,'" 117, 119; van der Toorn, "Judaean Necromancy," 202-03; Stewart, "The Covenant with Death," 376; C. R. Seitz, *Isaiah 1-39* (Interpretation; Louisville: Westminster/John Knox Press, 1993) 210. Eichrodt thinks it is Osiris, while Vermeylen envisions both Mot and Osiris (referred to as "Sheol"); see W. Eichrodt, *Der Herr der Geschichte: Jesaja 13-23 und 28-39* (Die Botschaft des Alten Testaments: Erläuterungen alttestamentlicher Schriften 17; Stuttgart: Calwer Verlag, 1967) 128-29; Vermeylen, *Du Prophète Isaïe*, 393n1, 395n2. Whether one or two deities, both authors envision divine witness(es) to a human treaty, but there is no treaty in the passage. Verses 15 and 18 are seen simply as hyperbolic metaphors for the leaders' confidence that they will escape destruction by Cheyne, *Isaiah*, 1.165-66; Kissane, *Isaiah*, 306; Young, *Isaiah*, 282; Fohrer, *Jesaja 2*, 59-60; Driver, "'Another Little Drink,'" 58; Kaiser, *Isaiah 13-39*, 251, but the surrounding religious connections suggest otherwise.

[99] The LXX (συνθήκη) and the Vulgate (*pactum*) both understood these terms as comparable in meaning to "covenant." While this fits the parallelism, the basic meaning of the Hebrew is "vision." Köhler emends to חֶסֶד and Driver explains the versions by deriving the Hebrew words from the same root as חָזֶה ("breast") on analogy with the South-Arabic *ḥdyt*, "agreement"; see L. Köhler, "Zu Jes 28,15a und 18b," *ZAW* 48 (1930) 227-28; Driver, "'Another Little Drink,'" 58. But neither approach is necessary, since the idea of "agreement" can be derived from the basic semantic field of "seeing," as shown on the basis of Akkadian *naplusu* ("look favourably on"; cf. Exod 2:24-25) by M. Weinfeld, "Covenant Terminology in the Ancient Near East and Its Influence on the West," *JAOS* 93 (1973) 196n87; he also notes (p. 196) the word חזי with this connotation in a letter from Elephantine; see also Wildberger, *Jesaja 28-39*, 1065. Since the covenant is with a deity, the term חֹזֶה was probably chosen for the interplay between the agreement itself and its mediation through a vision.

[100] See Jackson, "Style," 93, for the details. I would make a minor adjustment to Jackson's analysis that does not alter the end result. He identifies vv. 9 and 15 as quotations of the drunkards and scoffers respectively, but I view the former as continuing Isaiah's words. None the less, the "he" in v. 9 refers to the source of

resolution of initial ambiguity. For instance, since the first two lines in v. 7 lack explicit subjects, we do not learn who is being described until line c. Similarly, it is not revealed until 7f-g that their drunkenness occurs during, and affects, their official duties.[101] The same pattern of clarification is also at work in the larger unit: their location in Jerusalem is not specified until v. 14 and the identity of "he" in v. 10-11 is delayed until Mot is mentioned in v. 15.[102] The end result is that Isa 28:7-22 is an integrated unit which forms the interpretative context for vv. 7-8. Since the latter verses are most relevant to the *marzēaḥ*, only they have been reproduced above, but other portions of the larger unit will shed light on the interpretation of those two verses.[103]

It remains to consider proposed deletions from Isa 28:7-8 that would eliminate possible *marzēaḥ* elements. For instance, instead of just "these also," all of 7a-b is considered a redactional link by some.[104] In contrast, Kissane considers 7a-b original, with 7c-g a gloss on the first two lines.[105] These excisions are predicated on the repetitiveness of the verse, which is considered a sign of editorial activity. That repetitiveness may, however, reflect the poet's artistry: the repetition of ideas, combined with the alteration of verbs, nouns and prepositions and the shifts in rhythm, reflect the impaired yet

---

their revelation (see van der Toorn, "Judaean Necromancy," 205), which corresponds to Mot in v. 15 (see further below). Thus the structural pattern can be retained, and with it the interconnection of vv. 7-22.

[101] The primary force of the preposition in 7f, which also governs 7g, is temporal, but a secondary meaning is that they also "go astray" in how they perform their specific roles.

[102] On the delayed identifications in the larger unit (but not within v. 7) see the discussions by Petersen, "Isaiah 28," 117; Exum, "Isaiah 28," 109-10 and 118 and especially W. A. M. Beuken, "Isaiah 28: Is It Only Schismatics That Drink Heavily? Beyond the Synchronic Versus Diachronic Controversy," *Synchronic or Diachronic? A Debate on Method in Old Testament Exegesis: Papers Read at the Ninth Joint Meeting of Het Oudtestamentisch Werkgezalschap in Nederland en België and the Society for Old Testament Study, Held at Kampen, 1994* (OTS 34; ed. J. C. de Moor; Leiden/New York/Cologne: E. J. Brill, 1995) 31-37.

[103] Some critics who consider vv. 7-13 and 14-22 separate units still date them to the same period and consider them addressed to the same audience. Thus, e.g., Marti, *Jesaja*, 207; Procksch, *Jesaia I*, 360; Kissane, *Isaiah*, 299; see also Wildberger, *Jesaja 28-39*, 1068-69; Halpern, "'The Excremental Vision,'" 112; van der Toorn, "Judaean Necromancy," 199; Stewart, "The Covenant with Death," 376. As such, the interpretive significance of the latter portion remains.

[104] Kaiser, *Isaiah 13-39*, 246-47; Vermeylen, *Du Prophète Isaïe*, 390; Petersen, "Isaiah 28," 108-09; Wildberger, *Jesaja 28-39*, 1056.

[105] Kissane, *Isaiah*, 303, 305. Lines 7e-g are rejected by Kaiser, *Isaiah 13-39*, 247-48.

garrulous speech, and the stumbling gait, of the drunkards.[106] Moreover, the individual lines are structurally integrated into the verse. For instance, in 7a-d the words "wine" and "strong drink" are repeated in reverse order, forming a unifying mirror pattern. By itself, this could be attributed to an editor, but 7a-b seems an excessively long redactional link; the same result could be achieved by simply adding וְגַם ("and even") to the beginning of 7c. Furthermore, the verbs in 7a-d combine with those in the rest of the verse to form a concentric pattern on the basis of sound: lines a-c and e-g contain two-syllable *qal* perfect verbs with the vowels *ā* and *û*, while in the central line d, נִבְלְעוּ is a *niphal*, and therefore longer and with different initial vowel sounds.[107] Finally, since each line of v. 7 contributes to the developmental pattern of both the verse and the larger unit,[108] they should all be retained, together with v. 8, as original parts of the larger unit.

## C. *Discussion*

Isa 28:7-8 has been identified as a *marzēaḥ* allusion for three reasons. First, there is the drunkenness motif shared with Amos 6:1, 3-7. Second, the mention of vomit and excrement in v. 8 reminds some of El collapsing in his own excretions after hosting a *marzēaḥ*.[109] Third, the "covenant with Death" in vv. 15 and 18 is often taken to reflect a connection between the *marzēaḥ* and the cult of the dead.[110]

None of these factors, either individually or in combination, is conclusive, though. To begin with, comparable content does not necessarily mean identical situations are being described. A shared fo-

[106] Over one hundred years ago, Delitzsch, *Isaiah*, 439, commented: "The language imitates the tottering and stumbling of the topers . . . ." The alteration of verbs and nouns is noted by Exum, "Isaiah 28," 119, and the role of the rhythm by Landy, "Isaiah 28," 152; both link them to drunken staggering. Oswalt, *Isaiah 1-39*, 510, also comments that the repetition of verbs and objects "seems to imitate the stumblings and gigglings of the drunk." None of them recognize the mimetic function of the shifting prepositions or the parallel between the repetitions and drunken verbosity.

[107] Jackson, "Style," 90. Irwin, *Isaiah 28–33*, 14, also notes an A:B:A pattern in the first there verbs (שָׁגוּ, תָּעוּ, שָׁגוּ).

[108] See p. 175.

[109] See the references in n. 4. Sweeney, *Isaiah 1-39*, 369, mentions El's indecorous posture but does not connect it with v. 8. Cf. the discussion of *CAT* 1.114 in chapter 1.

[110] See the references in n. 5.

cus on drunkenness does not, by itself, mean Isaiah is describing a *marzēaḥ*, as Amos did, any more than lack of control over one's bodily functions is evidence of similar situations, much less continuity, in Isa 28:7-8 and *CAT* 1.114. With respect to the latter two texts in particular, at least five hundred years passed between Ugarit's destruction (and the loss of the tablet) and this Isaian oracle. Moreover, the similarity between El's drunken collapse and v. 8 is not as close as suggested. Not only is the location of the expelled material and of the main character(s) in relationship to it different in the two texts, but only one of two items is comparable (excrement), and even then different terms are used.[111]

At the same time, it is illegitimate to pronounce this passage a *marzēaḥ* allusion only on the basis of references to Mot, the God of the underworld. Since there is no evidence of a necessary connection between the *marzēaḥ* and the cult of the dead prior to this time,[112] that cannot be used to establish this text as a *marzēaḥ*. This does not mean a connection between a *marzēaḥ* and the cult of the dead in Isa 28:7-8 is impossible. It is obvious from vv. 15 and 18 that the larger unit deals with Mot, and therefore has funerary associations, but whether it also deals with the *marzēaḥ* must be established on other grounds. I return, therefore, to the criteria of copious upper-class drinking in a religious context.

Each of these elements is easily detected in Isa 28:7-8. For instance, v. 7 describes the immediate physical effect of excessive alcohol consumption while v. 8 deals with subsequent vomiting and diarrhea,

---

[111] In *CAT* 1.114 the material emerges only after El leaves his *marzēaḥ* whereas here it is found in the same location as the (proposed) *marzēaḥ* (Dennis Pardee, personal communication). Moreover, in the Ugaritic text it is on the floor but in Isaiah the vomit, at least, is on the table, and even though the priests and prophets are most likely surrounded by the excrement, there is no indication they are floundering in it like El. Similarly, both texts allude to excrement, but not only is the vocabulary different (*ḫri'* and צֹאָה) but the two words occur as the first term at Ugarit but the second in Isa 28:8. Also, the Ugaritic text refers to urine (*ṯnt*) while Isa 28:8 has vomit (קִיא) as the other term. Pope seeks a closer connection between the two texts by emending בראה in v. 7f to בחרא, matching the Ugaritic text, and by suggesting a now lost term indicating human liquid waste, comparable to Ugaritic *ṯnt*, underlying פְּלִילִיָּה in 7g; see Pope, "Divine Banquet," 196; *idem*, *Song of Songs*, 217. But *contra* Pope, those terms in Isa 28:7f-g are neither "meaningless" nor "bizarre." They indicate the functions of the priest and prophet mentioned in 7c and anticipate the revelatory terms in v. 9a-b, so there is no reason to emend them.

[112] See the discussion in the three preceding chapters.

and the verb forms suggest this was not an isolated occurance.[113] Secondly, "priest and prophet" are mentioned in 7c, and the juxtaposition of these two functionaries suggests the prophets are cultic ones attached to the temple alongside the priests. As such, the protagonists here are a definable group among the elite of Jerusalem. Thirdly, their corresponding duties are mentioned in 7f and g ("seeing" and "judgment"), confirming a religious context for their drunken party: intoxication coincides with the performance of their religious duties.[114]

In sum, Isa 28:7-8 reflects the basic elements of a *marzēaḥ*. But further information about the religious component of this particular *marzēaḥ* can be derived from the larger context of those verses. Specifically, in v. 15 they acknowledge making a pact with Mot, the god of death. Assuming this "covenant with Death" was either initiated or celebrated during their *marzēaḥ*, Mot would be its patron deity.[115]

This can be supported from vv. 9-11. Those verses encompass a famous *crux interpretum* which has elicited a variety of explanations. Verse 10 has been variously interpreted as the drunken ramblings of the priests and prophets,[116] their comparison of Isaiah's message to a child's alphabet lesson,[117] the reduction of that message to a

[113] Delitzsch, *Isaiah*, 439, thought the perfect verbs "intimate that drunkenness has become the habit of the bearers of these offices"; see also Oswalt, *Isaiah 1-39*, 503n9. The *plene* spelling of the substantive "vomit" (קִיא) only occurs in connection with drunkenness (here and at Isa 19:14; Jer 48:26); see Wildberger, *Jesaja 28-39*, 1057; cf. Irwin, *Isaiah 28–33*, 19.

[114] Whether this banquet was essentially sacrificial (thus Cheyne, *Isaiah*, 1.164; Kaiser, *Isaiah 13-39*, 244; Herbert, *Isaiah*, 162; Jensen, *Isaiah 1-39*, 216; Floß, "Jes 28,7-12," 71), is not specified. *Contra* E. A. Leslie, *Isaiah: Chronologically Arranged, Translated and Interpreted* (New York: Abingdon Press, 1963) 83; Fohrer, *Jesaja 2*, 51, the table in 8a is not necessarily a sacrificial one.

[115] "Lie" and "deceit" in the latter part of v. 15 are taken as disguised references to Chemosh and Milcom by van der Toorn, "Judaean Necromancy," 203-04. In contrast, Irwin, *Isaiah 28–33*, 28, capitalizes the words as alternative names for Death (Mot) and Sheol, while Scott thinks they simply indicate the illusory power of other gods (R. B. Y. Scott, "Isaiah 1-39," 317). Van der Toorn's proposal is speculative, and in light of the chthonic connections of those deities, would not shift the primary locus of the *marzēaḥ*'s divine patron.

[116] Cheyne, *Isaiah*, 1.165; Driver, "'Another Little Drink,'" 55-57; Watts, *Isaiah 1-33*, 363; E. W. Conrad, *Reading Isaiah* (OBT 27; Minneapolis: Fortress Press, 1991) 125; V. Tanghe, "Dichtung und Ekel in Jes xxviii 7-13," *VT* 43 (1993) 236-39, 245-46.

[117] E.g., W. W. Hallo, "Isaiah 28:9-13 and the Ugaritic Abecedaries," *JBL* 77 (1958) 324-38; G. Pfeifer, "Entwöhnung und Entwöhnungsfest im Alten

monotonously repeated exhortation,[118] Assyrian commands addressed to exiles leaving the destroyed city,[119] or vulgar variants of the words קִיא ("vomit") and צֹאָה ("excrement") from v. 8.[120] But none of these fully integrate the verse with what precedes and follows.[121] Most proposals require a new speaker in v. 9 in order to make sense, only the third proposal reflects the revelatory terminology of v. 9, and none takes Mot's connection with the feast into account. But without any indication of a speaker other than Isaiah in v. 9, what follows should relate to the activities of the priest and prophet in v. 7, which means "he" in v. 9 must indicate the source of their revelation. Some consider this to be Yahweh,[122] but "his" word is contrasted with Yahweh's in v. 13. More directly, since Mot is their patron, he is the more probable source of a revelation. Thus, I think Karel van der Toorn is correct when he suggests that the syllables in v. 10 are a slightly deformed reproduction of that revelation.[123] This produces an interpretation that fits the larger context and is consistent with its development from ambiguity to greater clarity:[124] after denouncing their *marzēaḥ*, in which religious functionaries receive revelations while in a state of inebriation (vv. 7-8), Isaiah mocks the means through which that revelation is expressed (vv. 9-11), contrasts it with

Testament: der Schlüssel zu Jesaja 28,7-13?" *ZAW* 84 (1972) 341-47.

[118] I.e., "Command upon command, command upon command, rule upon rule, rule upon rule, here a little, there a little." Thus, e.g., Cheyne, *Isaiah*, 1.164-65; Kissane, *Isaiah*, 306; Young, *Isaiah*, 276-77; Eichrodt, *Der Herr der Geschichte*, 124; Oswalt, *Isaiah 1-39*, 512.

[119] "Go out! Let him go out! Go out! Let him go out! Wait! Let him wait! Wait! Let him wait! Servant, listen! Servant, listen!" See van Selms, "Isaiah 28:9-13," 332-39. André Lemaire suggests the "alphabet" interpretation for v. 10 and van Selms' proposal for v. 13; see A. Lemaire, *Les écoles et la formation de la bible dans l'ancien Israël* (OBO 39; Fribourg: Éditions Universitaires; Göttingen: Vandenhoeck & Ruprecht, 1981) 38-39.

[120] M. Görg, "Jesaja als 'Kinderlehrer?' Beobachtungen zur Sprache und Semantik in Jes 28,10(13)," *BN* 29 (1985) 12-16.

[121] Cf. the critique of Halpern, "'The Excremental Vision,'" 112-13. Van Selms completely divorces vv 9-13 from vv. 7-8.

[122] E.g., Petersen, "Isaiah 28," 109; Exum, "Isaiah 28," 120; Halpern, "'The Excremental Vision,'" 114.

[123] Van der Toorn, "Judaean Necromancy," 205-12; he builds upon the earlier suggestion of S. Daiches, "Isaiah and Spiritualism," *The Jewish Chonicle Supplement* (July 1921) 6. Van der Toorn points to connections between birds, revelations, and the dead in the ancient Near East in general, and the specific comparison of ghosts' voices to "chirping" in Isa 8:19; 29:4 to support his view that v. 10 indicates necromantic messages which imitate bird calls.

[124] See p. 175 above.

their refusal to listen to Yahweh's clear revelation, which therefore will become equally unintelligible, leading to their downfall (vv. 12-13), explicitly denounces the source of their message, namely Mot (vv. 14-15), and concludes by clearly announcing Yahweh's "cornerstone," which will obliterate the "covenant with death" (vv. 16-22).

In conclusion, vv. 7-8 reflect the basic elements of a *marzēaḥ*, namely a definable portion of the elite getting drunk in an explicitly religious context. At the same time, the larger context presents the first clear connection between a *marzēaḥ* and the cult of the dead.[125] This latter point is significant for the historical development of the institution. As such, a brief comment on the text's relative date are in order.

### D. *Dating the Text*

The Isaianic origin of the larger unit in general, and vv. 7-8 in particular, is not in doubt. Although individual lines are occasionally deleted, no one denies the core of the passage to the prophet himself.[126] The general consensus is that this text dates from shortly before 700 BCE,[127] which places it after the references and allusions by Amos and Hosea and before those to be examined in the following chapters.

## IV. Isa 56:9-57:13

The final text to consider in this chapter is Isa 56:9-57:13. Jared Jackson has linked this passage with Amos 6:1-7 on the basis of the drinking and the reference to "beds" in both places, and characterizes Isa 57:8 in particular as "a *mrzḥ*, where behind closed doors a memorial for absent members is held."[128]

---

[125] In addition to the necromantic consultation of Mot already noted, the "bed" and "covering" in v. 20 are taken as a funeral bed and shroud by Halpern, "'The Excremental Vision,'" 117; see also Sweeney, *Isaiah 1-39*, 371. This would be further confirmation of the funerary nature of this *marzēaḥ*, but contrast Beuken, "Isaiah 28," 27, who considers v. 20 an unconnected proverb.

[126] See the commentaries. Deletions from vv. 7-8 were considered and rejected above.

[127] The scholarship on the passage's dating is conveniently summarized by Wildberger, *Jesaja 28-39*, 1056-57.

[128] Jackson, "Style," 96.

This proposal can be dealt with much more quickly than previous ones because of fundamental flaws in Jackson's argument. First, while a funerary context for a *marzēaḥ* is not impossible here, especially in light of the preceding discussion of Isa 28:7-8,[129] the only dead in this passage are children (v. 5), who are unlikely members of a *marzēaḥ* association. Secondly, the beds' purposes are different in the two passages: in Amos 6:4 they indicate where the *marzēaḥ* members sprawl while in Isa 57:7-8 it refers to the place the prostitute practices her trade.[130] Thirdly, and most importantly, Jackson fails to take into account the major division in the passage at 57:3, which separates the drinking from the beds and the funerary language.[131]

The precise compositional structure of Isa 56:9-57:13 is disputed,[132] but there is widespread recognition that וְאַתֶּם ("but as for you") in Isa 57:3 initiates a new section.[133] Hanson claims that the word provides the transition in an hybrid salvation-judgment form, but still concludes that "56:9-57:2 was originally an independent composi-

---

[129] Jackson, "Style," 96n87, draws a parallel between חָזִית in Isa 57:8 and the word חָזוּת parallel to בְּרִית, used to designate the covenant/agreement with Mot/Sheol in Isa 28:18 (cf. Isa 28:15 as well); the connection is also noted by T. J. Lewis, *Cults of the Dead in Ancient Israel and Ugarit* (HSM 39; Atlanta: Scholars Press, 1989) 150; since "you cut" at the beginning of 57:8 is probably an elliptical reference to "cutting a covenant" (thus J. L. McKenzie, *Second Isaiah: A New Translation with Introduction and Commentary* [AB 20; Garden City: Doubleday, 1968] 157) this interpretation of חָזִית is plausible. Jackson treated the preceding יָד as a verb (he refers to A. Fitzgerald, "Hebrew *yd* = 'Love' and 'Beloved'," *CBQ* 29 [1967] 368-74, for support; cf. אָהַבְתְּ, "you loved" immediately before) and translated "(you) loved the pact."

[130] Verses 7-13 consist of 2nd singular feminine verbs and pronouns, referring to the personified prostitute mother of those addressed in vv. 3-6. Lewis, *Cults of the Dead*, 149-50, followed by S. Ackerman, *Under Every Green Tree: Popular Religion in Sixth-Century Judah* (HSM 46; Atlanta: Scholars Press, 1992) 153-54, sees a combined reference to her bed and a grave ("bed" has the latter meaning in v. 2), but that too distinguishes these beds from those in Amos 6:4. In contrast, Schmidt, *Israel's Beneficent Dead*, 258, argues for just a bed on the basis of the harlotry imagery in Isa 57:7-8.

[131] In light of this disjuncture I do not present the entire Hebrew text and translation as with other passages, since when it came to "establishing the unit" the two halves would be separated and the discussion ended.

[132] E.g., McKenzie considers 56:9-57:2 and 57:3-13 two unconnected units, Westermann (following Ewald and Volz) identifies four separate units (56:9-12; 57:1-2, 3-6, 7-13) and Whybray divides it into three (56:9-12; 57:1-2, 3-13); see McKenzie, *Second Isaiah*, 153-59, especially p. 158; C. Westermann, *Isaiah 40-66: A Commentary* (OTL; trans. D. M. G. Stalker; Philadelphia: Westminster Press, 1969) 301-02; R. N. Whybray, *Isaiah 40-66* (NCBC; Grand Rapids: Wm. B. Eerdmans Publishing Co., 1975) 200.

[133] Even Oswalt, who considers the whole passage a unit, subdivides it at 57:3;

tion, representing an attack on the leaders of the community by the prophetic group, and that someone within that same group later expanded that composition with the addition of 57:3-13."[134] The separation of these two sections is confirmed by the lack of thematic continuity between them. Isa 56:9-57:2 attacks the community's leaders[135] for their drunken self-centredness that fails to consider the plight of the righteous. In contrast, although Isa 57:3-13 may deal with these same leaders,[136] those verses focus on cultic aberrations. Also, the only vocabulary shared by the two sections is the word "bed" (מִשְׁכָּב), but it has different nuances in each: a grave and a harlot's bed.[137] Thus, Ackerman is correct in identifying it as a *Stichwort* that "binds the two units together but, because of its different meanings, indicates the independence of each stanza."[138]

As a result, even though the three basic *marzēaḥ* elements are present in the larger passage, they do not all occur together in either half. For instance, the leaders are described in 56:10-11,[139] and their[140] drinking in v. 12 is consistent with a *marzēaḥ*: "strong drink" (שֵׁכָר) was consumed in Isa 28:7 as well, the verb סָבָא connotes excessiveness,[141] and the second half of the verse implies this activity

---

see J. N. Oswalt, *The Book of Isaiah, Chapters 40-66* (NICOT; Grand Rapids: Wm. B. Eerdmans Publishing Co., 1998) 467.

[134] P. D. Hanson, *The Dawn of Apocalyptic: The Historical and Sociological Roots of Jewish Apocalyptic Eschatology* (Rev. ed.; Philadelphia: Fortress Press, 1975) 188-89. He sees the word effecting the same transition at Isa 65:11, 13, 14.

[135] "Watchmen" is used of prophets at Jer 6:17; Ezek 3:17; Hab 2:1, but most extend the meaning to include other leaders as well. Hanson and Oswalt both see a three-fold reference to priests, prophets and civic leaders, albeit on slightly different grounds; cf. Hanson, *The Dawn of Apocalyptic*, 196; Oswalt, *Isaiah 40-66*, 469.

[136] Most think this section also deals with the leaders, but it is addressed to the whole community by Cheyne, *Isaiah*, 2.66; Westermann, *Isaiah 40-66*, 302. Similarly, Whybray, *Isaiah 40-66*, 200, identifies "two distinct groups of people . . ., the leaders of the community (56:9-12) and idolators (57:3-13*a*)."

[137] See n. 130. I agree with Schmidt that the primary meaning in vv. 7-8 is a (figurative) prostitute's bed, but in light of the death language in the surrounding verse I would not rule out a play on the meaning "grave" as well (cf. Prov 2:16-17, cited by Lewis, *Cults of the Dead*, 158; cf. the references in his n. 104).

[138] Ackerman, *Under Every Green Tree*, 101n1.

[139] See n. 135.

[140] The opening words in v. 12 are from a single speaker ("Come, let me get [אֶקְחָה] wine"), but the following phrase ("let us guzzle strong drink") indicates more than one person is involved. The Vulgate, the Targum, the Peshitta and 1QIs[a] all change the singular to the plural, but the individual may simply be a representative who orders for the group.

[141] Three of its five other occurrences are in conjunction with זולל ("glutton"): Deut 21:20; Prov 23:21, 30; see also Ezek 23:42; Nah 1:10 and the noun סֹבֶא in Hos 4:18.

was ongoing. But there is no indication in those verses that the drinking occurred in a religious context. Similarly, while the second half of the passage describes religious activity,[142] there is no reference to drinking, and it is not even clear that the leaders are being addressed.[143] In short, nothing in the larger text connects the drinking in the first half and the religious practices condemned in the second half. Thus, even if Hanson is correct that the first half was expanded by the same authorial group,[144] this is not a case of a subsequent clarification by them that the first half alludes to a *marzēaḥ*. Since the two parts have not been integrated, even if the same group is being denounced in both parts, it is because of two distinct practices. This indicates that Isa 56:9-57:13 does not allude to a *marzēaḥ*, either before or after the fact.[145]

## V. Summary

Four Isaiah texts have been considered as possible *marzēaḥ* allusions, but only one can be accepted with any confidence. First, Isa 5:11-13 adapts Amos 6:1, 3-7 to a different situation. Although the text describes drunkenness by members of the upper-class, this did not occur in a religious context. Thus, Isaiah identified the episode as a "feast" (מִשְׁתֶּה) rather than the more specific *marzēaḥ* banquet. Second, like Amos 6:1, 3-7, Isa 28:1-4 denounces the drunken Samarian elite. But despite the similar audience, the two texts do not address an identical situation. Asen's attempt to link the latter to the *marzēaḥ*

[142] Since the passage does not allude to a *marzēaḥ*, the precise nature of this activity is secondary to my purpose, but it is clear from v. 5 that child sacrifice is involved. Recent proposals concerning the rest of the passage include those of Schmidt, who interprets the sexual language in terms of harlotry as a metaphor for idolatrous child sacrifice, Lewis, who views it as a metaphor for a necromantic cult of the dead, and Ackerman, who finds three cults intertwined in vv. 3-13: child sacrifice, fertility rites and the cult of the dead; see Schmidt, *Israel's Beneficent Dead*, 258-59; Lewis, *Cults of the Dead*, 145-58; Ackerman, *Under Every Green Tree*, 117-63, especially pp. 154-62.

[143] Cf. n. 136 above.

[144] See n. 134 above.

[145] Also, all of Isa 56:12 is absent from the LXX; for Lewis, *Cults of the Dead*, 143n50, this is "a sure sign that we are dealing with a later addition." While not conclusive (it is present in the other versions and at Qumran), it cautions against giving too much weight to the verse in determining an allusion. At the same time, even if the verse was added in imitation of Isa 28:7-8, as Lewis thinks, the lack of integration with the second half still argues against a *marzēaḥ* here.

through the participants' use of flowers proved unsuccessful, and the passage does not include all of the basic elements of a *marzēaḥ*. Specifically, it lacks a religious connection, without which the text may reflect nothing more than another example of general upper-class excess. Third, the references to leaders drinking in Isa 56:10-12 and religious activity in 57:3-13 occur in distinct sections of a larger passage which exhibits no integral connection between the two parts. As such there is no religious context for the drinking, which excludes it from classification as an assured *marzēaḥ* allusion.

In contrast, Isa 28:7-8 (and what follows) does reflect the elements necessary for a *marzēaḥ* allusion. Those verses attack the priests and prophets, members of the religious hierarchy. The excessiveness of their drinking while performing religious functions is clear in v. 7, and culminates in the description in v. 8 of vomit and excrement spread around the room. The subsequent verses indicate that the divine patron of their *marzēaḥ* is Mot, the god of the underworld, and that during the feast the priest and prophet receive revelatory messages from him. This has great importance for the *marzēaḥ*'s history. Isa 28:7-22 is the first instance of a *marzēaḥ* text that also exhibits an explicit link with the cult of the dead. As such it sets a precedent, but not a requirement, for subsequent instances of a *marzēaḥ*. Since this particular one was a means for contacting the realm of the dead, the possibility that later ones might be as well is increased. But that possibility should not be mistaken for a necessity. Funerary elements alone cannot establish a passage as a *marzēaḥ* allusion. Drinking in a religious context by a definable portion of the elite remain essential characteristics of a *marzēaḥ*, and subsequent texts will still have to be evaluated on the basis of those criteria.

CHAPTER FIVE

# THE *MARZĒAḤ* IN JEREMIAH

Jer 16:5 is one of two explicit biblical references to a *marzēaḥ*[1] (the other being Amos 6:7), but no one has proposed any *marzēaḥ* allusions in the book of Jeremiah. Therefore, the following discussion will elaborate the main points of Jer 16:5 within its context and clarify the nature of this particular *marzēaḥ*. But first, the verse and its context will be established.

## I. Jer 16:5-9

### A. *The Text*

כִּי[2]־כֹה אָמַר יהוה אַל־תָּבוֹא בֵּית מַרְזֵחַ וְאַל־תֵּלֵךְ לִסְפּוֹד וְאַל־תָּנֹד לָהֶם כִּי־
אָסַפְתִּי אֶת־שְׁלוֹמִי מֵאֵת הָעָם־הַזֶּה נְאֻם־יהוה אֶת־הַחֶסֶד וְאֶת־הָרַחֲמִים (6) וּמֵתוּ
גְדֹלִים וּקְטַנִּים בָּאָרֶץ הַזֹּאת לֹא יִקָּבֵרוּ[3] וְלֹא־יִסְפְּדוּ לָהֶם וְלֹא יִתְגֹּדַד וְלֹא יִקָּרֵחַ

[1] As such, the verse was discussed in D. B. Bryan, "Texts Relating to the *Marzeaḥ*: A Study of an Ancient Semitic Institution" (Ph.D. diss., Johns Hopkins University, 1973) 69-71.

[2] The initial כִּי is absent from the LXX and deleted by W. L. Holladay, *Jeremiah 1: A Commentary on the Book of the Prophet Jeremiah, Chapters 1-25* (Hermeneia; Philadelphia: Fortress Press, 1986) 467, 468. He argues it does not begin a motivation clause like the word's other occurrences at vv. 3, 5b, and especially v. 9. But the word may be intended to highlight the transition from vv. 1-4; thus F. Giesebrecht, *Das Buch Jeremia übersetzt und erklärt* (KHAT 13; 2nd ed.; Göttingen: Vandenhoeck & Ruprecht, 1907) 95, who translates as "denn also . . . ." Other translations in the same vein include "weiter" by P. Volz, *Der Prophet Jeremia übersetzt und erklärt* (KAT 10; 2nd ed.; Leipzig: A. Deichertsche Verlagsbuchhandlung, 1928) 178; "further" by J. Bright, *Jeremiah: A New Translation with Introduction and Commentary* (AB 21; Garden City: Doubleday, 1965) 107; "weiter . . . also" by A. Weiser, *Das Buch Jeremia* (ATD 21; Göttingen: Vandenhoeck & Ruprecht, 1966) 136; and "ferner . . . also" by W. Rudolph, *Jeremia* (HAT 12; 3rd ed.; Tübingen: J. C. B. Mohr [Paul Siebeck], 1968) 92]). See also p. 191 below.

[3] Pointed as a *qal* by Holladay, *Jeremiah* 1, 467, who is followed by J. A. Thompson, *The Book of Jeremiah* (NICOT; Grand Rapids: Wm. B. Eerdmans Publishing Co., 1980) 400n7; they claim that the subject of the following verbs is the survivors, not the dead. However, the survivors' actions are directed to the dead and the focus does not shift to actual concern for the former, specifically, a "mourner" (cf. p. 187 below) until v. 7. This verb occurs as a niphal in v. 4 as well.

> לָהֶם (7) וְלֹא־יִפְרְסוּ לֶחֶם[4] עַל־אָבֵל[5] לְנַחֲמוֹ[6] עַל־מֵת וְלֹא־יַשְׁקוּ אוֹתוֹ[7] כּוֹס תַּנְחוּמִים
> עַל־אָבִיו וְעַל־אִמּוֹ (8) וּבֵית־מִשְׁתֶּה לֹא[8]־תָבוֹא לָשֶׁבֶת אִתָּם[9] לֶאֱכֹל וְלִשְׁתּוֹת (9)
> כִּי כֹה אָמַר יהוה צְבָאוֹת אֱלֹהֵי יִשְׂרָאֵל הִנְנִי מַשְׁבִּית מִן־הַמָּקוֹם הַזֶּה לְעֵינֵיכֶם
> וּבִימֵיכֶם קוֹל שָׂשׂוֹן וְקוֹל שִׂמְחָה קוֹל חָתָן וְקוֹל כַּלָּה
>
> Furthermore, thus says Yahweh: Do not enter the *marzēaḥ* house; do not go to lament and do not grieve for them. For I have taken away my peace from this people, (Yahweh's utterance), my steadfast love and mercy. (6) Great and small will die in this land. They will not be buried, and no one will lament for them; no one will gash himself or make himself bald for them. (7) They will not break bread for the mourner, to comfort him for the dead. They will not give him the cup of consolation to drink for his father or his mother. (8) You shall not enter the drinking house to sit with them, to eat and drink. (9) For thus says Yahweh of hosts, the God of Israel: I am going to banish from this place, in your days and before your eyes, the sound of mirth and the sound of gladness, the voice of the bridegroom and the voice of the bride.

As is often the case in the book of Jeremiah, the LXX for this passage is shorter than the MT. The only substantial portion is 5b-6a (נְאֻם־יהוה . . . לֹא יִקָּבֵרוּ), but it does not contain anything of significance concerning this *marzēaḥ* that is not duplicated elsewhere in the text,[10] nor does "for them" at the end of v. 6 or "(Yahweh) of hosts" in v. 9 affect the passage as a whole. However, since v. 6a prepares for what follows, Janzen concludes that the MT represents the orig-

---

[4] Instead of לָהֶם in the MT; see the discussion on p. 187.

[5] The MT vocalizes this word as אֵבֶל; see p 187.

[6] The suffix is deleted by K. H. Cornhill, *The Book of the Prophet Jeremiah: Critical Edition of the Hebrew Text Arranged in Chronological Order, with Notes* (SBOT 11; trans. C. Johnston; Leipzig: J. C. Hinrichs'sche Buchhandlung, 1895) 58-59, but it fits the sense of the passage and is repeated three more times in the verse (one involves emendation; see p. 187 below) .

[7] The MT reads אוֹתָם; see p. 187.

[8] Changed to אַל by Holladay, *Jeremiah 1*, 467 and O. Loretz, "*Marziḥu* im ugaritischen und biblischen Ahnenkult: zu Ps 23; 133; Am 6,1-7 und Jer 16,5.8," *Mesopotamica, Ugaritica, Biblica: Festschrift für Kurt Bergerhof zur Vollendung seines 70. Lebensjahres am 7. Mai 1992* (AOAT 232; eds. M. Dietrich and O. Loretz; Kevelaer: Verlag Butzon and Bercker; Neukirchen-Vluyn: Neukirchener Verlag, 1993) 139n85. אַל does provide a better parallel with v. 5, but a different negative here may be meant to highlight a distinction between the two verses; cf. pp. 189-91 below.

[9] In place of אוֹתָם in the MT; cf. p. 187.

[10] The mourning practices listed in vv. 6b-7 provide the same funerary connection as the references to death and burial in 6a.

inal text, with a line having fallen out of the LXX's *Vorlage*.[11]

Four changes have been made to the MT.[12] The phrase וְלֹא־יִפְרְסוּ לָהֶם עַל־אֵבֶל ("They will not break for them for mourning") at the start of v. 7 is obviously damaged. Changing לָהֵם to לֶחֶם yields a smoother first half of the phrase,[13] while repointing אֵבֶל as אָבֵל ("mourner"; cf. the Vulgate's *lugenti*) provides a referent for the masculine singular pronouns later in the verse. Granted, the second of those singular pronouns is achieved by emending אוֹתָם to אוֹתוֹ with the LXX, but the plural pronoun is inconsistent with the singular ones later in the verse. Finally, the command not to sit "them" (אוֹתָם) in v. 8 is problematic, but this is resolved if one accepts the variant reading of אִתָּם ("with them") found in some manuscripts and the LXX (μετ' αὐτῶν).

## B. *Establishing the Unit*

It was suggested above that v. 5 initiates an elaboration of the preceding verses,[14] and Holladay points to a number of thematic and linguistic repetitions in support of linking vv. 2-9.[15] Jer 16:1 intro-

---

[11] J. G. Janzen, *Studies in the Text of Jeremiah* (HSM 6; Cambridge: Harvard University Press, 1973) 98; see also L. Stulman, *The Other Text of Jeremiah: A Reconstruction of the Hebrew Text Underlying the Greek Version of the Prose Sections of Jeremiah with English Translation* (Lanham/New York/London: University Press of America, 1985) 30-33; *idem, The Prose Sermons of the Book of Jeremiah: A Redescription of the Correspondences with Deuteronomistic Literature in the Light of Recent Text-Critical Research* (SBLDS 83; Atlanta: Scholars Press, 1986) 67-70. "For them" at the end of v. 6 is consistent with the same words earlier in the verse.

[12] For a convenient summary of the textual witnesses, history of scholarship and modern translational choices for the first three see D. Barthélemy, *Critique textuelle de l'Ancien Testament. 2. Isaïe, Jérémie, Lamentations* (OBO 50; Fribourg: Editions Universitaires; Göttingen: Vandenhoeck & Ruprecht, 1986) 602-05.

[13] The change is accepted by virtually all scholars. The two words are very similar in appearance, and לֶחֶם is found in a few Hebrew manuscripts. Cornhill, *Jeremiah*, 59, suggests both words were originally present, and different ones dropped out of the MT and the LXX's *Vorlage*, but the LXX apparently read both words (ἄρτος . . . αὐτῶν), as did the Vulgate (*inter eos . . . panem*).

[14] See n. 2 above.

[15] Holladay, *Jeremiah 1*, 467-68; see also Thompson, *Jeremiah*, 400nn6, 9, 11. Both portions contain prohibitions addressed to an individual, each of which is followed by motivations introduced by כִּי. The first two motivations are linked by the failure to "bury" and "lament" (vv. 4 and 6), which occurs "in this land" (בָּאָרֶץ הַזֹּאת; vv. 3 and 6), while the first and third begin with "Thus says Yahweh . . ." (כֹּה אָמַר יהוה: vv. 3 and 9; v. 5a has נְאֻם יהוה ["Yahweh's utterance"] instead) and refer to "this place" (מָקוֹם הַזֶּה). Finally, the prohibition of marriage

duces a new word from the Lord, but the verse is absent from the LXX, leading Carroll to conclude it is a later addition meant to change the following address from the people to the prophet.[16] However, the second person singular masculine verb and pronouns in v. 2 (לֹא־תִקַּח and לְךָ [2x]) are echoed in vv. 5a and 8a, indicating that an individual is addressed throughout even though the fate of the populace is described in vv. 3-4, 5b-7, 9. In any case, the content of Jer 16:(1)2-9 is sufficiently distinctive from chapter 15 for the two to be separated for the purposes of interpretation.[17]

Some scholars extend the unit to encompass vv. 10-13,[18] but those verses do not share any vocabulary with the preceding ones.[19] Moreover, the address shifts from an individual to the larger community, and the various prohibitions of vv. 2-9 do not figure in vv. 10-13. As a result, most interpreters treat vv. 10-13 as a later interpretation of the anti-social behaviour called for in vv. 2-9.[20] Thus, Jer 16:5-9 is a subsection of a larger unit, namely Jer 16:1-9. But since the earlier verses do not add anything of substance to the issue of the *marzēaḥ* beyond what is already in vv. 5-9, the analysis will focus on the latter verses.

It is widely recognized that those verses have been the object of

---

in v. 2 is echoed in the wedding imagery of v. 9, and "mother(s)" and "father(s)" are mentioned in reverse order in vv. 3 and 7, as are "lament" and "bury" in vv. 4 and 6. The result is a mirror structure unifying vv. 2-9.

[16] R. P. Carroll, *Jeremiah: A Commentary* (OTL; Philadelphia: Westminster Press, 1986) 338-39. See further on p. 194 below.

[17] Jer 15:19-21 is a combined rebuke and reassurance to the prophet in response to the complaint of Jer 15:15-18. The former promises Yahweh's deliverance from "this people" while Jer 16:2-9 commands separation from them. Rudolph's suggestion that the latter passage was placed here as an illustration of the loneliness of Jer 15:17 is probably correct (see Rudolph, *Jeremia*, 93; he is followed by most commentators). In addition, the "sword and famine" theme in 14:11-18; 15:2 and 16:4 is noted by Bright, *Jeremiah*, 112, while Carroll and Kelley point to the "mother motif" in 15:8-9,10 and 16:3; see Carroll, *Jeremiah*, 338; P. C. Craigie, P. H. Kelley and J. F. Drinkard, Jr., *Jeremiah 1-25* (WBC 26; Dallas: Word Books, 1991) 215.

[18] E.g., Volz, *Jeremia*, 177-82; J. P. Hyatt, "The Book of Jeremiah: Introduction and Exegesis," *IB* 945-46; Bright, *Jeremiah*, 112; Rudolph, *Jeremia*, 93-95. Cf. Weiser, *Jeremia*, 139.

[19] Holladay, *Jeremiah 1*, 467. He also claims vv. 10-13 do not exhibit the characteristics of "rhythmic prose" (*Kunstprosa*) he identifies in vv. 2-9. See also H. Weippert, *Die Prosareden des Jeremiabuches* (BZAW 132; Berlin: Walter de Gruyter, 1973) 166-69.

[20] See the convenient summary of scholarship by W. McKane, *A Critical and Exegetical Commentary on Jeremiah. Vol. I: Introduction and Commentary on Jeremiah I-XXV* (ICC 20; Edinburgh: T. & T. Clark, 1986) 369.

editorial activity. Two redactional proposals in particular have implications for this study: Oswald Loretz offers a truncated form of v. 7[21] and H.-J. Fabry considers all but vv. 1, 5a and 8 to be secondary.[22] Since either suggestion, if accepted, drastically affects the nature of the *marzēaḥ* in this passage, they will be considered in conjunction with the analysis of the text itself.

## C. *Discussion*

Jer 16:5 refers to a *marzēaḥ* house (בֵּית מַרְזֵחַ), an institution already encountered in the material from Ugarit and still known as late as the 6th century CE.[23] The extra-biblical material indicates that the *marzēaḥ* house was owned by an identifiable upper-class group and was the location for the *marzēaḥ* feast itself, and there is nothing to indicate a different context here. Whatever else can be determined about this specific *marzēaḥ* house depends on its connection with the following verses.

Whether or not the *marzēaḥ* house in v. 5 and the "drinking house" in v. 8 are identical is central to the proper interpretation of this passage. If they are the same, a link with more than "social drinking" exists, but if they are distinct then vv. 8-9 have little bearing on the meaning of vv. 5-7, except by way of contrast. Scholarly opinion diverges as to the relationship between the two buildings.[24]

---

[21] O. Loretz, "Ugaritisch-biblisch *mrzḥ* 'Kultmahl, Kultverein' in Jer 16,5 und Am 6,7. Bemerkungen zur Geschichte des Totenkultes in Israel," *Künder des Wortes. Beiträge zur Theologie der Propheten: Joseph Schreiner zum 60. Geburtstag* (eds. L. Ruppert, P. Weimar and E. Zenger; Würzburg: Echter-Verlag, 1982) 89.

[22] H.-J. Fabry, "מַרְזֵחַ *marzēaḥ*," *TWAT* 5.15.

[23] The Akkadian phrase *bît* amilM*mar-za-i/mar-ze-i* ("house of the men of the *marzēaḥ*") occurs in RS 15.70 and RS 15.88, and ΒΗΤΟΜΑΡΣΕΑ is found on the Madeba Map. See Chapter 1 for discussion of those instances, as well as for other buildings linked to *marzēaḥ*s in *CAT* 1.21.II.1-9; 1.114.15-17; 3.9, the Moabite papyrus and the Palmyrene contract.

[24] They are considered synonymous by Bright, *Jeremiah*, 110-11; B. Porten, *Archives from Elephantine: The Life of an Ancient Jewish Military Colony* (Berkeley: University of California Press, 1968) 181; Bryan, "Texts," 69; M. H. Pope, *Song of Songs: A New Translation with Introduction and Commentary* (AB 7C; Garden City: Doubleday, 1977) 216, 222; *idem*, "Le *MRZḤ* à l'Ugarit et ailleurs," *AAAS* 29-30 (1979-1980) 141; *idem*, "The Cult of the Dead at Ugarit," *Ugarit in Retrospect* (ed. G. D. Young; Winona Lake: Eisenbrauns, 1981) 176; T. J. Lewis, *Cults of the Dead in Ancient Israel and Ugarit* (HSM 39; Atlanta: Scholars Press, 1989) 89, 138-39; S. Ackerman, *Under Every Green Tree: Popular Religion in Sixth-Century Judah* (HSM 46; Atlanta: Scholars Press, 1992) 72; D. R. Jones, *Jeremiah* (NCBC; Grand Rapids: Wm. B. Eerd-

At first glance, the parallels between vv. 5-7 and 8-9 seem to support linking the two "houses." Both sections begin with a command not to enter one or the other type of house, followed by a reason for the prohibition that is rooted in God's imminent action. But in fact, a new command and motivation, as in v. 8, suggests something new is being introduced,[25] which is confirmed by the variations between the two sections. In v. 5 the negated verb comes before the reference to the house, while the order is reversed in v. 8; this, combined with the disjunctive *waw* at the beginning of v. 8, indicates a new topic.[26] This is supported by the use of different negatives (אל and לא) and the divergent content of the two motivations, namely funerary and marriage imagery.[27] Finally, the structure of the larg-

---

mans Publishing Co., 1992) 231; P. J. King, *Jeremiah: An Archaeological Companion* (Louisville: Westminster/John Knox Press, 1993) 141; Loretz, "*Marziḥu*," 139-40; F. Gangloff and J.-C. Haelewyck, "Osée 4,17-19: un marzeah en l'honneur de la déesse ʿAnat" *ETL* 71 (1995) 378; H. M. Barstad, "Some Reflections on the Meaning of the Expression בית מרזח in Jer 16:5," *Built on Solid Rock: Studies in Honour of Professor Ebbe Egede Knudsen on the Occasion of His 65th Birthday April 11th 1997* (Instituttet for Sammenlignende Kulturforskning Serie B: Skrifter XCVIII; ed. E. Wardini; Oslo: Novus Forlag, 1997) 24-26; Fabry, "מַרְזֵחַ *marzēaḥ*," 5.15. The Vulgate translates both terms as *domum convivii* ("house of banqueting").

The two houses are distinguished by K. F. Keil, *Biblical Commentary on the Prophecies of Jeremiah* (CFTL; Edinburgh: T. & T. Clark, 1880) 1.268; Giesebrecht, *Jeremia*, 94; Volz, *Jeremia*, 179; O. Eissfeldt, "Etymologische und archäologische Erklärung alttestamentlicher Wörter," *OrAnt* 5 (1966) 171; Thompson, *Jeremiah*, 406; L. Boadt, *Jeremiah 1-25* (OTMS 9; Wilmington: Michael Glazier, 1982) 124; Carroll, *Jeremiah*, 340; McKane, *Jeremiah I*, 365, 367; W. Brueggemann, *To Pluck up, to Tear Down: A Commentary on the Book of Jeremiah 1-25* (ITC; Grand Rapids: Wm. B. Eerdmans Publishing Co., 1988) 145; Craigie, Kelley and Drinkard, *Jeremiah 1-25*, 217; B. B. Schmidt, *Israel's Beneficent Dead: Ancestor Cult and Necromancy in Ancient Israelite Religion and Tradition* (Winona Lake: Eisenbrauns, 1996) 247. Most of these link the "drinking house" with a wedding; cf. vv. 2, 9 and Judg 10:14, 19. Separate terms are used for the two "houses" in the LXX, the Peshitta and the Targum.

For Holladay, *Jeremiah 1*, 470, "the question must remain open"; see his pp. 468, 471-72.

[25] Holladay, *Jeremiah 1*, 470.

[26] The word order is noted by Holladay, *Jeremiah 1*, 470; for the syntax involved see R. J. Williams, *Hebrew Syntax: An Outline* (2nd ed.; Toronto: University of Toronto Press, 1976) §573. On the disjunctive *waw* see T. O. Lambdin, *Introduction to Biblical Hebrew* (New York: Scribner's Sons, 1971) §132; B. K. Waltke and M. O'Connor, *An Introduction to Biblical Hebrew Syntax* (Winona Lake: Eisenbrauns, 1990) §39.2.3.

[27] Pope and Holladay seek to counter the latter point by appealing to rabbinic traditions in which the dead are referred to as bride and groom; see Pope, *Song of Songs*, 216; *idem*, "The Cult of the Dead," 177; Holladay, *Jeremiah 1*, 470. Apart from the difficulties inherent in using material from centuries later, this does not

er passage also argues against identifying the two "houses." Marriage is forbidden in v. 2 because the future will entail widespread, unlamented death (vv. 3-4). The marriage and death motifs are then developed in reverse order, with vv. 5-7 picking up the lack of burial and lamentation from v. 4 and v. 8-9 echoing the marriage imagery from v. 2. All of these factors indicate vv. 5-7 and 8-9 deal with different topics, death and marriage, which in turn are linked to different houses.[28]

This leaves vv. 5b-7 as the primary interpretive context for the *marzēaḥ* reference in 5a. Within those verses, Oswald Loretz finds the transition from sudden death, with no time for mourning in v. 6, to leisurely mourning ("friedlichen Trauer") in v. 7 too sudden to be original.[29] Instead, he proposes the original wording of v. 7 was, "Und man wird da 'Brot' für sie nicht brechen und man wird ihnen nicht zu trinken geben den Trostbecher." Having stripped the verse of supposed secondary material, he interprets breaking bread and the cup of consolation as sacrifices on behalf of the dead, and interprets the *marzēaḥ* as a ritual feeding of the dead with those sacrifices. There are problems with Loretz's proposal, however. A minor difficulty is that his translation includes both "bread" and "for them," whereas there is only one word in the MT.[30] More significantly, if there were no time for mourning then there would be no time for sacrifices either. Furthermore, v. 6 indicates no one will lament the dead or perform the mourning rituals of gashing and shaving oneself for them, so having someone feed the dead in v. 7 would run contrary to the point of v. 6. On the other hand, as it stands, v. 7 continues the perspective of v. 6: not only will the usual customs with respect to the dead not be observed (v. 6), but neither will the traditional efforts to comfort the survivors take place (v. 7). In short, Loretz's suggestion creates problems where none existed, and v. 7 should be retained intact.[31]

A more radical proposal comes from H.-J. Fabry, who suggests a

---

negate the disjunctive *waw* in v. 8 or the obvious difference between lament (v. 7) and "mirth and . . . gladness" (v. 9).

[28] The contrast is clearly reflected later in Qoh 7:2, where "drinking house" is in opposition to the "mourning house" (בֵּית־אֵבֶל).

[29] Loretz, "'Kultmahl,'" 89.

[30] There is no indication he follows Cornhill in viewing both as original (see n. 13 above).

[31] The role of the words "father" and "mother," which Loretz would delete, in the mirror structure of the larger unit (cf. n. 15 above), supports this decision.

three-stage development in the text. In his view, the oldest text consisted of vv. 1, 5a and 8; this was later supplemented with vv. 2, 6-7, after which the Deuteronomists inserted 3-4, 9. Having thus isolated what he considers the original text, he takes the commands not to lament and grieve in 5a as antithetical to the surrounding commands not to go (to celebrate) to the *marzēaḥ*/feasting house. Thus, what little funerary language is original is also antithetical to the *marzēaḥ*.[32] However, Fabry's proposal destroys the carefully balanced mirror structure of the larger passage. It is easier to envision that structure arising from a single hand than from the consecutive efforts of three individuals working separately. Finally, as was shown above,[33] within that structure the *marzēaḥ* house and the feasting house are antithetical, not synonymous as Fabry claims. In sum, his proposal is not convincing, and vv. 6-7 can and should be related to the *marzēaḥ* house in 5a.

Thus, vv. 5b-7 constitute the main source for more information about that *marzēaḥ* house. Drinking and ritual actions are mentioned in those verses, but they do not provide definitive evidence of the extensive drinking in a religious context encountered in previous *marzēaḥs*. Pope points to the rabbinic restriction of the cup of consolation to ten servings as evidence of drunkenness,[34] but without evidence that custom existed at the time of this text the use of such later material is problematic. In any case, the focus here is on comforting the mourner, not drunkenness. So too, with the self-laceration and shaving mentioned in v. 6. These actions are forbidden in Deut 14:1-2, with the implication they are part of non-Yahwistic practices[35] but there is no hint of disapproval in the Jeremiah text.[36]

---

[32] Fabry, "מַרְזֵחַ *marzēaḥ*," 5.15. The same proposal is found in Gangloff and Haelewyck, "Osée 4,17-19," 378, who incorrectly attribute the redactional analysis to Thiel (their n. 107). Fabry relies upon, but goes well beyond, Thiel's redactional analysis of the passage: she considers vv. 1-3a, 4a, 5-8,9 (minus "in your days and before your eyes") the earliest text, with only 3b and 4b as deuteronomistic additions; see W. Thiel, *Die deuteronomistische Redaktion von Jeremia 1-25* (WMANT 41; Neukirchen-Vluyn: Neukirchener Verlag, 1973) 195-98, 201. Loretz, "*Marziḫu*," 140, accepts Fabry's redactional analysis but retains funerary associations for this *marzēaḥ*.

[33] See pp. 189-91.

[34] Pope, *Song of Songs*, 216.

[35] Thus Bright, *Jeremiah*, 110; Thompson, *Jeremiah*, 405-06; Carroll, *Jeremiah*, 339-40; Lewis, *Cults of the Dead*, 101; Jones, *Jeremiah*, 231; see also Lev 19:27-28; 21:5. Contrast n. 36.

[36] Hyatt, "Jeremiah," 946; Holladay, *Jeremiah 1*, 471; Craigie, Kelley and

In any case, while the biblical evidence indicates that these rituals may occur within an organized cultic context, that is not necessarily the case. As a result, there is no certain evidence of either extensive drinking or a religious connection for this particular *marzēaḥ*. This is not to say they were not part of this *marzēaḥ*, only that they are not central to the passage. In light of their connection with *marzēaḥ*s before and after the period reflected here, the author may have thought it unnecessary to mention them, since the term itself was used.

On the other hand, the passage does provide another instance of a funerary connection for a *marzēaḥ*, subsequent to Isa 28:7-8. Since the various mourning rituals in Jer 16:6b-7 are mentioned after the *marzēaḥ* house, it is clear that this building was a place one could "go to lament and . . . grieve" (v. 5). Some consider the connection merely coincidental,[37] but various features of the text suggest otherwise. First and most importantly, grammatical and syntactical aspects of the text establish a contrast between the *marzēaḥ* house and the "drinking house":[38] just as the "drinking house" was a normal place for the "sound of mirth and the sound of gladness" (v. 9) so too the *marzēaḥ* house was a natural place for mourning. Moreover, in this passage the *marzēaḥ*'s funerary associations are taken for granted as something that requires no justification from the prophet, which suggests the connection was a common one in this period. But at the same time, this is not just a case of lamenting a deceased member of a *marzēaḥ* group as one of its many activities.[39] In v. 5 the prophet is

---

Drinkard, *Jeremiah 1-25*, 217; Jones, *Jeremiah*, 231. The claim that they "are forbidden here because they are a tacit acknowledgements of the gods and spirits of other cults . . ." (Carroll, *Jeremiah*, 339) is speculative. That these actions were widely practiced is reflected in Isa 3:24; 15:2-3; 22:12; Jer 7:29; 41:5; 47:5; 48:37; Ezek 7:18; Amos 8:10; Mic 1:16; Job 1:20; Ezra 9:13. Ritual baldness is actually called for by Yahweh in Jer 7:29; Isa 22:12; Mic 1:16) and in Jer 41:5 yahwistic worshipers appear gashed and shaven after the death of Gedaliah. Schmidt surveys biblical, Ugaritic and Mesopotamian texts dealing with both actions and concludes the negative attitude of the legal texts is a late development; see Schmidt, *Israel's Beneficent Dead*, 166-78, especially p. 176. See also S. M. Olyan, "What Do Shaving Rites Accomplish and What Do They Signal in Biblical Ritual Contexts?" *JBL* 117 (1998) 611-22.

[37] E.g., while he does acknowledge the connection, Bryan, "Texts," 69-70, argues that the funerary aspects of this *marzēaḥ* are accidental. See also n. 39 below.

[38] See pp. 189-91 above.

[39] *Contra* D. Pardee, "*Marziḥu*, *Kispu*, and the Ugaritic Funerary Cult: A Minimalist View," *Ugarit, Religion and Culture: Proceedings of the International Colloquium on Ugarit, Religion and Culture: Edinburgh, July 1994. Essays Presented in Honour of Professor*

ordered, "do not grieve for them (לָהֶם)," and the antecedent for this pronoun is the "sons and daughters," "mothers" and "fathers" of v. 3; in other words, it refers to "this people" who are the focus of vv. 6-7 and not the restricted membership of a *marzēaḥ* society. Therefore, at the time of Jeremiah the *marzēaḥ* house was a locus for mourning in general, not just for the coincidental memorial services of a specific group. Finally, the translation history of Jer 16:5 indicates the funerary aspect of this *marzēaḥ* house often, but not always, endured.[40]

## D. *Dating the Text*

It is difficult to establish a precise date for this text. Since v. 1 is absent from the LXX and v. 10 refers to an individual telling "this people all these words," Carroll thinks the individual in vv. 2-9 is a literary creation, representing the exilic community's concerns.[41] As such, the passage would post-date Jeremiah's prophetic ministry. But Carroll himself indicates that the placement of vv. 10-13 is redactional,[42] in which case those verses cannot be used to establish either the intention or provenance of vv. 1-9.[43] In contrast, while acknowledging the evidence of editorial activity, many commentators link the passage's underlying content to Jeremiah himself.[44] The prohi-

*John C. L. Gibson* (UBL 12; eds. N. Wyatt, W. G. E. Watson and J. B. Lloyd; Münster: Ugarit-Verlag, 1996) 279.

[40] Josephus described it as a "house where one celebrates funerary banquets" (οἶκον ἔνθα ἐπιτελοῦσι περίδειπνα), the Peshitta translated "house of sorrow" (*byt mrqwdt'*) and *Bab. Ketubah* 69ab uses Jer 16:5 to support the definition of *marzēaḥ* as "mourning" (מאי מרזחא אבל). In contrast, though, Aquila renders it simply as οἶκον ἑστιάσες ("banqueting house") and Symmachus translates οἶκον ἑταιρίας ("house of brotherhood"). The LXX occupies the middle ground by rendering בֵּית מַרְזֵחַ as θίασος, a voluntary association which sometimes celebrated a memorial meal for deceased members, although that was not its only *raison d'être*; see further J. S. Kloppenborg, "Collegia and *Thiasoi*: Issues in Function, Taxonomy and Membership," *Voluntary Associations in the Graeco-Roman World* (eds. J. S. Kloppenborg and S. G. Wilson; London/New York: Routledge Press, 1997) 17, 20-22.

[41] Carroll, *Jeremiah*, 338-41. A similar approach is taken by McKane, *Jeremiah I*, 366-67. On the communal interpretation of the "I" in the book of Jeremiah in general see H. G. Reventlow, *Liturgie und prophetisches Ich bei Jeremia* (Gütersloh: Gerd Mohn, 1963).

[42] Carroll, *Jeremiah*, 342; so too, McKane, *Jeremiah I*, 369, and most commentators.

[43] See also the succinct critique of Carroll in Jones, *Jeremiah*, 228.

[44] B. Duhm, *Das Buch Jeremia* (KHAT 11; Tübingen: J. C. B. Mohr, 1901) 138;

bition of marriage would have greatest relevance and symbolic value if given earlier rather than later in the prophet's career,[45] although most avoid suggesting anything more precise.[46]

The period between a possible Jeremianic origin for the nucleus of this passage and the exilic redaction into its final form by the Deuteronomists would be about 75 years (ca. 625-550 BCE). In terms of establishing the *marzēaḥ*'s chronological development in the prophetic literature, this would place the passage after those already considered in Chapters 2-4 and roughly contemporary with the Ezekiel texts to be considered in the next chapter.

## II. Summary

Jer 16:5 is one of only two direct references to the *marzēaḥ* in the Bible. The verse mentions a *marzēaḥ* house, which points to a wealthy social setting. Although the following verses allude to drinking and mourning rituals, neither drunkenness nor a religious setting for the lamentation are emphasized. On the other hand, in this text the *marzēaḥ* house is clearly located within a funerary setting. The connection is both more self-evident and more naturally asserted than was the case with the only other funerary *marzēaḥ* encountered thus far, at Isa 28:7-8. At the same time, the *marzēaḥ* house and the activities associated with it are not opposed in Jer 16:5 because of this or any other aspect of its nature. It is simply rejected along with other funerary practices as inappropriate, due to the widespread death that awaits the people of Judah.

---

Giesebrecht, *Jeremia*, 94; A. Condamin, *Le livre de Jérémie: traduction et commentaire* (EBib; 3me éd.; Paris: J. Gabalda, 1936) 146; S. Mowinckel, *Zur Komposition des Buches Jeremia* (Kristiania: Jacob Dybwad, 1914) 20, 39-40; E. A. Leslie, *Jeremiah: Chronologically Arranged, Translated and Interpreted* (New York: Abingdon Press, 1954) 88; Bright, *Jeremiah*, 112; Thiel, *Jeremia 1-25*, 198, 201; Thompson, *Jeremiah*, 407; R. E. Clements, *Jeremiah* (Interpretation; Atlanta: John Knox Press, 1988) 102. Holladay, *Jeremiah 1*, 467-72, appears to attribute the whole passage to Jeremiah, without any editorial activity. As evidence of editorial influence, Thiel notes the long-winded, repetitive prose style, deuteronomistic expressions and parallels to other editorial passages; for details see Thiel, *Jeremia 1-25*, 195; see also Stulman, *Prose Sermons*, 69-70.

[45] Craigie, Kelley and Drinkard, *Jeremiah 1-25*, 216; Jones, *Jeremiah*, 229. The element of sacrifice is less if one has already gone unmarried for a long time, or been married and widowed.

[46] An exception is Holladay, *Jeremiah 1*, 468, who dates the passage to "December 601 or early in 600."

CHAPTER SIX

# THE *MARZĒAḤ* IN EZEKIEL?

Two passages in Ezekiel have been proposed as *marzēaḥ* allusions.[1] First, Susan Ackerman has argued that Ezek 8:7-13 reflects *marzēaḥ* features encountered elsewhere, including a restricted aristocratic membership with a designated leader, a physical location dedicated to the group's purposes, and royal approval.[2] Second, in Ezek 39:19 Yahweh invites the birds and animals to feast on the corpses of Gog's army "to satiety" and to "drink . . . to drunkenness"; identical language in *CAT* 1.114.3-4, 16 has led Brian Irwin to suggest that Ezek 39:17-20 also reflects the *marzēaḥ* feast.[3]

## I. Ezek 8:7-13

Ackerman's proposal for a *marzēaḥ* allusion here is based on the similarity between elements of Ezek 8:7-13 and features of the extra-biblical *marzēaḥ*. Since her proposal hinges on her understanding of the word שֶׁקֶץ in v. 10 as "unclean food," the text and its context must be established before those similarities can be evaluated.

### A. *The Text*

וַיָּבֵא אֹתִי אֶל־פֶּתַח הֶחָצֵר וָאֶרְאֶה וְהִנֵּה חֹר־אֶחָד בַּקִּיר (8) וַיֹּאמֶר אֵלַי
בֶּן־אָדָם חֲתָר־נָא בַקִּיר וָאֶחְתֹּר בַּקִּיר וְהִנֵּה פֶּתַח אֶחָד (9) וַיֹּאמֶר אֵלָי בֹּא וּרְאֵה

---

[1] Since the word *marzēaḥ* itself does not appear in Ezekiel, Bryan did not consider that book.

[2] S. Ackerman, "A *MARZĒAḤ* in Ezekiel 8:7-13?" *HTR* 82 (1989) 267-81. This material subsequently appeared, slightly revised, in S. Ackerman, *Under Every Green Tree: Popular Religion in Sixth-Century Judah* (HSM 46; Atlanta: Scholars Press, 1992) 38, 41-44, 53-55, 67-79; the following discussion will refer to the latter.

[3] B. P. Irwin, "Molek Imagery and the Slaughter of Gog in Ezekiel 38 and 39," *JSOT* 65 (March 1995) 108-09 and his n. 40. Earlier, Marvin Pope had noted the parallels as a "literary cliche"; see M. H. Pope, "Notes on the Rephaim Texts from Ugarit," *Essays on the Ancient Near East in Memory of Jacob Joel Finkelstein* (Memoirs of the Connecticut Academy of Arts and Sciences 19; ed. M. de Jong Ellis; Hamden: Archon Books, 1977) 175.

אֶת־הַתּוֹעֵבוֹת[4] אֲשֶׁר הֵם עֹשִׂים פֹּה (10) וָאָבוֹא וָאֶרְאֶה וְהִנֵּה כָל־[5]שֶׁקֶץ וְכָל־גִּלּוּלֵי
בֵּית יִשְׂרָאֵל מְחֻקֶּה עַל־הַקִּיר סָבִיב סָבִיב[6] (11) וְשִׁבְעִים אִישׁ מִזִּקְנֵי
בֵית־יִשְׂרָאֵל וְיַאֲזַנְיָהוּ בֶן־שָׁפָן עֹמֵד בְּתוֹכָם עֹמְדִים לִפְנֵיהֶם וְאִישׁ מִקְטַרְתּוֹ בְּיָדוֹ
וַעֲתַר הַקְּטֹרֶת[7] עֹלֶה (12) וַיֹּאמֶר אֵלַי הֲרָאִיתָ בֶן־אָדָם אֲשֶׁר זִקְנֵי בֵית־יִשְׂרָאֵל
עֹשִׂים בַּחֹשֶׁךְ[8] אִישׁ בְּחַדְרֵי[9] מַשְׂכִּיתוֹ כִּי אֹמְרִים אֵין יְהוָה רֹאֶה[10] עָזַב יהוה

---

[4] The MT calls the abominations "evil" (הָרָעוֹת) but the LXX lacks the word here (see also at 6:11) and in v. 17. Most scholars delete it as superfluous, an exception being D. I. Block, *The Book of Ezekiel: Chapters 1-24* (NICOT; Grand Rapids: Wm. B. Eerdmans Publishing Co., 1997) 288n27.

[5] In the MT, the phrase תַּבְנִית רֶמֶשׂ וּבְהֵמָה ("image of a creeping thing and animal") occurs here, but it is absent from the LXX. The syntax is awkward (the words would fit better after שֶׁקֶץ) and most scholars consider the phrase a gloss influenced by Deut 4:17-18. The important point for Ackerman is that even without the words, the prophet sees something "detestable" (שֶׁקֶץ).

[6] The LXX only has a single word here (κύκλῳ), as is the translator's custom for double occurrences of סָבִיב in Ezekiel; see W. Zimmerli, *Ezekiel 1: A Commentary on the Book of the Prophet Ezekiel, Chapters 1-24* (Hermeneia; trans. R. E. Clements; Philadelphia: Fortress Press, 1979) 220. Thus, there is no reason to delete one instance of סָבִיב here, *contra* A. Bertholet, *Hesekiel* (HAT 13; mit einem Beitrag von Kurt Galling; Tübingen: J. C. B. Mohr [Paul Siebeck], 1936) 31; E. Balla, "Ezechiel 8, 1-9, 11; 11, 24-25," *Festschrift Rudolf Bultmann zum 65. Geburtstag überreicht* (Stuttgart/Köln: W. Kohlhammer Verlag, 1949) 8n12; G. Fohrer, *Die Hauptprobleme des Buches Ezekiel* (BZAW 72; Berlin: Alfred Töpelman, 1952) 174; *idem*, *Ezechiel* (HAT 13; mit einem Beitrag von Kurt Galling; Tübingen: J. C. B. Mohr [Paul Siebeck], 1955) 49.

[7] The MT attaches עֲנַן־ ("cloud") to the beginning of this word. Its deletion (with the LXX) as a gloss on the preceding *hapax legomenon* עֲתַר is widely accepted; again, Block, *Ezekiel 1-24*, 288n32 is an exception. Zimmerli, *Ezekiel 1*, 220, suggests influence from Lev 16:13. The *hapax* is best explained on the basis of the Syriac *ʿeṭra*, "vapour, fume"; see M. Greenberg, *Ezekiel 1-20: A New Translation with Introduction and Commentary* (AB 22; New York: Doubleday, 1983) 170; cf. the versions.

[8] This word is deleted by many commentators because it is absent from the LXX; see, e.g., Bertholet, *Hesekiel*, 31; Balla, "Ezechiel 8, 1-9, 11; 11, 24-25," 8n15; Fohrer, *Ezechiel*, 49; J. W. Wevers, *Ezekiel* (NCBC; Grand Rapids: Wm. B. Eerdmans Publishing Co., 1969) 81; W. Eichrodt, *Ezekiel: A Commentary* (OTL; trans. C. Quin; Philadelphia: Westminster Press, 1970) 108; K. W. Carley, *The Book of Ezekiel* (CBC; Cambridge: Cambridge University Press, 1974) 55; Zimmerli, *Ezekiel 1*, 220; Ackerman, *Under Every Green Tree*, 44n28; K.-F. Pohlmann, *Das Buch des Propheten Hesekiel (Ezekiel) Kapitel 1-19 übersetzt und erklärt* (ATD 22; Göttingen: Vandenhoeck & Ruprecht, 1996) 123. פֹּה ("here") is inserted in its place by J. Herrmann, *Ezechiel übsersetzt und erklärt* (KAT 11; Leipzig: A. Deichertsche Verlagsbuchhandlung, 1924) 52, and apparently Eichrodt, *Ezekiel*, 106, in conformity with vv. 6, 9, 17. But the phrase "in the dark" is consistent with the hidden, secret room in vv. 7-8 (see further below), and its connotations, at least, are retained in the LXX's subsequent ἕκαστος αὐτῶν ἐν τῷ κοιτῶνι τῷ κρυπτῷ αὐτῶν ("each in his hidden chamber"); see G. A. Cooke, *A Critical and Exegetical Commentary on the Book of Ezekiel* (ICC; Edinburgh: T. & T. Clark, 1936) 95; L. C. Allen, *Ezekiel 1-19* (WBC 28; Dallas: Word Books, 1994) 121. As such, the LXX may reflect an attempt at a smoother, more economical translation. In addition to Cooke and Allen, the word is retained by K. F. Keil, *Biblical Commentary on the Prophecies of Ezekiel* (trans. J. Martin; 1876; rpt. Grand Rapids: Wm. B. Eerdmans Publishing Co., 1950)

אֶת־הָאָרֶץ (13) וַיֹּאמֶר אֵלָי עוֹד תָּשׁוּב תִּרְאֶה תּוֹעֵבוֹת גְּדֹלוֹת אֲשֶׁר־הֵמָּה עֹשִׂים

> And he brought me to the entrance of the court; I looked, and there was a hole in the wall. (8) Then he said to me, "Mortal, dig through the wall"; and when I dug through the wall, there was an entrance. (9) He said to me, "Go in, and see the abominations that they are committing here." (10) So I went in and looked; there was every kind of detestable thing, all the idols of the house of Israel, engraved[11] upon the wall. (11) Seventy of the elders of the house of Israel (Jaazaniah, the son of Shaphan, was standing among them) stood before them. Each had his censer in his hand, and the incense smoke was ascending. (12) Then he said to me, "Mortal, have you seen what the elders of the house of Israel are doing in the dark, each in his room of images? For they say, 'Yahweh does not see, Yahweh has forsaken the land.'" (13) He also said to me, "You will see still greater abominations that they are committing."

The Masoretic and Greek versions of this text differ at a number of points. Most are minor variations that do not significantly affect the passage's meaning, and have been treated in the preceding footnotes. A more substantial difference is the second half of v. 7 (בַּקִּיר . . . וָאֶרְאֶה) and both instances of בַּקִּיר ("in/through the wall") in v. 8, all of which are lacking from the LXX. However, the wall might be reflected in the LXX at the end of v. 10, where "upon it" (ἐπ' αὐτοῦ) occurs in place of the MT's "upon the wall" (עַל־הַקִּיר). There is no antecedent for the pronoun in the LXX, although "wall" would be an appropriate one. Thus, the shorter LXX version of vv. 7b-8 may simply reflect confusion by the translator.[12] In any case, the difference

---

I.118; Greenberg, *Ezekiel 1-20*, 165, 170-71; W. H. Brownlee, *Ezekiel 1-19* (WBC 28; Waco: Word Books, 1986) 133; Block, *Ezekiel 1-24*, 289n39. Block's suggestion of spiritual as well as literal darkness fits the context; cf. 1 Sam 3:1-3.

[9] Reading the singular with the versions for the MT's grammatically difficult plural. See D. Barthélemy, *Critique textuelle de l'Ancien Testament. 3. Ezéchiel, Daniel et les Douze Prophètes* (OBO 50; Fribourg: Editions Universitaires; Göttingen: Vandenhoeck & Ruprecht, 1992) 56-57.

[10] Deleting אֹתָנוּ ("us") from the MT at this point with the LXX and Ezek 9:9; cf. Ps 94:7.

[11] Taking מְחֻקֶּה as a nominal predicate, with A. B. Ehrlich, *Randglossen zur Hebräischen Bibel* (Leipzig: J. C. Hinrichs, 1912) 5.26; Zimmerli, *Ezekiel 1*, 219.

[12] Thus G. R. Driver, "Ezekiel: Linguistic and Textual Problems," *Bib* 35 (1954) 149-50. Since the text describes a visionary experience we should not expect the same clarity as with a direct observation of the events; on this point see further, Greenberg, *Ezekiel 1-20*, 169; I. M. Duguid, *Ezekiel and the Leaders of Israel* (VTSup 56; Leiden/New York/Köln: E. J. Brill, 1994) 67-68; Block, *Ezekiel 1-24*, 289.

in meaning is slight. In both versions the prophet is instructed to dig,[13] with the MT clarifying that he is to dig into the wall, enlarging an already existing hole. In the LXX he would presumably dig down, but in either scenario, the prophet gains access to the site clandestinely.[14] Since there is no significant change in meaning, I prefer to retain the MT for the reasons given in n. 13.

The text given above matches Ackerman's, except that we differ concerning the word "darkness" in v. 12.[15] More significantly, though, we diverge drastically concerning the significance of the word שֶׁקֶץ, which is central to whether there is a *marzēaḥ* allusion in this text. But before addressing that matter, the limits of the text need to be considered.

## B. *Establishing the Unit*

Ezekiel 8-11 describes a visionary experience in which the prophet sees the sins of the Jerusalemites and their punishment,[16] and Ezek

---

[13] Balla, following V. Herntrich, *Ezekielprobleme* (BZAW 61; Giessen: Alfred Töpelmann, 1933), emends the root חתר in v. 8 to חפר; see Balla, "Ezechiel 8, 1-9, 11; 11, 24-25," 8n11; Balla in turn is followed by Fohrer, *Hauptprobleme*, 59, 174; *idem, Ezechiel*, 49; Eichrodt, *Ezekiel*, 108 note 1, 125; Carley, *Ezekiel*, 54. Balla explains the divergence in the two texts as follows: חָפַר means both "dig" and "look closely," and the second sense was meant here. Ezekiel was instructed to look closely, after which he sees a concealed door and enters. The LXX misunderstood the word with the first meaning and incorrectly rendered it with the verb ὀρύσσω. The Hebrew tradition misunderstood the word in the same way, and over time the root חתר replaced חפר, and the other words missing from the LXX were gradually added, perhaps under the influence of Ezek 12:5, 7, 12.

This proposal removes all the difficulties, but only by postulating complex textual histories in the Hebrew and Greek for which there is no manuscript support. On the other hand, there are good reasons for retaining the MT. In addition to the principle of *lectio difficilior* and the possible reflection of "wall" in the LXX's ἐπ' αὐτοῦ (noted above), the verb חָתַר, with its connotations of breaking into a location (BDB 369b; the cognate noun מַחְתֶּרֶת means "burglary" [see Exod 22:1; Jer 2:34]), is quite appropriate to the context of entering a restricted site; see D. J. Halperin, *Seeking Ezekiel: Text and Psychology* (University Park: Pennsylvania State University Press, 1993) 85-86; M. Dijkstra, "Goddess, Gods, Men and Women in Ezekiel 8," *On Reading Prophetic Texts: Gender Specific and Related Studies in Memory of Fokkelien Van Dijk-Hemmes* (BIS 18; eds. B. Becking and M. Dijkstra; Leiden: E. J. Brill, 1996) 94n37 (Halperin's sexual interpretation does not negate the cogency of his linguistic analysis). Job 1:13 and Ezekiel 12 are exceptions to this meaning of the verb; this argues against any influence here from Ezekiel 12:5, 7, 12.

[14] That would also be the case with the emendation rejected in n. 13.

[15] As argued in n. 8, its connotations are present elsewhere in the text anyway.

[16] The possible secondary nature of chapters 9-11 is irrelevant to this study;

8:7-13 depicts one of four "abominations" the prophet sees. The four scenes share a common structural pattern,[17] and some have tried to interpret them as part of a single ritual.[18] However, Cogan attributes a "disjointed, catalogue quality" to the four vignettes and Ackerman notes the scattered locations for each as arguments against a unified rite.[19] Apart from Ezekiel's role as observer and the repeated statement that the next abomination will be greater than the last (vv. 6, 13, 15; cf. v. 17), the scenes are not integrated with each other. In particular, the sins and sinners are different in each, with no indication of continuity, interaction or overlap. Thus, Ezek 8:7-13 is a self-contained passage within that sequence, and can be analyzed independently of the other three "abominations."

Within vv. 7-13, various deletions have been proposed. Most are based on the LXX and were dealt with when establishing the text

---

see the commentaries and Balla, "Ezechiel 8, 1-9, 11; 11, 24-25," 1-11. Contrast M. Greenberg, "The Vision of Jerusalem in Ezekiel 8-11: A Holistic Interpretation," *The Divine Helmsman: Studies on God's Control of Human Events, Presented to Lou H. Silberman* (eds. J. L. Crenshaw and S. Sandmel; New York: Ktav Publishing House, 1980) 143-64; *idem, Ezekiel 1-20*, 195-205; J. Becker, "Ez 8-11 als einheitliche Komposition in einem pseudepigraphischen Ezechielbuch," *Ezekiel and His Book: Textual and Literary Criticism and Their Interrelation* (BETL 74; ed. J. Lust; Leuven: University Press, 1986) 136-50.

[17] Although not all are present in every instance, five elements can be identified: (1) the prophet is taken to a site, (2) ordered to look, (3) the exclamation "behold" is followed by a description of specific sins and sinners, (4) the prophet is called "Mortal" and asked if he has seen, and (5) he is told he will see even worse things; see F. Horst, "Exilsgemeinde und Jerusalem in Ez viii-xi: Eine literarische Untersuchung," *VT* 3 (1953) 342-44.

[18] The earliest proposal was a celebration for Adonis, suggested by H. A. C. Haevernick, *Commentar über den Propheten Ezechiel* (Erlangen: C. Heyder, 1843); it is discussed by Zimmerli, *Ezekiel 1*, 237. The conclusion of the summer solstice was suggested by H. G. May, "The Departure of the Glory of Yahweh," *JBL* 56 (1937) 309-21. M. Nobile, "Lo sfondo cultuale di Ez 8-11," *Anton* 58 (1983) 185-200, also sees a solar festival here. Gaster interpreted Ezekiel 8 as a fall harvest ritual outlined in *CAT* 1.23; see T. H. Gaster, "Ezekiel and the Mysteries," *JBL* 60 (1941) 289-310, especially pp. 289-97; cf. Dijkstra, "Ezekiel 8," 113-14. Ezekiel 8 is related to a son's obligations to a father outlined in the story of Aqhat (see *CAT* 1.17.I.25-34 and parallels) by Y. Avishur, "The 'Duties of the Son' in the 'Story of Aqhat' and Ezekiel's Prophecy on Idolatry (Ch. 8)," *UF* 17 (1986) 49-60. None of these has found much acceptance; for a critique of Gaster in particular see W. F. Albright, *Archaeology and the Religion of Israel* (Baltimore: Johns Hopkins University Press, 1956) 165-68.

[19] M. Cogan, *Imperialism and Religion: Assyria, Judah and Israel in the Eighth and Seventh Centuries B.C.E.* (SBLMS 19; Missoula: Scholars Press, 1974) 86n116; Ackerman, *Under Every Green Tree*, 53-55.

itself.[20] However, two proposed deletions have implications for a possible *marzēaḥ* allusion in this text and must be considered. First, Ackerman takes the references to the seventy elders of Israel in vv. 11 and 12 as evidence of the social and political stature of the participants, and by extension, of their activity, but a few authors delete one or both instances of the word "elders."[21] They do not present arguments in support of the deletions, however, but simply label them explanatory glosses. Yet without the specification as "elders," the number seventy (v. 11) seems arbitrary, while with it the seventy men serve a representative role comparable to that in Exod 24:1, 9; Num 11:16, 24-25. Without any text-critical basis for deleting it, and especially in light of its presence in the usually shorter LXX version of this passage at both places, the word "elders" should be retained.

Secondly, Ackerman considers Jaazaniah, who stands in the midst of the seventy elders, to be the leader of the *marzēaḥ*,[22] but that entire clause is deleted as a later addition by some scholars because they feel it disturbs the flow of the Hebrew in v. 11.[23] However, as Block astutely observes, ". . . if smoothness were a test of authenticity, most parenthetical clauses would be eliminated."[24] Furthermore, there is no manuscript evidence for dropping this phrase either, and the LXX's minor change actually supports its authenticity.[25] Therefore, it has been kept, and the text given at the beginning of this chapter will be the basis of the following discussion.

---

[20] See notes 4-10.

[21] Ackerman, *Under Every Green Tree*, 71, 76. Both references are deleted by Balla, "Ezechiel 8, 1-9, 11; 11, 24-25," 8nn14 and 15; Fohrer, *Ezechiel*, 49; the second instance is dropped by Eichrodt, *Ezekiel*, 108 note q. Ackerman does not seem to be aware of their proposals.

[22] Ackerman, *Under Every Green Tree*, 76.

[23] Balla, "Ezechiel 8, 1-9, 11; 11, 24-25," 8n14; Fohrer, *Ezechiel*, 49; Wevers, *Ezekiel*, 82; Carley, *Ezekiel*, 55; Zimmerli, *Ezekiel 1*, 220; Pohlmann, *Hesekiel 1-19*, 139n650.

[24] Block, *Ezekiel 1-24*, 288n30; see also Brownlee, *Ezekiel 1-19*, 127; Allen, *Ezekiel 1-19*, 121. Cooke, *Ezekiel*, 93-94, solves the problem by rearranging the verse. Other instances of parenthetical statements interrupting the "flow" include Gen 13:7; 29:16; 1 Sam 1:9; see further, T. O. Lambdin, *Introduction to Biblical Hebrew* (New York: Scribner's Sons, 1971) §132; B. K. Waltke and M. O'Connor, *An Introduction to Biblical Hebrew Syntax* (Winona Lake: Eisenbrauns, 1990) §39.2.3.

[25] The LXX drops the plural participle "standing," producing the reading, "And seventy elders of the house of Israel (and Jaazaniah stood among them) before them." This has its own problems, but does indicate some difficulty with the Hebrew; most importantly, the fact that the Greek contains the clause but fails to improve the syntax more argues for its originality in the MT.

## C. *Discussion*

Ackerman's claim that Ezek 8:7-13 describes a *marzēaḥ* is based on her identification of parallels between this text and features known from the explicit biblical and extra-biblical *marzēaḥ* references. In her view, the passage describes the Jerusalem aristocracy (the seventy elders), with a recognizable leader (Jaazaniah), worshipping images at a banquet in a room dedicated to that purpose within the palace-temple complex.[26] The points of contact with the earlier Ugaritic *marzēaḥ* in particular are obvious: the seventy elders correspond to the "men of the *marzēaḥ*," Jaazaniah is the *rb mrzḥ*, the room is the equivalent of the *marzēaḥ* house, the idols represent the patron deities of the *marzēaḥ* and the physical location of the room indicates royal approval.[27] At the same time, two of the three criteria used throughout this study are clearly present. For instance, even if the number seventy is purely symbolic, as many suggest, it is obviously meant to indicate that those so identified serve a representative role as Jerusalem's leading citizens.[28] Similarly, the idols point to religious activity, which is reinforced by the nuance of "worship" for the phrase "stand before" in v. 11.[29]

Ackerman's proposal runs into difficulty, however, when it comes to the third criteria, i.e., extensive drinking. She recognizes the centrality of this element when she states, "It is clear that the *marzēaḥ* centered around feasting and *especially around drinking*."[30] But not only is there no reference to drinking in the passage, it does not even deal with feasting. Ackerman argues that elsewhere the term שֶׁקֶץ always refers to unclean food, and stripped of the secondary phrase "image of a creeping thing and animal" does here as well;[31] on that basis she sees a banquet consisting of unclean food in v. 10. But Ackerman's absolutism concerning the denotation of שֶׁקֶץ is not quite accurate. The word actually refers to hybrid animals that are forbidden as food *because* they are detestable.[32] In Lev 7:21 mere contact

[26] See Ackerman, *Under Every Green Tree*, 67-79, especially pp. 68-71, 76-77.

[27] See Chapter 1 for these elements at Ugarit in RS 15.70; 15.88; 18.01; *CAT* 4.399; 3.9; 1.114; 1.21, and in various combinations in the post-biblical evidence as well.

[28] See p. 201.

[29] See especially Zimmerli, *Ezekiel 1*, 220, and the biblical references he cites.

[30] Ackerman, *Under Every Green Tree*, 72 (emphasis added).

[31] Ibid., 69-71. Cf. n. 5 above.

[32] See Lev 11:10, 11, 12, 13, 20, 23, 41, 42; cf. Isa 66:17.

with things that are שֶׁקֶץ renders one ritually unfit to eat sacrificial food (cf. Lev 11:24-25), while in Lev 11:11 their dead carcasses, which few would venture to eat, are labeled שֶׁקֶץ. In other words, שֶׁקֶץ refers to the essential nature of such things, not their status as food; it is the former that makes them unsuitable as the latter.

Lest I be accused of being overly subtle on this issue, three points should be noted. First, Ezekiel is capable of criticizing unacceptable dining much more directly.[33] Second, the focus in the rest of the passage is on the religious activity, with no indication that a banquet is taking place.[34] Third, this is the only time שֶׁקֶץ occurs in the book of Ezekiel, whereas the comparable שִׁקּוּץ occurs eight times.[35] It makes sense, therefore, to interpret the solitary instance of the former term as a variant of the preferred usage in the book of Ezekiel, describing what the prophet perceives as cultic aberrations, rather than with a derived meaning of "unclean food" for שֶׁקֶץ.[36] If this is done, the banquet disappears, and all that is left is a reference to idol worship.[37] But if there is no banquet in this passage, then the only possible evidence of drinking is also gone. As a result, nothing in this passage connects the idol worship with a *marzēaḥ*, and Ackerman's proposal must be rejected.

---

[33] Dijkstra, "Ezekiel 8," 95; see Ezek 18:6, 11, 15; 22:9.

[34] Cf. Dijkstra, "Ezekiel 8," 96-97.

[35] This accounts for 35% of the word's total occurrences in the First Testament. Significantly, in Ezekiel they are evenly split between references to an "abomination" (תּוֹעֵבָה; Ezek 5:11; 7:20; 11:18, 21; cf. Ezek 8:9, 13) and an idol (גִּלּוּל; Ezek 20:7, 8, 30-31; 37:23; cf. Ezek 8:10). The word also refers to unacceptable cultic activities in Deut 29:16; 1 Kgs 11:5, 7 (2x); 2 Kgs 23:13 (2x), 24; Isa 66:3; Jer 4:1; 7:30//32:34; 13:27; 16:18; Dan 9:27; 11:31; 12:1; Hos 9:10; 2 Chr 15:8. See also Nah 3:6; Zech 9:7.

[36] Some emend it to the plural שִׁקּוּצִים with the Targum; see K. H. Cornhill, *Das Buch des Propheten Ezechiel* (Leipzig: Hinrich, 1886); C. H. Toy, *The Book of the Prophet Ezekiel* (SBOT 12; New York: Dodd, Mead, 1899); these scholars are cited in Zimmerli, *Ezekiel 1*, 219. It is simpler to take the word here as a collective noun. Dijkstra, "Ezekiel 8," 96, draws an analogy with the offering of incense to Nehushtan (2 Kgs 18:4), a cultic snake that would be "detestable" on the basis of Lev 11:41-42.

[37] A precise identification of the deities involved is secondary to my purpose. Scholarly opinion diverges between an Egyptian and a Babylonian background for the deities in question, with the attendant political ramifications of their cult being practiced in Israel. The former is argued by Keil, *Ezekiel*, I.121; Bertholet, *Hesekiel*, 31,32; J. Ziegler, *Ezekiel* (Würzburg: Echter Verlag, 1948) 29; Eichrodt, *Ezekiel*, 123-25; Carley, *Ezekiel*, 55; Zimmerli, *Ezekiel 1*, 241; Brownlee, *Ezekiel 1-19*, 134; J. Blenkinsopp, *Ezekiel* (Interpretation; Louisville: John Knox Press, 1990) 55; Duguid, *Ezekiel*, 113; Pohlmann, *Hesekiel 1-19*, 139; for the latter view see Cooke, *Ezekiel*, 94; Fohrer, *Hauptprobleme*, 175; *idem*, *Ezechiel*, 51; Albright, *Archaeology*, 166-

One other aspect of this passage supports rejecting Ezek 8:7-13 as a *marzēaḥ* allusion. Virtually all commentators agree that the passage deals with a hidden room and therefore a secret ritual.[38] The other three abominations in the chapter are open, public actions, but in this case the prophet can only observe what is going on by digging his way into the location. Ackerman suggests this is because he is not a member of the *marzēaḥ*,[39] but the visionary aspects of the text suggests otherwise. Ezek 8:3 suggests Ezekiel was not physically present in Jerusalem,[40] and there is no indication he was observed at any time in chapter 8. With respect to vv. 7-13 especially, if he can only gain entrance to the *marzēaḥ* clandestinely, then the participants' lack of reaction to his presence is surprising, to say the least. This confirms that his transference from Babylon to Israel is presented as being outside the normal realm of human experience, in which case there is no reason he could not have entered through the front door undetected. Thus, rather than reflecting his lack of credentials, Ezekiel's alternative mode of entrance is more likely meant to emphasize the secretive nature of the ritual. But although the *marzēaḥ* is a private and at times exclusive institution, there is no

---

67; H. L. Ellison, *Ezekiel: The Man and His Message* (Exeter: The Paternoster Press, 1956) 42-43; Greenberg, *Ezekiel 1-20*, 169-70). The arguments are based upon the secondary designation of the images as "creeping things and animals." Even if this is a correct interpretation of שֶׁקֶץ, (Wevers, *Ezekiel*, 81; Zimmerli, *Ezekiel 1*, 240-41; *contra* Ackerman, *Under Every Green Tree*, 69-70), the only thing that can be said for certain is that since the elders think Yahweh has abandoned the land (v. 12), they are appealing to other deities in this passage.

[38] See Keil, *Ezekiel*, I.119; Herrmann, *Ezechiel*, 60; Cooke, *Ezekiel*, 93; Ellison, *Ezekiel*, 43; Wevers, *Ezekiel*, 80-81; Eichrodt, *Ezekiel*, 124; R. M. Hals, *Ezekiel* (FOTL 19; Grand Rapids: Wm. B. Eerdmans Publishing Co., 1988) 52; Allen, *Ezekiel 1-19*, 143; Duguid, *Ezekiel*, 112. Greenberg, *Ezekiel 1-20*, 169, points to the nuance of "hiding place" for חֹר (v. 7) at 1 Sam 14:11; Job 30:6 in support of his statement, "a secret meeting place is meant." Ackerman allows for that possibility at least: ". . . the cult Ezekiel envisions in vv. 1-12 is private, *perhaps even secret*." (see Ackerman, *Under Every Green Tree*, 69, emphasis added).

[39] Ackerman, *Under Every Green Tree*, 69.

[40] He experiences the events of chapter 8 in a "divine vision"; see the discussions of Greenberg, *Ezekiel 1-20*, 168; Blenkinsopp, *Ezekiel*, 53; Block, *Ezekiel 1-24*, 280. For interpretations of Israelite prophecy in light of similar "soul travel" (the phrase is Blenkinsopp's) experiences in other cultures, especially shamanism, see J. Lindblom, *Prophecy in Ancient Israel* (Oxford: Basil Blackwell, 1963) 1-137; R. R. Wilson, *Prophecy and Society in Ancient Israel* (Philadelphia: Fortress Press, 1980) 21-88; T. W. Overholt, *Prophecy in Cross-Cultural Perspective: A Sourcebook for Biblical Researchers* (SBLSBS 17; Atlanta: Scholars Press, 1986); see also I. M. Lewis, *Ecstatic Religion: A Study of Shamanism and Spirit Possession* (2nd ed.; London; New York: Routledge Press, 1989).

indication from any place or time in its history that it was a secret one.[41] Nor is there any reason it should be here. The other "abominations" describe the public worship of other deities, thereby ruling out non-yahwistic divine patrons as a reason for the secrecy here, and Ackerman's suggestion that the room's location indicates royal approval[42] also argues against a secret *marzēaḥ*. In short, the secretive nature of the religious activity being practiced in Ezek 8:7-13,[43] as well as the absence of drinking in the passage, argue against it being a *marzēaḥ*.

## II. Ezek 39:17-20

In *CAT* 1.114.3-4, El invites the gods to a feast where they "drink (*tštn*) wine to satiety (*šbʿ*), new wine to drunkenness (*škr*)," and he drinks to the same effect in line 16. Similarly, in Ezek 39:19, after Gog's army is destroyed Yahweh invites birds and animals to a sacrificial feast where they will "eat fat to satiety (שָׂבְעָה) and drink (שְׁתִיתֶם) blood to drunkenness (שִׁכָּרוֹן)."[44] For Brian Irwin this repetition of vocabulary from El's *marzēaḥ* "opens up the possibility that the Ezekiel passage constitutes an additional OT reference to the *Marzeaḥ* banquet."[45] Since the focus of his article lies elsewhere, this statement is not developed, but it is worth further consideration. Although three vocabulary items from a text that was buried six centuries earlier are not enough to establish an allusion to the *marzēaḥ*, the fundamental content of the two texts is also comparable, and I will argue that

[41] The *marzēaḥ*'s widespread attestation alone would argue against a secret institution, as does the granting of official approval, its use as a reference point in dating other events, etc. (see in Chapter 1, *passim*). Moreover, none of the biblical instances of the *marzēaḥ* were secretive; see especially Jer 16:5, which is roughly contemporary with Ezekiel 8.

[42] Ackerman, *Under Every Green Tree*, 71.

[43] The reason for the secrecy is not immediately apparent, and any proposal in this regard would be highly speculative. In any case, my point here does not require identifying the reason, only that such secrecy is inconsistent with the nature of the *marzēaḥ*.

[44] Note too the root זבח, cognate with *dbḥ* used in *CAT* 1.114.1. The Ugaritic gods also eat, but different verbs are used for eating there (*tlḥmn*) and here (אָכַל). In any case, the emphasis in the Ugaritic text is on drinking, especially in the parallel in line 16.

[45] Irwin, "Molek Imagery," 109n40. See also his pp. 108-09 and Pope, "Notes," 175.

the Ezekiel passage alludes to the mythological tradition in general, rather than the Ugaritic text itself.

## A. *The Text*

וְאַתָּה בֶן־אָדָם[46] אֱמֹר לְצִפּוֹר כָּל־כָּנָף וּלְכֹל חַיַּת הַשָּׂדֶה כֹּה־אָמַר יהוה
הִקָּבְצוּ וָבֹאוּ הֵאָסְפוּ מִסָּבִיב עַל־זִבְחִי אֲשֶׁר אֲנִי זֹבֵחַ לָכֶם זֶבַח גָּדוֹל עַל
הָרֵי יִשְׂרָאֵל וַאֲכַלְתֶּם בָּשָׂר וּשְׁתִיתֶם דָּם (18) בְּשַׂר גִּבּוֹרִים תֹּאכֵלוּ
וְדַם־נְשִׂיאֵי הָאָרֶץ תִּשְׁתּוּ אֵילִים כָּרִים וְעַתּוּדִים פָּרִים מְרִיאֵי בָשָׁן כֻּלָּם
(19) וַאֲכַלְתֶּם־חֵלֶב לְשָׂבְעָה וּשְׁתִיתֶם דָּם לְשִׁכָּרוֹן מִזִּבְחִי אֲשֶׁר־זָבַחְתִּי
לָכֶם (20) וּשְׂבַעְתֶּם עַל־שֻׁלְחָנִי סוּס וָרֶכֶב גִּבּוֹר וְכָל־אִישׁ מִלְחָמָה
נְאֻם[47] יהוה

As for you, mortal, say to the birds of every kind and to all the wild animals, "Thus says Yahweh: 'Assemble and come, gather from all around to my sacrifice that I am sacrificing for you, a great sacrifice on the mountains of Israel. Eat[48] flesh and drink blood; (18) the flesh of the mighty, eat, and drink the blood of the princes of the earth: rams, lambs and goats, bulls, fatlings of Bashan[49]—all of them. (19) Eat fat to satiety and drink blood to drunkenness at my sacrifice that I am sacrificing for you. (20) Be filled at my table with horse and chariot horse,[50] with the mighty and all kinds of soldiers' (utterance of Yahweh)."

---

[46] Transposing כֹּה־אָמַר (אֲדֹנָי) יהוה to after הַשָּׂדֶה, where it directly introduces the actual message, but deleting אֲדֹנָי as superfluous. See the LXX and most commentators for both changes, but cf. the ambivalence concerning the expanded version of the divine name in W. Zimmerli, *Ezekiel 2: A Commentary on the Book of the Prophet Ezekiel, Chapters 25-48* (Hermeneia; trans. J. D. Martin; Philadelphia: Fortress Press, 1983) 293, 294 versus 556-62.

[47] Deleting אֲדֹנָי with the LXX.

[48] The 2nd person perfects and imperfects continue the force of the preceding imperatives; cf. Lambdin, *Biblical Hebrew*, §107; Waltke and O'Connor, *Biblical Hebrew Syntax*, §32.2.2.

[49] The use of animal names for leaders was common in the ancient semitic world; see P. D. Miller, Jr., "Animal Names as Designations in Ugaritic and Hebrew," *UF* 2 (1970) 177-86. The Targum abandons the metaphor completely: ". . .princes of the earth, *kings, rulers, and governors* all of them *mighty men, rich in possessions*"; this translation is taken from S. H. D. Levey, *The Targum of Ezekiel: Translated, with a Critical Introduction, Apparatus and Notes* (The Aramaic Bible 13; Wilmington: Michael Glazier, 1987) 108.

[50] The word רֶכֶב usually means "chariot," but that makes for a strange menu item, even for birds and wild animals. The word is revocalized as רֹכֵב ("rider") by Wevers, *Ezekiel*, 294; Eichrodt, *Ezekiel*, 517; D. I. Block, *The Book of Ezekiel: Chapters 25-48* (NICOT; Grand Rapids: Wm. B. Eerdmans Publishing Co., 1997) 473n67; the *BHS*; and apparently by Keil, *Ezekiel*, II.173; see also the LXX, the Vulgate,

This passage does not present any significant text-critical problems, either in terms of emendation or deletion.[51] Most importantly, the words "satiety" (שָׂבְעָה), "(you will) drink" (שְׁתִיתֶם) and "drunkenness" (שִׁכָּרוֹן), which were the initial basis for proposing a *marzēaḥ* allusion here, are an assured part of the text.

## II. *Establishing the Unit*

Ezek 39:17-20 opens and closes with a messenger formula, and this plus its content sets it apart from the immediately surrounding verses. The preceding verses describe the burial of Gog's army while the following section explains Israel's exile and describes the nation's subsequent restoration. At the same time, the idea of birds and animals feasting on Gog's fallen soldiers "on the mountains of Israel" is anticipated in v. 4. Some think the description of Israelites burying Gog's horde and disposing of their weapons is a later addition that interrupts the flow of the passage and even renders the feast of vv. 17-20 impossible.[52] However, if the chapter is not read as a strict chronological sequence, the intervening verses may be little more than a digression.[53] In any case, what is important is that the feeding mentioned in v. 4 is described in vv. 17-20 as a sacrificial feast for animals and birds hosted by Yahweh.

---

the Syriac, the *NAB*, the *NEB* and the *NRSV*. In a few instances, רֶכֶב itself can simply mean "rider" (e.g., 2 Kgs 7:14; Isa 21:7, 9; 22:6 [but cf. BDB 939 concerning the last three]), but it can also be a metonymy for the horses pulling the chariots (see 2 Sam 8:4 // 1 Chr 18:4); the latter view is taken by Herrmann, *Ezechiel*, 242; Cooke, *Ezekiel*, 422; Zimmerli, *Ezekiel 2*, 294; L. C. Allen, *Ezekiel 20-48* (WBC 29; Dallas: Word Books, 1990) 202; the *NJB*. Although either of the latter understandings of רֶכֶב eliminates the need for an emendation, the last provides a more "balanced diet" (two servings of animals and two of humans) and is followed here.

[51] Cody claims that all the sacrificial language is secondary, and that the text merely describes carrion eaters in the aftermath of the preceding carnage, but he provides no supporting evidence or argumentation; see A. Cody, *Ezekiel, with an Excursus on Old Testament Priesthood* (OTMS 11; Wilmington: Michael Glazier, 1984) 189. Wevers, *Ezekiel*, 293, considers v. 17b a condensed, and probably secondary, version of 18a; the primary content would remain even if the former were deleted.

[52] Herrmann, *Ezechiel*, 251; Eichrodt, *Ezekiel*, 521; Carley, *Ezekiel*, 265; Zimmerli, *Ezekiel 2*, 298, 308; Hals, *Ezekiel*, 281; Allen, *Ezekiel 20-48*, 203.

[53] Keil, *Ezekiel*, II.176, thinks this scene is described last for effect. See also H. G. May, "The Book of Ezekiel: Introduction and Exegesis," *IB* 6.281; Block, *Ezekiel 25-48*, 473.

## C. *Discussion*

As indicated above, Ezek 39:17-20 has been identified as a *marzēaḥ* allusion on the basis of vocabulary shared with El's *marzēaḥ* at Ugarit, specifically, the repetition of "drink," "satiety" and "drunkenness."[54] This contrasts with the usual interpretation of the passage in terms of holy war and divine warrior motifs.[55] For instance, Cook notes that in her infamous battle scene, Anat waded through the blood of battle "until she was sated."[56] Similarly, the association of blood and Yahweh's sword being sated in Isa 34:5-7 and Jer 46:10 is frequently adduced as a parallel to the Ezekiel text.[57] Finally, Ezek 39:17-20 is linked to the destruction of Gog's army, which itself draws heavily upon the holy war and divine warrior traditions.[58] However, the connection between those traditions and Ezek 39:17-20 is not as close as it appears. In the first place, although Yahweh's feast is contingent upon Gog's defeat, it is distinct from that event. The change in content coincides with a shift in the recipient of the divine address: throughout chapters 38-39 the prophet has spoken to Gog, but in 39:17 he addresses birds and animals. Thus, the passage itself has no military associations, but deals only with a subsequent feast. Secondly, the supposed parallels to the holy war and divine warrior motifs are actually fairly superficial. For instance, Anat's

---

[54] See p. 205.

[55] On the holy war traditions compare G. von Rad, *Holy War in Ancient Israel* (trans. & ed. M. J. Dawn; introd. by B. C. Ollenburger, bibliography by J. E. Sanderson; 1958; rpt. Grand Rapids: Wm. B. Eerdmans Publishing Co., 1991) and S.-M. Kang, *Divine War in the Ancient Near East* (BZAW 177; Berlin/New York: Walter de Gruyter, 1989); for the divine warrior see P. D. Miller, Jr., *The Divine Warrior in Early Israel* (HSM 5; Cambridge: Harvard University Press, 1973). Most interpreters do not seem to be aware of the lexical parallels with El's *marzēaḥ*. S. L. Cook, *Prophecy and Apocalypticism: The Postexilic Social Setting* (Minneapolis: Fortress Press, 1995) 89n19, does quote *CAT* 1.114.3-4, but only to contrast the Ugaritic gods' drinking with Yahweh's sobriety; he makes nothing of the shared vocabulary.

[56] *CAT* 1.3.II.29, using the root *šbʿ* as well. See Cook, *Prophecy and Apocalypticism*, 89; cf. May, "Ezekiel," 281.

[57] Both are noted by Keil, *Ezekiel*, II.176; H. Gressmann, *Der Ursprung der israelitisch-jüdischen Eschatologie* (FRLANT 6; Göttingen: Vandenhoeck & Ruprecht, 1905) 139; Herrmann, *Ezechiel*, 250; Cooke, *Ezekiel*, 421; May, "Ezekiel," 6.281; Zimmerli, *Ezekiel 2*, 309. Isa 34:5-7 only is mentioned by Cook, *Prophecy and Apocalypticism*, 89 and Jer 46:10 alone by Allen, *Ezekiel 20-48*, 208. Block, *Ezekiel 25-48*, 475, mentions Isa 34:6-8 and Zeph 1:7.

[58] See Cook, *Prophecy and Apocalypticism*, 88-91 and the biblical references he cites.

satiety is not related to anything she ingests. She beomes "sated with fighting" (*tšbʿ . tmtḫs*), but she does not drink the blood, nor does she become drunk. Similarly, the parallel with the other biblical texts breaks down upon closer inspection. In Jer 46:10, Yahweh's sword "eats" and becomes "sated," using the same verbs (אָכַל and שָׂבַע) as Ezek 39:19, but it only becomes "saturated" (רָוְתָה) with blood. Moreover, Isa 34:5-7 does not even contain any of the significant vocabulary from Ezek 39:19, speaking only of Yahweh's sword being "filled" (מָלְאָה) with blood in v. 6.[59] In other words, although Yahweh's sword metaphorically drinks blood, it does not become drunk. In fact, Ezek 39:19 is the only place in the entire Bible where blood causes drunkenness.[60] All of this suggests that something other than holy war traditions is involved in the passage.

In contrast to those militaristic traditions, the description of El's *marzēaḥ* from Ugarit provides a more suitable background for Ezek 39:17-20. Two points support using the former to illustrate the latter. First, the occurrence of three central words[61] in both texts establishes more points of contact than with any of the holy war texts considered above. Secondly, the parallels go beyond repeated vocabulary to encompass significantly similar content as well: in both texts a deity invites guests to a meal in order to get drunk. The guests are different, since having other gods at Yahweh's banquet would give them a legitimacy at odds with the rest of the book of Ezekiel,

[59] Although this might have a nuance comparable to "sated," the use of a different word is important for the point at hand. Similarly, while the parallel line does say that the sword "has engorged itself with fat (חֵלֶב)," the verb there is דָּשֵׁן, not שָׂבַע.

[60] *Contra* Cook, *Prophecy and Apocalypticism*, 89, Isa 63:1-6; Joel 4:13 [Eng 3:13]; Rev 14:19-20; 19:15 do not speak of "intoxicating blood." Those texts use the image of crushing grapes as a symbol for divine wrath, with blood as the metaphorical counterpart to grape juice. In each case the emphasis is on the destructive connotations of crushing grapes, not the effect of any wine that might be produced later, and none of those texts make any reference to drinking, and especially not to drunkenness.

BDB 924, cites Isa 34:5 and 7 as its only examples of the meaning "be intoxicated" for רָוָה; in the latter verse it is directly linked with blood and is in the former by analogy with v. 6. However, since in v. 7 it is paralleled with "their soil will be engorged with fat" (cf. v. 6), a more natural translation for the line is, "Their land will be saturated with blood." Unless a known intoxicant is consumed, the normal meaning of "drink one's fill, be saturated" for this verb should be retained; this holds for Isa 34:5 (the parallel in v. 6 uses the verb "be full") and Jer 46:10 as well.

[61] זבח/*dbḥ* can also be included, although it is peripheral to the Ugaritic text's central motif.

but otherwise the basic content and purpose remains the same. Simply put, the common vocabulary and content point to El's *marzēaḥ* as the primary background for Ezek 39:17-20. However, the only known copy of *CAT* 1.114 was buried when Ugarit was destroyed ca. 1200, about six hundred years before the traditional time of Ezekiel's prophetic call. This makes direct literary dependence on that text by Ezek 39:17-20 implausible, if not impossible. But the interpretive value of the Ugaritic text does not depend upon the Ezekiel author using the text itself, but rather his use of the traditions it contains. It would be sufficient if the idea of a god extending an invitation to get drunk survived independently of the Ugaritic text, and was adapted into the Ezekiel passage as we have it.[62]

Two aspects of the passage suggest that this is, in fact, what happened. In itself, most of the passage is neither surprising nor without parallel in the First Testament. For instance, Yahweh calls upon birds of prey and wild animals to devour his "heritage" Israel, in Jer 12:9. References to satiety and drinking at a banquet are not unexpected either, and those words alone could be explained as coincidental. However, this is the only place animals are invited to partake of a sacrificial feast,[63] and, as has been noted, Ezek 39:19 is unique in having blood as an intoxicant. Moreover, Isa 34:5,7 and Jer 46:10 show that the root רָוָה is an established parallel to the root

[62] The genre of the passage is relevant to this matter. The nature of the feast, as well as its connection with the preceding Gog and Magog material, establishes points of contact with proto-apocalyptic; on the genre of Ezekiel 38-39, including 39:17-20, see especially B. Erling, "Ezekiel 38-39 and the Origins of Jewish Apocalyptic," *Ex Orbe Religionum* (SHR; ed. G. Widengren; Leiden: E. J. Brill, 1972) 1.104-114; Cook, *Prophecy and Apocalypticism*, 85-97. This is significant because of the tendency within the apocalyptic tradition to reinterpret ancient material; on this point see further J. J. Collins, *The Apocalyptic Imagination: An Introduction to Jewish Apocalyptic Literature* (BRS; 2nd ed.; Grand Rapids: Wm. B. Eerdmans Publishing Co., 1998) 17-19; note especially his comments on p. 19 concerning the indirect reuse of Ugaritic material in the book of Daniel. In the same way, Rev 20:7-10 uses the material from Ezekiel 38-39, but reinterprets Gog and Magog as Satan's army, while Rev 19:17-21 is based on Ezek 39:17-20 itself. Similarly, the defeat of Satan in the form of a seven-headed dragon (Rev 12:3, 9; cf. the "beast" in Rev 13:1; 17:3) draws upon Yahweh overcoming Leviathan in Isa 27:1 (see also Ps 74:14; Job 26:13), which in turn is based upon Baʿal's conquest of Lītānū in the Ugaritic mythology (*CAT* 1.5.I.1; cf. Anat's claim to have done the same in *CAT* 1.3.III.40-42). Such examples could be greatly multiplied. For comparable reinterpretations of older traditions by non-biblical millennarian groups see the references cited in Cook, *Prophecy and Apocalypticism*, 28n34.

[63] Herrmann, *Ezechiel*, 251.

שָׂבַע, without the connotations of drunkenness,[64] and would be even more suitable in relationship to drinking by non-humans. But instead, the author uses the root שׁכר, thereby establishing drunkenness as a primary purpose for the feast itself. I think this was intentional, because he wanted to make Yahweh's banquet for the animals conform to the tradition of a deity inviting guests to a meal with the express purpose of getting drunk. Moreover, Jer 16:5 shows the *marzēaḥ* itself endured to approximately this time within the biblical record, and well beyond in non-biblical references. Therefore, both the author and his audience would probably have understood the scene in Ezek 39:17-20 in terms of that well-known institution.

But even if this reconstruction of the text's tradition-historical background is accepted, in the absence of the term itself it is appropriate to evaluate the passage according to the criteria used previously for identifying *marzēaḥ* allusions. Two of the requisite *marzēaḥ* elements are clearly represented, i.e., copious drinking in a religious setting. Verse 19 explicitly identifies drunkenness as one purpose for the feast, and since Yahweh extends an invitation to "my sacrifice," the feast has religious connotations; Yahweh could even be understood as its patron deity. But there is no indication here of the third constitutive element of the *marzēaḥ*, namely, upper-class participation in the debauchery. However, their absence can be easily explained on the basis of the feast's menu. Since Gog's fallen army is the main course, having human guests would entail cannibalism, so the birds of the air and the beasts of the field are invited instead.[65] But this results in two things not found elsewhere in the biblical literature: animals are invited to a sacrificial feast and blood intoxicates. I suggest their combination in a single text is not accidental, but rather a conscious adaptation to *marzēaḥ* traditions. In the same vein, the variation from its usual upper-class nature can be attributed to the literary requirements of this particular allusion. As such, it does not outweigh the

[64] See also Jer 31:14; Lam 3:15.

[65] This also avoids concern over the prohibition of blood to humans and the restriction of the fat and blood from a sacrifice to Yahweh; see, e.g., Gen 9:4; Lev 3:16-17; 17:10-14; Ezek 44:7, 15. There is also an ironic reversal in having these aristocrats (cf. n. 49) as the meal itself rather than guests at it (suggested to me by William H. Irwin). If the author is playing on funerary connections for the *marzēaḥ* as in Jer 16:5, the irony would be even greater: rather than a *marzēaḥ* feast to mourn their passing, they themselves are the main course at a celebratory *marzēaḥ*. However, in the absence of explicit funerary language here, that must remain a tantalizing possibility.

arguments presented above for interpreting this passage in terms of the mythological tradition of a divine *marzēaḥ*.

### D. *Dating the Text*

The question of the passage's date is linked to its relationship to the preceding material. Yet because of the difficulties involved in identifying a possible historical identity for Gog, and therefore a timeframe for the events connected with him, agreement on even a general date is probably impossible.[66] Hals' advice concerning chapters 38-39 is applicable to this particular section as well: "The problems which confront us in this unusual passage are far more responsibly handled in the present, limited state of our knowledge by restricting ourselves to facing them than by speculative attempts at their resolution."[67] Thus I only offer a tentative date for the passage, in relative relationship to the others considered previously. In that respect, Ezek 39:17-20 is later than all of the other biblical instances of the *marzēaḥ*, with the possible exception of Jer 16:5, which itself cannot be dated with certainty. However, the apocalyptic-like elements in the Ezekiel passage[68] suggest that it occupies a place further along in the development of biblical traditions, and therefore is more likely to be the latest of the biblical *marzēaḥ* texts considered in this study.

## III. Summary

In this chapter I evaluated two possible *marzēaḥ* allusions, but only accepted one. Despite Ackerman's arguments that Ezek 8:7-13 reflects the features of a *marzēaḥ*, it lacks a central element of that institution: drinking. Ackerman's interpretation of this passage is ultimately dependent on her view that the word שֶׁקֶץ always means "unclean food" and that therefore the text describes a banquet. But the word actually refers to the essential nature of "detestable" things; it is their basic nature that renders them unsuitable as food. Moreover, שֶׁקֶץ occurs only here in Ezekiel, while the cognate שִׁקּוּץ is found

---

[66] For instance, Zimmerli, *Ezekiel 2*, 302-04, argues for a date close to Ezekiel himself, Eichrodt, *Ezekiel*, 520-21, suggests the early post-exilic period, and Cooke, *Ezekiel*, 421, points to the Persian or Hellenistic period.

[67] Hals, *Ezekiel*, 285.

[68] See n. 62 above.

eight times, always in connection with "abominations" or idols, but never with food. Reading the first Hebrew term in light of the second eliminates any basis for a banquet in the passage, and with it, any grounds for a *marzēaḥ* allusion. Ezek 8:7-13 simply describes the prophet's revulsion at the sight of a secret ritual in Jerusalem, whose very secretive nature also argues against it being a *marzēaḥ*.

On the other hand, Ezek 39:17-20 draws upon mythological *marzēaḥ* traditions to describe the birds and animals feasting on the bodies of Gog's soldiers. I propose that although the Ugaritic text describing El's *marzēaḥ* was buried until a few decades ago, the underlying concept of a deity inviting guests to a banquet at which they get drunk survived independently. In Ezek 39:17-20, the food for the feast made it impossible for the author to have upper-class humans participate, as in a normal *marzēaḥ*, and he substituted carrion eaters. Nevertheless, it is identified as a religious feast hosted by Yahweh, and the author describes the birds and animals getting "drunk" on blood, rather than using a more neutral term, semantically parallel to "satiety," for the consumption of liquid. The result is that two elements unique in the First Testament are combined in a single text: non-humans are the guests at a sacrificial feast where blood causes drunkenness. I think this reflects the author's efforts to evoke essential elements of a *marzēaḥ*. Combined with the echoes of the divine *marzēaḥ* tradition from Ugarit, the unique elements in the text more than compensate for the non-aristocratic status of the guests, which was necessitated by the exigencies of the text itself. In short, Ezek 39:17-20 does allude to a *marzēaḥ*.

# CONCLUSION

Literary and epigraphic references to the *marzēaḥ* occur in a variety of geographical locations over a span of three thousand years. It is surprising, therefore, that such a widespread and long-lasting institution is only mentioned twice in the biblical literature, at Amos 6:7 and Jer 16:5. Consequently, a number of scholars have suggested that various texts in the First Testament are allusions that refer to the *marzēaḥ* without using the word itself. However, those proposals are offered on a number of different grounds, which begs the question whether there are fundamental aspects of the *marzēaḥ* that should be present before a text that does not use the term can justifiably be classified as an allusion.

The examination in Chapter 1 of all extra-biblical references identified three elements that are present in both early and late attestations of the *marzēaḥ*, namely: (1) extensive alcohol consumption (2) by members of the upper class (3) in a religious context. Inasmuch as these features are characteristic of the *marzēaḥ* throughout its history in the semitic world, they can be considered constitutive aspects of the *marzēaḥ*, and therefore used as fundamental criteria for evaluating proposed *marzēaḥ* allusions in the prophetic literature. Using these three features as the minimum requirements for any *marzēaḥ* allusion resulted in the identification of a restricted but more certain *corpus* of *marzēaḥ* texts in the prophetic literature than had previously been established.

The preceding study has shown that the *marzēaḥ* is more prevalent in the prophetic literature than the two instances of the word itself would suggest, although it is not as extensive as some scholars have proposed. In addition to the explicit references at Amos 6:7 and Jer 16:5, ten possible allusions to the *marzēaḥ* were considered, of which only four have been accepted as definitely alluding to the *marzēaḥ*: Amos 4:1; Hos 4:16-19; Isa 28:7-8(22) and Ezek 39:17-20. While this might seem like a meagre result from the preceding pages, it should be remembered that it derives from very minimalistic criteria and methodology. The *marzēaḥ* may actually figure more extensively in the prophetic literature than these six references and allusions, but they constitute a solid starting point that can serve as the basis for evaluating other possibilities.

Together with the references in Amos 6:7 and Jer 16:5, those four allusions fill a gap in the history of the *marzēaḥ*. The prophetic works in question have traditionally been dated between the eighth and sixth centuries BCE, and with the exception of the Moabite papyrus, all of the extra-biblical *marzēaḥ* references occur either before or after that period. The two prophetic references provided some information about the *marzēaḥ* in that interval, which can now be supplemented by the allusions. In particular, the relative chronology of the prophetic references and allusions allows one to see both continuity and development with respect to the *marzēaḥ* during that period and as well as in relationship to the earlier and later extra-biblical references.

On the one hand, the *marzēaḥ*'s nature in the prophetic literature is consistent with the extra-biblical literature, and even permits a slight elaboration concerning one aspect. In Amos 6:7 the word probably refers to an association of upper-class individuals who celebrated religious feasts characterized by excessive drinking. The mention of a *marzēaḥ* house in Jer 16:5 reflects a similar economic context; on the other hand, that text does not emphasize drinking, although this may be because the focus is on mourning rituals. Nonetheless, the allusions in Amos 4:1, Hos 4:16-19, Isa 28:7-8 and Ezek 39:17-20 all reflect the basic elements of a *marzēaḥ*: copious upper-class drinking in a religious context (allowing for an adaptation with respect to the participants in Ezek 39:17-20). Furthermore, in Amos 6:7, Isa 28:7-8 and Ezek 39:17-20 it is clear that this drinking is to the point of drunkenness, and the same result is implied in Amos 4:1 and Hos 4:16-19. This provides further support for the suggestion in Chapter 1 that drunkenness was a major *raison d'être* of the *marzēaḥ*.

On the other hand, there is also evidence of some innovation in the prophetic period. Although many consider the *marzēaḥ* to be essentially funerary in nature, Isa 28:7-8(22) is the earliest instance in the biblical and extra-biblical references and allusions where such a connection can be established for a *marzēaḥ* text. A century-and-a-half later, a funerary context seems commonplace in Jer 16:5, so such an association for the *marzēaḥ* may have actually begun in the late 8th century BCE. Still, as Ezek 39:17-20 and the post-biblical references show, that is only one possible context for the *marzēaḥ*.

There is no uniform prophetic attitude towards the *marzēaḥ*. Amos, Hosea and Isaiah all view it negatively, but for different reasons. For Amos, the *marzēaḥ* association and its feasts reflect the societal injustice of northern Israel in the mid-eighth century BCE, but in Hos 4:16-19 the issue was that a particular *marzēaḥ* had Anat as its patron. On the other hand, in Isa 28:7-8 the issue seems to be twofold: religious figures are drunk while performing their duties, and they also acknowledge a divine patron other than Yahweh. In contrast, later prophets do not directly oppose the *marzēaḥ* itself. In Jer 16:5, the *marzēaḥ* house is simply listed as a place where one might enact mourning rituals, but it is not denounced for that reason or even in itself. Rather, the point there is that the coming destruction will be so great that the usual mourning customs, including those occuring in the *marzēaḥ* house, are to be abandoned. In contrast, Ezek 39:17-20 uses the *marzēaḥ* traditions positively, with Yahweh as the host of a *marzēaḥ* feast celebrating the defeat of Israel's enemies. Thus, one cannot speak of a unified "prophetic attitude" towards the *marzēaḥ*; instead, their response to the *marzēaḥ* is determined by their own social, economic and religious context. This in itself confirms the stance taken in this study against a uniform perspective on the *marzēaḥ*, either in the Bible or outside.

There is still room for further study of the *marzēaḥ*. For instance, although Greek parallels such as the *thiasos* and *symposium* were excluded from the present study, they are a legitimate field of investigation that will surely shed light on the *marzēaḥ* itself. Similarly, possible biblical allusions outside the prophetic literature have been proposed,[1] and the criteria developed in this work can provide a basis for evaluating such suggestions. Finally, the possible continuation of the *marzēaḥ* into the Second Testament has yet to be considered. Tentative connections between the *marzēaḥ* and the early christian eucharist have been suggested, but none have been developed in any detail.[2] Unfortunately, that too is a topic for another study.

---

[1] See the Introduction, n. 5.

[2] A correlation with St. Paul's condemnation of the rich getting drunk before the Lord's Supper (see especially 1 Cor 11:21-22) has been suggested by M. H. Pope, "A Divine Banquet at Ugarit," *The Use of the Old Testament in the New and Other Essays: Studies in Honor of W. F. Stinespring* (ed. J. M. Efird; Durham: Duke University Press, 1972) 202; *idem, Song of Songs: A New Translation with Introduction and Commentary* (AB 7C; Garden City: Doubleday, 1977) 220. Similarly, a link between the *marzēaḥ* and 1 Cor 10:18-21 has been proposed by H. Gressmann, "῾Η ΚΟΙΝΩΝΙΑ ΤΩΝ ΔΑΙΜΟΝΙΩΝ," *ZNW* 20 (1921) 224-30; M. H. Pope, "The Cult of the Dead at Ugarit," *Ugarit in Retrospect* (ed. G. D. Young; Winona Lake: Eisenbrauns, 1981) 178. For a link between the eucharist and the Greek *thiasos* (used to translate "*marzēaḥ* house" in the LXX at Jer 16:5) see C. F. D. Moule, *Worship in the New Testament* (Richmond: John Knox Press, 1961) 28.

To conclude, the *marzēaḥ* in the prophetic literature encompasses more than the word itself. Other texts allude to the *marzēaḥ* as well, and need to be considered in determining its nature. It is my hope that the present study contributes to that scholarly enterprise.

# BIBLIOGRAPHY


Ackerman, Susan. "A *MARZĒAḤ* in Ezekiel 8:7-13?" *HTR* 82 (1989): 267-81.

———. *Under Every Green Tree: Popular Religion in Sixth-Century Judah*. HSM 46. Atlanta: Scholars Press, 1992.

Albright, William Foxwell. *Archaeology and the Religion of Israel*. Baltimore: Johns Hopkins University Press, 1956.

Allen, Leslie C. *Ezekiel 1-19*. WBC 28. Dallas: Word Books, 1994.

———. *Ezekiel 20-48*. WBC 29. Dallas: Word Books, 1990.

Ameling, W. "ΚΟΙΝΟΝ ΤΩΝ ΣΙΔΩΝΙΩΝ," *ZPE* 81 (1990): 189-99.

Amsler, Samuel. "Amos." In *Osée Joël Amos Abdias Jonas*. 2nd ed. CAT 11a, 157-247. Genève: Labor et Fides, 1982.

*An Aramaic Handbook*. Edited by Franz Rosenthal. PLO 10. Wiesbaden: Otto Harrassowitz, 1967.

Andersen, Francis I., and David Noel Freedman. *Amos: A New Translation with Introduction and Commentary*. AB 24A. New York/London/Toronto: Doubleday, 1989.

———. *Hosea: A New Translation with Introduction and Commentary*. AB 24. New York/London/Toronto: Doubleday, 1980.

Archi, Alfonso. "Cult of the Ancestors and Tutelary God at Ebla." In *Fucus: A Semitic/Afrasian Gathering in Remembrance of Albert Ehrman*, edited by Yoël L. Arbeitman. Current Issues in Linguistic Theory 58, 103-12. Amsterdam/Philadelphia: John Benjamins Publishing Company, 1988.

———. *Testi amministrativi: assegnazioni di tessuti (archivio L. 2769)*. ARET I. Roma: Missione archeologica italiana in Siria, 1985.

Arnaud, Daniel. *Recherches au pays d'Aštata. Emar VI.3: textes sumériens et accadiens*. Synthèse 18. Paris: Éditions Recherche sur les Civilisations, 1986.

Asen, Bernhard A. "The Garlands of Ephraim: Isaiah 28:1-6 and the *marzēaḥ*." *JSOT* 71 (September 1996): 73-87.

Audet, Jean-Paul. "Origines comparées de la double tradition de la loi et de la sagesse dans le Proche-Orient ancien." *Acten Internationalen Orientalistenkongresses (Moscow)* 1 (1960): 352-57.

Austin, J. L. *How to Do Things with Words*. Oxford: Oxford University Press, 1962.

Avi-Yonah, Michael. *The Madaba Mosaic Map with Introduction and Commentary*. Jerusalem: Israel Exploration Society, 1954.

Avigad, N., and Jonas C. Greenfield. "A Bronze *phialē* with a Phoenician Dedicatory Inscription." *IEJ* 32 (1982): 118-28.

Avishur, Yitshak. "The 'Duties of the Son' in the 'Story of Aqhat' and Ezekiel's Prophecy on Idolatry (Ch. 8)." *UF* 17 (1986): 49-60.

Bach, Robert. "Gottesrecht und weltliches Recht in der Verkündigung des Propheten Amos." In *Festschrift für Günther Dehn*, edited by W. Schneemelcher, 23-34. Neukirchen-Vluyn: Kreis Moers, 1957.

Baker, David W. "Leviticus 1-7 and the Punic Tariffs: A Form Critical Comparison." *ZAW* 99 (1987): 188-97.

Balla, Emil. "Ezechiel 8, 1-9, 11; 11, 24-25." In *Festschrift Rudolf Bultmann zum 65. Geburtstag überreicht*, 1-11. Stuttgart/Köln: W. Kohlhammer Verlag, 1949.

Balz-Cochois, Helgard. *Gomer: Der Höhenkult Israels im Selbstverständnis der Volksfrömmigkeit. Untersuchungen zu Hosea 4,1-5,7*. Europäische Hochschulschriften Reihe XXIII: Theologie 191. Frankfurt am Main/Bern: Peter Lang, 1982.

Bardtke, Hans. "Die Latifundien in Juda während der zweiten Hälfte des achten Jahrhunderts v. Chr. (zum Verständnis von Jes 5, 8-10)." In *Hommages à André Dupont-Sommer*, edited by André Caquot, 235-54. Paris: Librairie Adrien Maisonneuve, 1971.

Barnett, Richard D. *A Catalogue of the Nimrud Ivories, with Other Examples of Ancient Near Eastern Ivories in the British Museum*. London: Trustees of the British Museum, 1957.

———. *Ancient Ivories in the Middle East*. Jerusalem: Institute of Archaeology, 1982.

———. "Assurbanipal's Feast." *EI* 18 (1985): 1*-6*.

Barstad, Hans M. "Die Basankühe in Amos 4:1." *VT* 25 (1975): 286-97.

———. "Festmahl und Übersättigung. Der 'Sitz im Leben' von RS 24.258." *AcOr* 39 (1978): 23-30.

———. "Some Reflections on the Meaning of the Expression בית מרזח in Jer 16:5." In *Built on Solid Rock: Studies in Honour of Professor Ebbe Egede Knudsen on the Occasion of His 65th Birthday April 11th 1997*, edited by Elie Wardini. Instituttet for Sammenlignende Kulturforskning Serie B: Skrifter XCVIII, 17-26. Oslo: Novus Forlag, 1997.

———. *The Religious Polemics of Amos: Studies in the Preaching of Am 2,7B-8; 4,1-13; 5,1-27; 6,4-7; 8,14*. VTSup 34. Leiden: E. J. Brill, 1984.

Barthélemy, Dominique. *Critique textuelle de l'Ancien Testament. 2. Isaïe, Jérémie, Lamentations*. OBO 50. Fribourg: Editions Universitaires; Göttingen: Vandenhoeck & Ruprecht, 1986.

———. *Critique textuelle de l'Ancien Testament. 3. Ezéchiel, Daniel et les Douze Prophètes*. OBO 50. Fribourg: Editions Universitaires; Göttingen: Vandenhoeck & Ruprecht, 1992.

Barton, John. *Amos' Oracles Against the Nations: A Study of Amos 1:3–2:5*. SOTSMS 6. Cambridge: Cambridge University Press, 1980.

Baslez, M. F., and F. Briquel-Chatonnet. "Un exemple d'intégration phénicienne au monde grec: les Sidoniens au Pirée à la fin du IVe siècle." In *Atti del II congresso internazionale di studi fenici e punici: Roma, 9-14 novembre 1987*, edited by Enrico Acquaro, Piero Bartoloni, *et al.* Instituto per la civiltà fenicia e punica. Collezione di studi fenici 30, I.229-40. Roma: Consiglio nazionale delle richerche, 1991.

Baumann, Eberhard. *Der Aufbau der Amosreden*. BZAW 7. Giessen: J. Ricker, 1903.

Beach, Eleanor Ferris. "The Samaria Ivories, *Marzeaḥ* and Biblical Texts." *BA* 55 (1992): 130-39.

Becker, J. "Ez 8-11 als einheitliche Komposition in einem pseudepigraphischen Ezechielbuch." In *Ezekiel and His Book: Textual and Literary Criticism and Their Interrelation*, edited by Johan Lust. BETL 74, 136-50. Leuven: University Press, 1986.

Beek, Martinus Adrianus. "The Religious Background of Amos ii 6-8." *OTS* 5 (1948): 132-41.

Bertholet, Alfred. *Hesekiel*. Mit einem Beitrag von Kurt Galling. HAT 13. Tübingen: J. C. B. Mohr [Paul Siebeck], 1936.

Beuken, Willem A. M. "Isaiah 28: Is It Only Schismatics That Drink Heavily? Beyond the Synchronic Versus Diachronic Controversy." In *Synchronic or Diachronic? A Debate on Method in Old Testament Exegesis: Papers Read at the Ninth Joint Meeting of Het Oudtestamentisch Werkgezalschap in Nederland en België and the Society for Old Testament Study, Held at Kampen, 1994*, edited by Johannes C. de Moor. OTS 34, 15-38. Leiden/New York/Cologne: E. J. Brill, 1995.

Bič, Miloš. *Das Buch Amos*. Berlin: Evangelische-Verlagsanstalt, 1969.

Biggs, Robert D. "Ebla Texts." *ABD* 2.263-70.

Binger, Tilde. *Asherah: Goddess in Ugarit, Israel and the Old Testament.* JSOTSup 232. Sheffield: Sheffield Academic Press, 1997.
Birch, Bruce C. *Hosea, Joel, and Amos.* Westminster Bible Companion. Louisville: Westminster/John Knox Press, 1997.
Blenkinsopp, Joseph. *Ezekiel.* Interpretation. Louisville: John Knox Press, 1990.
Block, Daniel Isaac. *The Book of Ezekiel: Chapters 1-24.* NICOT. Grand Rapids: Wm. B. Eerdmans Publishing Co., 1997.
———. *The Book of Ezekiel: Chapters 25-48.* NICOT. Grand Rapids: Wm. B. Eerdmans Publishing Co., 1997.
Blum, Erhard. "'Amos' in Jerusalem: Beobachtungen zu Am 6,1-7." *Hen* 16 (1994): 23-47.
Boadt, Lawrence. *Jeremiah 1-25.* OTMS 9. Wilmington: Michael Glazier, 1982.
Bohlen, Reinhold. "Zur Sozialkritik des Propheten Amos." *TTZ* 95 (1986): 282-301.
Bonnet, C. "Le dieu solaire Shamash dans le monde phénico-punique." *SEL* 6 (1989): 97-115.
Bordreuil, Pierre, and Dennis Pardee. "Le papyrus du *marzeaḥ*." *Sem* 38 (1990): 49-68, pl. VII-X.
Botterweck, G. Johannes. "'Sie verkaufen den Unschuldigen um Geld.' Zur sozialen Kritik des Propheten Amos." *BibLeb* 12 (1971): 215-31.
Bovati, Pietro, and Roland Meynet. *Le livre du prophète Amos.* Rhétorique Biblique 2. Paris: Les Éditions du Cerf, 1994.
Bright, John. *Jeremiah: A New Translation with Introduction and Commentary.* AB 21. Garden City: Doubleday, 1965.
Briquel-Chatonnet, F. *Studia Phoenicia XII: Les relations entre les cités de la côte phénicienne et les royaumes d'Israël et de Juda.* OLA 46. Leuven: Departement Oriëntalistiek/Uitgeverij Peeters, 1992.
Brownlee, William Hugh. *Ezekiel 1-19.* WBC 28. Waco: Word Books, 1986.
Brueggemann, Walter. *To Pluck up, to Tear Down: A Commentary on the Book of Jeremiah 1-25.* ITC. Grand Rapids: Wm. B. Eerdmans Publishing Co., 1988.
Bryan, David Burton. "Texts Relating to the *Marzeaḥ*: A Study of an Ancient Semitic Institution." Ph.D. diss., Johns Hopkins University, 1973.
Buccellati, Giorgio. "Due noti di testi accadici di Ugarit: MAŠKIM-*sākinu*." *OrAnt* 2 (1963): 223-28.
Büchler, Adolph. "Une localité énigmatique mentionnée sur la mosaïque de Madaba." *REJ* 42 (1901): 125-28.
Budde, Karl. "Zu Text und Auslegung des Buches Amos." *JBL* 43 (1924): 46-131.
———. "Zu Text und Auslegung des Buches Hosea." *JBL* 45 (1926): 280-97.
Buhl, Marie-Louise. "Hamath." *ABD* 3.33-36
Cantineau, Jean. "Inscriptions palmyréniennes." *RA* 27 (1930): 27-51.
———. *Inventaire des inscriptions de Palmyre.* Vol. 9, *Le sanctuaire de Bêl.* Publications du Musée National Syrien de Damas 1. Beyrouth: Imprimerie Catholique, 1933.
———. *Le Nabatéen.* Paris: Ernest Leroux, 1930-32.
———. "Textes palmyréniens provenant de la fouille du temple de Bêl." *Syria* 12 (1931): 116-41.
Carley, Keith W. *The Book of Ezekiel.* CBC. Cambridge: Cambridge University Press, 1974.
Carroll, Mark Daniel. *Contexts for Amos: Prophetic Poetics in Latin American Perspective.* JSOTSup 132. Sheffield: JSOT Press, 1992.
Carroll, Robert P. *Jeremiah: A Commentary.* OTL. Philadelphia: Westminster Press, 1986.

Caspari, W. "Hebräisch בין temporal." *OLZ* 16 (1913): 337-41.
Catastini, Allesandro. "Una nuova iscrizione fenicia e la 'Coppa di Yahweh'." In *Studi in onore di Edda Bresciani*, edited by Sandro Filippo Bondi *et al.*, 111-18. Pisa: Giardini, 1985.
Cathcart, Kevin J. "Ilu, Yariḫu and the One with the Two Horns and a Tail." In *Ugarit, Religion and Culture: Proceedings of the International Colloquium on Ugarit, Religion and Culture: Edinburgh, July 1994. Essays Presented in Honour of Professor John C. L. Gibson*, edited by N. Wyatt, W. G. E. Watson, and J. B. Lloyd. UBL 12, 1-7. Münster: Ugarit-Verlag, 1996.
——— and Robert P. Gordon. *The Targum of the Minor Prophets: Translated, with a Critical Apparatus, and Notes*. The Aramaic Bible 14. Wilmington: Michael Glazier, 1989.
Cathcart, Kevin J., and Wilfred G. E. Watson. "Weathering a Wake: A Cure for Carousal. A Revised Translation of *Ugaritica V* Text 1." *PIBA* 4 (1980): 35-58.
Cavalletti, S. "Il dio ebbro di vino." *RBR* 15 (1981): 135-36.
Chabot, J.-B. "Séance du 10 novembre." *CRAIBL* (1911): 670.
Cheyne, Thomas Kelly. "Gleanings in Biblical Criticism and Geography." *JQR* 10 (1898): 565-83.
———. *The Prophecies of Isaiah: A New Translation with Commentary and Appendices*. Rev. 4th ed. New York: Thomas Whittaker, 1886.
Chisholm, Robert B., Jr. "Structure, Style, and the Prophetic Message: An Analysis of Isaiah 5:8-30." *BSac* 143 (1986): 46-60.
Clements, Ronald E. *Isaiah 1-39*. NCBC. Grand Rapids: Wm. B. Eerdmans Publishing Co., 1980.
———. *Jeremiah*. Interpretation. Atlanta: John Knox Press, 1988.
———. "The Form and Character of Prophetic Woe Oracles." *Semitics* 8 (1982): 17-29.
Clermont-Ganneau, Charles. "Épigraphie palmyrénienne." *JA* 10e Sér 5 (1905): 383-408.
———. "Note sur les deux inscriptions religieuses de Palmyre publiées par M. E. Littmann." *JA* 9e Sér 18 (1901): 521-28.
Clifford, Richard J. *The Cosmic Mountain in Canaan and the Old Testament*. HSM 4. Cambridge: Harvard University Press, 1972.
———. "The Use of *HÔY* in the Prophets." *CBQ* 28 (1966): 458-64.
Cody, Aelred. *Ezekiel, with an Excursus on Old Testament Priesthood*. OTMS 11. Wilmington: Michael Glazier, 1984.
Cogan, Mordechai. *Imperialism and Religion: Assyria, Judah and Israel in the Eighth and Seventh Centuries B.C.E.* SBLMS 19. Missoula: Scholars Press, 1974.
Collins, John J. *The Apocalyptic Imagination: An Introduction to Jewish Apocalyptic Literature*. 2nd ed. BRS. Grand Rapids: Wm. B. Eerdmans Publishing Co., 1998.
Condamin, Albert. *Le livre de Jérémie: traduction et commentaire*. 3me éd. EBib. Paris: J. Gabalda, 1936.
Conrad, Edgar W. *Reading Isaiah*. OBT 27. Minneapolis: Fortress Press, 1991.
Cook, Stephen L. *Prophecy and Apocalypticism: The Postexilic Social Setting*. Minneapolis: Fortress Press, 1995.
Cooke, George Albert. *A Critical and Exegetical Commentary on the Book of Ezekiel*. ICC. Edinburgh: T. & T. Clark, 1936.
———. *Textbook of North-Semitic Inscriptions: Moabite, Hebrew, Phoenician, Aramaic, Nabataean, Palmyrene, Jewish*. Oxford: Clarendon Press, 1903.
Cooper, Alan. "Divine Names and Epithets in the Ugaritic Texts." In *Ras Shamra Parallels III: The Texts from Ugarit and the Hebrew Bible*, edited by S. Rummel.

AnOr 51, 331-500. Rome: Pontifical Biblical Institute, 1981.

Coote, Robert B. *Amos Among the Prophets: Composition and Theology*. Philadelphia: Fortress Press, 1981.

Cornhill, Carl Heinrich. *Das Buch des Propheten Ezechiel*. Leipzig: Hinrich, 1886.

———. *The Book of the Prophet Jeremiah: Critical Edition of the Hebrew Text Arranged in Chronological Order, with Notes*. Translated by C. Johnston. SBOT 11. Leipzig: J. C. Hinrichs'sche Buchhandlung, 1895.

Craigie, Peter C. *Ugarit and the Old Testament*. Grand Rapids: Wm. B. Eerdmans Publishing Co., 1983.

———, Page H. Kelley, and Joel F. Drinkard, Jr. *Jeremiah 1-25*. WBC 26. Dallas: Word Books, 1991.

Creason, S. "The Syntax of אם and the Structure of the Marseille Tariff." *RSF* 20 (1992): 143-59.

Crenshaw, James L. "Method in Determining Wisdom Influence Upon 'Historical' Literature." *JBL* 88 (1969): 129-42.

Cripps, Richard S. *A Critical and Exegetical Commentary on the Book of Amos: The Text of the Revised Version Edited with Introduction, Notes and Excursuses*. 2nd ed. With a foreword by R. H. Kennett. London: SPCK, 1955.

Crowfoot, J. W., and G. M. Crowfoot. *Early Ivories from Samaria*. Samaria-Sebaste 2. London: Palestine Exploration Fund, 1938.

Crowfoot, J. W., K. Kenyon, and E. L. Sukenik. *The Buildings at Samaria*. Samaria-Sebaste 1. London: Palestine Exploration Fund, 1942.

Curtis, Adrian H. *Ugarit (Ras Shamra)*. Cities of the Biblical World. Grand Rapids: Wm. B. Eerdmans Publishing Co., 1985.

Dahmen, Ulrich. "Zur Text- und Literarkritik von Amos 6:6a." *BN* 31 (1986): 7-10.

Dahood, Mitchel J. "Additional Notes on the *MRZḤ* Text." In *The Claremont Ras Shamra Texts*, edited by Loren R. Fisher. AnOr 48, 51-54. Rome: Pontifical Biblical Institute, 1971.

———. "Love and Death at Ebla and Their Biblical Reflections." In *Love and Death in the Ancient Near East: Essays in Honor of Marvin H. Pope*, edited by John H. Marks and Robert M. Good, 93-99. Winona Lake: Eisenbrauns, 1987.

———. *Proverbs and Northwest Semitic Philology*. Rome: Biblical Institute Press, 1963.

———. *Psalms I: 1-50. A New Translation with Introduction and Commentary*. AB 16. New York: Doubleday, 1968.

———. *Psalms II: 51-100. A New Translation with Introduction and Commentary*. 3rd ed. AB 17. New York: Doubleday, 1968.

———. *Psalms III: 101-150. A New Translation with Introduction and Commentary*. AB 17A. New York: Doubleday, 1970.

———. "The Minor Prophets and Ebla." In *The Word of the Lord Shall Go Forth: Essays in Honor of David Noel Freedman in Celebration of His Sixtieth Birthday*, edited by Carole L. Meyers and Michael O'Connor, 47-67. Winona Lake: Eisenbrauns, 1983.

———. "'To Pawn One's Cloak'." *Bib* 42 (1961): 359-66.

———. "Ugaritic-Hebrew Parallel Pairs." In *Ras Shamra Parallels I: The Texts from Ugarit and the Hebrew Bible*, edited by Loren Fisher. AnOr 49, 71-382. Rome: Biblical Institute Press, 1972.

——— and Tadeusz Penar. "The Grammar of the Psalter." In *Psalms III: 101-150. A New Translation with Introduction and Commentary*. AB 17A, 361-456. New York: Doubleday, 1970.

Daiches, S. "Amos VI.5." *ExpTim* 26 (1914-15): 521-22.

———. "Isaiah and Spiritualism." *The Jewish Chonicle Supplement* July (1921): 6.

Dalman, Gustaf. *Neue Petra-Forschungen und der heilige Felsen von Jerusalem*. PFAT 2. Leipzig: J. C. Heinrich, 1912.

———. *Petra und seine Felsheiligtümer*. PFAT 1. Leipzig: J. C. Hinrichs, 1908.

Davies, Eryl W. *Prophecy and Ethics: Isaiah and the Ethical Traditions of Israel*. JSOTSup 16. Sheffield: JSOT Press, 1981.

Davies, G. Henton. "Amos—the Prophet of Re-Union: An Essay in Honour of the Eightieth Birthday of Professor Aubrey R. Johnson, F.B.A." *ExpTim* 92 (1981): 196-200.

Davies, G. I. *Hosea*. NCBC. Grand Rapids: Wm. B. Eerdmans Publishing Co., 1992.

Day, Peggy L. "Anat עֲנָת." *DDD* 36-43.

Dearman, John Andrew. *Property Rights in the Eighth-Century Prophets: The Conflict and Its Background*. SBLDS 106. Atlanta: Scholars Press, 1988.

Delcor, Mathias. "Le tarif de Marseille (CIS I, 165). Aspects du système sacrifiel punique." *Semitica* 38 (1990): 87-93.

Delitzsch, Franz. *Biblical Commentary on the Prophecies of Isaiah*. 4th ed. Edinburgh: T. & T. Clark, 1890.

de Moor, Johannes C. "Henbane and KTU 1.114." *UF* 16 (1984): 355-56.

———. "Rāpi'ūma—Rephaim." *ZAW* 88 (1976): 323-45.

———. "Studies in the New Alphabetic Texts from Ras Shamra." *UF* 1 (1969): 167-75.

de Tarragon, Jean-Michel. *Le culte à Ugarit d'après les textes de la pratique en cunéiformes alphabétiques*. CahRB 19. Paris: J. Gabalda, 1980.

de Vaux, Roland. *Ancient Israel: Its Life and Institutions*. New York/Toronto: McGraw-Hill, 1961.

de Waard, Jan. "The Chiastic Structure of Amos V:1-17." *VT* 27 (1977): 170-77.

Dietrich, Manfred, and Oswald Loretz. "Der Vertrag eines MRZḤ-Klubs in Ugarit. Zum Verständis von KTU 3.9." *UF* 14 (1982): 71-76.

———. *"Jahwe und seine Aschera": Anthropomorphes Kultbild in Mesopotamien, Ugarit und Israels: Das biblische Bilderverbot*. UBL. Münster: Ugarit-Verlag, 1992.

———. "KTU 1.114, ein 'Palimpsest'." *UF* 25 (1993): 133-36.

———. "Neue Studien zu den Ritualtexten aus Ugarit (I). Ein Forschungsbericht" *UF* 13 (1981): 63-100.

———. "Neue Studien zu den Ritualtexten aus Ugarit (II)—Nr. 6—Epigraphische und inhaltliche Probleme in KTU 1.161." *UF* 15 (1983): 17-24.

———. "'Siehe, da war er (wieder) munter!' Die mythologische Begründung für eine medikamentöse Behandlung in KTU 1.114 (RS 24.258)." In *Boundaries of the Ancient Near Eastern World: A Tribute to Cyrus H. Gordon*, edited by Meir Lubetski, Claire Gottlieb, and Sharon Keller. JSOTSup 273, 174-98. Sheffield: Sheffield Academic Press, 1998.

——— and J. Sanmartín. "Der Stichometrische Aufbau von RS 24.258 (= Ug. 5, S. 545 NR. 1)." *UF* 7 (1976): 109-14.

Dijkstra, Meindert. "Goddess, Gods, Men and Women in Ezekiel 8." In *On Reading Prophetic Texts: Gender Specific and Related Studies in Memory of Fokkelien Van Dijk-Hemmes*, edited by Bob Becking and Meindert Dijkstra. BIS 18, 83-114. Leiden: E. J. Brill, 1996.

Dommershausen, W. "חלל *ḥll* I; חֹל *chōl*; חָלִיל *chālîl*." *TDOT* 4.409-421

Donner, Herbert. *The Mosaic Map of Madaba: An Introductory Guide*. PA 7. Kampen: Kok Pharos Publishing House, 1992.

——— and Heinz Cüppers. *Die Mosaikkarte von Madeba*. Tafelband. Abhandlungen des deutschen Palästinavereins. Weisbaden: Otto Harrassowitz, 1977.

Drexler, W. "Maioumas." In *Ausfürliches Lexicon der griecheschen und römischen Mythologie* 2:2, edited by Wilheim Heinrich Roscher, cols. 2286-88. Leipzig: B. G.

Teubner, 1894-1897; rpt. Hildesheim: Georg Olms, 1965.

Driver, G. R. "'Another Little Drink'—Isaiah 28:1-22." In *Words and Meanings: Essays Presented to David Winton Thomas on His Retirement from the Regius Professorship of Hebrew in the University of Cambridge, 1968*, edited by Peter R. Ackroyd and Barnabas Lindars, 47-67. Cambridge: Cambridge University Press, 1968.

———. "Babylonian and Hebrew Notes." *WO* 2 (1954): 19-26.

———. "Ezekiel: Linguistic and Textual Problems." *Bib* 35 (1954): 145-59.

———. "Linguistic and Textual Problems: Minor Prophets I." *JTS* 39 (1939): 154-86.

———. *Studies in Old Testament Prophecy*. Edited by Harold Henry Rowley. Edinburgh: T. & T. Clark, 1950.

———. "Studies in the Vocabulary of the Old Testament VI." *JTS* 34 (1933): 375-85.

Driver, Samuel Rolles. *The Books of Joel and Amos*. 2nd ed. Adapted and supplemented by H. C. O. Lanchester. The Cambridge Bible for Schools and Colleges. Cambridge: Cambridge University Press, 1915.

Duguid, Iain M. *Ezekiel and the Leaders of Israel*. VTSup 56. Leiden/New York/Köln: E. J. Brill, 1994.

Duhm, Bernhard. "Anmerkungen zu den Zwölf Propheten I: Buch Amos." *ZAW* 31 (1911): 1-18.

———. *Das Buch Jeremia*. KHAT 11. Tübingen: J. C. B. Mohr, 1901.

———. *Das Buch Jesaia übersetzt und erklärt*. 4th ed. HAT 3. Göttingen: Vandenhoeck & Ruprecht, 1922.

du Mesnil du Buisson, Comte R. *Les tessères et les monnaies de Palmyre: un art, une culture et une philosophie grecs dans les moules d'une cité et d'une religion sémitiques*. Inventaire des Collections du Cabinet des Médailes de la Bibliothèque Nationale. Paris: Éditions E. du Boccard, 1962.

Dunant, Christiane. *Le sanctuaire de Baalshamin à Palmyre*. Vol. 3, *Les inscriptions*. BHR 10. Rome: Institut suisse de Rome, 1971.

———. "Nouvelles tessères de Palmyre." *Syria* 36 (1959): 102-10.

Edghill, Ernest Arthur. *The Book of Amos, with Notes*. 2nd ed. Edited and introduced by G. A. Cooke. Westminster Commentaries. London: Methuen & Co. Ltd., 1926.

Ehrlich, Arnold B. *Randglossen zur Hebräischen Bibel*. Leipzig: J. C. Hinrichs, 1912.

Eichrodt, Walther. *Der Herr der Geschichte: Jesaja 13-23 und 28-39*. Die Botschaft des Alten Testaments: Erläuterungen alttestamentlicher Schriften 17. Stuttgart: Calwer Verlag, 1967.

———. *Ezekiel: A Commentary*. Translated by C. Quin. OTL. Philadelphia: Westminster Press, 1970.

Eidevall, Göran. *Grapes in the Desert: Metaphors, Models and Themes in Hosea 4-14*. ConBOT 43. Stockholm: Almqvist & Wiksell, 1996.

Eissfeldt, Otto. "Etymologische und archäologische Erklärung alttestamentlicher Wörter." *OrAnt* 5 (1966): 165-76.

———. "Kultvereine in Ugarit." In *Ugaritica VI*, edited by C. F. A. Schaeffer. MRS 17, 187-95. Paris: Geuthner, 1969.

———. "Neue Belege für nabatäische Kultgenossenschaften." *MIO* 15 (1969): 217-27.

———. "Sohnespflichten im Alten Orient." *Syria* 43 (1966): 39-47.

———. "מַרְזֵחַ und מַרְזְחָא 'Kultmahlgenossenschaft' im spätjüdischen Schrifttum." In *Kleine Schriften zum Alten Testament* 5, edited by Rudolf Sellheim and Fritz Maass, 136-42. Tübingen: J. C. B. Mohr, 1973.

Elhorst, Hendrik Jan. "Amos 6 5." *ZAW* 35 (1915): 62-63.

Ellison, Henry Leopold. *Ezekiel: The Man and His Message*. Exeter: The Paternoster Press, 1956.
Emerton, J. A. "'Yahweh and His Asherah': The Goddess or Her Symbol," *VT* 49 (1999): 315-37.
Emmerson, Grace I. "A Fertility Goddess in Hosea IV 17-19?" *VT* 24 (1974): 492-97.
Erling, B. "Ezekiel 38-39 and the Origins of Jewish Apocalyptic." In *Ex Orbe Religionum*, edited by Geo Widengren. SHR, 1.104-14. Leiden: E. J. Brill, 1972.
Exum, J. Cheryl. "'Whom Will He Teach Knowledge?' A Literary Approach to Isaiah 28." In *Art and Meaning: Rhetoric in Biblical Literature*, edited by David J. A. Clines, David M. Gunn, and Alan J. Hauser. JSOTSup 19, 108-39. Sheffield: JSOT Press, 1982.
Fabry, Heinz-Josef. "מַרְזֵחַ *marzēaḥ*." *TWAT* 5.11-16
Fendler, Marlene. "Zur Sozialkritik des Amos: Versuch einer wirtschafts- und sozialgeschichtlichen Interpretation alttestamentlicher Texte." *EvT* 33 (1973): 32-53.
Fenton, T. L. "The Claremont 'MRZḤ' Tablet, Its Text and Meaning." *UF* 9 (1977): 71-75.
Février, James Germain. *La religion des Palmyréniens*. Paris: J. Vrin, 1931.
Fey, Reinhard. *Amos und Jesaja: Abhängigkeit und Eigenständigkeit des Jesaja*. WMANT 12. Neukirchen-Vluyn: Neukirchener Verlag, 1963.
Fichtner, J. "Isaiah Among the Wise." In *Studies in Ancient Israelite Wisdom*, edited by James L. Crenshaw, 429-39. New York: Ktav Publishing House, 1976.
Fitzgerald, Aloysius. "Hebrew *yd* = 'Love' and 'Beloved'." *CBQ* 29 (1967): 368-74.
Fleischer, Gunter. *Von Menschen verkaüfern, Baschankühen und Rechtsverkehrern: die Sozialkritik des Amosbuches in historisch-kritischer, sozialgeschichtlicher und archäologischer Perspektive*. BBB 74. Frankfurt am Main: Athenäum Verlag, 1989.
Fleming, Daniel E. "More Help From Syria: Introducing Emar to Biblical Study." *BA* 58 (1995): 139-47.
———. *The Installation of Baal's High Priest at Emar: A Window on Ancient Syrian Religion*. HSS 42. Atlanta: Scholars Press, 1992.
Floß, Johannes Peter. "Biblische Theologie als Sprecherin der 'Gefährlichen Erinnerung' dargestellt an Jes 28,7-12." *BN* 54 (1990): 60-80.
Fohrer, Georg. *Das Buch Jesaja Bd. 1: Kap. 1-23*. 2nd ed. Zürcher Bibelkommentare. Zürich/Stuttgart: Zwingli Verlag, 1966.
———. *Das Buch Jesaja, Bd. 2: Kap. 24-39*. 2nd ed. Zürcher Bibelkommentare. Zürich/Stuttgart: Zwingli Verlag, 1967.
———.*Die Hauptprobleme des Buches Ezekiel*. BZAW 72. Berlin: Alfred Töpelman, 1952.
———. *Ezechiel*. Mit einem Beitrag von Kurt Galling. HAT 13. Tübingen: J. C. B. Mohr [Paul Siebeck], 1955.
———. "Zion-Jerusalem in the Old Testament." *TDNT* 7.293-319.
Fosbroke, Hughell E. W. "The Book of Amos: Introduction and Exegesis." *IB* 6.761-853.
Freedman, David Noel. "But Did King David Invent Musical Instruments?" *BRev* 1/2 (1985): 49-51.
Frevel, Christian. *Aschera und der Ausschließlichkeitsanspruch YHWHs: Beiträge zu literarischen, religionsgeschichtlichen und ikonographischen Aspekten der Ascheradiskussion*. BBB 94. Weinheim: Beltz Athenäum, 1995.
Friedman, Richard Elliot. "The *MRZḤ* Tablet from Ugarit." *Maarav* 2 (1979-80): 187-206.

Gangloff, Frédéric, and Jean-Claude Haelewyck. "Osée 4,17-19: un marzeah en l'honneur de la déesse 'Anat" *ETL* 71 (1995): 370-82.

Gaster, T. H. "Ezekiel and the Mysteries." *JBL* 60 (1941): 289-310.

Gawlikowski, Michel. "Inscriptions de Palmyre." *Syria* 48 (1971): 407-26, plates 23-24.

Gerstenberger, Erhard S. "The Woe-Oracles of the Prophets." *JBL* 81 (1962): 249-63.

Gese, Hartmut. "Komposition bei Amos." In *Congress Volume: Vienna*, edited by J. Emerton. VTSup 32, 74-95. Leiden: E. J. Brill, 1981.

Gibson, J. C. L. *Canaanite Myths and Legends*. 2nd ed. Edinburgh: T. &. T. Clark, 1978.

Giesebrecht, Friedrich. *Das Buch Jeremia übersetzt und erklärt*. 2nd ed. KHAT 13. Göttingen: Vandenhoeck & Ruprecht, 1907.

Ginsberg, H. Louis. "Some Emendations in Isaiah." *JBL* 69 (1950): 51-60.

———. *The Israelian Heritage of Judaism*. TSTJSA 24. New York: The Jewish Theological Seminary of America, 1982.

Glück, J. J. "Some Semantic Complexities in the Book of Hosea." In *Die O.T. Werkgemeenskap in Suid-Afrika: Studies on the Books of Hosea and Amos*. Pretoria: Potchefstroom Herald, 1966.

Good, Edwin M. "The Composition of Hosea." *SEÅ* 31 (1966): 21-63.

Good, R. M. "The Carthaginian MAYUMAS." *SEL* 3 (1986): 99-114.

Goody, Jack. *The Culture of Flowers*. Cambridge: Cambridge University Press, 1993.

Görg, Manfred. "Jesaja als 'Kinderlehrer?' Beobachtungen zur Sprache und Semantik in Jes 28,10(13)." *BN* 29 (1985): 12-16.

Gray, George Buchanan. *A Critical and Exegetical Commentary on the Book of Isaiah. Vol. I: Introduction and Commentary on I-XXVII*. ICC. Edinburgh: T. & T. Clark, 1912.

Greenberg, Moshe. *Ezekiel 1-20: A New Translation with Introduction and Commentary*. AB 22. New York: Doubleday, 1983.

———. "The Vision of Jerusalem in Ezekiel 8-11: A Holistic Interpretation." In *The Divine Helmsman: Studies on God's Control of Human Events, Presented to Lou H. Silberman*, edited by James L. Crenshaw and Samuel Sandmel, 143-64. New York: Ktav Publishing House, 1980.

Greenfield, Jonas C. "The *Marzeaḥ* as a Social Institution." In *Wirtschaft und Gesellschaft im Alten Vorderasien*, edited by J. Harmatta and G. Komoróczy, 451-55. Budapest: Åkadémiai Kiadó, 1976.

———. "Une rite religieux araméen et ses parallèles." *RB* 80 (1973): 46-52.

Grelot, Pierre. *Documents araméens d'Égypte: introduction, traduction, présentation*. LAPO 5. Paris: Les Éditions du Cerf, 1972.

Gressmann, Hugo. *Der Ursprung der israelitisch-jüdischen Eschatologie*. FRLANT 6. Göttingen: Vandenhoeck & Ruprecht, 1905.

———. "'Η ΚΟΙΝΩΝΙΑ ΤΩΝ ΔΑΙΜΟΝΙΩΝ." *ZNW* 20 (1921): 224-30.

Gubel, Eric. "À propos du *marzeaḥ* d'Assurbanipal." In *Reflets des deux fleuves: volume de mélanges offerts à André Finet*, edited by Marc Lebeau and Philippe Talon. AS 6, 47-53. Leuven: Peeters, 1989.

Guzzo Amadasi, Maria Giulia. *Le iscrizioni fenicie e puniche delle colonie in Occidente*. SS 28. Roma: Università di Roma, Instituto di studi del vicino Oriente, 1967.

———. "Under Western Eyes." *SEL* 4 (1987): 121-28.

Hadley, Judith M. "Yahweh and 'His Asherah': Archaeological and Textual Evidence for the Cult of the Goddess." In *Ein Gott allein? JHWH-Verehrung und biblisher Monotheismus im Kontext der israelitischen und altorientalischen Religionsgeschichte*, edited by Walter Dietrich and Martin A. Klopfenstein. OBO 139, 235-68.

Göttingen: Vandenhoeck & Ruprecht; Freiburg: Universitätsverlag, 1994.
Haevernick, H. A. C. *Commentar über den Propheten Ezechiel.* Erlangen: C. Heyder, 1843.
Halévy, J. *RevSém* 21 (1913): 5.
Hallo, William W. "Isaiah 28:9-13 and the Ugaritic Abecedaries." *JBL* 77 (1958): 324-38.
Halperin, David J. *Seeking Ezekiel: Text and Psychology.* University Park: Pennsylvania State University Press, 1993.
Halpern, Baruch. "A Landlord-Tenant Dispute at Ugarit?" *Maarav* 2 (1979-80): 121-40.
———. "'The Excremental Vision': The Doomed Priests of Doom in Isaiah 28." *HAR* 10 (1987): 109-21.
Hals, Ronald M. *Ezekiel.* FOTL 19. Grand Rapids: Wm. B. Eerdmans Publishing Co., 1988.
Hammershaimb, Erling. *The Book of Amos: A Commentary.* Translated by John Sturdy. New York: Schocken Books, 1970.
Hanson, Paul D. *The Dawn of Apocalyptic: The Historical and Sociological Roots of Jewish Apocalyptic Eschatology.* Rev. ed. Philadelphia: Fortress Press, 1975.
Haran, Menahem. "The Rise and Decline of the Empire of Jeroboam Ben Joash." *VT* 17 (1967): 266-97.
Harper, William Rainey. *A Critical and Exegetical Commentary on the Books of Amos and Hosea.* ICC 18. Edinburgh: T. & T. Clark, 1912.
Harvey, Dorothea Ward. "Rejoice Not, O Israel." In *Israel's Prophetic Heritage: Essays in Honor of James Muilenburg*, edited by Bernhard W. Anderson and Walter Harrelson, 115-27. New York: Harper & Brothers, 1962.
Hauret, Charles. *Amos et Osée.* Verbum Salutis, Ancien Testament 5. Paris: Beauchesne, 1970.
Hayes, John Haralson. *Amos the Eighth-Century Prophet: His Times and His Preaching.* Nashville: Abingdon Press, 1988.
——— and Stuart A. Irvine. *Isaiah the Eighth-Century Prophet: His Times and His Preaching.* Nashville: Abingdon Press, 1987.
Heidenheim, M. *Bibliotheca Samaritana.* Leipzig: Schulze, 1885.
Heider, George C. *The Cult of Molek: A Reassessment.* JSOTSup 43. Sheffield: JSOT Press, 1985.
Heltzer, Michael. *Goods, Prices and the Organization of Trade in Ugarit (Marketing and Transportation in the Eastern Mediterranean in the Socond* [sic] *Half of the II Millenium* [sic] *B.C.E.* Weisbaden: Reichert, 1978.
———. *The Internal Organization of the Kingdom of Ugarit (Royal Service-Systems, Taxes, Royal Economy, Army and Administration).* Weisbaden: Reichert, 1982.
———. *The Rural Community in Ancient Ugarit.* Weisbaden: Reichert, 1976.
Herbert, A. S. *The Book of the Prophet Isaiah: Chapters 1-39.* CBC. Cambridge: Cambridge University Press, 1973.
Herntrich, Volkmar. *Ezekielprobleme.* BZAW 61. Giessen: Alfred Töpelmann, 1933.
Herrmann, Johannes. *Ezechiel übsersetzt und erklärt.* KAT 11. Leipzig: A. Deichertsche Verlagsbuchhandlung, 1924.
Hillers, Delbert Roy. "*Hôy* and *Hôy*-Oracles: A Neglected Syntactical Aspect." In *The Word of the Lord Shall Go Forth: Essays in Honor of David Noel Freedman in Celebration of His Sixtieth Birthday*, edited by Carole L. Meyers and Michael O'Connor, 185-88. Winona Lake: Eisenbrauns, 1983.
———. "Palmyrene Aramaic Inscriptions and the Old Testament, Especially Amos 2:8." *ZAH* 8 (1995): 55-62.

———. "Some Books Recently Received (Cont.)." *BASOR* 198 (April 1970): 43-46.

Hitzig, Ferdinand. *Der Prophet Jesaja, übersetzt und ausgelegt*. Heidelberg: C. F. Winter, 1833.

Holladay, William L. "Amos VI 1bβ: a Suggested Solution." *VT* 22 (1972): 107-10.

———. *Isaiah: Scroll of a Prophetic Heritage*. New York: Pilgrim Press, 1978.

———. *Jeremiah 1: A Commentary on the Book of the Prophet Jeremiah, Chapters 1-25*. Hermeneia. Philadelphia: Fortress Press, 1986.

Horst, Friedrich. "Exilsgemeinde und Jerusalem in Ez viii-xi: Eine literarische Untersuchung." *VT* 3 (1953): 337-60.

Houtsma, M. T. "Bijdrage tot de kritiek en verklaring van Hosea." *ThT* 9 (1875): 55-75.

Huffmon, Herbert B. "The Social Role of Amos' Message." In *The Quest for the Kingdom of God: Studies in Honor of George E. Mendenhall*, edited by H. B. Huffmon, F. A. Spina, and A. R. W. Green, 109-16. Winona Lake: Eisenbrauns, 1983.

Humbert, P. "Laetari et exultare dans le vocabulaire religieux de l'Ancien Testament." *RHPR* 22 (1942): 185-214.

Hummel, H. D. "Enclitic *mem* in Early Northwest Semitic, Especially Hebrew." *JBL* 76 (1957): 85-107.

Hyatt, J. Philip. "The Book of Jeremiah: Introduction and Exegesis." *IB* 5.777-1142.

Ingholt, Harald. "Les thiases à Palmyre d'après une inscription inédite." *CRAIBL* (1925): 355-62.

———. "Un nouveau thiase à Palmyre." *Syria* 7 (1926): 128-41.

———, Henri Seyrig and Jean Starcky. *Recueil des tessères de Palmyre*. Institut Français d'Archéologie de Beyrouth, Bibliothèque Archéologique et Historique 58. Paris: Imprimerie Nationale, 1955.

Irwin, Brian P. "Molek Imagery and the Slaughter of Gog in Ezekiel 38 and 39." *JSOT* 65 (March 1995): 93-112.

Irwin, William H. "Isaiah 24-39." *NJBC* 244-48.

———. *Isaiah 28–33: Translation with Philological Notes*. BibOr 30. Rome: Biblical Institute Press, 1977.

Jackson, Jared Judd. "Style in Isaiah 28 and a Drinking Bout of the Gods (RS 24.258)." In *Rhetorical Criticism: Essays in Honor of James Muilenburg*, edited by Jared Judd Jackson and Martin Kessler. PTMS 1, 85-98. Pittsburgh: Pickwick, 1974.

Jacob, Edmond. *Esaïe 1-12*. CAT 8a. Genève: Labor et Fides, 1987.

———. "Osée." In *Osée Joël Amos Abdias Jonas*. 2nd ed. CAT 11a, 7-98. Genève: Labor et Fides, 1982.

Jacobs, Paul E. "'Cows of Bashan'—A Note on the Interpretation of Amos 4:1." *JBL* 104 (1985): 109-10.

Janzen, J. Gerald. *Studies in the Text of Jeremiah*. HSM 6. Cambridge: Harvard University Press, 1973.

Janzen, Waldemar. *Mourning Cry and Woe Oracle*. BZAW 125. Berlin/New York: Walter de Gruyter, 1972.

Jaruzelska, Izabela. "Social Structure in the Kingdom of Israel in the Eighth Century B.C. as Reflected in the Book of Amos." *FO* 29 (1992-93): 91-117.

Jensen, Joseph. *Isaiah 1-39*. OTMS 8. Wilmington: Michael Glazier, 1984.

Jeremias, Jörg. "Amos 3—6: From the Oral Word to the Text." Translated by Stuart A. Irvine. In *Canon, Theology, and Old Testament Interpretation: Essays in*

*Honor of Brevard S. Childs*, edited by Gene M. Tucker, David L. Petersen, and Robert R. Wilson, 217-29. Philadelphia: Fortress Press, 1988.

———. *Der Prophet Amos*. ATD 24. Göttingen: Vandenhoeck & Ruprecht, 1995.

———. *Der Prophet Hosea*. ATD 24. Göttingen: Vandenhoeck & Ruprecht, 1983.

——— and Friedhelm Hartenstein. "'JHWH und seine Aschera,' 'Offizielle Religion,' und 'Volksreligion' zur Zeit der klassischen Propheten." In *Religionsgeschichte Israels: Formale und materiale Aspekte*, edited by Bernd Janowski and Matthias Köckert. VWGT 15, 79-138. Gütersloh: Christopher Kaiser Verlag/Gütersloher Verlagshaus, 1999.

Jones, Douglas Rawlinson. *Jeremiah*. NCBC. Grand Rapids: Wm. B. Eerdmans Publishing Co., 1992.

Kaiser, Otto. *Isaiah 1-12: A Commentary*. Revised and completely rewritten. 2nd ed. Translated by John Bowden. OTL. Philadelphia: Westminster Press, 1983.

———. *Isaiah 13-39: A Commentary*. Translated by R. A. Wilson. OTL. Philadelphia: Westminster Press, 1974.

Kang, Sa-Moon. *Divine War in the Ancient Near East*. BZAW 177. Berlin/New York: Walter de Gruyter, 1989.

Kapelrud, Arvid S. *Central Ideas in Amos*. Oslo: W. Nygaard, 1956.

Keil, Karl Friedrich. *Biblical Commentary on the Prophecies of Ezekiel*. Translated by James Martin. 1876; rpt. Grand Rapids: Wm. B. Eerdmans Publishing Co., 1950.

———. *Biblical Commentary on the Prophecies of Jeremiah*. CFTL. Edinburgh: T. & T. Clark, 1880.

Kennett, Robert Hatch. *Ancient Hebrew Social Life and Custom as Indicated in Law, Narrative and Metaphor*. The Schweich Lectures on Biblical Archaeology, 1931. London: Oxford University Press, 1931.

Kenyon, Kathleen. *Royal Cities of the Old Testament*. London: Barric & Jenkins, 1971.

Key, A. F. "The Magical Background of Is 6:9-13." *JBL* 86 (1967): 198-204.

King, Philip J. *Amos, Hosea, Micah—An Archaeological Commentary*. Philadelphia: Westminster Press, 1988.

———. *Jeremiah: An Archaeological Companion*. Louisville: Westminster/John Knox Press, 1993.

———. "Using Archaeology to Interpret a Biblical Text—The *marzēaḥ* Amos Denounces." *BARev* 14/4 (July/August 1988): 34-44.

Kissane, Edward Joseph. *The Book of Isaiah: Translated from a Critically Revised Hebrew Text with Commentary*. Rev. ed. Dublin: Richview, 1960.

Kitchen, Kevin A. "The King List of Ugarit." *UF* 9 (1977): 131-42.

Kloppenborg, John S. "Collegia and *Thiasoi*: Issues in Function, Taxonomy and Membership." In *Voluntary Associations in the Graeco-Roman World*, edited by John S. Kloppenborg and Stephen G. Wilson, 16-30. London/New York: Routledge Press, 1997.

Koch, Klaus. *The Prophets, Vol. I: The Assyrian Period*. Translated by Margaret Kohl. Philadelphia: Fortress Press, 1983.

Köhler, L. "Zu Jes 28,15a und 18b." *ZAW* 48 (1930): 227-28.

Korpel, Marjo C. A. "Structural Analysis as a Tool for Redaction Criticism: The Example of Isaiah 5 and 10.1-6." *JSOT* 69 (March 1996): 53-71.

Kraus, Hans-Joachim. "Die prophetische Botschaft gegen das sociale Unrecht Israels." *EvT* 15 (1955): 295-307.

———. "הוי als prophetische Leichenklage über das eigene Volk im 8. Jahrhundert." *ZAW* 85 (1973): 15-46.

Kuhnigk, Willibald. *Nordwestsemitische Studien zum Hoseabuch*. BibOr 27. Rome: Biblical Institute Press, 1974.

L'Heureux, Conrad E. *Rank Among the Canaanite Gods: El, Baʿal and the Rephaʾim*. HSM 21. Missoula: Scholars Press, 1979.

———. "The Redactional History of Isaiah 5:1-10:4." In *In the Shelter of Elyon: Essays on Ancient Palestinian Life and Literature in Honor of G. W. Ahlström*, edited by W. Boyd Barrick and John R. Spencer. JSOTSup 31, 99-119. Sheffield: JSOT Press, 1984.

Lambdin, Thomas O. *Introduction to Biblical Hebrew*. New York: Scribner's Sons, 1971.

Landy, Francis. *Hosea*. Readings: A New Biblical Commentary. Sheffield: JSOT Press, 1995.

———. "Tracing the Voice of the Other: Isaiah 28 and the Covenant with Death." In *The New Literary Criticism and the Hebrew Bible*, edited by J. Cheryl Exum and David J. A. Clines. JSOTSup 143, 140-62. Sheffield: JSOT Press, 1994.

Lang, Bernhard. *Monotheism and the Prophetic Minority*. SWBA 1. Sheffield: The Almond Press, 1983.

Lemaire, André. *Les écoles et la formation de la bible dans l'ancien Israël*. OBO 39. Fribourg: Éditions Universitaires; Göttingen: Vandenhoeck & Ruprecht, 1981.

———. "Oracles, politique et littérature dans les royaumes araméens et transjordaniens." In *Oracles et prophéties dans l'antiquité: Actes du Colloque de Strasbourg 15-17 juin 1995*, edited by Jean-Georges Heintz. Publications du Centre de Recherce sur le Proche-Orient et la Grèce Antiques 15, 171-93. Paris: Diffusion de Boccard, 1997.

Leslie, Elmer Archibald. *Isaiah: Chronologically Arranged, Translated and Interpreted*. New York: Abingdon Press, 1963.

———. *Jeremiah: Chronologically Arranged, Translated and Interpreted*. New York: Abingdon Press, 1954.

Levey, S. H. D. *The Targum of Ezekiel: Translated, with a Critical Introduction, Apparatus and Notes*. The Aramaic Bible 13. Wilmington: Michael Glazier, 1987.

Lewis, Ioan M. *Ecstatic Religion: A Study of Shamanism and Spirit Possession*. 2nd ed. London/New York: Routledge Press, 1989.

Lewis, Theodore J. *Cults of the Dead in Ancient Israel and Ugarit*. HSM 39. Atlanta: Scholars Press, 1989.

———. "El's Divine Feast." In *Ugaritic Narrative Poetry*, edited by Simon B. Parker. SBLWAW 9, 193-96. Atlanta: Scholars Press, 1997.

———. "The Disappearance of the Goddess Anat: The 1995 West Semitic Research Project on Ugaritic Epigraphy." *BA* 59 (1996): 115-21.

———. "The Rapiuma." In *Ugaritic Narrative Poetry*, edited by Simon B. Parker. SBLWAW 9, 196-205. Atlanta: Scholars Press, 1997.

———. "Toward a Literary Translation of the Rapiuma Texts." In *Ugarit, Religion and Culture: Proceedings of the International Colloquium on Ugarit, Religion and Culture: Edinburgh, July 1994. Essays Presented in Honour of Professor John C. L. Gibson*, edited by N. Wyatt, W. G. E. Watson, and J. B. Lloyd. UBL 12, 115-49. Münster: Ugarit-Verlag, 1996.

Lidzbarski, Mark. *Ephemeris für semitische Epigraphik*. New York: Stechert, 1902.

Lindblom, Johannes. *Prophecy in Ancient Israel*. Oxford: Basil Blackwell, 1963.

Lindenberger, James M. *Ancient Aramaic and Hebrew Letters*. Edited by Kent Harold Richards. SBLWAW 4. Atlanta: Scholars Press, 1994.

Lipiński, Edward. *Studia Phoenicia XIV: Dieux et déesses de l'univers phénicien et punique*. OLA 64; Leuven: Peeters, 1995.

Littmann, Enno. "Deux inscriptions religieuses de Palmyre, le dieu שיע אלקום." *JA* 9e Sér 18 (1901): 374-90.

Liverani, M. "Review of *Ugaritica V*," *OrAnt* 8 (1969): 338-40.

Loewenstamm, Samuel E. "Eine lehrhafte ugaritische Trinkburleske." *UF* 1 (1969): 71-77.

Löhr, M. *Untersuchungen zum Buch Amos*. BZAW 4. Giessen: J. Ricker, 1901.

Loretz, Oswald. "Das Prophetenwort über das Ende der Königsstadt Samaria (Jes 28,1-4)." *UF* 9 (1977): 361-63.

———. "*Marziḥu* im ugaritischen und biblischen Ahnenkult: zu Ps 23; 133; Am 6,1-7 und Jer 16,5.8." In *Mesopotamica, Ugaritica, Biblica: Festschrift für Kurt Bergerhof zur Vollendung seines 70. Lebensjahres am 7. Mai 1992*, edited by Manfred Dietrich and Oswald Loretz. AOAT 232, 93-144. Kevelaer: Verlag Butzon and Bercker; Neukirchen-Vluyn: Neukirchener Verlag, 1993.

———. "Ugaritisch-biblisch *mrzḥ* 'Kultmahl, Kultverein' in Jer 16,5 und Am 6,7. Bemerkungen zur Geschichte des Totenkultes in Israel." In *Künder des Wortes. Beiträge zur Theologie der Propheten: Joseph Schreiner zum 60. Geburtstag*, edited by Lothar Ruppert, Peter Weimar, and Erich Zenger, 87-93. Würzburg: Echter-Verlag, 1982.

Lust, Johan. "Remarks on the Redaction of Amos V 4-6, 14-15." *OTS* 21 (1981): 129-54.

Maag, Victor. *Text, Wortschaft und Begriffswelt des Buches Amos*. Leiden: E. J. Brill, 1951.

Macintosh, Andrew A. *A Critical and Exegetical Commentary on Hosea*. ICC. Edinburgh: T. & T. Clark, 1997.

Maier, Christl, and Ernst Michael Dörrfuß. "'Um mit ihnen zu sitzen, zu essen und zu trinken': Am 6,7; Jer 16,5 und die Bedeutung von *marzeaḥ*." *ZAW* 111 (1999): 45-57.

Maier, Walter A., III. "Anath (DIETY) [Heb *ʿănāt* עֲנָת]" *ABD* 1.225-27

Margalit, Baruch. *A Matter of "Life" and "Death": A Study of the Baal-Mot Epic (CTA 4—5—6)*. AOAT 206. Kevelaer: Verlag Butzon and Bercker; Neukirchen-Vluyn: Neukirchener Verlag, 1980.

———. "K-R-T Studies," *UF* 27 (1995): 215-315.

———. "The Ugaritic Feast of the Drunken Gods: Another Look at RS 24.258 (KTU 1.114)." *Maarav* 2 (1979-80): 65-120.

———. *The Ugaritic Poem of AQHT: Text, Translation, Commentary*. BZAW 182. Berlin/New York: Walter de Gruyter, 1989.

Margueron, Jean-Claude. "Emar." *ABD* 2.488-90.

Margulis, Baruch. "A New Ugaritic Farce (RS 24.252)." *UF* 2 (1970): 131-38.

Marti, Karl. *Das Buch Jesaja erklärt*. KHAT 10. Tübingen: J. C. B. Mohr [Paul Siebeck], 1900.

———. *Das Dodekapropheton erklärt*. KHAT 13. Tübingen: J. C. B. Mohr [Paul Siebeck], 1904.

Martin-Achard, Robert, and S. Paul Re'emi. *God's People in Crisis: A Commentary on the Books of Amos and Lamentation*. ITC. Grand Rapids: Wm. B. Eerdmans Publishing Co., 1984.

Mauchline, J. *Isaiah 1-39: Confidence in God*. Torch Bible Commentaries. London: SCM Press, 1962.

———. "The Book of Hosea." *IB* 6.551-725.

May, Herbert Gordon. "The Book of Ezekiel: Introduction and Exegesis." *IB* 6.39-338.

———. "The Departure of the Glory of Yahweh." *JBL* 56 (1937): 309-21.

Mays, James Luther. *Amos: A Commentary*. OTL. Philadelphia: Westminster Press, 1969.

———. *Hosea: A Commentary*. OTL. Philadelphia: Westminster Press, 1969.

Mazar, Amihai. *Archaeology of the Land of the Bible: 10,000—586 B.C.E.* ABRL. New

York: Doubleday, 1992.
McKane, William. *A Critical and Exegetical Commentary on Jeremiah. Vol. I: Introduction and Commentary on Jeremiah I-XXV.* ICC 20. Edinburgh: T. & T. Clark, 1986.
———. *A Critical and Exegetical Commentary on Jeremiah. Vol. II: Commentary on Jeremiah XXVI-LII.* ICC 20. Edinburgh: T. & T. Clark, 1996.
McKeating, Henry. *The Books of Amos, Hosea and Micah.* CBC. Cambridge: Cambridge University Press, 1971.
McKenzie, John L. *Second Isaiah: A New Translation with Introduction and Commentary.* AB 20. Garden City: Doubleday, 1968.
McLaughlin, John L. "The *marzeaḥ* at Ugarit: A Textual and Contextual Study." *UF* 23 (1991): 265-81.
Meier, Samuel A. "Calneh." *ABD* 1.823-24.
Melugin, Roy F. "The Conventional and the Creative in Isaiah's Judgement Oracles." *CBQ* 36 (1974): 301-11.
Meshel, Zeev. "Kuntillet 'Ajrud (M.R. 094954)." *ABD* 4.103-09.
Milgrom, Jacob. "The Missing Thief in Leviticus 5:20ff." *RIDA*[3] 22 (1975): 71-85.
Milik, J. T. *Recherches d'épigraphie proche-orientale I: Dédicaces faites par des dieux (Palmyre, Hatra, Tyr) et des thiases sémitiques a l'époque romaine.* Institut Français d'Archéologie de Beyrouth, Bibliothèque Archéologique et Historique 92. Paris: Librairie Orientaliste Paul Geuthner, 1972.
Miller, Patrick D., Jr. "Animal Names as Designations in Ugaritic and Hebrew." *UF* 2 (1970): 177-86.
———. *The Divine Warrior in Early Israel.* HSM 5. Cambridge: Harvard University Press, 1973.
———. "The *MRZḤ* Text." In *The Claremont Ras Shamra Tablets*, edited by Loren R. Fisher. AnOr 48, 37-48. Rome: Biblical Institute Press, 1971.
Miscall, Peter D. *Isaiah.* Readings: A New Biblical Commentary. Sheffield: JSOT Press, 1993.
Montgomery, J. "Notes from the Samaritan: The Root פרט—Amos 6:5." *JBL* 25 (1906): 51-52.
Moran, William L. *The Amarna Letters.* Baltimore: Johns Hopkins University Press, 1992.
Morgenstern, Julian. "Amos Studies IV: The Addresses of Amos—Text and Commentary." *HUCA* 32 (1961): 295-350.
Moule, C. F. D. *Worship in the New Testament.* Richmond: John Knox Press, 1961.
Mowinckel, Sigmund. *Psalmenstudien.* Kristiania: Jacob Dybwad, 1922.
———. *The Psalms in Israel's Worship.* Translated by D. R. Ap-Thomas. 1962; rpt. The Biblical Seminar 14. Sheffield: JSOT Press, 1992.
———. *Zur Komposition des Buches Jeremia.* Kristiania: Jacob Dybwad, 1914.
Mullen, E. Theodore, Jr. *The Assembly of the Gods: The Divine Council in Canaanite and Early Hebrew Literature.* HSM 24. Chico: Scholars Press, 1980.
Naumann, Thomas. *Hoseas Erben: Strukturen der Nachinterpretation im Buch Hosea.* BWANT 131. Stuttgart/Berlin/Cologne: Kohlhammer, 1991.
Naveh, Joseph. "Some Notes on Nabatean Inscriptions from 'Avdat." *IEJ* 17 (1967): 187-89.
Negev, A. "Nabatean Inscriptions from 'Avdat (Oboda) I." *IEJ* 13 (1961): 127-38, pls. 130-31.
———. "Nabatean Inscriptions from 'Avdat (Oboda) II." *IEJ* 13 (1963): 113-24, pls. 17-18.
Neher, André. *Amos: contribution à l'étude du prophétisme.* Paris: Librairie Philosophique J. Vrin, 1950.

Niehr, Herbert. *Religionen in Israels Umwelt: Einführung in die nordwestsemitischen Religionen Syrien-Palästinas*. Die Neue Echter Bibel, Ergänzungbund zum Alten Testament 5. Würzburg: Echter Verlag, 1998.

Nissinen, Marti. *Prophetie, Redaktion und Fortschreibung im Hoseabuch: Studien zum Werdegang eines Prophetenbuches im Lichte von Hos 4 und 11*. AOAT 231. Neukirchen-Vluyn: Neukirchener Verlag, 1991.

Nobile, M. "Lo sfondo cultuale di Ez 8-11." *Anton* 58 (1983): 185-200.

Nowack, Wilhelm. *Die Kleinen Propheten übersetzt und erklärt*. 3rd ed. HAT 3. Göttingen: Vandenhoeck & Ruprecht, 1922.

Nyberg, H. S. *Studien zum Hoseabuche. Zugleich ein Beitrag zur Klärung des Problems der alttestamentlichen Textkritik*. UUÅ 6. Uppsala: Almqvist & Wiksell, 1935.

O'Callaghan, R. T. "Madaba (Carte de)." In *Supplément au Dictionaire de la Bible* 5, edited by Louis Pirot, A. Robert, and Henri Cazelles, cols. 627-704. Paris: Librairie Letouzey et Ané, 1957.

O'Connor, Michael. "Northwest Semitic Designations for Elective Social Affinities." *JANES* 18 (1986): 67-80.

Oettli, S. *Amos und Hosea. Zwei Zeugen gegen die Anwendung der Evolutionstheorie die Religion Israels*. BFCT 5. Gütersloh: Bertelsmann, 1901.

Olyan, Saul M. *Asherah and the Cult of Yahweh in Israel*. SBLMS 34. Atlanta: Scholars Press, 1988.

———. "What Do Shaving Rites Accomplish and What Do They Signal in Biblical Ritual Contexts?" *JBL* 117 (1998): 611-22.

Oswalt, John N. *The Book of Isaiah, Chapters 1-39*. NICOT. Grand Rapids: Wm. B. Eerdmans Publishing Co., 1986.

———. *The Book of Isaiah, Chapters 40-66*. NICOT. Grand Rapids: Wm. B. Eerdmans Publishing Co., 1998.

Overholt, Thomas W. *Prophecy in Cross-Cultural Perspective: A Sourcebook for Biblical Researchers*. SBLSBS 17. Atlanta: Scholars Press, 1986.

Pardee, Dennis. *Les textes para-mythologiques de la 24e campagne (1961)*. RSO IV. Paris: Éditions Recherche sur les Civilisations, 1988.

———. "*Marziḫu, Kispu*, and the Ugaritic Funerary Cult: A Minimalist View." In *Ugarit, Religion and Culture: Proceedings of the International Colloquium on Ugarit, Religion and Culture: Edinburgh, July 1994. Essays Presented in Honour of Professor John C. L. Gibson*, edited by N Wyatt, W. G. E. Watson, and J. B. Lloyd. UBL 12, 273-87. Münster: Ugarit-Verlag, 1996.

———. "The Preposition in Ugaritic." *UF* 7 (1975): 329-378; 8 (1976): 215-322.

———. "Ugaritic." *AfO* 28 (1981-82): 259-72.

——— and Pierre Bordreuil. "Ugarit: Texts and Literature." *ABD* 6.706-21.

Parrot, André. *Samaria, the Capital of the Kingdom of Israel*. Translated by S. R. Hooke. SBA 7. London: SCM Press, 1958.

Paul, Shalom M. *Amos: A Commentary on the Book of Amos*. Edited by Frank Moore Cross. Hermeneia. Minneapolis: Fortress Press, 1991.

———. "Two Cognate Semitic Terms for Mating and Copulation." *VT* 32 (1982): 492-94.

Peckham, Brian. "Phoenicia and the Religion of Israel: The Epigraphic Evidence." In *Ancient Israelite Religion: Essays in Honor of Frank Moore Cross*, edited by Patrick D. Miller, Jr., Paul D. Hanson, and Dean S. McBride, 79-99. Philadelphia: Fortress Press, 1987.

Peckham, J. Brian. *The Development of the Late Phoenician Scripts*. Cambridge: Harvard University Press, 1968.

Perles, Joseph. *Etymologische Studien zur Kund der rabbinischen Sprache und Altertümer*. Breslau: Schletter, 1871.

———. "Miscellen zur rabbinischen Sprach- und Altertumskunde." *MGWJ* 21 (1872): 251-73.

Peters, J. P. *The Psalms as Liturgies*. New York: Macmillan, 1922.

Petersen, David L. "Isaiah 28: A Redaction Critical Study." *SBLSP* 17 (1979): 2:101-122.

Pettey, Richard J. *Asherah, Goddess of Israel*. American University Studies, Series 7: Theology and Religion 74. Frankfurt am Main/Bern/New York: Peter Lang, 1990.

Pettinato, Giovanni. *Ebla: A New Look at History*. Translated by C. Faith Richardson. Baltimore/London: Johns Hopkins University Press, 1991.

———. *Testi amministrativi della biblioteca L. 2769*. MEE 2. Napoli: Instituto Universitario Orientale di Napoli, 1980.

Pfeifer, Gerhard. "Entwöhnung und Entwöhnungsfest im Alten Testament: der Schlüssel zu Jesaja 28,7-13?" *ZAW* 84 (1972): 341-47.

Pitard, Wayne T. "A New Edition of the Rāpiʾūma texts: *KTU* 1.20-22." *BASOR* 285 (February 1992): 33-77.

Pohlmann, Karl-Friedrich. *Das Buch des Propheten Hesekiel (Ezekiel) Kapitel 1-19 übersetzt und erklärt*. ATD 22. Göttingen: Vandenhoeck & Ruprecht, 1996.

Polley, Max E. *Amos and the Davidic Empire: A Socio-Historical Approach*. New York: Oxford University Press, 1989.

Pope, Marvin H. "A Divine Banquet at Ugarit." In *The Use of the Old Testament in the New and Other Essays: Studies in Honor of W. F. Stinespring*, edited by J. M. Efird, 170-203. Durham: Duke University Press, 1972.

———. "Le *MRZH* à l'Ugarit et ailleurs." *AAAS* 29-30 (1979-80): 141-43.

———. "Notes on the Rephaim Texts from Ugarit." In *Essays on the Ancient Near East in Memory of Jacob Joel Finkelstein*, edited by Maria de Jong Ellis. Memoirs of the Connecticut Academy of Arts and Sciences 19, 163-82. Hamden: Archon Books, 1977.

———. *Song of Songs: A New Translation with Introduction and Commentary*. AB 7C. Garden City: Doubleday, 1977.

———. "The Cult of the Dead at Ugarit." In *Ugarit in Retrospect*, edited by G. D. Young, 159-79. Winona Lake: Eisenbrauns, 1981.

Porath, Renatus. *Die Sozialkritik im Jesajabuch: Redaktionsgeschichtliche Analyse*. Europäische Hochschulschriften Reihe XXIII: Theologie 503. Frankfurt am Main: Peter Lang, 1994.

Porten, Bezalel. *Archives from Elephantine: The Life of an Ancient Jewish Military Colony*. Berkeley: University of California Press, 1968.

Preisendenz, K. "Maioumas." In *Paulys Real-Encyclopädie der classischen Altertumwissenschaft: Neue Bearbeitung begonnen von George Wissowa unter Mitwirkung zahlreicher Fachgenossen* 14:1, edited by W. Kroll, cols. 610-12. Stuttgart: Metzler, 1928.

Procksch, Otto. *Jesaia I übersetzt und erklärt*. KAT 9. Leipzig: Deichert, 1930.

Rainey, Anson F. "The Social Stratification of Ugarit." Ph.D. diss., Brandeis University, 1962.

———. "The Ugaritic Texts in Ugaritica 5." *JAOS* 94 (1974): 184-87.

Reider, Joseph. "Etymological Studies in Biblical Hebrew." *VT* 2 (1952): 113-30.

Reisner, G. A. *Israelite Ostraca from Samaria*. Cambridge: Harvard University, 1924.

Reventlow, Henning Graf. *Liturgie und prophetisches Ich bei Jeremia*. Gütersloh: Gerd Mohn, 1963.

Riessler, P. *Der Kleinen Propheten oder das Zwölfprophetenbuch nach dem Urtext übersetzt und erklärt*. Rottenburg: Bader, 1911.

Roberts, J. J. M. "Amos 6:1-7." In *Understanding the Word: Essays in Honor of Bernhard W. Anderson*, edited by James T. Butler, Edgar W. Conrad, and Ben C.

Ollenburger. JSOTSup 37, 155-66. Sheffield: JSOT Press, 1985.
Robinson, Theodore H., and Friedrich Horst. *Die zwölf Kleinen Propheten*. HAT 1. Tübingen: J. C. B. Mohr, 1964.
Robinson, Thomas H. *Prophecy and the Prophets in Ancient Israel*. 3rd ed. London: Duckworth, 1953.
Rodd, C. S. "Modern Issues in Biblical Study: Rediscovered Hebrew Meanings." *ExpTim* 71 (1959-60): 131-34.
Rosenbaum, Stanley Ned. עָמוֹס הַיִּשְׂרְאֵלִי *Amos of Israel: A New Interpretation*. Macon: Mercer University Press, 1990.
Rost, Leonhard. "Zu Jesaja 28:1ff." *ZAW* 12 (1935): 292.
Rottzoll, Dirk U. *Studien zur Redaktion und Komposition des Amosbuchs*. BZAW 243. Berlin/New York: Walter de Gruyter, 1996.
Rudolph, Wilhelm. *Hosea*. KAT 13. Gütersloh: Gütersloher Verlagshaus/Gerd Mohn, 1966.
———. "Hosea 4,15-19." In *Gottes Wort und Gottes Land: Hans-Wilhelm Hertzberg zum 70. Gerburtstag am 16. Januar 1965 dargebracht von Kollegen, Freunden und Schülern*, edited by Henning Graf Reventlow, 193-99. Göttingen: Vandenhoeck & Ruprecht, 1965.
———. *Jeremia*. 3rd ed. HAT 12. Tübingen: J. C. B. Mohr [Paul Siebeck], 1968.
———. *Joel–Amos–Obadja–Jona*. KAT 13. Gütersloh: Gütersloher Verlagshaus/ Gerd Mohn, 1971.
Rüger, Hans Peter. "Zu RS 24.258." *UF* 1 (1969): 203-06.
Savignac, R. "Chronique: notes de voyage de Suez au Sinaï et à Pétra." *RB* 10 (1913): 429-42.
Sayce, Archibald Henry. "An Aramaic Ostracon from Elephantine." *PSBA* 31 (1909): 154-55.
Schmidt, Brian B. *Israel's Beneficent Dead: Ancestor Cult and Necromancy in Ancient Israelite Religion and Tradition*. Winona Lake: Eisenbrauns, 1996.
Schottroff, Willy. "The Prophet Amos: A Socio-Historical Assessment of His Ministry." In *The God of the Lowly: Socio-Historical Interpretations of the Bible*, edited by Willy Schottroff and Wolfgang Stegemann, translated by Matthew J. O'Connell, 27-46. Maryknoll: Orbis Books, 1984.
Scott, M. *Textual Discoveries in Proverbs, Psalms and Isaiah*. London: S.P.C.K., 1927.
Scott, R. B. Y. "Isaiah Chapters 1-39: Introduction and Exegesis." *IB* 5.149-381.
Seger, Joe D. "Gath." *ABD* 2.908-09.
Segert, Stanislav. *A Basic Grammar of the Ugaritic Language with Selected Texts and Glossary*. Berkeley: University of California Press, 1984.
———. *A Grammar of Phoenician and Punic*. Munich: Verlag C. H. Beck, 1976.
Seitz, Christopher R. *Isaiah 1-39*. Interpretation. Louisville: Westminster/John Knox Press, 1993.
Sellin, Ernst. *Das Zwölfprophetenbuch übersetzt und erklärt*. 1st ed. KAT 12. Leipzig: Deichert, 1922.
———. *Das Zwölfprophetenbuch übersetzt und erklärt*. 2nd ed. KAT 12. Leipzig: Deichert, 1929.
Seyrig, Henri. "Antiquités syriennes: 37—Postes romains sur la route de Médine; 38—Inscriptions grecques de l'agora de Palmyre." *Syria* 22 (1941): 218-70.
———. "Les tessères palmyréniennes et le banquet rituel." In *Memorial Lagrange*, edited by L. Vincent. Cinquantenaire de L'École Biblique et Archéologique Française de Jerusalem (15 Novembre 1890—15 Novembre 1940), 51-58. Paris: J. Gabalda, 1940.
Shanks, Hershel. "Ancient Ivory: The Story of Wealth, Decadence, and Beauty." *BARev* 11/5 (1985): 40-53.

Sheppard, Gerald T. "Isaiah 1-39." In *Harper's Bible Commentary*, edited by James L. Mays *et al.*, 542-70. San Francisco: Harper, 1988.

Silver, Morris. *Prophets and Markets: The Political Economy of Ancient Israel.* Social Dimensions of Economics. Boston/The Hague/London: Kluwer-Nijhoff Publishing, 1983.

Slayton, Joel C. "Bashan (PLACE) [Heb *Bāshān*]." *ABD* 1.623-24.

Smith, Gary V. *Amos: A Commentary.* LBI. Grand Rapids: Zondervan Publishing House, 1989.

Smith, George Adam. *The Book of the Twelve Prophets. Vol. I: Amos, Hosea, Micah.* The Expositors Bible, 8th Series. London: Hodder & Stoughton, 1896.

Smith, Mark S. "*CAT* 1.96." In *Ugaritic Narrative Poetry*, edited by Simon B. Parker. SBLWAW 9, 224-28. Atlanta: Scholars Press, 1997.

———. "The Baal Cycle." In *Ugaritic Narrative Poetry*, edited by Simon B. Parker. SBLWAW 9, 81-180. Atlanta: Scholars Press, 1997.

———. *The Early History of God: Yahweh and the Other Deities of Canaan.* San Francisco: Harper & Row, 1990.

———. *The Ugaritic Baal Cycle. Vol. 1: Introduction with Text, Translation and Commentary of KTU 1:1-1.2.* VTSup 55. Leiden/New York/Cologne: E. J. Brill, 1994.

Smith, Morton. *Palestinian Parties and Politics That Shaped the Old Testament.* 2nd ed. London: SCM Press, 1987.

Snaith, Norman Henry. *Amos, Hosea and Micah.* Epworth Preacher's Commentaries. London: The Epworth Press, 1956.

———. *The Book of Amos.* London: The Epworth Press, 1945-46.

Snyman, S. D. "'Violence' in Amos 3,10 and 6,3." *ETL* 71 (1995): 30-47.

Sobernheim, Moritz. "Palmyrenische Inschriften." *MVAG* 10/2 (1905): 17-73, 25 plates.

Soggin, J. Alberto. *The Prophet Amos: A Translation and Commentary.* Translated by John Bowden. London: SCM Press, 1987.

Speier, Salomon. "Bermerkungen zu Amos." *VT* 3 (1953): 305-10.

Spronk, Klaas. *Beatific Afterlife in Ancient Israel and in the Ancient Near East.* AOAT 219. Kevelaer: Verlag Butzon and Bercker; Neukirchen-Vluyn: Neukirchener Verlag, 1986.

Stager, Lawrence E. "The Finest Olive Oil in Samaria." *JSS* 28 (1983): 241-45.

Stansell, Gary. *Micah and Isaiah: A Form and Tradition Historical Comparison.* SBLDS 85. Atlanta: Scholars Press, 1988.

Starcky, Jean. "Autour d'une dédicace palmyrénienne à Šadrafa et à Duʿanat" *Syria* 26 (1949): 43-85.

———. "Pétra et la Nabatène." In *Supplément au Dictionaire de la Bible* 7, edited by Louis Pirot, A. Robert, Henri Cazelles, and André Feuillet, cols. 886-1018. Paris: Librairie Letouzey et Ané, 1966.

Stewart, Alistair C. "The Covenant with Death in Isaiah 28." *ExpTim* 100 (1989): 375-77.

Stieglitz, Robert R. "Commodity Prices at Ugarit." *JAOS* 99 (1979): 15-23.

Stulman, Louis. *The Other Text of Jeremiah: A Reconstruction of the Hebrew Text Underlying the Greek Version of the Prose Sections of Jeremiah with English Translation.* Lanham/New York/London: University Press of America, 1985.

———. *The Prose Sermons of the Book of Jeremiah: A Redescription of the Correspondences with Deuteronomistic Literature in the Light of Recent Text-Critical Research.* SBLDS 83. Atlanta: Scholars Press, 1986.

Sutcliffe, Thomas Henry. *The Book of Amos.* London: SPCK, 1939.

Sweeney, Marvin A. *Isaiah 1-39, with an Introduction to Prophetic Literature.* FOTL 16. Grand Rapids: Wm. B. Eerdmans Publishing Co., 1996.

Talmon, Shemeryahu. "Biblical *rĕpā'îm* and Ugaritic *rpu/i(m)*." In *Biblical and Other Studies in Honor of Robert Gordis*, edited by R. Aharoni. HAR 7, 235-49. Columbus: Ohio State University, 1983.

Tanghe, V. "Dichtung und Ekel in Jes xxviii 7-13." *VT* 43 (1993): 235-60.

Teixidor, Javier. "Bulletin d'épigraphie sémitique." *Syria* 48 (1971): 453-85.

———. "L'assemblée législative en Phénicie d'après les inscriptions." *Syria* 57 (1980): 453-64.

———. "Le thiase de Bêlastor et de Beelshamên d'après une inscription récemment découverte à Palmyre." *CRAIBL* (1981): 306-14.

Thiel, Winfried. *Die deuteronomistische Redaktion von Jeremia 1-25*. WMANT 41. Neukirchen-Vluyn: Neukirchener Verlag, 1973.

Thomas, D. Winton. "A Consideration of Isaiah LIII in the Light of Recent Textual and Philological Study." *ETL* 44 (1968): 79-86.

Thompson, John Arthur. *The Book of Jeremiah*. NICOT. Grand Rapids: Wm. B. Eerdmans Publishing Co., 1980.

Thorogood, Bernard. *A Guide to the Book of Amos with Theme Discussions on Judgement, Social Justice, Priest and Prophet*. Theological Education Fund Study Guides 4. London: SPCK, 1971.

Toews, Wesley I. *Monarchy and Religious Institution in Israel Under Jeroboam I*. SBLMS 47. Atlanta: Scholars Press, 1993.

Tomback, Richard S. *A Comparative Semitic Lexicon of the Phoenician and Punic Languages*. SBLDS 32. Missoula: Scholars Press, 1978.

Torczyner, Harry. "Dunkle Bibelstellen." In *Vom Alten Testament. Karl Marti zum siebzigsten Geburtstage gewidmet von Freunden, Fachgenossen und Schülern*, edited by Karl Budde. BZAW 41, 274-80. Giessen: Alfred Töpelmann, 1925.

Torrey, Charles Cutler. "On the Text of Am 5:25; 6:1,2; 7:2." *JBL* 13 (1894): 61-63.

Toy, C. H. *The Book of the Prophet Ezekiel*. SBOT 12. New York: Dodd, Mead, 1899.

Tsukimoto, Akio. *Untersuchungen zur Totenpflege (kispum) im alten Mesopotamien*. AOAT 216. Kevelaer: Verlag Butzon and Bercker; Neukirchen-Vluyn: Neukirchener Verlag, 1985.

Utzschneider, Helmut. *Hosea, Prophet vor dem Ende: Zum Verhältnis von Geschichte und Institution in der alttestamentlichen Prophetie*. OBO 31. Freiburg: Universitätsverlag; Göttingen: Vandenhoeck & Ruprecht, 1980.

van den Branden, A. "Lévitique 1-7 et le tarif de Marseille, *CIS* I 165." *RSO* 40 (1965): 107-30.

———. "Notes phéniciennes." *Bulletin du Musée de Beyrouth* 13 (1956): 87-95.

van der Toorn, Karel. "Echoes of Judaean Necromancy in Isaiah 28:7-22." *ZAW* 100 (1988): 199-217.

———. "Prostitution [Heb *Zenût, Zenûnîm, Taznût*]: Cultic Prostitution." *ABD* 5.510-13.

van Selms, Adrian. "Isaiah 28:9-13: An Attempt to Give a New Interpretation." *ZAW* 85 (1973): 332-39.

van Soldt, Wilfred. "Studies in the Topography of Ugarit (1): The Spelling of the Ugaritic Toponyms." *UF* 28 (1996): 653-92.

Vawter, Bruce. *Amos, Hosea, Micah, with an Introduction to Classical Prophecy*. OTMS 7. Wilmington: Michael Glazier, 1981.

Vermeylen, Jacques. *Du prophète Isaïe à l'apocalyptique: Isaïe I-XXXV, miroir d'un demi-millénaire d'expérience religieuse en Israël*. EBib. Paris: J. Gabalda, 1978.

Vesco, Jean-Luc. "Amos de Téqoa, défenseur de l'homme." *RB* 87 (1980): 481-513.

Virolleaud, Charles. "Les nouveaux textes mythologiques et liturgiques de Ras Shamra." *CRAIBL* (1962): 105-13.

———. "Les nouveaux textes mythologiques et liturgiques de Ras Shamra (XX-IV$^{e}$ campagne, 1961)." In *Ugaritica V*, edited by C. F. A. Schaeffer *et al.* MRS 16, 545-55. Paris: Geuthner, 1968.

———. "Les Rephaïm: Fragments de poèmes de Ras Shamra." *Syria* 22 (1941): 1-30.

———. "Six textes de Ras Shamra provenant de la XIV$^{e}$ campagne (1950)." *Syria* 28 (1951): 173-79.

Vogt, Ernst. "Das Prophetenwort Jes 28,1-4 und das Ende der Königsstadt Samaria." In *Homenaje a Juan Prado: Miscelanea de Estudios Biblicos y Hebraicos*, edited by L. Alvarez Verdes and E. J. Alonso Hernandez, 109-30. Madrid: Consejo Superior de Investigaciones Cientificas, 1975.

Volz, Paul. *Der Prophet Jeremia übersetzt und erklärt.* 2nd ed. KAT 10. Leipzig: A. Deichertsche Verlagsbuchhandlung, 1928.

von Rad, Gerhard. *Holy War in Ancient Israel.* Translated and edited by Marva J. Dawn. With an introduction by Ben C. Ollenburger, bibliography by Judith E. Sanderson. 1958; rpt. Grand Rapids: Wm. B. Eerdmans Publishing Co., 1991.

von Soden, Wolfram. "Zu Einigen Ortsbenennungen bei Amos und Micha." *ZAH* 3 (1990): 214-20.

Vuilleumier-Bessard, René. *La tradition cultuelle d'Israël dans la prophétie d'Amos et d'Osée.* CT 45. Neuchatel: Éditions Delachaux & Niestlé, 1960.

Wacker, Marie-Theres. *Figurationen des weiblichen im Hosea-Buch.* HBS 8. Freiburg: Herder, 1996.

Walls, Neal H. *The Goddess Anat in Ugaritic Myth.* SBLDS 135. Atlanta: Scholars Press, 1992.

Waltke, Bruce K., and Michael O'Connor. *An Introduction to Biblical Hebrew Syntax.* Winona Lake: Eisenbrauns, 1990.

Wanke, Günther. "אוי und הוי." *ZAW* 78 (1966): 215-18.

Ward, James M. *Amos and Isaiah: Prophets of the Word of God.* New York: Abingdon Press, 1969.

———. *Hosea: A Theological Commentary.* New York: Harper & Row, 1966.

———. "The Message of Hosea." *Int* 23 (1969): 387-407.

Watson, Wilfred G. E. *Classical Hebrew Poetry: A Guide to Its Techniques.* JSOTSup 26. Sheffield: JSOT Press, 1984.

Watts, John D. W. "A Critical Analysis of Amos 4:1ff." In *Society of Biblical Literature Proceedings* 2, 489-500. Missoula: Scholars Press, 1972.

———. *Isaiah 1-33.* WBC 24. Waco: Word Books, 1985.

Weinfeld, Moshe. "Covenant Terminology in the Ancient Near East and Its Influence on the West." *JAOS* 93 (1973): 190-99.

Weippert, Helga. "Amos: Seine Bilder und ihr Milieu." In *Beiträge zur prophetischen Bildsprache in Israel und Assyrien*, edited by Helga Weippert, Klaus Seybold, and Manfred Weippert. OBO 64, 1-29. Freiburg: Universitätsverlag; Göttingen: Vandenhoeck & Ruprecht, 1985.

———. *Die Prosareden des Jeremiabuches.* BZAW 132. Berlin: Walter de Gruyter, 1973.

Weiser, Artur. *Das Buch der zwölf Kleinen Propheten.* ATD 24. Göttingen: Vandenhoeck & Ruprecht, 1949.

———. *Das Buch Jeremia.* ATD 21. Göttingen: Vandenhoeck & Ruprecht, 1966.

———. *Die Prophetie des Amos.* BZAW 53. Giessen: A. Topelmann, 1929.

Weisman, Ze'ev. *Political Satire in the Bible.* SBLSS 32. Atlanta: Scholars Press, 1998.

Wellhausen, Julius. *Die Kleinen Propheten übersetzt und erklärt.* 4th ed. Berlin: Walter de Gruyter, 1963.
Westermann, Claus. *Basic Forms of Prophetic Speech.* Translated by Hugh Clayton White, with a foreword by Gene M. Tucker. 1967; rpt. Cambridge: The Lutterworth Press; Louisville: Westminster/John Knox Press, 1991.
———. *Isaiah 40-66: A Commentary.* Translated by David M. G. Stalker. OTL. Philadelphia: Westminster Press, 1969.
Wevers, John William. *Ezekiel.* NCBC. Grand Rapids: Wm. B. Eerdmans Publishing Co., 1969.
Whedbee, J. William. *Isaiah and Wisdom.* Nashville: Abingdon Press, 1971.
Whybray, R. N. *Isaiah 40-66.* NCBC. Grand Rapids: Wm. B. Eerdmans Publishing Co., 1975.
Wiggins, Steve A. *A Reassessment of "Asherah": A Study According to the Textual Sources of the First Two Millennia B.C.E.* AOAT 235. Kevelaer: Verlag Butzon und Bercker; Neukirchen-Vluyn: Neukirchener Verlag, 1993.
Wildberger, Hans. *Isaiah 1-12: A Commentary.* Translated by Thomas H. Trapp. Continental Commentaries. Minneapolis: Fortress Press, 1991.
———. *Jesaja 28-39: das Buch, der Prophet und seine Botschaft.* BKAT 10. Neukirchen-Vluyn: Neukirchener Verlag, 1982.
Williams, James G. "Irony and Lament: Clues to Prophetic Consciousness." *Semeia* 8 (1977): 51-74.
———. "The Alas-Oracles of the Eighth Century Prophets." *HUCA* 38 (1967): 75-91.
Williams, Ronald J. *Hebrew Syntax: An Outline.* 2nd ed. Toronto: University of Toronto Press, 1976.
Willi-Plein, Ina. *Vorformen der Schriftexegese innerhalb des Alten Testaments: Untersuchungen zum literarischen Werden der auf Amos, Hosea und Micha zurückgehenden Bücher im hebräischen Zwölfprophetenbuch.* BZAW 123. Berlin: Walter de Gruyter, 1971.
Wilson, Robert R. *Prophecy and Society in Ancient Israel.* Philadelphia: Fortress Press, 1980.
Wittenberg, G. H. "Amos 6:1-7: 'They Dismiss the Day of Disaster but You Bring Near the Rule of Violence'." *JTSA* 58 (March 1987): 57-69.
Wolff, Hans Walter. *Amos the Prophet: The Man and His Background.* Edited by John Reumann. Translated by Foster R. McCurley. Philadelphia: Fortress Press, 1973.
———. *Die Stunde des Amos: Prophetie und Protest.* München: Christopher Kaiser Verlag, 1969.
———. *Hosea: A Commentary on the Book of the Prophet Hosea.* Translated by G. Stansell. Hermeneia. Philadelphia: Fortress Press, 1974.
———. *Joel and Amos: A Commentary on the Books of the Prophets Joel and Amos.* Edited by S. D. McBride. Translated by W. Janzen. Hermeneia. Philadelphia: Fortress Press, 1977.
Wood, Joyce Rillet. "Amos: Prophecy as a Performing Art and Its Transformation in Book Culture." Ph.D. diss., University of St. Michael's College, 1993.
Würthwein, Ernst. "Amos-Studien." *ZAW* 62 (1950): 10-52.
Wyatt, N. *Religious Texts from Ugarit: The Words of Ilimilku and His Colleagues.* The Biblical Seminar 53. Sheffield: Sheffield Academic Press, 1998.
Xella, Paolo. "Studi sulla religione della Siria antica I: El e il vino (RS 24.258)," *SSR* 1 (1977): 229-61.
———. "Un antecedente eblaita del 'demone' ugaritico *ḥby*?" *SEL* 3 (1986): 17-25.
Yee, Gale A. *Composition and Tradition in the Book of Hosea: A Redactional Critical In-*

*vestigation.* SBLDS 102. Atlanta: Scholars Press, 1987.

Yon, Marguerite. "L'archéologie d'Ougarit," In *Ugarit—ein ostmediterranes Kulturzentrum im Alten Orient: Ergebnisse und Perspektiven der Forschung, Band 1—Ugarit und seine altorientalische Umwelt*, edited by Manfried Dietrich and Oswald Loretz. ALASPM 7, 267-79. Münster: Ugarit-Verlag, 1995.

———. "Les stèles en pierre," In *Arts et industries de la pierre*, edited by Marguerite Yon. RSO VI, 273-344. Paris: Éditions Recherche sur les Civilisations, 1991.

———. "The Temple of the Rhytons at Ugarit." In *Ugarit, Religion and Culture: Proceedings of the International Colloquium on Ugarit, Religion and Culture: Edinburgh, July 1994. Essays Presented in Honour of Professor John C. L. Gibson*, edited by N. Wyatt, W. G. E. Watson, and J. B. Lloyd. UBL 12, 405-16. Münster: Ugarit-Verlag, 1996.

———. "Ugarit: History and Archaeology." *ABD* 6.695-706.

Young, Edward J. *The Book of Isaiah: The English Text, with Introduction, Exposition, and Notes.* NICOT. Grand Rapids: Wm. B. Eerdmans Publishing Co., 1965.

Ziegler, Joseph. *Ezekiel.* Würzburg: Echter Verlag, 1948.

Zimmerli, Walther. *Ezekiel 1: A Commentary on the Book of the Prophet Ezekiel, Chapters 1-24.* Translated by R. E. Clements. Hermeneia. Philadelphia: Fortress Press, 1979.

———. *Ezekiel 2: A Commentary on the Book of the Prophet Ezekiel, Chapters 25-48.* Translated by James D. Martin. Hermeneia. Philadelphia: Fortress Press, 1983.

Zobel, H.-J. "הוֹי *hôy*." *TDOT* 3.359-64.

Zolli, I. "Hosea 4 17-18." *ZAW* 15 (1938): 175.

# INDEXES

## ANCIENT TEXTS

Page numbers in bold indicate the starting point of the full text in the original language with English translation, plus discussion.

### A. Biblical Texts

**Deuterocanonical/ Apocryphal**



**Versions/Translations**



**Second Testament**

B. Extra-Biblical Texts

**Phoenicia**



**Rabbinic Texts**

# AUTHORS

# SUPPLEMENTS TO VETUS TESTAMENTUM

2. Pope, M.H. *El in the Ugaritic texts.* 1955. ISBN 90 04 04000 5
3. *Wisdom in Israel and in the Ancient Near East.* Presented to Harold Henry Rowley by the Editorial Board of Vetus Testamentum in celebration of his 65th birthday, 24 March 1955. Edited by M. Noth and D. Winton Thomas. 2nd reprint of the first (1955) ed. 1969. ISBN 90 04 02326 7
4. *Volume du Congrès* [International pour l'étude de l'Ancien Testament]. Strasbourg 1956. 1957. ISBN 90 04 02327 5
8. Bernhardt, K.-H. *Das Problem der alt-orientalischen Königsideologie im Alten Testament.* Unter besonderer Berücksichtigung der Geschichte der Psalmenexegese dargestellt und kritisch gewürdigt. 1961. ISBN 90 04 02331 3
9. *Congress Volume,* Bonn 1962. 1963. ISBN 90 04 02332 1
11. Donner, H. *Israel unter den Völkern.* Die Stellung der klassischen Propheten des 8. Jahrhunderts v. Chr. zur Aussenpolitik der Könige von Israel und Juda. 1964. ISBN 90 04 02334 8
12. Reider, J. *An Index to Aquila.* Completed and revised by N. Turner. 1966. ISBN 90 04 02335 6
13. Roth, W.M.W. *Numerical sayings in the Old Testament.* A form-critical study. 1965. ISBN 90 04 02336 4
14. Orlinsky, H.M. *Studies on the second part of the Book of Isaiah.* — The so-called 'Servant of the Lord' and 'Suffering Servant' in Second Isaiah. — Snaith, N.H. Isaiah 40-66. A study of the teaching of the Second Isaiah and its consequences. Repr. with additions and corrections. 1977. ISBN 90 04 05437 5
15. *Volume du Congrès* [International pour l'étude de l'Ancien Testament]. Genève 1965. 1966. ISBN 90 04 02337 2
17. *Congress Volume,* Rome 1968. 1969. ISBN 90 04 02339 9
19. Thompson, R.J. *Moses and the Law in a century of criticism since Graf.* 1970. ISBN 90 04 02341 0
20. Redford, D.B. *A study of the biblical story of Joseph.* 1970. ISBN 90 04 02342 9
21. Ahlström, G.W. *Joel and the temple cult of Jerusalem.* 1971. ISBN 90 04 02620 7
22. *Congress Volume,* Uppsala 1971. 1972. ISBN 90 04 03521 4
23. *Studies in the religion of ancient Israel.* 1972. ISBN 90 04 03525 7
24. Schoors, A. *I am God your Saviour.* A form-critical study of the main genres in Is. xl-lv. 1973. ISBN 90 04 03792 2
25. Allen, L.C. *The Greek Chronicles.* The relation of the Septuagint I and II Chronicles to the Massoretic text. Part 1. The translator's craft. 1974. ISBN 90 04 03913 9
26. *Studies on prophecy.* A collection of twelve papers. 1974. ISBN 90 04 03877 9
27. Allen, L.C. *The Greek Chronicles.* Part 2. Textual criticism. 1974. ISBN 90 04 03933 3
28. *Congress Volume,* Edinburgh 1974. 1975. ISBN 90 04 04321 7
29. *Congress Volume,* Göttingen 1977. 1978. ISBN 90 04 05835 4
30. Emerton, J.A. (ed.). *Studies in the historical books of the Old Testament.* 1979. ISBN 90 04 06017 0
31. Meredino, R.P. *Der Erste und der Letzte.* Eine Untersuchung von Jes 40-48. 1981. ISBN 90 04 06199 1
32. Emerton, J.A. (ed.). *Congress Vienna* 1980. 1981. ISBN 90 04 06514 8
33. Koenig, J. *L'herméneutique analogique du Judaïsme antique d'après les témoins textuels d'Isaïe.* 1982. ISBN 90 04 06762 0

34. Barstad, H.M. *The religious polemics of Amos.* Studies in the preachings of Amos ii 7B-8, iv 1-13, v 1-27, vi 4-7, viii 14. 1984. ISBN 90 04 07017 6
35. Krašovec, J. *Antithetic structure in Biblical Hebrew poetry.* 1984. ISBN 90 04 07244 6
36. Emerton, J.A. (ed.). *Congress Volume,* Salamanca 1983. 1985. ISBN 90 04 07281 0
37. Lemche, N.P. *Early Israel.* Anthropological and historical studies on the Israelite society before the monarchy. 1985. ISBN 90 04 07853 3
38. Nielsen, K. *Incense in Ancient Israel.* 1986. ISBN 90 04 07702 2
39. Pardee, D. *Ugaritic and Hebrew poetic parallelism.* A trial cut. 1988. ISBN 90 04 08368 5
40. Emerton, J.A. (ed.). *Congress Volume,* Jerusalem 1986. 1988. ISBN 90 04 08499 1
41. Emerton, J.A. (ed.). *Studies in the Pentateuch.* 1990. ISBN 90 04 09195 5
42. McKenzie, S.L. *The trouble with Kings.* The composition of the Book of Kings in the Deuteronomistic History. 1991. ISBN 90 04 09402 4
43. Emerton, J.A. (ed.). *Congress Volume,* Leuven 1989. 1991. ISBN 90 04 09398 2
44. Haak, R.D. *Habakkuk.* 1992. ISBN 90 04 09506 3
45. Beyerlin, W. *Im Licht der Traditionen.* Psalm LXVII und CXV. Ein Entwicklungszusammenhang. 1992. ISBN 90 04 09635 3
46. Meier, S.A. *Speaking of Speaking.* Marking direct discourse in the Hebrew Bible. 1992. ISBN 90 04 09602 7
47. Kessler, R. *Staat und Gesellschaft im vorexilischen Juda.* Vom 8. Jahrhundert bis zum Exil. 1992. ISBN 90 04 09646 9
48. Auffret, P. *Voyez de vos yeux.* Étude structurelle de vingt psaumes, dont le psaume 119. 1993. ISBN 90 04 09707 4
49. García Martínez, F., A. Hilhorst and C.J. Labuschagne (eds.). *The Scriptures and the Scrolls.* Studies in honour of A.S. van der Woude on the occasion of his 65th birthday. 1992. ISBN 90 04 09746 5
50. Lemaire, A. and B. Otzen (eds.). *History and Traditions of Early Israel.* Studies presented to Eduard Nielsen, May 8th, 1993. 1993. ISBN 90 04 09851 8
51. Gordon, R.P. *Studies in the Targum to the Twelve Prophets.* From Nahum to Malachi. 1994. ISBN 90 04 09987 5
52. Hugenberger, G.P. *Marriage as a Covenant.* A Study of Biblical Law and Ethics Governing Marriage Developed from the Perspective of Malachi. 1994. ISBN 90 04 09977 8
53. García Martínez, F., A. Hilhorst, J.T.A.G.M. van Ruiten, A.S. van der Woude. *Studies in Deuteronomy.* In Honour of C.J. Labuschagne on the Occasion of His 65th Birthday. 1994. ISBN 90 04 10052 0
54. Fernández Marcos, N. *Septuagint and Old Latin in the Book of Kings.* 1994. ISBN 90 04 10043 1
55. Smith, M.S. *The Ugaritic Baal Cycle. Volume 1.* Introduction with text, translation and commentary of KTU 1.1-1.2. 1994. ISBN 90 04 09995 6
56. Duguid, I.M. *Ezekiel and the Leaders of Israel.* 1994. ISBN 90 04 10074 1
57. Marx, A. *Les offrandes végétales dans l'Ancien Testament.* Du tribut d'hommage au repas eschatologique. 1994. ISBN 90 04 10136 5
58. Schäfer-Lichtenberger, C. *Josua und Salomo.* Eine Studie zu Autorität und Legitimität des Nachfolgers im Alten Testament. 1995. ISBN 90 04 10064 4
59. Lasserre, G. *Synopse des lois du Pentateuque.* 1994. ISBN 90 04 10202 7
60. Dogniez, C. *Bibliography of the Septuagint – Bibliographie de la Septante (1970-1993).* Avec une préface de Pierre-Maurice Bogaert. 1995. ISBN 90 04 10192 6
61. Emerton, J.A. (ed.). *Congress Volume,* Paris 1992. 1995. ISBN 90 04 10259 0

62. Smith, P.A. *Rhetoric and Redaction in Trito-Isaiah.* The Structure, Growth and Authorship of Isaiah 56-66. 1995. ISBN 90 04 10306 6
63. O'Connell, R.H. *The Rhetoric of the Book of Judges.* 1996. ISBN 90 04 10104 7
64. Harland, P.J. *The Value of Human Life.* A Study of the Story of the Flood (Genesis 6-9). 1996. ISBN 90 04 10534 4
65. Roland Page Jr., H. *The Myth of Cosmic Rebellion.* A Study of its Reflexes in Ugaritic and Biblical Literature. 1996. ISBN 90 04 10563 8
66. Emerton, J.A. (ed.). *Congress Volume.* Cambridge 1995. 1997. ISBN 90 04 106871
67. Joosten, J. *People and Land in the Holiness Code.* An Exegetical Study of the Ideational Framework of the Law in Leviticus 17–26. 1996. ISBN 90 04 10557 3
68. Beentjes, P.C. *The Book of Ben Sira in Hebrew.* A Text Edition of all Extant Hebrew Manuscripts and a Synopsis of all Parallel Hebrew Ben Sira Texts. 1997. ISBN 90 04 10767 3
69. Cook, J. *The Septuagint of Proverbs – Jewish and/or Hellenistic Proverbs?* Concerning the Hellenistic Colouring of LXX Proverbs. 1997. ISBN 90 04 10879 3

70,1 Broyles, G. and C. Evans (eds.). *Writing and Reading the Scroll of Isaiah.* Studies of an Interpretive Tradition, I. 1997. ISBN 90 04 10936 6 (*Vol.* I); ISBN 90 04 11027 5 (*Set*)

70,2 Broyles, G. and C. Evans (eds.). *Writing and Reading the Scroll of Isaiah.* Studies of an Interpretive Tradition, II. 1997. ISBN 90 04 11026 7 (*Vol.* II); ISBN 90 04 11027 5 (*Set*)

71. Kooij, A. van der. *The Oracle of Tyre.* The Septuagint of Isaiah 23 as Version and Vision. 1998. ISBN 90 04 11152 2
72. Tov, E. *The Greek and Hebrew Bible.* Collected Essays on the Septuagint. 1999. ISBN 90 04 11309 6
73. García Martínez, F. and Noort, E. (eds.). *Perspectives in the Study of the Old Testament and Early Judaism.* A Symposium in honour of Adam S. van der Woude on the occasion of his 70th birthday. 1998. ISBN 90 04 11322 3
74. Kassis, R.A. *The Book of Proverbs and Arabic Proverbial Works.* 1999. ISBN 90 04 11305 3
75. Rösel, H.N. *Von Josua bis Jojachin.* Untersuchungen zu den deuteronomistischen Geschichtsbüchern des Alten Testaments. 1999. ISBN 90 04 11355 5
76. Renz, Th. *The Rhetorical Function of the Book of Ezekiel.* 1999. ISBN 90 04 11362 2
77. Harland, P.J. and Hayward, C.T.R. (eds.). *New Heaven and New Earth Prophecy and the Millenium.* Essays in Honour of Anthony Gelston. 1999. ISBN 90 04 10841 6
78. Krašovec, J. *Reward, Punishment, and Forgiveness.* The Thinking and Beliefs of Ancient Israel in the Light of Greek and Modern Views. 1999. ISBN 90 04 11443 2.
79. Kossmann, R. *Die Esthernovelle – Vom Erzählten zur Erzählung.* Studien zur Traditions- und Redaktionsgeschichte des Estherbuches. 2000. ISBN 90 04 11556 0.
80. Lemaire, A. and M. Sæbø (eds.). *Congress Volume.* Oslo 1998. 2000. ISBN 90 04 11598 6.
81. Galil, G. and M. Weinfeld (eds.). *Studies in Historical Geography and Biblical Historiography.* Presented to Zecharia Kallai. 2000. ISBN 90 04 11608 7
82. Collins, N.L. *The library in Alexandria and the Bible in Greek.* 2001. ISBN 90 04 11866 7

83,1 Collins, J.J. and P.W. Flint (eds.). *The Book of Daniel.* Composition and Reception, I. 2001. ISBN 90 04 11675 3 (*Vol.* I);
ISBN 90 04 12202 8 (*Set*)

83,2 Collins, J.J. and P.W. Flint (eds.). *The Book of Daniel.* Composition and Reception, II. 2001. ISBN 90 04 12200 1 (*Vol.* II); ISBN 90 04 12202 8 (*Set*).

84. Cohen, C.H.R. *Contextual Priority in Biblical Hebrew Philology.* An Application of the Held Method for Comparative Semitic Philology. 2001. ISBN 90 04 11670 2 (In preparation).

85. Wagenaar, J.A. *Judgement and Salvation.* The Composition and Redaction of Micah 2-5. 2001. ISBN 90 04 11936 1

86. McLaughlin, J.L. *The* Marzēaḥ *in the Prophetic Literature.* References and Allusions in Light of the Extra-Biblical Evidence. 2001. ISBN 90 04 12006 8